ANNUAL EDITIONS

Human Development 12/13
Forty-First Edition

EDITOR

Karen L. Freiberg
University of Maryland, Baltimore County

Dr. Karen Freiberg has an interdisciplinary educational and employment background in nursing, education, and developmental psychology. She received her BS from the State University of New York at Plattsburgh, her MS from Cornell University, and her PhD from Syracuse University. Dr. Freiberg has worked as a school nurse, a pediatric nurse, a public health nurse for the Navajo Indians, an associate project director for a child development clinic, a researcher in several areas of child development, and a university professor. She authored an award-winning textbook, *Human Development: A Life-Span Approach.* Dr. Freiberg has edited compendiums about *Educating Children with Exceptionalities and Adolescent Development,* as well as 17 editions of *Human Development.*

McGraw Hill

Connect
Learn
Succeed™

ANNUAL EDITIONS: HUMAN DEVELOPMENT, FORTY-FIRST EDITION

Published by McGraw-Hill, a business unit of The McGraw-Hill Companies, Inc., 1221 Avenue of the Americas, New York, NY 10020. Copyright © 2013 by The McGraw-Hill Companies, Inc. All rights reserved. Previous edition(s) © 2012, 2011, 2010, and 2009. Printed in the United States of America. No part of this publication may be reproduced or distributed in any form or by any means, or stored in a database or retrieval system, without the prior written consent of The McGraw-Hill Companies, Inc., including, but not limited to, in any network or other electronic storage or transmission, or broadcast for distance learning.

Some ancillaries, including electronic and print components, may not be available to customers outside the United States.

This book is printed on acid-free paper.

Annual Editions® is a registered trademark of the McGraw-Hill Companies, Inc.
Annual Editions is published by the **Contemporary Learning Series** group within the McGraw-Hill Higher Education division.

1 2 3 4 5 6 7 8 9 0 QDB/QDB 1 0 9 8 7 6 5 4 3 2

ISBN 978-0-07-805128-9
MHID 0-07-805128-2
ISSN 0278-4661 (print)
ISSN 2159-1075 (online)

HQ
768
.A55
2012/13

Managing Editor: *Larry Loeppke*
Developmental Editor: *Jade Benedict*
Permissions Coordinator: *DeAnna Dausener*
Marketing Specialist: *Alice Link*
Project Manager: *Joyce Watters*
Design Coordinator: *Margarite Reynolds*
Cover Graphics: *Studio Montage, St. Louis, Missouri*
Buyer: *Susan K. Culbertson*
Media Project Manager: *Sridevi Palani*

Compositor: Laserwords Private Limited
Cover Images: © 2009 Jupiterimages Corporation (inset); Comstock/PictureQuest (background)

Editors/Academic Advisory Board

Members of the Academic Advisory Board are instrumental in the final selection of articles for each edition of ANNUAL EDITIONS. Their review of articles for content, level, and appropriateness provides critical direction to the editors and staff. We think that you will find their careful consideration well reflected in this volume.

ANNUAL EDITIONS: Human Development 12/13
41st Edition

EDITOR

Karen L. Freiberg
University of Maryland, Baltimore County

ACADEMIC ADVISORY BOARD MEMBERS

Editors/Academic Advisory Board continued

Preface

In publishing ANNUAL EDITIONS we recognize the enormous role played by the magazines, newspapers, and journals of the public press in providing current, first-rate educational information in a broad spectrum of interest areas. Many of these articles are appropriate for students, researchers, and professionals seeking accurate, current material to help bridge the gap between principles and theories and the real world. These articles, however, become more useful for study when those of lasting value are carefully collected, organized, indexed, and reproduced in a low-cost format, which provides easy and permanent access when the material is needed. That is the role played by ANNUAL EDITIONS.

In these times of economic uncertainty, students may want to obtain a degree as quickly and as easily as possible. Students may prefer rote memorization to deep processing of information. Creativity, however, requires a mastery of concepts such that new insights can occur. In order to become proficient thinkers, students must be exposed to multiple concepts.

The articles chosen for this compendium will help students use the full power of their reasoning abilities. Learning Outcomes will focus on the knowledge to be acquired in each selection, and the consequences of possessing this information. Critical Thinking questions for each article will help students evaluate their own understanding of the materials which have been read.

As humans develop through the circle of life, it is customary to track changes from infancy through old age. The arrangement of articles in this collection follows this chronology. However, many subjects are treated in abridged form in many units because they are not age specific. Some examples are intelligence, emotional responsivity, socialization, culture, spirituality, education, gender, and nutrition. A Topic Guide is included in this publication to help readers find current, appropriate educational information in the many areas of development which transcend age boundaries.

At conception a new human being is created, but each unique individual carries genetic materials from biological relatives alive and dead, and may pass them on to future generations. The first articles in this anthology make the science of genetics, and the possibility of tracing one's ancestry, easier to understand.

Development through infancy proceeds from sensory and motor responses to verbal communication, thinking, conceptualizing, and learning from others.

Childhood brings rapid physical growth, improved cognition, and many types of social learning.

In adolescence the individual's values and identity are questioned. Separation from parents occurs. Under the influence of sex hormones, the brain undergoes multiple changes. Emotions may fluctuate rapidly.

Early adulthood usually establishes the individual as an independent person. Employment, further education, and the beginning of one's own family are all aspects of setting up a distinct life, with both its own characteristics and the characteristics and customs of previous generations.

During middle adulthood persons have new situations to face, new transitions to cope with. Children grow up and leave home. Signs of aging become apparent. Relationships change, roles shift. New abilities may be found and opportunities created.

Finally, during late adulthood, people assess what they've accomplished. Some are pleased. Some feel they could have done more or lived differently. In the best of instances, individuals accept who they are and are comfortable with themselves.

As you explore this anthology, you will discover that many articles ask questions that have no answers. As a student, I felt frustrated by such writing. I wanted answers, right answers, right away. However, over time I learned that maturity includes accepting relativity and acknowledging extenuatory circumstances. Life frequently has no right or wrong answers, but rather various alternatives with multiple consequences. Instead of right versus wrong, a more helpful consideration is "What will bring about the greater good for the greater number?" Controversies, whether about terrorism, stem cells, or global warming, can promote healthy discussions. Different viewpoints should be weighed against societal standards. Different philosophies should be celebrated for what they offer in creating intellectual abilities in human beings to allow them to adapt to changing circumstances.

The Greek sophists were philosophers who specialized in argumentation, rhetoric (using language persuasively), and dialectics (finding synthesis or common ground between contradictory ideas). This was sophistication. However, from their skilled thinking came the derogatory term "sophism," suggesting that some argumentation was deceptive rather than wise. The term sophomore, which now means second-year student, comes from this variation of sophism, combining "sophos" (wise) with "moros" (dull or foolish). "Sophomoric" translates to exhibiting immaturity and lack of judgment, while "sophisticated" translates to having acquired knowledge. Educators strive to have their students move from knowing all the answers (sophomoric) to asking intelligent questions (sophisticated).

This anthology is dedicated to seekers of knowledge and searchers for what is true, right, or lasting. To this end, those articles have been selected that provide you with information that will stimulate discussion and give your thoughts direction, but not those that tell you what to think. May you be "seeking" learners all through your own years of human development. May each suggestive answer you discover open your mind to more erudite (instructive) learning, questioning, and sophistication.

Karen Freiberg

Karen Freiberg, PhD
Editor

The Annual Editions Series

VOLUMES AVAILABLE

Adolescent Psychology

Aging

American Foreign Policy

American Government

Anthropology

Archaeology

Assessment and Evaluation

Business Ethics

Child Growth and Development

Comparative Politics

Criminal Justice

Developing World

Drugs, Society, and Behavior

Dying, Death, and Bereavement

Early Childhood Education

Economics

Educating Children with Exceptionalities

Education

Educational Psychology

Entrepreneurship

Environment

The Family

Gender

Geography

Global Issues

Health

Homeland Security

Human Development

Human Resources

Human Sexualities

International Business

Management

Marketing

Mass Media

Microbiology

Multicultural Education

Nursing

Nutrition

Physical Anthropology

Psychology

Race and Ethnic Relations

Social Problems

Sociology

State and Local Government

Sustainability

Technologies, Social Media, and Society

United States History, Volume 1

United States History, Volume 2

Urban Society

Violence and Terrorism

Western Civilization, Volume 1

World History, Volume 1

World History, Volume 2

World Politics

Contents

UNIT 1
Genetic and Prenatal Influences on Development

Unit Overview   xxii

Part A. Genetic Influences

1. **Your DNA, Decoded,** Mark Anderson, *Delta Skymagazine,* August 2010
   This article explains the six billion **genes** (half from father, half from mother), made up of base pairs (A, C, G and T), which comprise each unique human's instruction manual. One's **health, emotions,** and **personality** are influenced by one's genome **prenatally.** Environmental factors after birth also affect human functioning.   3

2. **Seeking Genetic Fate,** Patrick Barry, Science News, July 4, 2009
   The cost of having small variations in your **genes** analyzed (over 99% of all human genes are identical), has dropped precipitously. Several genomic **technology** companies now offer to forecast your personal disease risks. Most **health** hazards also involve diet, exercise, and environmental factors. The **ethics** of predicting complex maladies from saliva are questionable.   7

Part B. Prenatal Influences

3. **The Prematurity Puzzle,** Jeneen Interlandi, *Newsweek,* November 1, 2010
   Research scientists are focusing on the placenta (an organ) to learn why **premature infants** are more likely to have autism, cerebral palsy, mental retardation, and other developmental disabilities. **Brain development, physical health,** and **cognitive** abilities are stimulated by placental hormones over 40 weeks of **pregnancy.** The role of **genes** may be less crucial.   13

4. **Thanks, Dad,** *The Economist,* January 8, 2011
   The fact that a woman's **prenatal** environment has a profound impact on her **children's** future has been known for over 70 years. A **man's** effects on future offspring is finally coming of age. **Infants** fathered by starving male mice produced offspring with **genes** associated with obesity (active fat synthesis). A human father's **nutrition** may also contribute to his children's weight **health.**   15

UNIT 2
Development during Infancy and Early Childhood

Unit Overview   16

Part A. Infancy

5. **Keys to Quality Infant Care: Nurturing Every Baby's Life Journey,**
   Alice Sterling Honig, *Young Children,* September 2010
   Dr. Honig, an expert on **infant** caregiving, shares 11 keys to enhancing baby's **brain development, physical status, language** skills, **emotional** regulation, and **social** abilities. She explains different infant temperaments and advises on how **parents** and teachers can shape behaviors to accommodate **personalities.**   19

The concepts in bold italics are developed in the article. For further expansion, please refer to the Topic Guide.

UNIT 3
Development during Childhood: Cognition and Schooling

The concepts in bold italics are developed in the article. For further expansion, please refer to the Topic Guide.

UNIT 4
Development during Childhood: Family and Culture

The concepts in bold italics are developed in the article. For further expansion, please refer to the Topic Guide.

UNIT 5
Development during Adolescence and Young Adulthood

The concepts in bold italics are developed in the article. For further expansion, please refer to the Topic Guide.

UNIT 6
Development during Middle and Late Adulthood

The concepts in bold italics are developed in the article. For further expansion, please refer to the Topic Guide.

The concepts in bold italics are developed in the article. For further expansion, please refer to the Topic Guide.

Correlation Guide

The *Annual Editions* series provides students with convenient, inexpensive access to current, carefully selected articles from the public press. **Annual Editions: Human Development 12/13** is an easy-to-use reader that presents articles on important topics such as *genetics and prenatal development, school-age development, family and culture's roles in development, later-life development,* and many more. For more information on *Annual Editions* and other *McGraw-Hill Contemporary Learning Series* titles, visit www.mhhe.com/cls.

This convenient guide matches the units in **Annual Editions: Human Development 12/13** with the corresponding chapters in three of our best-selling McGraw-Hill Human Development textbooks by Crandall, Santrock, and Papalia.

Annual Editions: Human Development 12/13	Human Development, 10/e by Crandell	A Topical Approach to Life-span Development, 6/e by Santrock	Experience Human Development, 12/e by Papalia/Feldman
Unit 1: Genetic and Prenatal Influences on Development	**Chapter 2:** Theories of Development **Chapter 3:** Reproduction, Heredity, and Prenatal Development	**Chapter 2:** Biological Beginnings	**Chapter 2:** Theory and Research **Chapter 3:** Forming a New Life
Unit 2: Development During Infancy and Early Childhood	**Chapter 4:** Birth and Physical Development: The First Two Years **Chapter 5:** Infancy: Cognitive and Language Development **Chapter 7:** Early Childhood: Physical and Cognitive Development	**Chapter 2:** Biological Beginnings **Chapter 4:** Health **Chapter 5:** Motor, Sensory, and Perceptual Development **Chapter 7:** Information Processing **Chapter 8:** Intelligence **Chapter 9:** Language Development **Chapter 10:** Emotional Development **Chapter 12:** Gender and Sexuality **Chapter 15:** Peers and the Sociocultural World	**Chapter 4:** Birth and Physical Development during the First Three Years **Chapter 5:** Cognitive Development during the First Three Years **Chapter 6:** Psychosocial Development during the First Three Years **Chapter 8:** Psychosocial Development in Early Childhood
Unit 3: Development During Childhood: Cognition and Schooling	**Chapter 8:** Early Childhood: Emotional and Social Development **Chapter 9:** Middle Childhood: Physical and Cognitive Development	**Chapter 3:** Physical Development and Biological Aging **Chapter 6:** Cognitive Developmental Approaches **Chapter 7:** Information Processing **Chapter 8:** Intelligence **Chapter 16:** Schools, Achievement, and Work	**Chapter 9:** Physical and Cognitive Development in Middle Childhood **Chapter 10:** Psychosocial Development in Middle Childhood
Unit 4: Development During Childhood: Family and Culture	**Chapter 10:** Middle Childhood: Emotional and Social Development	**Chapter 2:** Biological Beginnings **Chapter 3:** Physical Development and Biological Aging **Chapter 4:** Health **Chapter 9:** Language Development **Chapter 10:** Emotional Development **Chapter 12:** Gender and Sexuality **Chapter 16:** Schools, Achievement, and Work	**Chapter 9:** Physical and Cognitive Development in Middle Childhood **Chapter 10:** Psychosocial Development in Middle Childhood

Correlation Guide

Annual Editions: Human Development 12/13	Human Development, 10/e by Crandell	A Topical Approach to Life-span Development, 6/e by Santrock	Experience Human Development, 12/e by Papalia/Feldman
Unit 5: Development During Adolescence and Young Adulthood	**Chapter 12:** Adolescence: Emotional and Social Development **Chapter 13:** Early Adulthood: Physical and Cognitive Development **Chapter 14:** Early Adulthood: Emotional and Social Development	**Chapter 3:** Physical Development and Biological Aging **Chapter 4:** Health **Chapter 7:** Information Processing **Chapter 8:** Intelligence **Chapter 9:** Language Development **Chapter 10:** Emotional Development **Chapter 12:** Gender and Sexuality **Chapter 14:** Families, Lifestyles, and Parenting **Chapter 15:** Peers and the Sociocultural World	**Chapter 9:** Physical and Cognitive Development in Adolescence **Chapter 12:** Psychosocial Development in Adolescence
Unit 6: Development During Middle and Late Adulthood	**Chapter 16:** Middle Adulthood: Emotional and Social Development **Chapter 17:** Late Adulthood: Physical and Cognitive Development **Chapter 18:** Late Adulthood: Emotional and Social Development	**Chapter 3:** Physical Development and Biological Aging **Chapter 4:** Health **Chapter 7:** Information Processing **Chapter 8:** Intelligence **Chapter 9:** Language Development **Chapter 10:** Emotional Development **Chapter 12:** Gender and Sexuality **Chapter 15:** Peers and the Sociocultural World **Chapter 17:** Death, Dying, and Grieving	**Chapter 15:** Physical and Cognitive Development in Middle Adulthood **Chapter 16:** Psychosocial Development in Middle Adulthood **Chapter 17:** Physical and Cognitive Development in Late Adulthood **Chapter 18:** Psychosocial Development in Late Adulthood

Topic Guide

This topic guide suggests how the selections in this book relate to the subjects covered in your course. You may want to use the topics listed on these pages to search the Web more easily.

On the following pages a number of websites have been gathered specifically for this book. They are arranged to reflect the units of this Annual Editions reader. You can link to these sites by going to www.mhhe.com/cls

All the articles that relate to each topic are listed below the bold-faced term.

Adolescence
13. In Defense of Distraction
14. What Really Motivates Kids
17. From Lockers to Lockup
24. Foresight Conquers Fear of the Future
26. Offsetting Risks: High School Gay-Straight Alliances and Lesbian, Gay, Bisexual, and Transgender (LGBT) Youth
27. Portrait of a Hunger Artist

Adulthood
18. Role Reversal
24. Foresight Conquers Fear of the Future
32. Heartbreak and Home Runs: The Power of First Experiences
33. All Joy and No Fun: Why Parents Hate Parenting
35. I Survived
36. The New Survivors
37. Curing Cancer
38. Can You Build a Better Brain?
39. Why Do Men Die Earlier?

Aggression
19. The Angry Smile
24. Foresight Conquers Fear of the Future
39. Why Do Men Die Earlier?

Aging
38. Can You Build a Better Brain?
39. Why Do Men Die Earlier?
41. This Is Your Brain. Aging.

Brain development
4. The Prematurity Puzzle
9. Five Skills Kids Need Before They Read
13. In Defense of Distraction
28. 53.1% of You Already Know What This Story's About, Or Do You?
30. I Can't Think!
34. Good Morning, Heartache
38. Can You Build a Better Brain?
41. This Is Your Brain. Aging.

Career
18. Role Reversal
24. Foresight Conquers Fear of the Future
29. How to "Ace" Your Freshman Year in the Workplace with C's
31. Are We There Yet?
35. I Survived

Children
5. Thanks, Dad
9. Five Skills Kids Need Before They Read
10. Little by Little
11. "Early Sprouts": Establishing Healthy Food Choices for Young Children
14. What Really Motivates Kids
16. What I've Learned
17. From Lockers to Lockup
18. Role Reversal
19. The Angry Smile
20. Fast Times

21. Engaging Young Children in Activities and Conversations about Race and Social Class
22. Use the Science of What Works to Change the Odds for Children at Risk
23. Culture of Corpulence
26. Offsetting Risks: High School Gay-Straight Alliances and LGBT Youth
33. All Joy and No Fun: Why Parents Hate Parenting
35. I Survived
37. Curing Cancer

Cognition
4. The Prematurity Puzzle
13. In Defense of Distraction
14. What Really Motivates Kids
22. Use the Science of What Works to Change the Odds for Children at Risk
28. 53.1% of You Already Know What This Story's About, Or Do You?
30. I Can't Think!
34. Good Morning, Heartache
38. Can You Build a Better Brain?
41. This Is Your Brain. Aging.

Creativity
14. What Really Motivates Kids
24. Foresight Conquers Fear of the Future
30. I Can't Think!
34. Good Morning, Heartache

Culture
9. Five Skills Kids Need Before They Read
10. Little by Little
13. In Defense of Distraction
16. What I've Learned
19. The Angry Smile
20. Fast Times
22. Use the Science of What Works to Change the Odds for Children at Risk
23. Culture of Corpulence
30. I Can't Think!
31. Are We There Yet?
35. I Survived
39. Why Do Men Die Earlier?
40. More Good Years

Death
17. From Lockers to Lockup
34. Good Morning, Heartache
35. I Survived
36. The New Survivors
37. Curing Cancer
39. Why Do Men Die Earlier?

Drug abuse
3. The Womb. Your Mother. Yourself
24. Foresight Conquers Fear of the Future
26. Offsetting Risks: High School Gay-Straight Alliances and Lesbian, Gay, Bisexual, and Transgender (LGBT) Youth
34. Good Morning, Heartache
39. Why Do Men Die Earlier?

Internet References

The following Internet sites have been selected to support the articles found in this reader. These sites were available at the time of publication. However, because websites often change their structure and content, the information listed may no longer be available. We invite you to visit www.mhhe.com/cls for easy access to these sites.

Annual Editions: Human Development 12/13

General Sources

Association for Moral Education
www.amenetwork.org/

This association is dedicated to fostering communication, cooperation, training, curriculum development, and research that links moral theory to educational practices.

Behavior Analysis Resources
www.coedu.usf.edu/behavior/bares.htm

Dedicated to promoting the experimental, theoretical, and applied analysis of behavior, this site encompasses contemporary scientific and social issues, theoretical advances, and the dissemination of professional and public information.

Healthfinder
www.healthfinder.gov

Healthfinder is a consumer health site that contains the latest health news, prevention and care choices, and information about every phase of human development.

UNIT 1: Genetic and Prenatal Influences on Development

American Academy of Pediatrics (AAP)
www.aap.org

AAP provides data on optimal physical, mental, and social health for all children. The site links to professional educational sources and current research.

Basic Neural Processes
www.psych.hanover.edu/Krantz/neurotut.html

An extensive tutorial on brain structures is provided here.

Center for Evolutionary Psychology
www.psych.ucsb.edu/research/cep/

A link to an evolutionary psychology primer is available on this site. Extensive background information is included.

Columbia Center for Children's Environmental Health
www.cumc.columbia.edu/dept/mailman/ccceh

The research center studies the effects of prenatal exposure to pollutants.

Conception
www.thefertilitydiet.com

The *Fertility Diet* guides couples toward diet and lifestyle choices that can make a real difference in fertility.

Genetics Education Center
www.kumc.edu/gec/

The University of Kansas Medical Center provides information on human genetics and the human genome project at this site. Included are a number of links to research areas.

Genetic Science Learning Center
www.learn.genetics.utah.edu

The University of Utah provides current scientific information about genome sequencing and genetic studies.

Harvard Heart Letter
www.health.harvard.edu/newsweek

The Harvard Heart Letter provides monthly advice on the latest developments in heart health, new treatments, prevention, and research breakthroughs.

International HapMap Project
www.hapmap.org

Scientists from six countries work together to catalog human genetic variations that affect health and disease.

MedlinePlus Health Information/Prenatal Care
www.nlm.nih.gov/medlineplus/prenatalcare.html

On this site of the National Library of Medicine and the National Institutes of Health, you'll find prenatal-related sections such as General Information, Diagnosis/Symptoms, Nutrition, Organizations, and more.

National Children's Study
www.nationalchildrensstudy.gov

In 2009, pregnant women began enrolling in a study of 100,000 U.S. children from before birth to age 21.

Project Viva
www.dacp.org/viva

For more than a decade, researchers have tracked 2,000 Boston-area kids from the time they were fetuses.

UNIT 2: Development during Infancy and Early Childhood

Autism
www.autism-society.org

ASA, the nation's leading grassroots autism organization, exists to improve the lives of all affected by autism. It has many excellent resources for those needing more information about autism.

BabyCenter
www.babycenter.com

This well-organized site offers quick access to practical information on a variety of baby-related topics that span the period from preconception to toddlerhood.

Center for Childhood Obesity Research (CCOR)
www.hhdev.psu.edu/ccor/index.html

CCOR reports on obesity in toddlers and school-age children.

Children's Nutrition Research Center (CNRC)
www.kidsnutrition.org

CNRC is dedicated to defining the nutrient needs of healthy children, from conception through adolescence, and of pregnant and nursing mothers.

Early Childhood Care and Development
www.ecdgroup.com

Child development theory, programming and parenting data, and research can be found on this site of the Consultative Group. It is dedicated to the improvement of conditions of young children at risk.

Internet References

The National Association for the Education of Young Children (NAEYC)
www.naeyc.org

NAEYC is the nation's largest organization of early childhood professionals. It is devoted to improving the quality of early childhood education programs for children from birth through the age of eight.

The Penn Resiliency Project
www.ppc.sas.upenn.edu

Helps children develop healthy attribution styles and authentic happiness.

Tech and Young Children
www.techandyoungchildren.org

Helps staff and teachers use technology to communicate with parents of young children.

Turnaround for Children
www.turnaroundusa.org

Partners with low performing schools to boost academic achievement.

Zero to Three: National Center for Infants, Toddlers, and Families
www.zerotothree.org

Zero to Three is dedicated solely to infants, toddlers, and their families. Organized by recognized experts in the field, it provides technical assistance to communities, states, and the federal government.

UNIT 3: Development during Childhood: Cognition and Schooling

Children Now
www.childrennow.org

Children Now focuses on improving conditions for children who are poor or at risk. Articles include information on education, the influence of media, health, and security.

Council for Exceptional Children
www.cec.sped.org

This is the home page of the Council for Exceptional Children, which is dedicated to improving education for exceptional children and the gifted child.

Cyberbullying Research Center
www.cyberbullying.us/aboutus.php

This is a clearinghouse of information concerning the use and abuse of technology. It includes facts and figures about online aggression and resources to help adults respond to and prevent cyberbullying.

Educational Resources Information Center (ERIC)
www.eric.ed.gov/

Sponsored by the U.S. Department of Education, this site will lead to numerous documents related to elementary and early childhood education.

Federation of Behavioral, Psychological, and Cognitive Science
www.thefederationonline.org

The federation's mission is fulfilled through legislative and regulatory advocacy, education, and information dissemination to the scientific community. Hotlink to the National Institutes of Health's Project on the Decade of the Brain.

JumpStart Coalition for Personal Financial Literacy
www.jumpstart.org

The coalition provides 12 financial principles all children can learn.

Project Zero
pzweb.harvard.edu

Following 30 years of research on the development of learning processes in children and adults, Project Zero is now helping to create communities of reflective, independent learners; to enhance deep understanding within disciplines; and to promote critical and creative thinking.

Students First
www.studentsfirst.org

This describes the movement to transform public education by retaining the best teachers.

Teaching Technologies
www.inspiringteachers.com/bttindex.html

This is an excellent website for aspiring as well as experienced teachers.

UNIT 4: Development during Childhood: Family and Culture

Harborview Injury Prevention and Research Center
depts.washington.edu/hiprc/

Systematic reviews of childhood injury prevention and interventions on such diverse subjects as adolescent suicide, child abuse, accidental injuries, and youth violence are offered on this site.

Families and Work Institute
www.familiesandwork.org/index.html

The Families and Work Institute conducts policy research on issues related to the changing workforce, and it operates a national clearinghouse on work and family life.

Optimal Weight for Life (OWL) Program
www.childrenshospital.org/clinicalservices/site1896

This site describes multidisciplinary treatment for childhood obesity including weight management, exercise, nutritional counseling, and behavior modification for psychological factors.

Parentsplace.com: Single Parenting
www.parentsplace.com

This site provides links to resources valuable to parents, with topics ranging from pregnancy to teens.

Passive Aggressive Diaries
www.PassiveAggressiveDiaries.com

Passive Aggressive Diaries is a website blog that invites people to share their stories of passive aggressive behavior.

UNIT 5: Development during Adolescence and Young Adulthood

Alcohol & Drug Addiction Resource Center
www.addict-help.com/

An online source for questions regarding alcohol and drug addiction.

ADOL: Adolescent Directory On-Line
http://site.educ.indiana.edu/aboutus/AdolescenceDirectoryonLine ADOL/tabid/4785/Default.aspx

Internet References

The ADOL site contains a wide array of Web documents that address adolescent development. Specific content ranges from mental health issues to counselor resources.

AMA—Adolescent Health On-Line
www.ama-assn.org/ama/pub/category/1947.html

This AMA adolescent health initiative describes clinical preventive services that primary care physicians and other health professionals can provide to young people.

American Academy of Child and Adolescent Psychiatry
www.aacap.org/

Up-to-date data on a host of topics that include facts for families, public health, and clinical practice may be found here.

Depression
www.depression-primarycare.org

This site provides depression-related information for clinicians, organizations, and patients.

UNIT 6: Development during Middle and Late Adulthood

Alzheimer's Disease Research Center
http://alzheimer.wustl.edu/

ADRC facilitates advanced research on clinical, genetic, neuropathological, neuroanatomical, biomedical, neuropsychological, and psychosocial aspects of Alzheimer's disease and related brain disorders.

American Association of Retired Persons
www.aarp.org

Founded in 1958, AARP is a nonprofit, nonpartisan membership organization that helps people 50 and over improve the quality of their lives. AARP has 40 million members and has offices in all 50 states, the District of Columbia, Puerto Rico and the U.S. Virgin Islands.

Lifestyle Factors Affecting Late Adulthood
www.school-for-champions.com/health/lifestyle_elderly.htm

The way a person lives his or her life in the later years can affect the quality of life. Find here information to improve a senior's lifestyle plus a few relevant links.

National Aging Information and Referral Support Center
www.nausa.org/informationandreferral/index-ir.php

This service by the States United for Action in Aging is a central source of data on demographic, health, economic, and social status of older Americans.

Department of Health and Human Services—Aging
www.hhs.gov/aging/index.html

This is a complete site, with links and topics on aging.

UNIT 1

Genetic and Prenatal Influences on Development

Unit Selections

1. **Your DNA, Decoded,** Mark Anderson
2. **Seeking Genetic Fate,** Patrick Barry
3. **The Prematurity Puzzle,** Jeneen Interlandi
4. **Thanks, Dad,** *The Economist*

Learning Outcomes

After reading this Unit you should be able to:

- Illustrate the pros and cons of having your own DNA decoded.

- Examine the impact on health care if everyone's genome is known.

- Choose which genetic-related conditions you want to explore about yourself.

- Counsel a person with a known genetic risk about having DNA testing done.

- Point out which experiences before birth can affect one's entire lifespan.

- Identify developmental disabilities more common in children born prematurely.

- Summarize some of the factors contributing to the steady rise in preterm births.

- Tell how a father's diet before conception affects genes involved in later offspring obesity.

- Point out how genes and environment have interactive effects.

Student Website

www.mhhe.com/cls

Internet References

American Academy of Pediatrics (AAP)
www.aap.org

Basic Neural Processes
http://psych.hanover.edu/Krantz/neurotut.html

Center for Evolutionary Psychology
www.psych.ucsb.edu/research/cep/

Columbia Center for Children's Environmental Health
www.cumc.columbia.edu/dept/mailman/ccceh

Conception
www.thefertilitydiet.com

Genetics Education Center
www.kumc.edu/gec/

Genetic Science Learning Center
www.learn.genetics.utah.edu

Harvard Heart Letter
www.health.harvard.edu/newsweek

International Hap Map Project
www. hapmap.org

MedlinePlus Health Information/Prenatal Care
www.nlm.nih.gov/medlineplus/prenatalcare.html

National Children's Study
www.nationalchildrensstudy.gov

Project Viva
www.dacp.org/viva

Globalization makes it imperative that all humans learn to think broadly, communicate clearly, and look at the world with a critical eye. How life begins plays a vital role in the kind of human each of us will become in our future. Genetic scientists have made quantum leaps recently, finding ways to prevent or treat abnormal human conditions by manipulating cells, genes, and the immune system. The total human genome was mapped in 2003. This knowledge of the human complement of twenty-three pairs of chromosomes with their associated genes in the nucleus of every cell has the potential for allowing cures for previously incurable diseases. The use of stem cells (undifferentiated embryonic cells) in animal research has enabled the possibility of morphing stem cells into any kind of human cells. Stem cells will turn into desired tissue cells when the gene sequences of cytosine, adenine, thymine, and guanine (CATG) of the desired tissues are expressed. Scientists are using their knowledge of the human genome and embryonic stem cells to alter behaviors as well as to cure diseases. Cloning (complete reproduction) of a human already exists when one egg fertilized by one sperm separates into identical twins. Monozygotic twin research suggests that one's genetic CATG sequencing does not determine human behaviors, diseases, and traits without environmental input. Nature versus nurture is better phrased nature plus nurture. Genes appear to have mechanisms by which environmental factors can turn them on or leave them dormant.

Genetic precursors of human development and the use of stem cells, morphing, and cloning will be hot topics of the next several years as more genetic manipulation becomes feasible. As DNA sequences associated with particular human traits (genetic markers) are uncovered, pressure will appear to alter these traits. Will the focus be on altering the CATG sequencing, or altering the environmental factors that will "operate" on the genes?

Human embryology (the study of the first through seventh weeks after conception) and human fetology (the study of the eighth week of pregnancy through birth) have provided verification for the idea that behavior precedes birth. The genetic hardwiring of CATG directs much of this behavior. However, the developing embryo/fetus reacts to the internal and external environments provided by the mother as well. Substances diffuse through the placental barrier from the mother's body. The embryo reacts to toxins (viruses, antigens) that pass through the umbilical cord. The fetus reacts to an enormous number of other stimuli, such as the sounds from the mother's body (digestive rumblings, heartbeat) and the mother's movements, moods, and medicines. How the embryo/fetus reacts (weakly to strongly, positively to negatively) depends, in large part, on his or her genetic preprogramming. Genes and environment are so inextricably intertwined that the effect of each cannot be studied separately. Prenatal development always has strong environmental influences and vice versa. A new science of fetal origins is demonstrating this.

© Erica Simone Leeds

The two articles in the genetic influences section of this unit describe how decoding of the human genome will affect our future views about human development. The information in them is central to many ongoing discussions of human development. Should everyone know his or her own genetic map, including disease risks? How will health care be affected by genomic information in medical charts? Will insurance companies deny coverage based on DNA results? We all need to understand what is happening. We need to make knowledgeable and well-thought-out choices for our futures.

The first article, "Your DNA, Decoded," describes genetic testing and the costs associated with having one's genome sequenced. Television programs such as "African American Lives," "Faces of America," and "Who Do You Think You Are" have featured persons who have traced their roots through DNA.

The second article, "Seeking Genetic Fate," discusses the possibility of having one's own DNA mapped in order to understand more about one's ancestry, geographical origins, and health risks. While humans share about 99.5% of their genes in common, the last 0.5 percent is of interest in that it produces human variations. Scientists have developed ways to look at single nucleotide polymorphisms, or SNPs, which can reveal much of these genetic variations. While personal genomics is possible, the technology is still evolving. There is no way at present to be absolutely sure the predictive power of SNPs is accurate. Many genetic diseases, for example, are triggered by environmental factors. Having the tag SNP does not always result in becoming diseased.

The first article in the Prenatal Influences section, "The Prematurity Puzzle," focuses on developmental disabilities such as autism, cerebral palsy, and mental retardation, and the positive correlation of these problems with preterm births. Correlation does not prove cause and effect. It does suggest areas that need further exploration. The number of babies born prematurely in the United States has increased by 40 percent since 1980. Most brain cell synthesis stops after birth when the baby and the placenta are separated. Two factors—less pre-term birth, and discovering how to provide placental hormones to premature infants—may be able to stave off many neurological disorders in the future.

The next article goes beyond pregnancy and the mother's womb as very influential to lifespan development. "Thanks, Dad" provides tentative evidence that a father's diet, before his sperm impregnate an egg, can tweak the genes involved in fat and cholesterol synthesis. The paternal sperm, therefore, may contribute to the offspring's problems with obesity.

Your DNA, Decoded

Ten years ago, it cost billions of dollars to map a single human genome. Today, it's about $20,000 and likely to get even cheaper. If the average consumer can afford to have her own genetic map drawn up, what will it mean for medicine and how we approach our health care?

MARK ANDERSON

In early 2008, Henry Louis Gates Jr. stepped off his flight at LaGuardia Airport and began the process of having an elaborate set of blueprints drawn up: the map of himself, his entire human genome.

The Harvard professor of African American studies had at the time just hosted PBS' successful miniseries, *African American Lives 1 & 2*. The miniseries, which Gates jokingly calls "Roots in a Test Tube," traced the genealogical and genetic heritage of prominent figures and celebrities such as Oprah Winfrey, Morgan Freeman, Tina Turner and Chris Rock.

Also on Gates' flight were officials from the Cambridge, Massachusetts-based genetics company Knome, who told Gates they were interested in working with him on other projects involving DNA testing. Already prompted by the miniseries' fans to do a show about all Americans, Gates told the Knome representatives that this time he wanted to make a PBS series based on testing the full DNA (or "genome") of some of his guests.

Every living thing on Earth is built from instruction manuals—an organism's genes—found inside its cells. The complete set of instruction manuals is called a genome. For humans, the complete set is 6 billion characters long. We all inherit half of our body's instruction manual (3 billion characters) from our mother and half from our father. When these strands bond together, the connections create units of information called "base-pairs." Base-pairs can take on one of four values, signified by the names of the molecules from which they're made: A, C, G or T.

Sequencing a person's genome means discovering the value of all 3 billion DNA base-pairs—every A, C, G and T—in your body's instruction manual. It's the full host of biological blueprints that encodes uniquely who you are.

In 2003, only one human genome had been sequenced in the world, and it cost 50 cents per character. Today, just seven years later, the price has dropped to an astonishing 1/300,000 of a dollar per character. Within two to four years, because of rapidly advancing technology and economies of scale, the price is expected to fall by another factor of 10 or more—bringing the total cost of a full genome down to about $2,000.

The era of affordable genomes hasn't yet arrived, but it isn't far off—and mapping personal genomes at the price point of a laptop computer will change the face of medicine and, in a sense, the world.

For his 2009 series *Faces of America,* Gates traced the genealogical and genetic heritage of guests such as Eva Longoria Parker, Yo-Yo Ma, Meryl Streep, Stephen Colbert, Dr. Mehmet Oz and figure skater Kristi Yamaguchi. And, although Gates wanted to do full genomes of two of his guests, his scientific advisers recommended instead sequencing the genomes of both Gates and his father, 97-year-old Henry Louis Gates Sr. (Scientists hadn't yet sequenced any African American's genomes, nor had they sequenced a father-son pair.)

In fact, perhaps the most heart-wrenching moment in *Faces of America* comes when the program's genetic experts subtract Gates Sr.'s 3 billion DNA base-pairs from Gates Jr.'s genome. And there, in bold blue and yellow lines, lies the stark genetic outline of the younger Gates' mother, who died in 1987. "I put my father in this series," Gates says. "And the big shock is, I got my mother back." What Gates discovered about his mother was largely symbolic. He, like everyone, carries the blueprint of each of his parents inside his every cell for every moment of his life.

However, Gates also learned a boatload of information about his own life and health. A person's genome carries crucial information about individual weaknesses to disease, susceptibility to various cancers, the effectiveness and ineffectiveness of various drugs and, ominously, some of a person's more likely ultimate causes of death.

Human Genome Project

In 2000, President Bill Clinton announced that the government had created the first draft of the entire human genome. Ten years later, scientists still haven't been able to apply the $3 billion Human Genome Project to curing some of our deadly, elusive diseases.

Synthetic Genome

In May, genomic researcher J. Craig Venter announced that he and his colleagues had created the first synthetic cell. Using chemicals, they recreated the genetic code of a species of bacterium and then transplanted the manufactured genome into a closely related bacterium. Then the synthetic DNA took over.

The genetic counselors Gates hired for *Faces of America* told him he carried an innate resistance to certain forms of malaria and that caffeine breaks down quickly in his digestive system. So coffee has less effect on him than it does on most people. "For years I hadn't drunk [coffee] after noontime, being afraid it'd keep me awake," he says. But emboldened by his genome results, Gates tried drinking a cup of joe one night before bed. "I went right to sleep," he says.

Other than a variant of sickle cell anemia that makes him more susceptible to a stroke at high altitudes, Gates also learned that no unexpected ticking time bombs awaited him. Thanks to the lack of grave surprises in his DNA, Gates joined a project by his colleague George Church of Harvard Medical School that posts a patient's entire genome on the Internet (at http://snp.med.harvard.edu) for scientists—and anyone else—to study.

The need for publicly accessible genomes to compare and study became evident in *Faces of America*. An initial analysis of a single character in one of Gates' genes suggested he also had an exceptionally good ability to digest dairy products. But Gates is lactose intolerant. "I'm the one with the stomach for 59 years," he said. "I know I can't drink milk."

It was only on a closer examination of Gates' genome—enabled by more detailed analysis of his own genes and comparisons to other peoples' genes—that Knome researchers discovered the source of Gates' difficulty with dairy products. His particular DNA blueprint, they discovered, also makes it hard for him to process a dairy digestive by-product, called galactose. This is why he can drink plenty of coffee, but not with milk.

One of the first full families—mother, father and children—to sequence their genomes was the West family of Cupertino, California. John West, the father, is a former executive of one of the leading genome sequencing companies in the world—Illumina of San Diego. West, his wife, Judy, and children, Anne and Paul, had blood samples drawn late last year and in January received an iMac that contained all 24 billion A's, C's, T's and G's which represented the whole West family genome.

Although the family is keeping the kids' genomic results private, 17-year-old Anne has given a public presentation about inheriting a genetic defect from her father that in 2004 resulted in a trip to the emergency room for him. Raced to the hospital with a blood clot in his lung, John West endured a painful and frightening few days staring at his own mortality.

But now he and his daughter know the likely cause of his hospitalization. They also know the diet to follow and medications

Cloning

Many will remember Dolly, a Finn Dorset ewe that in 1996 became the first mammal to be successfully cloned from an adult cell. She was cloned at the Roslin Institute in Scotland and lived there until her death in 2003. Before that, however, a tadpole was the first vertebrate to be cloned, in 1952. Since Dolly's death, many animals have been cloned, including a camel and a water buffalo.

to take to drastically reduce the chances of anything like this happening to either of them in the future. West says his Illumina genome fortunately revealed no bombshells other than the

Genetics in Pop Culture

Spit Parties

Spitting isn't au courant at New York Fashion Week, but that's what notables such as Rupert Murdoch and Ivanka Trump were doing in 2008 at 23 and Me's genetic testing spit party, hosted by founders Anne Wojcicki (wife of Google co-founder Sergey Brin) and Linda Avey.

Mapping Your Past

The **Genographic Project,** driven by National Geographic Explorer-in-Residence Dr. Spencer Wells, is "seeking to chart new knowledge about the migratory history of the human species." If you wish to participate, a $99.95 kit is available to test your DNA and determine your ancestry along your maternal or paternal line.

Ancestry on TV

Two shows on television this spring, *Faces of America* and *Who Do You Think You Are,* featured prominent people who went looking for their lineage. NBC's *Who Do You Think* used old-fashioned, document-based genealogy, while PBS' *Faces* paired genealogy with genetic testing.

DNA Portraits

Talk about one-of-a-kind art. DNA 11 takes a sample of your DNA and reproduces it in color on a canvas you can hang on your wall. You can even mingle your DNA with your spouse's, for a truly unique anniversary gift. It's genetics as home décor.

Ozzy, Decoded

After years on the road with Black Sabbath and a 40-year "bender," how has Ozzy Osbourne survived? That's what DNA research company Knome is going to try to find out by sequencing the 61-year-old's entire genetic code. The company is reportedly interested in Osbourne because of his "extreme medical history."

known "misspelling" in a gene of his called "Factor 5." Such genetic errors, resulting from single-character transcription mistakes soon after a child is conceived in the womb, are sprinkled throughout everyone's genome. Most DNA mutations are harmless. But just one well-positioned mistake—imagine a car repair manual containing the typo "plug the fuel line" instead of "plumb the fuel line"—can wreak havoc.

Although genetic testing is still in its infancy, West says there is one way to enjoy access to every genetic test in the world—and every one yet to come. "There are hundreds of genetic tests. And if you were to take every single one of them separately, it'd cost you a fortune and you'd have to pay attention to all these individual pieces," he says. "The advantage of having your genome sequenced is you're doing all possible genetic tests all in one shot."

There are hundreds of genetic tests. And if you were to take every single one of them separately, it'd cost you a fortune and you'd have to pay attention to all these individual pieces. The advantage of having your genome sequenced is you're doing all possible genetic tests, all in one shot.

Mike Spear, communications director for Genome Alberta, a genetics funding organization in Calgary, Canada, has had small snippets of his genome tested by genetic-test companies deCODE and 23andMe. He learned, for one, that he's at high risk for early onset Alzheimer's disease. And he already knew that longevity runs in his family—a grandmother lived to be 101 and his father is still in the work-force at age 85.

"So I'm going to live long, but the last 30 years will be in a corner," he says. He also says, though, that most genetic test results just weigh the dice a little, so it's important not to get too carried away.

Spear learned, for instance, that he has twice the risk of baldness compared to the average man. "Your genome is what you are, but there are so many factors involved," he says. "So I'm at higher risk for baldness, but ... I have a full head of hair, and I'm 56. I'm at very low 'risk' for asthma, but I have always been an asthmatic."

Spear says anyone who already tends toward hypochondria or excessive worrying might want to think twice about personal genome sequencing or genetic testing—especially since the marketplace is still so new and people are still only beginning to learn how to interpret the results. "When you get these tests done, you sign a lot of pieces of paper that say you know what you're walking into," he says. "They even at one point in your waivers say, in caps, 'You may find out things you don't want to know.' "

Knome founder George Church of Harvard Medical School says the U.S. Genetic Information Nondiscrimination Act of 2008 prevents insurance companies from upping their premiums or dropping consumers who discover bad things from genetic testing. However, he adds, the act "doesn't stop

Genetics in Criminology

DNA Testing

While it's common practice now, DNA evidence wasn't used to convict or exonerate criminal suspects until 1986, when Richard Buckland was exonerated despite having confessed to rape and murder near Leicestershire, England. A year later, the first person was convicted in America on the basis of DNA evidence. According to the Innocence Project, more than 250 people in the U.S. have been exonerated through postconviction DNA testing since 1989.

consumers from gaming the system." If a patient finds out her genome gives her a clean bill of health, she might cut back on insurance coverage—reducing the pool of money insurance companies use to pay for expensive care for sick subscribers. Or if a patient learns he's at a high risk for something such as Lou Gehrig's disease, he may preemptively sign up for all the medical coverage money can buy. Such scenarios ultimately aren't fair to insurance companies, Church says. He suggests that the insurance industry now needs to team up with geneticists to brainstorm ways to work within GINA while still discouraging abuses of the system.

Victor McElheny, author of the new book *Drawing the Map of Life: Inside the Human Genome Project* (Basic Books), says some cancer patients today are already having parts of their genome—and sometimes a tumor's genome—sequenced. "When you do cancer chemotherapy, you're operating pretty much by guess and by God," he says. "An awful lot of cancer drugs only help maybe one-third of the people who get them. ... You'd like to know what the person's own genetic predispositions are, so you can start picking the right drug the first time."

Cancer treatments are the first in a line of predicted "personalized medicine" breakthroughs, in which a person's genetic information helps doctors tailor the treatment to the patient's specific body chemistry. One big problem, however, is that well-trained doctors in genetics are still a rare breed today. And patients, more and more, will need good genetic advice.

Matthew Bower, a genetic counselor at the University of Minnesota Medical Center in Minneapolis, says his field is entering an age of data overload. A's, C's, G's and T's can crowd out useful medical knowledge and counseling as much as it can help bring it on. "There are not enough genetics professionals to be managing everyone's genome out there," he says. And without good counseling, he says, people can still make bad decisions.

For instance, Bower says he recently spoke to two journalists who had small parts of their genome sequenced and learned that they didn't have one particular gene mutation that increases the risk of breast cancer. "They said, 'At least I don't have to worry about breast cancer,' " Bower recalls. But breast cancer is caused by both environmental and genetic factors. And its genetic causes alone, he says, could come from dozens or hundreds of possible mutations in a person's genome.

"People tend to perceive genetic information as black-and-white, all-or-nothing," he says. "So if they don't have the Parkinson's marker, then they're not going to get Parkinson's. That's false. Or if they have the Parkinson's marker, then they're going to get Parkinson's. That's also false."

The likelihood for confusion as the personal genome marketplace heats up has recently inspired the federal government to act. In June, the U.S. Food and Drug Administration informed the top consumer genetic-sequencing companies in the country—such as Knome and Illumina—that the agency could soon be regulating the personal genome and consumer genetics marketplace.

Regulation, says Church, could entwine companies in red tape and slow the market down. On the other hand, he adds, it may not hurt much. The FDA's intervention could actually help the fledgling genome industry: "Reading about this in the news and seeing the FDA seal of approval," he says, might also lead consumers to want to try out consumer genetic testing.

Grant Campany, senior director of the Archon X-Prize for Genomics, says the FDA's move itself constitutes a kind of endorsement. "The industry is going through a natural state of evolution," he says. "It's in everybody's best interest that there's a certain standard or benchmark—what quality really means." FDA regulation of the marketplace also means that the June 2010 price tag for complete genome sequencing from the top two companies—Knome ($39,500, which includes genetic counseling) and Illumina ($19,500)—may soon be subject to change.

Campany particularly has his eyes on the future of the marketplace, as he's supervising the privately funded $10 million "X-Prize," which will be awarded to the first company that can sequence 100 genomes in 10 days or less at no more than $10,000 per genome.

Biotech journalist David Ewing Duncan says it's still early, but at least a subset of the world is fascinated at the prospect of being the first generation in human history to read their own blueprint. In 2009, he published *Experimental Man,* a book that traces his sometimes enlightening, sometimes-confounding experiences subjecting himself to genetic tests from companies such as 23andMe and deCODE. (Duncan hasn't yet had his whole genome sequenced, however.)

His conclusion, in short, is that a lot of genetic and genomic tests are scattershot: A little bit of information here, a little bit there and a lot of confusion elsewhere. Yet the field is progressing at great speed, too. It's not just looking at individual DNA base-pairs, but also making sense of larger patterns within the genome—discovering, for instance, that one DNA base-pair may suggest that a person is good at digesting milk, but a larger grouping suggests he's actually, on balance, lactose intolerant.

"We're a lot closer than I'd have thought. But it's like a thousand points of light that need to be connected," he says. "We took apart the human body. Now we have to put it back together."

Critical Thinking

1. Give examples of how knowing your genome could save your life.
2. Point out ways that lifestyle modifications can reduce the chance that a genetic error will become harmful.
3. Predict a person whose knowledge of personal genome might do more harm than good.

Seeking Genetic Fate

Personal genomics companies offer forecasts of disease risk, but the science behind the packaging is still evolving.

Patrick Barry

"Resistant!!!" shouts the title of Lindsay Richman's post. Apparently, she was elated to learn that her DNA reduces her susceptibility to norovirus infections, the principal cause of the common stomach flu.

So she posted a comment on a discussion board on the website for 23andMe, a company based in Mountain View, Calif., that specializes in the fledgling industry of personal genomics. To get a glimpse of her own DNA, Richman had sent the company $400 and a vial of her spit. From her point of view, what happened next was a mystery—a black box. But a few weeks later, out popped her results on a password-protected website, complete with social networking tools for sharing and discussing her genetic inheritance with other customers.

In the string of online responses to Richman's post, others who share her genetic good fortune compared notes on the last time they'd had any symptoms of stomach flu. Richman, a 26-year-old real estate agent in New York City, hasn't had stomach flu since she was 8, she wrote.

In other discussions, people compared their genetic profiles and brainstormed on how lifestyle choices and environmental exposures might influence their risks for various conditions, such as Parkinson's disease and prostate cancer.

Now that prices charged by personal genomics companies such as 23andMe, Navigenics, deCODE genetics and DNA Direct have dropped, ranging from a few hundred to a few thousand dollars, many people curious about their genetic inheritance, and how it relates to their health, have easier access to DNA testing.

Serving to "crowdsource" the search for new links among genes, behavior and disease, these companies' customers represent a small army of amateur genome sleuths who could prove to be a new force in pushing genomic research forward. But the genetic report cards these amateurs are reading may not be as definitive as they assume. Despite progress in linking genetic differences with disease risk and other traits, the predictive power of these links has fallen short of expectations.

In April, the *New England Journal of Medicine* published a review and a set of essays grappling with this shortfall in DNA's predictive power and searching for the best way to take research forward. An essay by Peter Kraft and David Hunter, epidemiologists at the Harvard School of Public Health in Boston, was revealingly titled, "Genetic risk prediction—are we there yet?"

Their answer, in a nutshell: No. Which leads to the crucial question of what, exactly, customers of personal genomics companies are looking at when logging on to the digital oracle to peek at their genetic fates.

The leap from a tube of saliva to a ledger of traits, health risks and ancestral history involves a lot of science—some credible, some flimsy. As more and more people become consumers of genetic information services, these people may want to first open that black box and take a good look inside.

The Black Box

It's certainly not the most dignified way to join the genomics era.

Inside the small, brightly colored DNA-sample kit that arrives in the mail lies a clear plastic tube capped by a blue plastic funnel—the easier to spit into. Users are instructed to fill the tube to a little line, which the directions say can take five minutes or more. Five minutes of repetitive spitting.

In that saliva float cheek cells that have sloughed off from the soft tissue lining the mouth. Snapping the tube's lid shut releases a preservative that keeps the cells intact during their voyage to the lab.

"The reason we collect so much spit is to get a lot of your DNA," explains Brian Naughton, a founding scientist at 23andMe. The machines that read the sequence of DNA chemical "letters" of the genetic code are quite accurate and robust against noise. Repeat the scan with DNA from the same person, and the two results will be more than 99.9 percent identical, according to the company.

"It's clearly reproducible," says George M. Church, a geneticist at Harvard Medical School in Boston. Testing a person again with another company's service using a different model of DNA reading machine will also produce nearly identical results. Church says.

Spit and Learn

The technology that personal genomics companies use does not read the sequence of genetic code letter by letter. Instead, the machines look for single-letter variations at specific locations. From a person's vial of spit, DNA is extracted from cells. The gene chip takes it from there.

DNA on a Chip

Resembling a computer chip, a gene chip has millions of microscopic spots. Each contains anchored, single DNA strands with specific sequences of genetic code with common single-letter variations.

Get Together

When spread over the gene chip, DNA from a person's spit sample joins with strands already attached to the chip that have the complementary genetic sequence. A fluorescent molecule marks joined strands.

Revealing Spots

Thanks to the fluorescent tags, glowing dots signal where a sample DNA strand has the matching genetic sequence to the known sequence of a pre-attached strand. A computer analyzes the results, producing a list of single-letter variations.

These machines use gene chips to read up to a million letters of genetic code at once. Since the first gene chips that could skim the entire genome debuted in 2005, the cost to scan a person's DNA has dropped dramatically.

Despite what some customers might assume, most personal genomics companies do *not* produce a complete sequence of a customer's genome. An entire human genome contains about 6 billion letters of genetic code distributed among a person's 23 pairs of chromosomes (the inspiration for the name 23andMe). These machines don't read every DNA letter. Instead, they read individual letters at 500,000 to a million different spots in the genome, capturing just 8 to 16 *thousandths* of one percent of the full genome.

But that genome sliver is carefully selected to represent much of the genetic variation among people. "It's really coverage of that genetic variation that you're going for," Naughton explains.

Nearly all of a person's genetic code is identical to that of every other person—roughly 99.5 percent of it matches up letter for letter. At certain spots along the length of a person's chromosomes, though, the genetic code can differ from other people's by a single letter. In the sequence of the familiar A's, T's, C's and G's, the four information-carrying nucleotides in DNA, some people might have a T at a certain location while others have a C. These small variations are called single nucleotide polymorphisms, or SNPs (pronounced "snips").

The human genome contains about 10 million known SNPs. That estimate is the latest from the International HapMap Project, an ongoing scientific collaboration that's mapping these genetic variations. But SNPs near each other on a chromosome tend to get inherited together, making it possible to group neighboring SNPs into units of inheritance called haplotypes. A few tag SNPs are enough to identify each group, so it takes only about 500,000 tag SNPs to reveal a person's haplotypes. That's why most gene chips test for at least 500,000 SNPs, and why checking this tiny sliver of the genome—these tag SNPs—can reveal much of the genetic variation that makes a person unique.

Tag SNPs usually aren't part of any known gene. But the surrounding DNA inherited along with a SNP can contain one or more genes important for various diseases. The SNP is often a proxy.

This much of the black box is fairly reliable: the raw data on at least hundreds of thousands of a person's SNPs. Some personal genomics companies make this mountain of raw data directly available to their customers.

But that's the easy part. The other, more problematic half of the black box is interpretation. What exactly does having one SNP variant or another mean for a person's risk for heart disease, diabetes, colon cancer?

In short, there's no single answer for how reliable these interpretations are. Some SNPs have clear, strong and well-understood links with specific traits or diseases. Many others have only small effects, and the biological mechanisms for the links are often unknown.

Reviewing the available scientific evidence for each disease or trait is the biggest challenge for these companies, says Michele Cargill, director of human genetics for Navigenics. "You really have to read each [study] very, very carefully. It takes a lot of time and it's all done manually."

For example, the resistance to norovirus infection that Richman enjoys is linked to a SNP called rs601338, which is located on each of the two chromosome 19s she inherited from her parents. At this location, a person can have either an A or a G for this SNR Chromosomes with an A lack a functioning copy of a gene called *FUT2*. This gene produces a certain molecule on the outer surfaces of the cells that line the intestines. As it turns out, noroviruses must bind to this molecule in order to enter and infect the cells. People like Richman, who inherited the ASNP from both of her parents, do not have a working copy of the *FUT2* gene, so their intestinal cells lack the molecule that noroviruses need to cause an infection.

In this case, the link is strong. A single SNP can indicate whether a person has a working copy of a certain gene, and the biological mechanisms tying this gene to the virus's ability to enter the person's cells are well understood. In nearly all studies, people who lacked a functional copy of the *FUT2* gene didn't get sick, even when deliberately exposed to this

Chances Are

Writer Patrick Barry sent his own vial of spit to 23andMe and in return had access to an online summary, featured in this Web screenshot, of his risk for type 2 diabetes. Also, the company's chart of Marker Effects illustrates how risk can change from one variation on a genome to another. The genetic answer to the risk for this disease is not straightforward.

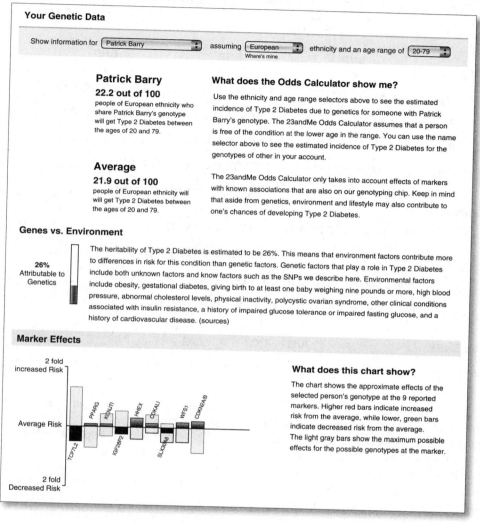

Your Genetic Data

Show information for [Patrick Barry] assuming [European] ethnicity and an age range of [20-79]
Where's mine

Patrick Barry
22.2 out of 100
people of European ethnicity who share Patrick Barry's genotype will get Type 2 Diabetes between the ages of 20 and 79.

Average
21.9 out of 100
people of European ethnicity will will get Type 2 Diabetes between the ages of 20 and 79.

What does the Odds Calculator show me?

Use the ethnicity and age range selectors above to see the estimated incidence of Type 2 Diabetes due to genetics for someone with Patrick Barry's genotype. The 23andMe Odds Calculator assumes that a person is free of the condition at the lower age in the range. You can use the name selector above to see the estimated incidence of Type 2 Diabetes for the genotypes of other in your account.

The 23andMe Odds Calculator only takes into account effects of markers with known associations that are also on our genotyping chip. Keep in mind that aside from genetics, environment and lifestyle may also contribute to one's chances of developing Type 2 Diabetes.

Genes vs. Environment

26%
Attributable to Genetics

The heritability of Type 2 Diabetes is estimated to be 26%. This means that environment factors contribute more to differences in risk for this condition than genetic factors. Genetic factors that play a role in Type 2 Diabetes include both unknown factors and know factors such as the SNPs we describe here. Environmental factors include obesity, gestational diabetes, giving birth to at least one baby weighing nine pounds or more, high blood pressure, abnormal cholesterol levels, physical inactivity, polycystic ovarian syndrome, other clinical conditions associated with insulin resistance, a history of impaired glucose tolerance or impaired fasting glucose, and a history of cardiovascular disease. (sources)

Marker Effects

2 fold increased Risk

Average Risk

2 fold Decreased Risk

TCF7L2 PPARG KCNJ11 IGF2BP2 HHEX CDKAL1 SLC30A8 WFS1 CDKN2A/B

What does this chart show?

The chart shows the approximate effects of the selected person's genotype at the 9 reported markers. Higher red bars indicate increased risk from the average, while lower, green bars indicate decreased risk from the average. The light gray bars show the maximum possible effects for the possible genotypes at the marker.

---

type of virus. It's as close as one ever gets in biology to a slam dunk.

About 1,300 genes have known, strong links to medical conditions, Church notes. Some disorders, such as sickle-cell anemia, are truly genetic diseases that a person has from birth. Others such as Parkinson's disease, macular degeneration, Alzheimer's disease and breast cancer arise later in life and can be influenced by environment and lifestyle, even though some genes are known to significantly change the odds that a person will get the disease.

But the relatively clear-cut cases are the exception, not the rule. For many traits and diseases, finding reasonably strong and reliable links with SNPs has proven more difficult than many scientists had expected.

Beware Weak Links

To search for these links, researchers use gene chips similar to those used by personal genomics companies. With these gene chips, scientists scan the DNA of two groups of people: a few hundred or thousand people with the disease in question and a few hundred or thousand without it. If the two groups are well matched in terms of other important traits such as age, ethnicity, smoking habits and so on, a SNP that appears more frequently among people with the disease than among the control group may be associated with the disease.

At first, these studies tended to "discover" a lot of illusory links—false connections that crop up by pure chance in the mountains of data produced by these studies *(SN: 6/21/08, p. 20)*.

Haplotype in a Haystack

Personal genomics companies read only a tiny portion of a person's genome. But it's a telling portion, with efforts focused on identifying SNPs and haplotypes. SNPs are spots in the DNA where one person has a different chemical letter than another. Certain congregations of SNPs are flags for haplotypes, which are patterns of genetic variation found in different populations. The illustration maps tag SNPs: (a) shows differences among four people in the same genetic sequence in part of one chromosome; (b) shows three SNPs highlighted in four haplotypes. The tag SNPs (c) can identify the haplotypes of the individuals.

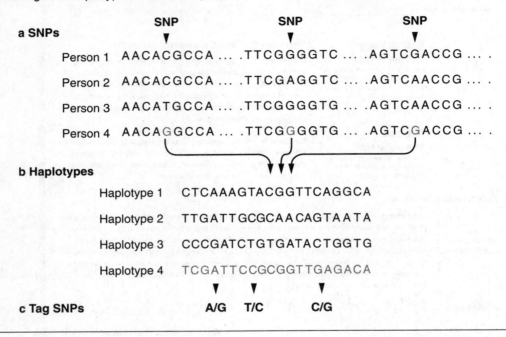

In the last few years, scientists have learned to correct for these statistical sins, but even with most false positives weeded out, these studies often point to large numbers of potentially suspect SNPs. For example, dozens of well-established SNPs contribute to the risk for Type 2 Diabetes, the form of the disease that emerges in late adulthood and is hastened by a diet high in sugar.

Unfortunately, most of these SNPs alter risk by only a tiny amount—a 2 percent change in risk for this one, a 5 percent change for that one, a 10 percent change for a third. Even a 10 percent change would mean that the odds of developing diabetes sometime in that person's lifetime would increase from the typical 22 percent to 24 percent. Not exactly a crystal ball–caliber revelation.

"People will tell you that if they know that they have a slightly higher risk for diabetes, then they could change their diet," Kraft says. "But you don't really need an expensive genome test to tell you that."

Even more problematic, though, is the fact that new links continue to trickle in. When the risks from individual SNPs are added, a person's overall risk of the disease could be slightly positive. But a newly discovered SNP could tilt the balance in the other direction.

"Our best guess about your risk today might turn out to be very different five years from now," Kraft says. "Your risk as a function of time is a random walk. It bounces up and down as we learn more."

These problems also plague other common illnesses such as heart disease, as well as complex traits such as height and intelligence. In each of these cases, large numbers of SNPs are involved because the underlying biology is complicated. Heart disease, for example, is an umbrella term for various cardiovascular problems that could depend on genes for heart muscle proteins, blood vessel strength and elasticity, cholesterol metabolism, blood clotting and others. And each of these functions often arises from webs of interactions among dozens or hundreds of genes. These interactions produce the feedback loops that fine-tune a cell's behavior and make it robust, and these interactions add to genetic complexity *(SN: 12/6/08, p. 22)*.

"It's very early days in terms of what we've learned about common, complex diseases," Kraft says.

Some in the genome research community say that studies with ever larger numbers of subjects are needed to find SNPs that have even weaker links but that many people have. The hope is that the cumulative effects will point to significant predictions. Others suggest that studies have already found all the important, common SNPs that there are to find, and that new studies should instead search for SNPs that are held by a small minority of people but that exert a stronger influence on disease.

Seeking Genetic Roots

DNA holds clues not only to an individual's medical future, but also to their family's past. Genetic profiles offered by many companies can show customers their ancestral histories.

After all, DNA is the ultimate genealogical record. A mutation that arose in the DNA of a person who lived 10,000 years ago could have been passed down to his or her children and grandchildren, becoming a kind of hidden family heirloom. Because the odds of that same single-letter mutation occurring again independently are negligibly small, somebody alive today who has that particular SNP almost certainly descended from that person who lived 10,000 years ago.

Of course, a DNA test can't pinpoint who that ancestor was. But by mapping where in the world a particular SNP is common among indigenous people, scientists can make a fairly good estimate of where its primogenitor lived.

DNA in small organelles called mitocnondria is inherited only from a person's mother. So a mitochondrial DNA SNP must have come from the mother, and her mother, and her mother, and so on for perhaps hundreds of generations. And DNA in the Y sex chromosome can come only from a boy's father and each previous father. Retracing the lineage of a mutation on other chromosomes is messy, since other chromosomes are shuffled at each generation. But mitochondrial DNA and Y chromosomes each offer a straight line of descent.

Modern tests look at more than 2,000 SNPs on both the mitochondrial DNA and—if the customer is male—the Y chromosome. The science behind these results is fairly robust, and estimates of geographical ancestry will only improve as scientists gather more DNA samples from people around the world.

—Patrick Barry

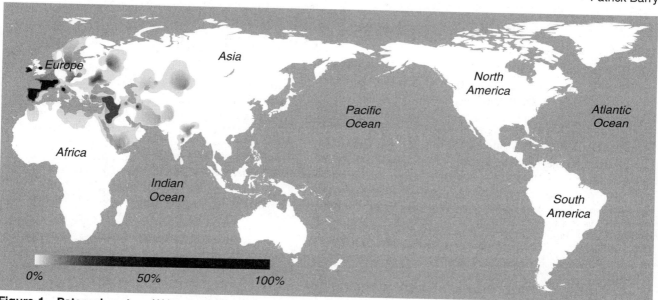

Figure 1   Paternal roots: Writer Patrick Barry discovered that his distant paternal ancestors most likely lived in western Europe. The map's color spectrum shows the probabilities that his father's family line, as identified by haplotype groups, originated in certain geographic regions.

Selling, Knowing Risk

Until more progress is made, some scientists say, selling risk information about complex diseases is premature.

"The justification is just not there for claiming that these [SNPs] have any clinical utility at this stage" for complex diseases, says Allan Balmain, a cancer geneticist at the University of California, San Francisco. He says that, in his opinion, personal genomics companies are "just exploiting the naïveté in the general population."

These companies plan to use their growing databases of DNA samples—and their legions of curious customers—for novel research. Other research scientists are cautiously optimistic.

Customers who have sent their DNA samples to these companies are not a random sample of the population, a fact that could bias the results. And information about family history, health habits and environmental exposures are gathered through unmonitored online surveys, rather than by professional clinicians. With careful study design and quality control for the data, though, these obstacles could be surmountable. "Their data set is not in itself bad," Balmain says. "Some of these things may turn out to be very useful."

Eventually, though, these companies may need to move beyond SNPs, as many researchers have begun to do. Much of the genetic variation among people comes in forms other than changes to single letters of code. Some people have long

Sometimes Even the Best Minds Need a Little R&R

So, pull the shades, turn off the PDA, and enjoy a guilty pleasure . . . *SCI FI* Magazine. We take you unblushingly into the world of the future . . . the world of what may be . . . and we have FUN with it. After all, who doesn't love those effects from the *Transformers* movies, or the gossip about a possible new *Star Trek* TV series, or those *Stargate Universe* secrets? Don't you deserve a little "me" time to pour over the paparazzi spread to see what kind of trouble the Hollywood sci fi set is getting into? Or even the review on the latest sci fi online game?

Yes, we know it's bubble-gum, it's popular media, it's psycho-babble. But its just so darn cool! . . . Next time someone scoffs that sci fi is useless, mind numbing drivel, you might want to remind them how many of those miraculous gadgets from the original *Star Trek* are now in everyday use.

Go ahead. Order a subscription for yourself today. It can be just our little secret.

Modified gene chips can detect some small insertions and deletions, but the best way to tally these changes is with the more thorough, and more expensive, approach of DNA sequencing.

Current state-of-the-art technologies can sequence an entire human genome for about $5,000, compared with millions of dollars just four years ago. "I think nobody anticipated just how fast the cost of sequencing would change," Church says. "I think we're already at the tipping point. It's already getting feasible to sequence large portions of genomes, maybe all the coding regions, for studies and for individuals."

Unfortunately, Naughton says, 23andMe doesn't store frozen saliva samples for most customers, only for those participating in research projects. So if Richman someday wants to upgrade to a full genome sequence to learn even more about her genetic inheritance, she'll have to go through all that spitting again.

Explore More

International HapMap Project: www.hapmap.org

Critical Thinking

1. Identify potential problems with predicting who is at risk of various disease conditions.
2. Appraise Dr. Allan Balmain's opinion that genomic companies are "just exploiting the naiveté in the general population." Do you agree or disagree with his opinion?

PATRICK BARRY is a science writer based in San Francisco.

chunks of DNA within their genomes that other people lack. Along with these insertions and deletions, the number of copies of some genes varies from person to person. While these kinds of structural differences are far less numerous than SNPs, each of them can involve hundreds or thousands of letters of genetic code, so together they account for about four times more genetic variation than SNPs do (*SN: 4/25/09, p. 16*).

From *Science News*, July 4, 2009, vol. 176, No. 1, pp. 16–21. Copyright © by Society for Science & the Public. Reprinted by permission.

The Prematurity Puzzle

Research on early births could hold clues to disorders like autism and cerebral palsy.

JENEEN INTERLANDI

Every year approximately 12.9 million babies—roughly 10 percent of all newborns around the world—are born too early, which is to say, before 37 weeks in utero. Despite a heroic, costly, and decades-long effort by doctors and scientists to understand and prevent preterm birth, that number has climbed steadily for the past three decades. In the U.S. alone, premature births are up 40 percent since 1980. Meanwhile, as modern medicine helps more and more of those babies survive, doctors and scientists have found themselves confronted with a new dilemma: how to prevent the string of neurological problems and developmental disabilities that plague many premature babies as they grow into children and adults.

Some of the factors behind the rise in preterm births are obvious: more women having children later in life (the risk of delivering prematurely increases as women get older), more families using in vitro fertilization (with its tendency toward multiple births), and more doctors opting for Caesarean sections at the first signs of fetal distress. But even among women who do none of these things, preterm births are still increasingly common. The fluid-filled membrane that surrounds the uterus ruptures decidedly ahead of schedule, sending mother into labor before baby is fully developed. Doctors still have no idea why this happens or how to prevent it. "Preterm birth is a huge, thriving area of research," says Amy McKenney, a perinatal pathologist at Stanford University Medical Center. "But for all of it, we haven't made much of a dent."

A $75 million educational campaign by the March of Dimes has managed to reduce incidence by a smidgen, from 12.8 percent in 2006 to 12.3 percent in 2008, mostly by persuading more pregnant women to quit smoking and more doctors to avoid elective C-sections in all but the direst cases.

But other efforts have failed spectacularly. "The most common interventions recommended to prevent or treat preterm labor have proved to be of little or no benefit," says Louis Muglia, a neonatologist at Vanderbilt University. For example, doctors learned in 2000 that certain bacterial infections increase a mother's chances of delivering early. But treating those infections with antibiotics does not reduce the risk of preterm

delivery or improve the baby's prognosis. Likewise, women whose cervixes have shortened to less than 25mm in length by their second trimester are three times as likely to deliver early, according to studies done in 2001. But placing a cerclage, or stitch, in the cervix to help prevent further shortening has proved to be of almost no value. And while several clues point to a genetic component—preterm births tend to run in families and are higher in certain ethnic populations—the hunt for offending genes has been inconclusive at best.

Preemies who survive the neonatal intensive-care unit frequently go on to experience a range of developmental disabilities as they grow.

Where we have improved is in keeping preemies alive. As recently as 1940, babies who were born too early or too small were often listed as stillborn and left for dead. Today we devote entire hospital wings—not to mention $26 billion in annual health-care costs—to keeping the frailest of newborns alive. Like giant mechanical wombs, neonatal intensive-care units employ a vast array of machinery to protect preterm babies from the outside world: incubators isolate them from pathogens while a host of machines and medications regulates body temperature and keeps tiny lungs working until baby is strong enough to do those things on her own. The result: 80 to 98 percent of preemies born in the U.S. now survive.

But so far, not even the best hospital in the world can fully substitute for a mother's womb. Preemies who survive the neonatal intensive-care unit frequently go on to experience a range of developmental disabilities as they grow. Some suffer from behavioral problems like attention-deficit/hyperactivity disorder, others develop more serious conditions, including mental retardation, cerebral palsy, and, according to two recent studies, autism. And unlike lung or heart problems, which are immediately apparent, neurological impairment can take years to show up. "We are delivering more and more babies preterm, and we are saving more and more of them," says Anna Penn, a neonatologist at Packard Children's Hospital in California. "But neurological outcomes are not improving in tandem." To change this, scientists will have to figure out what forces guide fetal brain development in the first place. Penn and her colleagues are betting on the placenta, a thick layer of cells that envelops part of the fetus.

Ancient civilizations, at least, were keenly aware of the placenta's significance, even if they lacked the scientific tools to probe its depths. Convinced of its mythical powers, the Egyptians built a cult around royal afterbirth—preserving and protecting the pharaoh's placenta while the king was alive, and burying it with him when he died. The latter custom—placenta burial—is still practiced by dozens of religious groups around the world today.

But as far as organs go, the placenta has ranked pretty far down on the totem pole for most of the modern medical era. Doctors recognized its ability to protect the fetus from a range of potential assaults and to usher a few basic chemicals, like oxygen and carbon dioxide, across the mother-fetus divide, but never suspected it was an actual organ capable of interacting with both mother and fetus. In fact, most doctors still toss the blubbery disc-shaped mass into an incinerator-bound bucket almost as soon as the mother expels it from the womb.

It turns out that the placenta is an organ, and a complicated one at that. Genetically all fetus but intricately bound to the mother's blood vessels, it facilitates a constant chemical dialogue between expecting mother and unborn child. It's this dialogue—nutrients, gasses, and hundreds of placenta-made hormones streaming back and forth—that transforms a fetus into a sufficiently developed infant.

A steady beat of emerging research suggests that crucial instructions for later neurodevelopment may also be included in that conversation. By manufacturing a vast array of chemicals and deploying them to the fetus, where they cross the blood-brain barrier, the placenta sets in motion a cascade of chemical events whose effects won't be fully realized for years to come.

Penn and her colleagues reason that cutting the conversation short leaves the developing brain in the lurch. "Without the placental signposts, development is hobbled," she says. "If we can figure out exactly what directions have been lost, we can chart an identical map and help keep development on course."

Using a small army of genetically engineered mice, Penn's team is turning off one hormone gene at a time in the hopes of determining which of them has the biggest impact on neural development. On top of that, they are collecting blood and spinal fluid from human babies—both premature and full term—so that they can compare hormone profiles between groups.

The placenta facilitate a constant chemical dialogue between expecting mother and unborn child.

So far, two particular chemicals have emerged as potential culprits. Both progesterone, which helps nerve cells to grow, and oxytocin, which protects fetal neurons from becoming over-excited and dying, appear to reach peak concentrations late in pregnancy. That means a baby who's born even a few weeks prematurely could be missing out on a crucial dose.

Oxytocin—sometimes called the cuddling hormone for its role in emotional attachment and maternal behavior—has also been implicated in autism. In young children, low concentrations of the hormone have been linked to social and behavioral difficulties, and signaling pathways for oxytocin have been shown to be impaired in autistic children.

That's not the only factor placing autism and preterm labor in the same orbit; both autism and the worst developmental effects of premature birth are more than twice as prevalent in males. And in a study published last year, children who were born significantly prematurely (before 27 weeks in utero) were twice as likely to develop autism. Penn and her Stanford colleagues are comparing oxytocin levels between 2-year-olds with autism and 2-year-olds without the disorder who were all born prematurely. "We want to see if the two groups have similar hormone profiles," says Penn. "It could mean that both are caused by some unique placental malfunction."

Once doctors understand which hormones are essential to fetal brain development, Penn hopes they will be able to measure the level of those hormones in the premature baby's blood and replace what's missing quickly enough to stave off neurological disaster.

Before they get there, many more human placentas will have to be studied. Penn's team is vying to build a large placenta repository, like the ones cancer biologists use to share and study tumor samples. Until that happens, some of the most valuable clues to brain development will continue to be tossed into the trash.

Critical Thinking

1. How are mental retardation, cerebral palsy, and autism related to prenatal brain development?

2. Summarize how the placenta transforms an embryo/fetus into an infant capable of sustaining life.

3. What are the role of the hormones progesterone and oxytocin?

Thanks, Dad

Fathers, as well as mothers, can pass on a propensity to obesity if they themselves have been starved.

THE ECONOMIST

That a gestating mother's environment can have a permanent effect on the physiology of her offspring is well established. The children of Dutch women who were pregnant during the "Hunger Winter" of 1944, for example, suffer much higher rates of obesity, diabetes and cardiovascular disease than those born a year or two earlier. Similar observations in other famines, together with experiments on rodents, suggest this is an accidental consequence of an evolutionary adaptation to food scarcity. The offspring of starving mothers, anticipating hard times during their own future lives, adjust their metabolisms to hoard calories. If the hard times then go away, the result is a tendency to put on weight, with the unpleasant consequences that entails.

Part of this adaptation is a response by the embryo to the nutrition it receives through the placenta. In some cases, though, the unfertilised ovum itself is believed to be affected. Its DNA is reprogrammed, the theory goes, by a process called cytosine methylation. This switches genes on and off in a way that is maintained when DNA replicates during the process of cell division—and can thus be passed down the generations. It is, moreover, a process that could apply equally to the sperm of putative fathers who were starved around the time of mating.

There are hints that it does. In particular, a recent paper by Sheau-Fang Ng of the University of New South Wales showed that gene activity in the pancreases of mice sired by fat fathers is abnormal. That is significant because the pancreas makes insulin, which regulates blood sugar. Abnormal insulin levels cause diabetes.

Oliver Rando of the University of Massachusetts and his colleagues have now looked at another metabolically crucial organ, the liver, and found a similar effect. To mimic starvation, they fed half of a group of male mice a diet that contained 11%

protein, which is low for such rodents. The others were fed a normal diet, containing 20% protein. After between nine and 12 weeks on these diets, each male was given a couple of days' access to a female who had been raised on a normal diet, to allow him to mate. The males were then taken away from their females, to limit any influence they might have on their progeny. After birth, those progeny were reared by their mothers until they were three weeks old, at which point they were killed and their livers analysed to study the activity of genes involved in metabolism.

As they report in *Cell*, Dr Rando and his team found 445 genes whose expression appeared to depend strongly on the diet of the father. In particular, genes associated with fat and cholesterol synthesis were much more active in the offspring of fathers who had been fed low-protein diets than in those sired by males who had been on normal diets. That, it might reasonably be assumed, would have allowed the mice in question to lay down any surplus calories as fat more easily than the offspring of well-fed fathers could have done.

Whether cytosine methylation is the explanation for this difference has yet to be tested, but something is clearly happening. Fathers, as well as mothers, it seems, can pass on the benefits of their experiences by subtle tweaking of their genes.

Critical Thinking

1. Support the theory that a father's sperm may affect the development of an embryo/fetus.

2. What advice would you give a father-to-be about food choices before impregnating his partner?

3. How can food scarcity and malnutrition affect a developing embryo/fetus?

UNIT 2

Development during Infancy and Early Childhood

Unit Selections

Learning Outcomes

After reading this Unit you should be able to:

- Distinguish between three infant temperament types and explain why each baby's unique personality should be explored.

- Defend the pro-vaccine group's position of "Every Child by Two."

- Explain the apparent increase in autistic spectrum disorders today.

- Rearrange the ten tasks of empathy nurturance in their order of importance to you.

- Contrast popular vs. rejected children in terms of their empathy abilities.

- Justify Peg Tyre's belief that young children need to be taught emotional skills.

- Analyze the relationship between trust and persistence at learning tasks.

- Summarize the steps by which a child develops an allergy.

- Suggest several ways to alleviate childhood allergies in the future.

- Defend the idea that parents need to be involved in their child's early education.

- Summarize ways to foster healthy eating habits in young children.

- Prepare a one-week snack plan for preschoolers and suggest how to make it exciting.

Student Website

www.mhhe.com/cls

Development during infancy and early childhood is more rapid than in any other life stage, excluding the prenatal period. Newborns are quite well developed in some areas, and incredibly deficient in others. Babies' higher cerebral hemispheres already have their full complement of neurons (worker cells). The neuroglia (supportive cells) are almost completely developed and will reach their final numbers by age one. In contrast, babies' legs and feet are tiny, weak, and barely functional. Look at newborns from another perspective, however, and their brains seem somewhat less superior. The neurons and neuroglia present at birth must be protected. By contrast, the cells of the baby's legs and feet (skin, fat, muscles, bones, blood vessels) are able to replace themselves by mitosis indefinitely. Their numbers will continue to grow through early adulthood; then their quantity and quality can be regenerated through advanced old age.

The developing brain in infancy is a truly fascinating organ. At birth it is poorly organized. The lower (primitive) brain parts (brain stem, pons, medulla, cerebellum) are developed enough to allow the infant to live. The lower brain directs vital organ systems (heart, lungs, kidneys, etc.). The higher (advanced) brain parts (cerebral hemispheres) have allocated neurons, but the nerve cells and cell processes (axons, dendrites) are small, underdeveloped, and unorganized. During infancy, these higher (cerebral) nerve cells (that allow the baby to think, reason, and remember) grow at astronomical rates. They migrate to permanent locations in the hemispheres, develop myelin sheathing (insulation), and conduct messages. Many 20th century researchers, including Jean Piaget, the father of cognitive psychology, believed that all brain activities in the newborn were reflexive, based on instincts for survival. They underestimated babies. New research has documented that fetuses can learn, and newborns can think as well as learn.

The role played by electrical and chemical activity of neurons in actively shaping the physical structure of the brain is particularly awe-inspiring. The neurons are produced prenatally. After birth, the flood of sensory inputs from the environment (sights, sounds, smells, tastes, touch, balance, and kinesthetic sensations) drives the neurons to form circuits and become wired to each other. Trillions of connections are established in a baby's brain. During childhood, the connections that are seldom or never used are eliminated or pruned. The first three years are critical for establishing these connections. Environments that provide both good nutrition and lots of sensory stimulation actually produce richer, more connected brains.

The first article selected for this unit, "Keys to Quality Infant Care," focuses on eleven important ways to stimulate the brain as it is developing in infancy and early childhood. The author, Alice Honig, has taught workshops in infant/toddler caregiving for 34 years and is an expert in this area. She cautions that all babies are different, and advice must be tailored to uniquely distinct personalities. Love and intimate emotional connections are paramount requirements.

The second infancy article, "Vaccination Nation," by Chris Mooney, explains how the fear of vaccinations developed in America. "Vaccines do not cause autism." This is the opening sentence. Ample research by unbiased scientists, working pro

© Getty Images/Blend Images

bono, is reviewed. However, once a claim is made and people become frightened, it is hard to contain their fears. Thimerosal, once blamed for causing brain damage, has been removed from vaccines since 2001! The sad result of the unsupported assertions about poisons in vaccines is that fewer children are getting inoculations. Polio, measles, mumps, diphtheria, tetanus, pertussis, and rubella, largely unknown diseases, can become epidemic again and cause unprecedented loss of life. The question remains, "How can people be persuaded that vaccines are safe and that they can prevent devastating diseases?"

"How to Help Your Toddler Begin Developing Empathy" explains that toddlers can understand that other people have feelings, separate from those the young child is experiencing. The ability to comprehend this is the foundation for developing empathy with others. Rebecca Pariakian and Claire Lerner explain how to encourage youngsters to think about others. This takes time, and a lot of patience. Moving from "I, me, and mine" to "you and yours" is a complex skill that continues to develop over one's lifetime.

The second selection for early childhood deals with "Five Skills Kids Need before They Read." The author, Peg Tyre, is an expert on developmental issues of early childhood. She makes a convincing case in this article for helping children feel good about themselves as a prerequisite for feeling good about school and learning. Ms. Tyre reviews relevant literature about socialization in early childhood. She also suggests resources for interested readers.

The third paper chosen for inclusion in this section on early childhood addresses what is quickly becoming a leading cause of disability in toddlers and preschoolers: food allergies. The increased prevalence is not well understood. There are multiple factors which may be involved. The author, Laura Beil, explains how children develop allergic reactions to certain foods. She gives hopeful information about what might be used to prevent allergies in the future, or at least make them less life-threatening.

The fourth article for the unit about young children addresses the need for family involvement in each child's early education. The authors suggest use of the Internet to keep communication alive and frequent. Even parents without computers can be included. They can be taught how to access technology in libraries and in other free sources. Hard copies of emails and website announcements can also be printed and sent home to such parents to keep them in the loop. The earlier parents feel a part of their child's education, the greater the probability of continued involvement throughout development and schooling.

The last selected writing for this collection of articles about infancy and early childhood addresses the importance of a healthy diet. High nutritional value foods are necessary for the rapid growth in this stage of life. Healthy development is promoted by eating lean proteins, whole grains, calcium-rich foods and beverages, and plenty of vegetables and fruits. Empty calorie snacks, excess sugar and salt, and artificially flavored beverages dull the appetite for more nutritious choices. The authors of "Early Sprouts: Establishing Healthy Food Choices for Young Children" have many exciting suggestions for helping young children really like the foods that are best for them.

Internet References

Autism
www.autism-society.org

BabyCenter
www.babycenter.com

Center for Childhood Obesity Research (CCOR)
www.hhdev.psu.edu/ccor/index.html

Children's Nutrition Research Center (CNRC)
www.kidsnutrition.org

Early Childhood Care and Development
www.ecdgroup.com

The National Association for the Education of Young Children (NAEYC)
www.naeyc.org

The Penn Resiliency Project
www.ppc.sas.upenn.edu

Tech and Young Children
www.techandyoungchildren.org

Turnaround for Children
www.turnaroundusa.org

Zero to Three: National Center for Infants, Toddlers, and Families
www.zerotothree.org

Keys to Quality Infant Care
Nurturing Every Baby's Life Journey

ALICE STERLING HONIG

Teachers of infants need a large bunch of key ideas and activities of all kinds to unlock in each child the treasures of loving kindness, thoughtful and eloquent use of language, intense active curiosity to learn, willingness to cooperate, and the deep desire to work hard to master new tasks. Here are some ideas that teachers can use during interactions with infants to optimize each child's development.

Get to Know Each Baby's Unique Personality

At 4 months, Luci holds her hands in front of her face and turns them back and forth so she can see the curious visual difference between the palms and backs. Jackson, an 8-month-old, bounces happily in accurate rhythm as his teacher bangs on a drum and chants, "Mary had a little lamb whose fleece was white as snow!" Outdoors, 1-year-old Jamie sits in an infant swing peering down at his feet sticking out of the leg holes. How interesting! Those are the same feet he has watched waving in the air while being diapered and has triumphantly brought to his mouth to chew on.

Teachers can tune in to each child's special personality—especially the child's temperament. There are three primary, mostly inborn, styles of temperament (Honig 1997). Some babies are more low-key; they tend to be slow to warm up to new caregivers, new foods, and new surroundings. They need reassuring hand-holding and more physical supports to try a new activity. Others are more feisty and sometimes irritable. They tend to be impetuous, intense in their emotional reactions, whether of anger or of joy. Easygoing babies are typically friendly, happy, accept new foods and caregivers without much fuss, and adapt fairly quickly and more flexibly after experiencing distress or sudden change. Try to find out whether each baby in your care tends to be shy and slow to warm up *or* mostly feisty and intense *or* easygoing. A caring adult's perceptive responses in tune with individual temperament will ease a child's ability to adapt and flourish in the group setting.

Physical Loving

Your body is a safe haven for an infant. Indeed, some babies will stay happy as a clam when draped over a shoulder, across your belly as you rock in a rocking chair, or, especially for a very young baby, snuggled in a sling or carrier for hours. As Montagu (1971) taught decades ago, babies need *body loving:* "To be tender, loving, and caring, human beings must be tenderly loved and cared for in their earliest years. . . . caressed, cuddled, and comforted" (p. 138).

As you carry them, some babies might pinch your neck, lick your salty arm, pull at your hair, tug at eyeglasses, or show you in other ways how powerfully important your body is as a sacred and special playground. Teach gentleness by calmly telling a baby you need your glasses on to read a story. Use the word *gently* over and over and over. Dance cheek-to-cheek with a young child in arms to slow waltz music—good for dreary days! Also carry the baby while you do a routine task such as walking to another room to get something.

Provide lap and touch times generously to nourish a child's sense of well-being. Slowly caress a baby's hair. Rub a tense shoulder soothingly. Kiss one finger and watch as a baby offers every other finger to kiss. Rock a child with your arms wrapped around him for secure comfort. Babies learn to become independent as we confirm and meet their dependency needs in infancy. A sense of well-being and somatic certainty flows from cherishing adults who generously hold, caress, and drape babies on shoulders and tummies.

Create Intimate Emotional Connections

Scan the environment so you can be close to every baby. Notice the quiet baby sitting alone, mouthing a toy piece and rocking back and forth with vacant eyes. Notice shy bids for attention, such as a brief smile with lowered lids. The child with an easy or cautious temperament needs your loving attention as much as the one who impulsively climbs all over you for attention.

A caring adult's perceptive responses in tune with individual temperament will ease a child's ability to adapt and flourish in the group setting.

Shine admiring eyes at the children, whether a baby is cooing as she lies in her crib, creeping purposefully toward a toy she desires, or feeding herself happily with messy fingers. Speak each child's name lovingly and frequently. Even if they are fussing, most babies will quiet when you chant and croon their names.

Although babies do not understand the meanings of the words, they do understand *tonal* nuances and love when your voice sounds admiring, enchanted with them, and happy to be talking with them. While diapering, tell the baby he is so delicious and you love his plump tummy and the few wispy hairs on that little head. Watch him thrust out his legs in delight on the diapering table. Your tone of voice entrances him into a deep sense of pleasure with his own body (Honig 2002).

Harmonizing Tempos

Tempo is important in human activities and is reflected in how abruptly or smoothly adults carry out daily routines. Because adults have so many tasks to do, sometimes we use impatient, too-quick motions, for example, while dressing a baby to play outdoors. When dressing or feeding, more leisurely actions are calming. They signal to children that we have time for them. Rub backs slowly and croon babies into soothing sleep.

A baby busily crawling across the rug sees a toy, grasps it, then plops himself into a sitting position to examine and try to pull it apart. He slowly looks back and forth at the toy as he leisurely passes it from hand to hand. He has no awareness that a teacher is about to interrupt because she is in a hurry to get him dressed because his daddy is coming to pick him up. Young children need time and cheerful supports to finish up an activity in which they are absorbed. If they are hurried, they may get frustrated and even have a tantrum.

Enhance Courage and Cooperation

Your presence can reassure a worried baby. Stay near and talk gently to help a child overcome his fear of the small infant slide. Pascal sits at the top, looking uncertain. Then he checks your face for a go-ahead signal, for reassurance that he can bravely try to slide down this slide that looks so long to him. Kneeling at the bottom of the slide, smile and tell him that you will be there to catch him when he is ready to slide down.

Be available as a "refueling station"—Margaret Mahler's felicitous term (Kaplan 1978). Sometimes a baby's independent learning adventure comes crashing down—literally. Your body and your lap provide the emotional support from which a baby regains courage to tackle the learning adventure again.

Create loving rituals during daily routines of dressing, bath times, nap times, feeding times. Babies like to know what will happen and when and where and how. Babies have been known to refuse lunch when their familiar, comfortable routines were changed. At cleanup times, older babies can be more flexible and helpful if you change some chores into games. Through the use of sing-song chants, putting toys away becomes an adventure in finding the big fat blocks that need to be placed together on a shelf and then the skinny blocks that go together in a different place.

Young children need time and cheerful supports to finish up an activity in which they are absorbed. If they are hurried, they may get frustrated and even have a tantrum.

Address Stress

Attachment research shows that babies who develop secure emotional relationships with a teacher have had their distress signals noticed, interpreted correctly, and responded to promptly and appropriately (Honig 2002). At morning arrival times, watch for separation anxiety. Sometimes holding and wordlessly commiserating with a baby's sad feelings can help more than a frenzied attempt to distract her (Klein, Kraft, & Shohet 2010). As you become more expert at interpreting a baby's body signals of distress and discomfort, you will become more sensitively attuned in your responses (Honig 2010).

Learn Developmental Milestones

Learning developmental norms helps teachers figure out when to wonder, when to worry, and when to relish and feel overjoyed about a child's milestone accomplishments. Day and night toilet learning can be completed anywhere from 18 months to 5 years. This is a *wide* time window for development. In contrast, learning to pick up a piece of cereal from a high chair tray with just thumb and forefinger in a fine pincer grasp is usually completed during a *narrow* time window well before 13 months. By 11 months, most babies become expert at using just the first two fingers.

Hone Your Detective Skills

If a baby is screaming and jerking knees up to his belly, you might suspect a painful gas bubble. Pick up the baby and jiggle and thump his back until you get that burp up. What a relief, for you as well as baby. Maybe an irritable, yowling baby just needs to be tucked in quietly and smoothly for a nap after an expert diaper change. Suppose baby is crying and thrashing about, and yet he has been burped and diapered. Use all your detective skills to determine the cause. Is it a hot day? He might be thirsty. A drink of water can help him calm down.

Notice Stress Signs

Scan a child's body for stress signs. Dull eyes can signal the need for more intimate loving interactions. Tense shoulders and a grave look often mean that a child is afraid or worried (Honig 2010). Compulsive rocking can mean a baby feels forlorn. Watch for lonesomeness and wilting.

Some babies melt down toward day's end. They need to be held and snuggled. Murmur sweet reassurances and provide a small snack of strained applesauce to soothe baby's taste buds and worries. Check his body from top to bottom for signs of stresses or tensions, such as eyes avoiding contact, teeth grinding, fingernail chewing, frequently clenched fists, so that you can develop an effective plan for soothing. Be alert, and tend to children's worrisome bodily signs; these will tell you what you need to know long before children have enough language to share what was stressful (Honig 2009).

Play Learning Games

Parents and teachers are a baby's preferred playmates. While playing learning games with infants, pay attention to their actions. Ask yourself if the game has become so familiar and easy that it is time to "dance up the developmental ladder" (Honig 1982) and increase the game's challenge. Or perhaps the game is still too baffling and you need to "dance down" and simplify the activity so that the child can succeed.

Provide safe mirrors at floor level and behind the diapering table so children can watch and learn about their own bodies. Hold babies in arms up to a mirror to reach out and pat the face in the mirror. Lying on the floor in front of a securely attached safety mirror, a young child twists and squirms to get an idea of where his body begins and ends.

Your body can serve as a comforting support for some early learning activities. Sit an infant on your lap and watch as he coordinates vision and grasp to reach and hold a toy you are dangling. Babies love "Peek-a-boo! I see you!" These games nurture the development of object permanence—the understanding that objects still exist even when they are out of sight. Peek-a-boo games also symbolically teach that even when a special adult is not seen, that dear person will reappear.

Provide Physical Play Experiences

Play pat-a-cake with babies starting even before 6 months. As you gently hold a baby's hands and bring them out and then back together, chant slowly and joyously, "Pat-a-cake, pat-a-cake, baker's man; bake me a cake just as fast as you can. Pat it, and roll it, and mark it with a *B*, and put it in the oven for [baby's name] and me." Smile with joy as you guide the baby's hands rhythmically and slowly through the game, and use a high-pitched voice as you emphasize her name in the sing-song chant. Over the next months, as soon as you begin chanting the words, the baby will begin to bring hands to the midline and do the hand motions that belong with this game. Babies who are 9 to 11 months old will even start copying the hand-rolling motions that belong with this game.

To encourage learning, try to arrange games with more physical actions. Sit on the floor with your toes touching the baby's toes, then model how to roll a ball back and forth.

Introduce Sensory Experiences

Safe sensory and tactile experiences are ideal for this age group. As he shifts a toy from hand to hand, turns it over, pokes, tastes, bangs, and even chews on it, a baby uses his senses to learn about the toy's physical properties. Teachers can blow bubbles so babies can reach for and crawl after them. Provide play-dough made with plenty of salt to discourage children from putting it in their mouths. Older babies enjoy exploring finger paints or nontoxic tempera paint and fat brushes.

Play Sociable Games

Give something appealing to a seated baby. Put out your hand, smile, and say "Give it to me, please." The baby may chew on the "gift," such as a safe wooden block or chunky plastic cylinder peg. After the baby passes it to you, say thank you, then give the object back with a smile. Give-and-take games with you are a sociable pleasure for babies and teach them turn-taking skills that are crucial for friendly social interchanges years later.

Seated on a chair, play a bouncing game, with the baby's back resting snuggly against your tummy. After you stop bouncing and chanting "Giddyup, horsie," a baby often bounces on his or her tush as if to remind you to start this game over and over. An older baby vigorously demands "More horsie!" to get you to restart this game. Babies enjoy kinesthetic stimulation too, such as when you swing them gently in a baby swing. A baby will grin with glee as you pull or push him in a wagon around the room or playground.

Observe Babies' Ways of Exploring and Learning

Observe a baby to learn what and how she is learning, then adapt the activity to offer greater challenge. Observation provides information that lets teachers determine when and how to arrange for the next step in a child's learning experience. Watch quietly as a baby tries with determination to put the round wood top piece for a ring stack set on the pole. His eyes widen in startled amazement as he gradually realizes that when the hole does not go through the middle, then that piece will not go down over the pole—a frustrating but important lesson. Calmly, a teacher can demonstrate how to place the piece on top of the pole while using simple words to describe how this piece is different. She can also gently guide the baby's hands so he feels successful at placing the piece on top.

Enhance Language and Literacy in Everyday Routines

Talk back and forth with babies; respond to their coos and babbles with positive talk. When the baby vocalizes, tell her, "What a terrific talker you are. Tell me some more."

The diapering table is a fine site for language games. With young babies, practice "parentese"—a high-pitched voice, drawn-out vowels, and slow and simple talk. This kind of talk fires up the brain neurons that carry messages to help a baby learn (Doidge 2007). Cascades of chemicals and electrical signals course down the baby's neural pathways. A baby responds when you are an attentive and delighted talking partner. Pause so the baby gets a turn to talk too, and bring the game to a graceful close when baby fatigue sets in.

Talk about body parts on dolls, stuffed animals, yourself, and the babies in the room. Talk about what the baby sees as you lift her onto your lap and then onto your shoulders. Talk at mealtimes. Use every daily routine as an opportunity to enhance oral language (Honig 2007).

Daily reading is an intimate one-on-one activity that young babies deeply enjoy in varied spaces and at varied times of the day (Honig 2004). Hook your babies on books as early as possible. Frequent shared picture-book experiences are priceless gifts. Early pleasurable reading experiences empower success in learning to read years later in grade school (Jalongo 2007).

Cuddle with one or several children as you read and share books together every day. Use dramatic tones along with loving and polite words. You are the master of the story as you read aloud. Feel free to add to or to shorten picture-book text according to a particular child's needs. Group reading times can be pleasurable when infants lean against you as you sit on the rug and share a picture book. Teachers often prefer the intimacy of individual reading times with babies (Honig & Shin 2001). Individual reading can help a tense or fussy baby relax in your lap as he becomes deeply absorbed in sharing the picture-book experience.

Encourage Mastery Experiences

Children master many linguistic, physical, and social skills in the first years of life. Watch the joy of mastery and self-appreciation as a baby succeeds at a task, such as successfully placing Montessori cylinders into their respective sockets. Babies enjoy clapping for their own efforts. Mastery experiences arranged in thoughtful doses bring much pleasure, such an eagerness to keep on exploring, trying, and learning. Watch the baby's joy as he proudly takes a long link chain out of a coffee can and then stuffs it slowly back in the can. He straightens his shoulders with such pride as he succeeds at this game of finding a way to put a long skinny chain into a round container with a small diameter opening.

Mastery experiences arranged in thoughtful doses bring much pleasure, such an eagerness to keep on exploring, trying, and learning.

Vygotsky taught that the *zone of proximal development* is crucial for adult-child coordination in learning activities. You the teacher are so important in helping a child to succeed when a task may be slightly too difficult for the child to solve alone. Hold the baby's elbow steady when she feels frustrated while trying to stack one block on top of another. For a difficult puppy puzzle, a teacher taped down a few of the pieces so a baby could succeed in getting the puppy's tail and head pieces in the right spaces. If a baby has been struggling with a slippery nesting cup for a while, just steady the stack of cups so he can successfully insert a smaller cup into the next largest one.

Promote Socioemotional Skills

Babies learn empathy and friendliness from those who nurture them. Empathy involves recognizing and feeling the distress of another and trying to help in some way. A young baby who sees another baby crying may look worried and suck his thumb to comfort himself. Fifteen-month-old Michael tussles over a toy with Paul, who starts to cry. Michael looks worried and lets go of the toy so Paul has it. As Paul keeps crying, Michael gives him his own teddy bear. But Paul continues crying. Michael pauses, then runs to the next room and gets Paul's security blanket for him. And Paul stops crying (Blum 1987).

When teachers showed deeply respectful caregiving, then they observed that babies did develop early empathy and internalize the friendly interactions they had experienced.

Friendliness includes making accommodations so children can play together. For example, move a child over to make room for a peer, or make overtures to invite other babies to engage in peer play. Perhaps they could take turns toddling in and out of a cardboard house. Babies act friendly when they sit near each other and companionably play with toys, happy to be close together. McMullen and colleagues (2009) observed that positive social-emotional interactions were rare in some infant rooms. But when teachers showed deeply respectful caregiving, then they observed that babies did develop early empathy and internalize the friendly interactions they had experienced. One teacher is described below:

> Her wonderful gentle manner, the way she speaks to the babies, how they are all her friends . . . only someone who utterly respects and values babies could put that kind of effort into this the way she does, almost like she is setting a beautiful table for honored guests each and every morning. (McMullen et al. 2009, p. 27)

Conclusion

Later in life, a baby will not remember your specific innumerable kindly caring actions in the earliest years. However, a child's *feelings* of being lovable and cherished will remain a body-memory for life. These feelings of having been loved will permeate positive emotional and social relationships decades later.

Keep your own joy pipes open. How brief are the years of babyhood. All too soon young children grow into the mysterious world of teenagers who prefer hanging out with peers to snuggling on an adult lap. Reflect with deep personal satisfaction on your confidence and delight in caring for tiny ones—hearing the first words, seeing the joy at a new accomplishment, watching the entranced look of an upturned face as you tell a story, feeling the trust as a baby sleepily settles onto your lap for refreshment of spirit, for a breath of the loving comfort that emanates from your body.

Life has grown more complicated in our technological, economically difficult, and more and more urbanized world. But you, the teacher, remain each baby's priceless tour guide into the world of "growing up!" You gently take each little person by the hand—literally and figuratively—and lure each and every baby into feeling the wonder and the somatic certainty of being loved, lovable, and cherished so that each baby can fully participate in the adventure of growing, loving, and learning.

Your nurturing strengthens a baby's determination to keep on learning, keep on cooperating, keep on being friendly, and keep on growing into a loving person—first in the world of the nursery and later in the wider world. You can give no greater gift to a child than to be the best guide possible as each child begins his or her unique life journey.

References

Blum, L. 1987. Particularity and responsiveness. In *The emergence of morality in young children,* eds. J. Kagan & S. Lamb, 306–37. Chicago: University of Chicago Press.

Doidge, N. 2007. *The brain that changes itself.* New York: Penguin.

Honig, A.S. 1982. *Playtime learning games for young children.* Syracuse, NY: Syracuse University Press.

Honig, A.S. 1997. Infant temperament and personality: What do we need to know? *Montessori Life* 9 (3): 18–21.

Honig, A.S. 2002. *Secure environments: Nurturing infant/toddler attachment in child care settings.* Washington, DC: NAEYC.

Honig, A.S. 2004. Twenty ways to boost your baby's brain power. *Scholastic Parent and Child* 11 (4): 55–56.

Honig, A.S. 2007. Oral language development. *Early Child Development and Care* 177 (6): 581–613.

Honig, A.S. 2009. Stress and young children. In *Informing our practice: Useful research on young children's development,* eds. E. Essa & M.M. Burnham, 71–88. Washington, DC: NAEYC.

Honig, A.S. 2010. *Little kids, big worries: Stress-busting tips for early childhood classrooms.* Baltimore: Brookes.

Honig, A.S., & M. Shin. 2001. Reading aloud to infants and toddlers in childcare settings: An observational study. *Early Childhood Education Journal* 28 (3): 193–97.

Jalongo, M.R. 2007. *Early childhood language arts.* 4th ed. New York: Pearson.

Kaplan, L. 1978. *Oneness and separateness: From infant to individual.* New York: Simon & Schuster.

Klein, P.S., R.R. Kraft, & C. Shohet. 2010. Behavior patterns in daily mother-child separations: Possible opportunites for stress reduction. *Early Child Development and Care* 180: 387–96.

McMullen, M.B., J.M. Addleman, A.M. Fulford, S. Moore, S.J. Mooney, S.S. Sisk, & J. Zachariah. 2009. Learning to be *me* while coming to understand *we.* Encouraging prosocial babies in group settings. *Young Children* 64 (4): 20–28. www.naeyc.org/files/yc/file/200907/McMullenWeb709.pdf

Montagu, A. 1971. *Touching: The human significance of the skin.* New York: Harper & Row.

Critical Thinking

1. Observe a parent or caregiver as they interact with an infant. Watch for one of the keys Dr. Honig discusses in her article. What did the adult do that made an impact on you and why?

2. Some of the key ideas are geared more to teachers than parents. Choose the ones that can be easily be adapted to the home environment and develop a one page handout that could be given to families to assist them in the home as they nurture their baby on his or her life journey.

ALICE STERLING HONIG, PhD, is professor emerita of child development in the College of Human Ecology at Syracuse University, where she has taught the QIC (Quality Infant/Toddler Caregiving) Workshop for 34 years. She is the author or editor of more than two dozen books and more than 500 articles and chapters on early childhood. As a licensed New York State clinician, she works with children and families coping with a variety of troubles, such as divorce or learning difficulties. ahonig@syr.edu.

From *Young Children,* Vol. 65, No. 5, September, 2010, pp. 40–47. Copyright © 2010 by National Association for the Education of Young Children. Reprinted by permission.

Vaccination Nation

**The decadelong controversy surrounding the safety of vaccines is over—
or is it? A fierce debate continues over what really puts our children at risk.**

CHRIS MOONEY

Vaccines do not cause autism. That was the ruling in each of three critical test cases handed down on February 12 by the U.S. Court of Federal Claims in Washington, D.C. After a decade of speculation, argument, and analysis—often filled with vitriol on both sides—the court specifically denied any link between the combination of the MMR vaccine and vaccines with thimerosal (a mercury-based preservative) and the spectrum of disorders associated with autism. But these rulings, though seemingly definitive, have done little to quell the angry debate, which has severe implications for American public health.

The idea that there is something wrong with our vaccines—that they have poisoned a generation of kids, driving an "epidemic" of autism—continues to be everywhere: on cable news, in celebrity magazines, on blogs, and in health news stories. It has had a particularly strong life on the Internet, including the heavily trafficked *Huffington Post,* and in pop culture, where it is supported by actors including Charlie Sheen and Jim Carrey, former *Playboy* playmate Jenny McCarthy, and numerous others. Despite repeated rejection by the scientific community, it has spawned a movement, led to thousands of legal claims, and even triggered occasional harassment and threats against scientists whose research appears to discredit it.

You can see where the emotion and sentiment come from. Autism can be a terrible condition, devastating to families. It can leave parents not only aggrieved but desperate to find any cure, any salvation. Medical services and behavioral therapy for severely autistic children can cost more than $100,000 a year, and these children often exhibit extremely difficult behavior. Moreover, the incidence of autism is apparently rising rapidly. Today one in every 150 children has been diagnosed on the autism spectrum; 20 years ago that statistic was one in 10,000. "Put yourself in the shoes of these parents," says journalist David Kirby, whose best-selling 2005 book, *Evidence of Harm,* dramatized the vaccine-autism movement. "They have perfectly normal kids who are walking and happy and everything—and then they regress." The irony is that vaccine skepticism—not the vaccines themselves—is now looking like the true public-health threat.

The decadelong vaccine-autism saga began in 1998, when British gastroenterologist Andrew Wakefield and his colleagues published evidence in *The Lancet* suggesting they had tracked down a shocking cause of autism. Examining the digestive tracts of 12 children with behavioral disorders, nine of them autistic, the researchers found intestinal inflammation, which they pinned on the MMR (measles, mumps, and rubella) vaccine. Wakefield had a specific theory of how the MMR shot could trigger autism: The upset intestines, he conjectured, let toxins loose in the bloodstream, which then traveled to the brain. The vaccine was, in this view, effectively a poison. In a dramatic press conference, Wakefield announced the findings and sparked an instant media frenzy. For the British public a retreat from the use of the MMR vaccine—and a rise in the incidence of measles—began.

In the United States, meanwhile, fears would soon arise concerning another means by which vaccines might induce autism. Many vaccines at the time contained thimerosal, a preservative introduced in the 1930s to make vaccines safer by preventing bacterial contamination. But thimerosal is 50 percent mercury by weight, and mercury is known to be a potent neurotoxin, at least in large doses. In 1999 new federal safety guidelines for mercury in fish stirred concerns about vaccines as well.

The U.S. government responded by ordering that thimerosal be removed from all vaccines administered to children under age 6, or reduced to trace amounts. (Some inactivated influenza vaccines were exempted.) The step was described as a "precautionary" measure. There was no proof of harm, government researchers said, just reason to worry that there might be. Meanwhile, scientists launched numerous studies to determine whether thimerosal had actually caused an autism epidemic, while some parents and their lawyers started pointing fingers and developing legal cases.

Within weeks of this year's federal court decisions—which examined and vindicated both the MMR vaccine and thimerosal environmental lawyer Robert F. Kennedy Jr. wrote a column in *The Huffington Post* in which he continued to press his case that the government had peddled unsafe vaccines to an unsuspecting public. It is a cause he has championed since 2005, when he published "Deadly Immunity" in *Rolling Stone* and *Salon* magazines. The article was a no-holds-barred denunciation of the U.S. public-health establishment, purporting to tell the story of how "government health agencies colluded with Big Pharma to hide the risks of thimerosal from the public . . . a chilling case study of institutional arrogance, power, and greed." Half a decade after the original thimerosal concerns were first raised, Kennedy claimed to have found the smoking gun: the transcript of a "secret" 2000 meeting of government, pharmaceutical, and independent researchers with expertise in vaccines. Kennedy's conclusion: The generational catastrophe was real; our kids had been poisoned. If true it would be perhaps the greatest biomedical catastrophe in modern history.

But for Kennedy to be right, a growing consensus in the medical establishment had to be wrong. Indeed, Kennedy blasted a leading organ of science that had just vindicated both the MMR vaccine and thimerosal, the Institute of Medicine (IOM). "The CDC [Centers for Disease Control and Prevention] paid the Institute of Medicine to conduct a new study to whitewash the risks of thimerosal," Kennedy wrote, "ordering researchers to 'rule out' the chemical's link to autism." In reality, the IOM—a branch of the National Academy of Sciences (NAS), the government's top independent scientific adviser—carefully creates firewalls between the funding it receives to conduct scientific assessments and the results it ultimately produces. "Funders don't control the composition of the committee, and they don't meet with the committee," says Harvard public-health researcher Marie McCormick, who chaired the IOM vaccine-safety committee in question. "And on no NAS or IOM committee are the members paid; they all work pro bono. There's no reason for them not to look at the data."

The same year Kennedy's article came out, journalist David Kirby published *Evidence of Harm—Mercury in Vaccines and the Autism Epidemic: A Medical Controversy*. He followed a group of parents from the Coalition for SafeMinds, an autism activist organization. They had grown convinced that vaccines and other environmental factors had caused their children's conditions. Kirby's chronicle of the parents' efforts to publicize the dangers of vaccines became a best seller and greatly advanced SafeMinds' cause.

"It's not hard to scare people," says pediatrician and leading vaccine advocate Paul Offit. "But it's extremely difficult to unscare them."

Yet even as vaccine hysteria reached a fever pitch in the wake of Kennedy's and Kirby's writings, the scientific evidence was leaning strongly in the other direction. In discounting the dangers of both the MMR vaccine and thimerosal, the IOM had multiple large epidemiological studies to rely on. For MMR, the IOM examined 16 studies. All but two, which were dismissed because of "serious methodological flaws," showed no evidence of a link. For thimerosal, the IOM looked at five studies, examining populations in Sweden, Denmark, the United Kingdom, and the United States (studies that vaccine critics contend were flawed). Since then, further research has strengthened and vindicated the committee's original conclusion. It is a conclusion that has been "independently reached by scientific and professional committees around the world," as a recent science journal commentary noted. Either the scientific community has found a clear, reassuring answer to the questions raised about thimerosal in vaccines, or there is a global scientific conspiracy to bury the truth.

Whether the public is hearing the scientific community's answer is another matter. "It's not hard to scare people," says pediatrician and leading vaccine advocate Paul Offit, who himself coinvented a vaccine. "But it's extremely difficult to unscare them."

A backlash against vaccine skeptics is beginning to mount. Standing up to fellow celebrities, actress Amanda Peet, who recently vaccinated her baby daughter, has become a spokeswoman for the provaccine group Every Child by Two. Offit's book *Autism's False Prophets* has further galvanized vaccine defenders—not only by debunking the science of those who claim vaccines are dangerous but also by contending that the parents of autistic children and the children themselves are indeed victims, not of vaccines but of medical misinformation.

The provaccine case starts with some undeniable facts: Vaccines are, as the IOM puts it, "one of the greatest achievements of public health." The CDC estimates that thanks to vaccines, we have reduced morbidity by 99 percent or more for smallpox, diphtheria, measles, polio, and rubella. Averaged over the course of the 20th century, these five diseases killed nearly 650,000 people annually. They now kill fewer than 100. That is not to say vaccines are perfectly safe; in rare cases they can cause serious, well-known adverse side effects. But what researchers consider unequivocally unsafe is to avoid them. As scientists at the Johns Hopkins Bloomberg School of Public Health recently found while investigating whooping cough outbreaks in and around Michigan, "geographic pockets of vaccine exemptors pose a risk to the whole community."

When it comes to autism, vaccine defenders make two central claims. First, the condition is likely to be mostly genetic rather than environmentally caused; and second, there are reasons to doubt whether there is really a rising autism epidemic at all.

It is misleading to think of autism as a single disorder. Rather, it is a spectrum of disorders showing great variability in symptoms and expression but fundamentally characterized by failed social development, inability to communicate, and obsessive repetitive behavior. Autism generally appears in children at early ages, sometimes suddenly, and its genetic component has long been recognized. Studies have shown that if one identical twin has autism, there is at least a 60 percent chance that the other also does. "From my point of view, it's a condition associated with genetic defects and developmental biology problems," says Peter Hotez, a George Washington University microbiologist and father of an autistic child. Hotez, who is also president of the Sabin Vaccine Institute, says, "I don't think it's possible to explain on the basis of any vaccine toxin that is acquired after the baby is born." Still, scientists cannot fully rule out environmental triggers—including various types of toxicity—that might interact with a given individual's preexisting genetic inclination. Autism is a complex disorder with multiple forms of expression and potentially multiple types of causation that are incompletely understood.

As for whether autism is rising, a number of experts say it is hard to know. Is the increase real, or is it largely the result of more attention to the condition, an expansion of the autism spectrum to embrace many different heterogeneous disorders, a new focus on children classified as autistic in federal special education programs during the 1990s, and other factors? It could be some combination of all these things.

But if environmental triggers of autism cannot be ruled out, the idea that those triggers can be found in the MMR vaccine or in thimerosal has crumbled under the weight of scientific refutation. Epidemiological studies have cast grave doubt on Andrew Wakefield's MMR hypothesis—and so have subsequent scandals. Nearly all of Wakefield's coauthors have since retracted the autism implications of their work; *The Lancet* has also backed away from the study. A series of investigative stories published in *The Times* of London unearthed Wakefield's undisclosed ties to vaccine litigation in the U.K. and, more recently, suggested he fabricated his data (which Wakefield denies).

As for thimerosal, government precautions notwithstanding, it was never clear how threatening it might be. The federal mercury standards that first heightened concern were developed for methylmercury, not ethylmercury, the form contained in thimerosal. Ethylmercury has less risk of accumulating to a toxic dose because it does not last as long in the body. And, according to the IOM's 2004 report, there had never been any evidence of a major incident of mercury poisoning leading to autism.

The strongest argument against the idea that thimerosal poisoned a generation of children does not emerge from the body of published studies alone. There is the added detail that although thimerosal is no longer present in any recommended childhood vaccines save the inactivated influenza vaccine—and hasn't been, beyond trace amounts, since 2001—no one is hailing the end of autism. "If you thought thimerosal was related to autism, then the incidence of autism should have gone down," Harvard's McCormick explains. "And it hasn't."

Children who would have been classified as mentally retarded or learning disabled were now being classified on the autism spectrum.

In 2005 David Kirby stated that if autism rates didn't begin to decline by 2007, "that would deal a severe blow to the autismthimerosal hypothesis." But as McCormick notes, despite the absence of thimerosal in vaccines, reports of autism cases have not fallen. In a 2008 study published in *Archives of General Psychiatry*, two researchers studying a California Department of Developmental Services database found that the prevalence of autism had actually continued increasing among the young. Kirby concedes that these findings about the California database represent a "pretty serious blow to the thimerosal-causes-autism hypothesis," though he does not think they thoroughly bury it. In an interview, he outlined many problems with relying on the California database, suggesting potential confounding factors such as the state's high level of immigration. "Look, I understand the desire to try to end this and not scare parents away from vaccination," Kirby says. "But I also feel that sometimes that desire to prove or disprove blinds people on both sides."

Kirby says—and even some vaccine defenders agree—that some small subgroup of children might have a particular vulnerability to vaccines and yet be missed by epidemiological studies. But the two sides disagree as to the possible size of that group. "If one or two or three children every year are getting autism from vaccines, you would never pick that up," Offit says. Kirby, in contrast, feels that while the idea of thimerosal as the "one and only cause of autism has gone out the window," he still believes there is an "epidemic" with many environmental triggers and with thimerosal as a possible contributing factor.

Meanwhile, in the face of powerful evidence against two of its strongest initial hypotheses—concerning MMR and thimerosal—the vaccine skeptic movement is morphing before our eyes. Advocates have begun moving the goalposts, now claiming, for instance, that the childhood vaccination schedule hits kids with too many vaccines at once, overwhelming their immune systems. Jenny McCarthy wants to "green our vaccines," pointing to many other alleged toxins that they contain. "I think it's definitely a response to the science, which has consistently shown no correlation," says David Gorski, a cancer surgeon funded by the National Institutes of Health who in his spare time blogs at Respectful Insolence, a top medical blog known for its provaccine stance. A hardening of antivaccine attitudes, mixed with the despair experienced by families living under the strain of autism, has heightened the debate—sometimes leading to blowback against scientific researchers.

Paul Shattuck did not set out to enrage vaccine skeptics and the parents of autistic children. Currently an assistant professor at the George Warren Brown School of Social Work at Washington University in St. Louis, he has dedicated the last decade of his professional life to helping people with autism in their families. "Some of my dearest friends have kids with autism," he says.

But in 2006 Shattuck came under fire after he published an article in the journal *Pediatrics* questioning the existence of an autism epidemic. No one doubts that since the early 1990s the number of children diagnosed with autism has dramatically increased, a trend reflected in U.S. special education programs, where children enrolled as autistic grew from 22,445 in 1994–1995 to 140,254 in 2003–2004. Yet Shattuck's study found reasons to doubt that these numbers were proof of an epidemic. Instead, he suggested that "diagnostic substitution"—in which children who previously would have been classified as mentally retarded or learning disabled were now being classified on the autism spectrum—played a significant role in the apparent increase.

Shattuck did not reject the idea that rising autism levels might be in part due to environmental causes; he merely showed the increase was largely an artifact of changing diagnostic practices, which themselves had been enabled by rising levels of attention to autism and its listing as a diagnostic category in special education. Yet simply by questioning autism epidemic claims in a prominent journal, he became a target. "People were obviously Googling me and tracking me down," he recalls. Shattuck emphasizes that most e-mails and calls merely delivered "heartfelt pleas from people with very sick kids who've been led to believe a particular theory of etiology." The bulk weren't menacing, but a few certainly were.

Others attacked Shattuck's research on the Web and insinuated that he had fabricated his data or committed scientific misconduct. "It was dismaying to feel like people were calling me a traitor to autistic kids and families," he says.

"If there has been a more harmful urban legend circulating in our society than the vaccine-autism link," University of Pennsylvania bioethicist Arthur Caplan wrote in *The Philadelphia Inquirer*, "it's hard to know what it might be." One type of harm, as Shattuck's story shows, is to individual scientists and the scientific process. There is a real risk that necessary research is being held back as scientists fear working in such a contested field. Shattuck's experience is not unique. Offit cannot go on a book tour to promote *Autism's False Prophets* because of the risk involved in making public appearances. He has received too many threats.

Yet another cost comes in the rush toward unproven, and potentially dangerous, alternative therapies to treat autism. It is easy to sympathize with parents of autistic children who desperately want to find a cure, but this has led to various pseudoremedies whose efficacy and safety have been challenged by science. These include facilitated communication, secretin infusion, chelation therapy (which involves pumping chemicals into the blood to bind with heavy metals such as mercury), and hormonal suppression. It is estimated that more than half of all children with autism are now using "complementary and alternative" treatments.

Disease, however, is the greatest danger associated with holding back vaccines amid the ongoing investigation of dubious claims. Both the vaccinated and the unvaccinated populations are placed at greater risk. Given enough vaccine exemptions and localized outbreaks, it is possible that largely vanquished diseases could become endemic again. (That is precisely what happened with measles in 2008 in the U.K., following the retreat from the MMR vaccine in the wake of the 1998 scare.) The public-health costs of such a development would be enormous—and they would not impact everyone equally. "If vaccine rates start to drop, who's going to get affected?" Peter Hotez asks. "It's going to be people who live in poor, crowded conditions. So it's going to affect the poorest people in our country."

Paradoxically, the great success of vaccines is a crucial reason why antivaccination sentiment has thrived, some scientists say. Most of the diseases that vaccines protect against have largely been licked. As a consequence, few people personally remember the devastation they can cause. So with less apparently on the line, it is easier to indulge in the seeming luxury of vaccine skepticism and avoidance. Even before the recent spike in attention to thimerosal, members of the public were alarmingly skeptical of vaccines. In a 1999 survey, 25 percent felt their children's immune systems could be harmed by too many vaccinations, and 23 percent shared the sentiment that children receive more vaccinations than are healthy. There is every reason to think that those numbers—gathered before the vaccine-autism controversy reached anything like its current intensity—have risen since.

In the United States, population pockets with low vaccination rates (such as in Boulder, Colorado, and Ashland, Oregon) have existed for some time, and the great fear among many governmental medical authorities is that high-profile claims about vaccine dangers will widen the phenomenon, with potentially disastrous consequences. Already, medical and religious vaccination exemptions are climbing: In New York State they totaled 4,037 in 2006, nearly twice as many as in 1999. In New Jersey they came to 1,923 in 2006 versus only 727 in 1990. It is not just exemptors: The far larger concern, according to McCormick and others, is those parents referred to as "vaccine hesitaters." They have heard all the noise about vaccines and will probably get their children shots because they feel they have to, but their skepticism is growing.

Offit points to still another threat: litigation. The wave of autism-related claims filed with the U.S. government's Vaccine Injury Compensation Program is unprecedented. Since 2001 autism claims have outnumbered nonautism cases almost four to one. Following the science, the court has now dismissed many of them, but there is the possibility that civil litigation will follow. "I still think it's going to be another 10 years before this really washes out in litigation," Offit says. If the legal atmosphere becomes too difficult for vaccine manufacturers, they could stop producing them or be forced out of business.

U ltimately, that is why the vaccineautism saga is so troubling— and why it is so important to explore how science and so many citizens fell out of touch.

"It wouldn't have been possible without the Internet," says journalist Arthur Allen, who has covered the vaccine-autism story since 2002, when he wrote a high-profile *New York Times Magazine* article that took the thimerosal risk seriously. Over time Allen changed his mind, coming to reject the idea that vaccines are to blame. Still, he recognizes why it persists. "If people believe something happened to them, there are so many people on the Web you can find who believe the same thing." The Internet has become a haven for a number of autism support groups that continually reinforce the vaccine-autism argument. This has led to the radicalization of some elements who have denounced scientists as "vaccine barbarians," "pharmaceutical and medical killers," and so on. And after all we have heard about environmental and chemical risks—some accurate, some not—people are now easily persuaded about all manner of toxin dangers.

But if the Internet has made it easier for pockets of antiscience feeling to grow and flourish, scientific authorities also deserve some of the blame. "I don't think they woke up that this was a serious problem until maybe 2008," David Gorski says about the growing antivaccine sentiment. George Washington University's Hotez notes that "the office of the surgeon general, the secretary of Health and Human Services, and the head of the CDC have not been very vocal on this issue." True, the CDC, the Food and Drug Administration, and other governmental organizations feature accurate and up-to-date information about vaccine risks on their websites. But that is very different from launching a concerted communications campaign to ensure that the public retains faith in vaccination.

Some outspoken scientists may have actually increased the polarization on this issue. For example, calling those against vaccines "scientifically illiterate"—or, as CDC vaccine expert Stephen Cochi reportedly put it to one journalist, "junk scientists and charlatans"— may just lead to a further circling of the wagons.

The most promising approach to the vaccine-autism issue comes from the government itself. Consider the work of Roger Bernier, a CDC scientist who turned to emphasizing the public-engagement aspects of the vaccine problem after hearing one parent declare any new government research on the topic "dead on arrival." The central problem Bernier has confronted: how to deal with a situation in which so many parents are unswervingly convinced that their children have been harmed, in which they could be harming their children even more by using untested therapies, and in which dangerous misinformation abounds.

"There's no end to the kind of noise people can make about vaccines," he observes. "And so if you're in the vaccine community, what's the best approach to this? I don't think it is ignoring people." Instead, Bernier has headed up a series of award-winning projects that bring together average citizens with scientists and policymakers to reach joint recommendations on vaccines, holding public dialogues across the country to break down boundaries between the experts and everybody else, literally putting multiple perspectives around a table. His example suggests that while science's first and greatest triumph in this area was to develop vaccinations to control or eradicate many diseases, the challenge now—not yet achieved, and in some ways even more difficult—is to preserve public support for vaccine programs long after these scourges have largely vanished from our everyday lives.

"The problem is not only research," Bernier says. "The problem is trust."

Critical Thinking

1. Explain why some people still believe that vaccinations cause autism.

2. Identify known factors which are correlated with autistic spectrum disorders.

3. Provide reasons why every child should have vaccinations.

CHRIS MOONEY will continue to report on the vaccineautism controversy on his blog. The Intersection, at blogs.discovermagazine.com/intersection.

How to Help Your Toddler Begin Developing Empathy

REBECCA PARIAKIAN AND CLAIRE LERNER

Empathy is the ability to imagine how someone else is feeling in a particular situation and respond with care. This is a very complex skill to develop. Being able to empathize with another person means that a child:

- Understands that he is a separate individual, his own person;
- Understands that others can have different thoughts and feelings than he has;
- Recognizes the common feelings that most people experience—happiness, surprise, anger, disappointment, sadness, etc.;
- Is able to look at a particular situation (such as watching a peer saying good-bye to a parent at child care) and imagine how he—and therefore his friend—might feel in this moment; and
- Can imagine what response might be appropriate or comforting in that particular situation—such as offering his friend a favorite toy or teddy bear to comfort her.

Understanding and showing empathy is the result of many social-emotional skills that are developing in the first years of life. Some especially important milestones include:

- Establishing a secure, strong, loving relationship with you. Feeling accepted and understood by you helps your child learn how to accept and understand others as he grows.
- Beginning to use social referencing, at about 6 months old. This is when a baby will look to a parent or other loved one to gauge his or her reaction to a person or situation. For example, a 7-month-old looks carefully at her father as he greets a visitor to their home to see if this new person is good and safe. The parent's response to the visitor influences how the baby responds. (This is why parents are encouraged to be upbeat and reassuring—not anxiously hover—when saying good-bye to children at child care. It sends the message that "this is a good place" and "you will be okay.") Social referencing, or being sensitive to a parent's reaction in new situations, helps the babies understand the world and the people around them.

- Developing a theory of mind. This is when a toddler (between 18 and 24 months old) first realizes that, just as he has his own thoughts, feelings and goals, others have their own thoughts and ideas, which may be different from his.
- Recognizing one's self in a mirror. This occurs between 18 and 24 months and signals that a child has a firm understanding of himself as a separate person.

What Can You Do: Nurturing Empathy in Your Toddler

Empathize with your child. *Are you feeling scared of that dog? He is a nice dog but he is barking really loud. That can be scary. I will hold you until he walks by.*

Talk about others' feelings. *Kayla is feeling sad because you took her toy car. Please give Kayla back her car and then you choose another one to play with.*

Suggest how children can show empathy. *Let's get Jason some ice for his boo-boo.*

Read stories about feelings. Some suggestions include:

- *I Am Happy: A Touch and Feel Book of Feelings* by Steve Light
- *My Many Colored Days* by Dr. Seuss
- *How Are You Feeling* by Saxton Freymann and Joost Elffers
- *Feelings* by Aliki
- *The Feelings Book* by Todd Parr
- *Baby Happy Baby Sad* by Leslie Patricelli
- *Baby Faces* by DK Publishing
- *When I Am/Cuando Estoy* by Gladys Rosa-Mendoza

Be a role model. When you have strong, respectful relationships and interact with others in a kind and caring way, your child learns from your example.

Use "I" messages. This type of communication models the importance of self-awareness: *I don't like it when you hit me. It hurts.*

Validate your child's difficult emotions. Sometimes when our child is sad, angry, or disappointed, we rush to try and fix it right away, to make the feelings go away because we want to protect him from any pain. However, these feelings are part of life and ones that children need to learn to cope with. In fact, labeling and validating difficult feelings actually helps children learn to handle them: *You are really mad that I turned off the TV. I understand. You love watching your animal show. It's okay to feel mad. When you are done being mad you can choose to help me make a yummy lunch or play in the kitchen while mommy makes our sandwiches.* This type of approach also helps children learn to empathize with others who are experiencing difficult feelings.

Use pretend play. Talk with older toddlers about feelings and empathy as you play. For example, you might have your child's stuffed hippo say that he does not want to take turns with his friend, the stuffed pony. Then ask your child: *How do you think pony feels? What should we tell this silly hippo?*

Think through the use of "I'm sorry." We often insist that our toddlers say "I'm sorry" as a way for them to take responsibility for their actions. But many toddlers don't fully understand what these words mean. While it may feel "right" for them to say "I'm sorry", it doesn't necessarily help toddlers learn empathy. A more meaningful approach can be to help children focus on the other person's feelings: *Chandra, look at Sierra—she's very sad. She's crying. She's rubbing her arm where you pushed her. Let's see if she is okay.* This helps children make the connection between the action (shoving) and the reaction (a friend who is sad and crying).

Be patient. Developing empathy takes time. Your child probably won't be a perfectly empathetic being by age three. (There are some teenagers and even adults who haven't mastered this skill completely either!) In fact, a big and very normal part of being a toddler is focusing on *me, mine,* and *I.* Remember, empathy is a complex skill and will continue to develop across your child's life.

Critical Thinking

1. Describe some of the attributes of empathy.
2. Name some of the social emotional milestones that foster the development of empathy.
3. Explain why some teenagers and adults do not know how to empathize with others.

From *Zero to Three*, July, 2009, pp. 1–3. Copyright © 2009 by Zero to Three. Reprinted by permission.

Five Skills Kids Need before They Read

How social and emotional development is making a comeback in the classroom.

PEG TYRE

When you enter PS 32 in the Belmont section of the Bronx, it's easy to see that emotions—and how students handle them—are as big a part of the curriculum in this school as math or reading. The walls are covered with colorful construction paper displays that highlight essays like "The Things I Love" and "What Makes Me Scream." In Melissa Locasto's kindergarten class, her 18 students sit on the rug while the teacher selects familiar puppets from a wicker basket for an end-of-the-year lesson. "What has Mr. Snail taught us?" she asks, holding up a soft puppet with a bright red-felt shell.

"How to come out of my Shell when I'm feeling shy," volunteers a quiet boy in the front. Locasto smiles, encouraging him.

"He's taught us that when we are afraid and embarrassed, or feeling shy, we sometimes go into our shell. But that's the time when we might need to take deep breaths to calm ourselves. Or to ask someone for help," she says, filling in.

The little boy nods, enthusiastically.

"And what about Mr. Grasshopper?" she asks.

Another little boy shouts, "How to pay attention when your body wants to—" Then he jostles other kids to demonstrate a world-class case of the fidgets.

Make no mistake. PS 32's principal, Esther Schwartz, like nearly every other public school principal in the nation, has a laser-like focus on improving test scores. But in the last five years, she's concluded that her 800 students need more than skills and drills. Nearly all come from very poor, stressed, and sometimes chaotic families. "Before they can begin to learn, our children often need help with basic social skills—sharing or taking a turn. Many need help regulating their attention, their emotions, or controlling their impulses," says Schwartz. Faced with dozens of disruptive children, Schwartz turned to an innovative group called Turnaround for Children, which helps failing schools improve their outcomes through emotional education.

Turnaround for Children helps administrators identify troubled kids, then works with teachers to build academically rigorous and emotionally healthy learning communities by making social and emotional skill-building part of the comprehensive curriculum. "We've discovered that social and emotional skill-building goes hand in hand with learning," says Schwartz. In the five years that Turnaround has been at PS 32, the number of disciplinary problems has plummeted and the percentage of kids deemed proficient in reading has risen from 30 to 72 percent.

Everything Old is New Again

In an era when high-stakes test scores rule, talking about social and emotional development in children can seem old-fashioned. But lately, the conversation about the so-called soft skills— the personal and interpersonal abilities kids need to maintain mental health and thrive socially, emotionally, and intellectually in a classroom—is being heard again around the nation. In 2004, Illinois adopted a roster of social and emotional goals teachers are expected to cover right along with mathematics and language arts. This year, New York state is expected to do the same. Schools in Singapore, which produce some of the highest-scoring mathematics students in the world, have made social and emotional learning a key component of their education formula.

Why did we stop talking about the social and emotional development of children? Blame the self-esteem movement of the 1980s. Back then, many administrators and teachers believed that classroom experiences should be structured around building a child's sense of self-worth, even at the expense of achievement. Posters announcing "Everyone Is Special" and advising children to "Learn to love yourself" could be found in almost every school. The programs were a success—sort of. Kids felt satisfied even when they failed and their opportunities for higher education withered. Eight years ago, when No Child Left Behind became law, measurable standards came into vogue and feel-good programs disappeared, taking with them the idea of emotional development in the classroom.

These days, academics, education researchers, principals, and teachers are discovering—or maybe rediscovering—that reading and math alone may not be enough. "We know that the emotional piece is really very important in terms of a child's overall well-being and capacity to learn and grow," says Dr. Jerlean Daniel, deputy director of the National Association for the Education of Young Children and chair of the Psychology in Education department at the University of Pittsburgh. But just what, exactly, is that emotional piece?

Researchers have begun to identify the soft skills that kids need to succeed. Here are the five most important, with some tips on what you can do in the classroom to help foster the growth of these skills.

1 Naming those Feelings

The ability to name feelings, understand them, and express them in a socially acceptable way is essential to a child's success. Most parents, caregivers, and, later, preschool and elementary school teachers provide this kind of instruction almost reflexively. If a toddler cries when a toy is taken away, his mother or teacher may ask, "Are you upset because you want that toy?" This soothes and provides a lexicon for the highly charged moment.

With kids from a deprived background or with older children, the job of helping a child sort and articulate shades of emotion becomes part of a teacher's job. Pam Cantor, a child psychologist and chief of Turnaround for Children, says the simple, puppet-based program featuring Mr. Snail and Mr. Grasshopper developed by her staff and taught once a week can help kids name what they're feeling so they can fend off tantrums and meltdowns.

If you aren't able to use such a program in your school, you can opt for a less formal approach involving classroom discussion. If a child refuses to speak during circle time out of shyness, for example, you might say, "That's okay, Andre. Sometimes I don't feel like talking, either. But if you want to share your ideas later, we'd love to hear them." Then talk to the child individually about ways to calm his anxiety, such as by taking deep breaths. Finally, you might host a whole-class discussion about how to overcome shyness.

2 Building Trusting Relationships

In his now-classic study, former Stanford University professor and current Carnegie Foundation for the Advancement of Teaching president Anthony Bryk found that trust is the emollient the keeps schools running smoothly. And nowhere is that element more important than in the classroom—particularly in the relationship between teacher and student. When teachers take the time to establish trusting relationships with their students, it can make a world of difference. "It makes learning more powerful," says Mary Utne O'Brien, a professor of psychology and education at the University of Illinois at Chicago and a researcher for the Collaborative for Academic, Social, and Emotional Learning. "Many teachers bemoan the fact that they don't feel like they have time to develop those relationships. I would argue that building trust is the first lesson before any others." Small gestures mean a lot, says O'Brien. She suggests that you be predictable, be consistent, and do what you say you will do. Articulate that you want the children to learn, and then show them that you are willing to go the extra mile to ensure that they do. These acts will help students learn to trust you and the larger community. "Children have to trust that their teacher cares about their education," says O'Brien. Having the capacity to trust allows a child to focus on what's important—learning.

Take the time to establish trusting relationships with your students . . . It makes learning more powerful.

3 Staying in Control

Several studies have shown that the ability to inhibit impulsive mental, verbal, and physical responses and remain engaged in goal-directed thinking without calling out, fidgeting, or responding to provocation is key for school success. In a study funded by the National Institute of Child Health and Human Development, researchers at Pennsylvania State University followed 141 3- to 5-year-olds from low-income homes. The children who had the strongest regulatory abilities tended to do as well and sometimes better than less regulated children who had higher IQs, says lead researcher Clancy Blair, an associate professor of human development at Penn State.

The same is true of older children. Researchers at the University of Pennsylvania studied 164 eighth graders and found that the least impulsive and most self-disciplined of the group had better grades and study habits and got into more selective high schools than their peers with higher IQs but less controlled behavior. "By the time children start school, they are expected to sufficiently regulate impulsivity in order to engage in learning experiences with teachers and classmates," says Blair.

Depending on the age of your students, introducing simple lessons in controlling impulsivity into your classroom can go

---

Resources for Soft Skills

Take a look at the following books and online resources for more information.

School Programs

The Penn Resiliency Project (www.ppc.sas.upenn.edu/prpsum.htm)

Turnaround for Children (www.turnaroundusa.org)

Collaborative for Academic, Social, and Emotional. Learning (www.casel.org/sel./families.php)

Books

The Optimistic Child by Martin Seligman. Harper Perennial, 1995.

Curious? Discover the Missing Ingredient to a Fulfilling Life by Todd Kashdan. William Morrow, 2009.

Articles

"Gratitude in Children and Adolescents" by Jeffrey Froh et al., *School Psychology Forum: Research in Practice,* Volume 2, Issue 1, pp. 1–13, Fall 2007.

"Old-Fashioned Play Builds Serious Skills" by Alix Spiegel (www.npr.org)

"Developing Self-Regulation in Kindergarten" by Elena Bodrova and Deborah J. Leong (www.journal .naeyc.org/btj/200803/pdf/BTJ_Primary_interest.pdf)

a long way toward helping kids learn to focus. One common approach is to encourage kids to "think aloud" as they complete a project or problem, saying or whispering each step they perform. This process can help boost the kind of silent self-talk that comes naturally to more disciplined kids.

4 Having Curiosity

Curiosity may be the key to success on a number of levels, academic and otherwise, and may even be more important overall than happiness. Curiosity leads to mindfulness, says Todd Kashdan, a professor at George Mason University and author of *Curious? Discover the Missing Ingredient to a Fulfilling Life*. Mindfulness is the engaged, satisfied state of being one feels when absorbed in a meaningful task, be it achieving an A in class or organizing a blood drive.

According to Kashdan, teachers are in a unique position to foster curiosity in the classroom and put their kids on the road to mindfulness and mental health. How to do it? Rote memorization of facts in a social studies class on the Civil War is the enemy of the curious mind, Kashdan says. Whenever possible, banish rote learning and help students understand events from different perspectives. A discussion on whether the Civil War might have been a bad or good thing for a Southern mill owner, a Northern shipping tycoon, a slave, or the President promotes the kind of thinking that will pay off down the road.

"Children who are taught that there is a difference in perspectives maintain the mental and emotional receptiveness they need to remain curious," says Kashdan. "High levels of curiosity translates into a child's ability to think critically, problem-solve more creatively, and even to recognize different strengths in different kinds of kids," he says.

If you're still not sure you want to rewrite your Civil War curriculum, think about this: According to Kashdan, as they grow, curious kids are better able to find things to be passionate about in life than their less curious classmates.

5 Expressing Gratitude

Even for star pupils, school can be difficult at times. But helping children balance some of the challenges of learning with an opportunity to express gratitude leads to warmer feelings toward the teacher and higher levels of school engagement—even among kids who struggle—which can translate to better GPAs. Fringe benefit: Grateful kids also experience less envy and are less materialistic.

How does it work? Kids get into trouble when they feel isolated. Jeffrey Froh, professor of psychology at Hofstra University and a gratitude researcher, says when teachers encourage kids (over 7 years of age) to regularly name and describe what they are grateful for in their lives, children see how interconnected they are to other people. "They see who is helping them," says Froh.

Not everyone benefits equally. "Some kids have more baseline gratitude than others," according to Froh. Others take to gratitude easily, and for some, it remains something of an effort. "But when you make the discussion of gratitude in the classroom more fluid and regular, everyone benefits at least a little," says Froh. Start by sharing your own thank-yous: "Thanks for walking to lunch so quietly." "Thank you for picking up your candy wrapper." By modeling gratitude—articulating how people are helping you and your feelings of warmth toward them for their help—you can support children in becoming more grateful themselves.

Critical Thinking

1. Restate the five skills kids need before they read.
2. Explain why stressed, chaotic families have children who learn poorly.
3. Predict N.C.L.B. test score results if public schools emphasize emotional skills.

Peg Tyre is a Spencer Fellow at Columbia University and a former senior writer at *Newsweek*. Her book *The Trouble With Boys* (Random House, 2008) is now available in paperback.

Little by Little

As food allergies proliferate, new strategies may help patients ingest their way to tolerance.

LAURA BEIL

Considering that food is full of foreign proteins, it makes sense that the intestine is the immune system's version of Grand Central station. It's the largest organ to regularly sweep up and annihilate molecules that don't belong. And because food comes from outside, it's no surprise that some people have allergies to it. The bigger mystery is why most don't. Somehow during evolution, the immune system and food components developed a secret handshake that allows munchables to pass without a fuss.

Most of the time, that is. Once relatively rare, serious allergies to peanuts, milk, shellfish and other foods appear to be afflicting a growing number of children. The U.S. Centers for Disease Control and Prevention reports that food allergies now affect about 4 percent of American children, almost 20 percent more than a decade ago. Scientists have ideas to explain the increase—from children raised with too few germs exercising their immune cells to modern food processing that alters natural proteins and adds nonfood substances never before consumed in large amounts. Some studies implicate the use of certain vitamins and even childhood obesity.

Despite the growing problem, doctors have had little to offer beyond advising patients to avoid allergic triggers. Recently, though, studies have raised hope that new approaches might one day treat food allergies and perhaps even prevent the next generation from developing them. "I think we're all encouraged that progress has happened relatively quickly," says Robert Wood of Johns Hopkins Children's Center in Baltimore. Nonetheless, he cautions, a true, effective therapy is still years away.

If nothing else, the experiments have shown for the first time that curing food allergies is at least possible, even if the long-term prospects aren't clear. Some children who began studies with immune reactions to even the smallest trace of peanut can now eat up to 13 nuts in one sitting. Similar dramatic gains have been seen for milk and egg allergies. Only a few children have been involved in each study so far, but researchers are cautiously increasing the number of enrollees and are emboldened to try other, more innovative methods.

"It's the beginning," says Andrew Saxon of UCLA's David Geffen School of Medicine. In a field with a history of false starts and disappointment, he says, "it's the *real* beginning this time."

New Strategies

Oral Tolerance
Eating tiny amounts of peanut protein can gradually retrain the immune system to tolerate allergens by avoiding the IgE antibody-mediated response.

Vaccines
Hiding a peanut protein in a bacterial cell or injecting a gene-based vaccine may help patients tolerate peanuts by avoiding IgE-activated response.

Tapping Parasites
Scientists are harnessing proteins from helminth parasites that block the activity of mast cells and other immune players to quell allergies.

Curing food allergies has been challenging, in part, because there are many ways to go wrong. No body process is simple, but the immune system is so terrifically complex that Nobel laureate Niels Jerne once likened it to a foreign language operating independently of the brain. Immunity (or allergy, which is essentially immunity run amok) involves legions of cells that not only chatter back and forth at lightning speed each time they encounter something new, but also remember their conversations for a lifetime.

Simply speaking, when an antigen such as peanut protein passes through the digestive tract, it is first greeted by an "antigen-presenting" cell. This cell functions like a maître d', escorting guests to their table and alerting the waiter. The waiters—it's a fancy establishment, so there are more than one—are the T cells, which help the body recognize friend from foe. When food allergy develops, the T cells, instead of welcoming the peanut as the valued customer it is, initiate a process that alerts another type of immune cell, called a B cell. B cells make antibodies—the body's bouncers. In the case of food allergies,

B cells start to make IgE antibodies, which when bound to a peanut protein summon mast cells. Mast cells come armed with chemical weapons. Substances released from mast cells, including histamines and cytokines, lead to the most frightening symptoms of food allergies: hives, vomiting and anaphylaxis, which can be deadly. Once the IgE antibodies are on patrol, the peanut protein finds itself on the blacklist, and will be violently ejected by security should it try to return.

Second Chance for a First Impression

Treatments for pollen, cat dander and other nonfood allergies can slowly refocus the immune system, starting with injections of antigen in amounts too minuscule to provoke IgE antibodies and gradually increasing the dose. In the presence of minute amounts of the antigen, immune responsibility gradually shifts back to the more friendly reception of T cells and antigen-presenting cells. The problem is, attempts in the 1980s to treat food allergies with shots produced severe, even life-threatening side effects. The risks from treatment exceeded the risks from the allergy itself. "With that, we quit trying for a while," says Wesley Burks of Duke University Medical Center in Durham, N.C.

But as the number of children with food allergies began to rise, so did renewed interest in research. (The U.S. National Institute of Allergy and Infectious Diseases alone increased funding for food allergy studies from $1.2 million in 2003 to more than $13 million in 2008.) Allergy experts spooked by the results of early experiments began to consider new approaches, among them giving allergy treatment orally rather than by injection.

Burks and others had long thought that the problem with previous treatment attempts was the shots themselves. Research suggested that the immune response to food particles introduced by mouth was safer and more likely to lead to tolerance. In 2003, for example, researchers writing in the *New England Journal of Medicine* noted that British infants were more likely to have peanut allergies if their skin had been exposed to creams containing peanut oil, instead of a first exposure through food. Experts believe that the human body is more inclined to tolerate substances introduced through the mouth, precisely because the digestive system must deal with the large amount of outside proteins in food and with the colonies of bacteria that live peacefully in the gut. "Understanding oral tolerance has been recognized as a key component in developing strategies for preventing and treating food allergies," Burks writes in the August issue of *Current Opinion in Allergy and Clinical Immunology.*

So guardedly, and under intense medical supervision, he and his colleagues began giving children infinitesimally small amounts of peanut powder to swallow (mixed with food), and increasing the dose in halting increments. In the August *Journal of Allergy and Clinical Immunology,* the researchers report that after months of treatment, 27 of 29 severely allergic children were able to eat about 13 peanuts. The most common reactions during the treatment were sneezing, itching and hives. Molecular analysis also revealed clues to explain how oral tolerance therapy might dampen the allergic response. Tests of the immune cells in the treated children found that after the experimental therapy, T cells were more likely to contain genes active in cellular suicide, or apoptosis, a finding that "is novel and may provide insight into the mechanism of oral immunotherapy," the scientists write.

Food Allergy Facts
Serving Size: U.S. Population

Children affected ≤ 4 years	6–8%
People affected ≥ 10 years	4%
Food-induced anaphylactic reactions per year	30,000
Percentage of ER visits for anaphylaxis food-allergy related	34–52%
Hospital admissions per year, food-allergy related	2,000
Deaths per year, food-allergy related	200
U.S. children affected ≤ 5 years by peanut allergy	1%
Total U.S. population affected by allergy to peanuts, tree nuts or both	3 million

COMMON FOOD ALLERGENS: FISH AND SHELLFISH SUCH AS SHRIMP, CRAYFISH, LOBSTER AND CRAB; EGGS; MILK; SOY; PEANUTS AND TREE NUTS SUCH AS WALNUTS.

RECOMMENDED TREATMENT: AVOIDANCE HALF OF PEOPLE WITH FOOD ALLERGIES DEVELOP A REACTION AFTER ACCIDENTAL EXPOSURE OVER A 2-YEAR PERIOD

Tolerance to a T

Under the oral tolerance scenario, almost any food antigen could be a candidate for therapy. For example, in October 2008, Wood from Johns Hopkins and his colleagues released results of the first randomized trial using oral tolerance to treat milk allergy—a study of 20 children that 19 completed. At the beginning, no child could drink more than about one-fourth of a teaspoon of cow's milk without a severe immune reaction. Writing in the *Journal of Allergy and Clinical Immunology,* the scientists reported that four months after starting treatment, children were able to tolerate from 2.5 to 8 ounces of milk. A follow-up published online in the journal this August described the experiences of more than a dozen children who were able to continue to gradually increase their intake of milk. While the results are encouraging, the team also noted that many of the children experienced side effects such as itching and hives that should be better understood before such a treatment becomes widespread.

Oral therapy isn't the only way scientists want to try to reeducate the immune systems of allergic children. For example, studies will soon be underway with a vaccine that encapsulates modified peanut proteins in *E. coli* bacteria. With the protein tucked inside a bacterium, researchers hope to sneak in under the IgE antibody radar, but still alert the nonallergic components of the immune system. "By altering the peanut proteins just a bit, but in very specific ways, it is hoped that the IgE will not as readily see the vaccine," says Scott Sicherer of Mount Sinai School of Medicine's Jaffe Food Allergy Institute in New York City. Other modifications should improve safety and effectiveness, he says.

Meanwhile, the idea of giving food-allergy shots has even been revived. UCLA's Saxon is trying to develop a genetic food-allergy vaccine—injecting not the peanut protein this time, but the gene that codes for it. The idea is to slip the gene into the maître d'/antigen-presenting cells and coax those cells to make the peanut protein. If the antigen-presenting cells produce the peanut protein robustly enough, the responsibility for the immune response might shift away from the IgE antibodies and mast cells.

"The idea of gene vaccines has been around a long time," Saxon says. "The biggest bugaboo is getting it where you want." If the introduced gene doesn't find the correct cell, the protein won't get made, or it won't get made in the right place. However, in July, he and his colleagues described a molecule they believe can deliver the gene straight to the antigen-presenting cells. The idea is still being tested in mice.

Promise from Parasites

Other future strategies take lessons from the past, by considering the origin of food allergies. Studies have long suggested that such allergies are a wayward version of the immune reaction to infection with human parasites such as helminths, the worms that cause river blindness, elephantiasis and other diseases. "If you study people in those countries where there are normally multiple parasites, the incidence of allergy is very low," says Marie-Hélène Jouvin of Beth Israel Deaconess Medical Center in Boston. Yet when children are treated for parasites, she says, the tendency for allergy rises.

Parasites survive by manipulating the immune system to grudgingly allow their presence. Since a helminth attaches itself to the inside of the intestine, the parasite's survival depends on creating a tolerant environment inside the body. One tactic was revealed in 2007: A research team led by scientists from the University of Strathclyde in Glasgow reported in *Nature Medicine* that a substance isolated from a helminth was able to disarm mast cells.

Jouvin and her colleagues hope to soon receive approval to study a kind of oral therapy that might mimic the natural protection from food allergies that follows a parasitic infection. Using helminth eggs, researchers hope to test a treatment designed to trick the immune system into reacting as if it were accommodating a parasite (minus the actual worm), and tempering the mast cell response.

The helminth experiments would also be consistent with the "hygiene hypothesis," one of the leading theories to explain the rise in the prevalence of allergies—that children raised in the indoor, antibacterial age lack the exposures to antigens of their ancestors, and so the children's immune systems don't always develop as nature intended. "Children are born with an immune system that is immature," Jouvin says.

Other clues, too, point to food allergies as a consequence of an immune system too bored in early life. Parents are often advised to avoid giving children foods that are particularly prone to causing allergies for about the first year of a child's life. But many studies are questioning that conventional wisdom, including one described late last year in the *Journal of Allergy and Clinical Immunology*. Researchers examined the prevalence of allergies among Jewish children in Israel and Great Britain, finding that the British elementary school children had almost 10 times the risk of peanut allergies (*SN: 12/6/08, p. 8*). The biggest difference in diets? Israeli children are fed peanuts earlier and more frequently than British children. The researchers also note that in the Middle East, Asia and Africa, peanuts are generally consumed in infancy and peanut allergies are uncommon.

"Our findings raise the question of whether early and frequent ingestion of high-dose peanut protein during infancy might prevent the development of peanut allergy," wrote an international research team funded in part by the National Peanut Board. "Paradoxically, past recommendations in the United States and current recommendations in the U.K. and Australia might be promoting the development of peanut allergy." Some countries, such as Sweden, have now abandoned the advice to avoid the introduction of certain foods early in life.

American doctors remain wary about early exposure to allergy-prone foods, believing the information still isn't conclusive enough to change official recommendations. "We will do the same things we've been doing until the ongoing studies have given us better guidance," Burks says. In particular, doctors are awaiting the results of a large study underway in Great Britain, in which children are being randomly assigned to eat peanuts in infancy or avoid them until later (for more information, see www.leapstudy.co.uk). Only when these and other studies conclude will experts know whether the secret weapon against food allergies ultimately lies in the culprit itself.

Critical Thinking

1. Explain how a little is helpful but more of the same is harmful in terms of allergens.

2. Review the cycle from T-cells, to B-cells, to IgE antibodies, to mast cells, to allergic response.

3. Differentiate between vaccines, helminth parasites, and oral tolerance therapies.

LAURA BEIL is a freelance science writer in Cedar Hill, Texas.

From *Science News*, September 12, 2009. Copyright © 2009 by Society for Science & the Public. Reprinted by permission.

Ten Tips for Involving Families through Internet-Based Communication

SASCHA MITCHELL, TERESA S. FOULGER, AND KEITH WETZEL

The research is clear that a family's involvement in their child's early education improves outcomes in areas such as the child's language, self-help, social, and motor skills (Connell & Prinz 2002; Henderson & Mapp 2002; Sheldon 2003; Epstein 2004; Weiss, Caspe, & Lopez 2006). The more frequent the contact between home and school, the more the child benefits (McWayne et al. 2004).

While traditional forms of home-school partnerships (for example, parents participating in class activities and teachers sending home children's work) are associated with positive results, they are limited in their ability to effectively reach all families. Some children divide their time between two house-holds as a result of divorce, and some parents cannot volunteer in the classroom due to daytime work hours. In such cases, teachers need to use different methods of home-program communication.

A variety of Internet-based communication methods exist to help increase the frequency and outreach of communication between families and early childhood programs. We recommend these strategies after observing and interviewing teachers who have successfully used them in their own classrooms.

Using Technology to Improve Home-school Communication

All of the following methods emphasize two-way communication. Unlike one-way communication approaches, in which families are merely informed of their child's progress, two-way communication approaches invite parents to participate in their child's learning process, thus creating an ongoing dialogue between home and program (Abdal-Haqq 2002; Vazquez-Nuttall, Li, & Kaplan 2006).

1. **Create a classroom Web site.** Many schools and programs have Web sites that teachers can add to. For teachers without this option, tools to create Web pages, such as Google Sites and Facebook, are free and accessible from any computer. In addition to using print sources to give families information about your classroom activities, post items on the Web site. Embed a calendar, your family handbook, newsletters, homework assignments (for primary grades), announcements, wish lists, permission slips, and volunteer opportunities. It is best if your Web site is password-protected and accessible only to the families of children in the class. Be sure to keep the information on the Web site current. If you have a large number of families whose home language is not English, post all key messages in families' home languages.

2. **Send individual e-mails to share positive information about a particular child's activities and accomplishments.** Teachers need to reach out to families when a child is facing challenges at school; e-mail can be too impersonal and too easily misinterpreted for these types of communications. On the other hand, teachers *can* send e-mails to share short anecdotes about children's developing interests, their newly acquired skills, or their ability to be a good friend that day. These types of positive, spontaneous communications can create two-way conversations when parents reply with similar anecdotes or questions.

3. **Post photo stories on the class Web site.** To help families focus on the process through which their child learns rather than just an end product, create photo essays—a series of photos with captions that capture children engaged in a project (for example, building with blocks, painting a picture, planting seeds). Post the photo essays for families to view; many software programs and Web sites provide easy ways to upload photos. (As photos can be copied on the Internet by anyone with access to the originating page, take special care to select photos for your Web site that do not show children's faces or names.) Sequenced photos give families a more accurate picture of their child's developmental progress. Also post photos of children's work. Change the photos often, and make sure to display each child's work at least once a month.

4. **Provide at-home educational activities.** Your Web site can help families use home computers as avenues for extended learning. Prepare a short list of activities

that use readily accessible materials and include links to age-appropriate sites related to classroom topics. For example, if the children are learning about birds, add a link to the National Audobon Society Web site, which familes can explore with their children. Encourage families to document their children's learning at home by keeping a portfolio of their work, taking photos, and jotting down their child's questions. Also ask them to share links to good sites they have found while investigating topics of interest to their children.

Teachers *can* send e-mails to share short anecdotes about children's developing interests, their newly acquired skills, or their ability to be a good friend that day.

---

5. **Create a family response link or form on the Web page to elicit comments, questions, and feedback.** This is a good strategy for inviting families to monitor and comment on their child's progress. Parents can complete a short online form to provide comments and questions and e-mail them directly to the teacher.

6. **Establish and moderate a family support discussion forum.** The purpose of discussion forums is to offer a place where families can share their thoughts and questions. As the discussion forum moderator, you can instigate forums, but work toward families becoming the major contributors. Check the forum regularly to highlight important points, pose follow-up questions, and delete contributions that are inappropriate. As new topics emerge, archive old forums for future reference. Examples of topics might include how to address challenging behavior or develop nutritious meal or snack ideas for children. Also share listings of upcoming family events in the community.

7. **Communicate logistical information through group e-mails.** In addition to using informal communication (conversations at drop-off and pickup) and formal communication (parent-teacher conferences, print), send group e-mails to remind all families of upcoming events, such as field trips and parent-teacher conferences.

Techniques for Addressing Challenges

While the above methods are opportunities to increase communication between programs and families of young children, they also raise concerns of equity. The following techniques offer ideas on how to increase access to computer technology for all teachers and families.

8. **Ensure families' access to technology.** To ensure that families who do not have computers at home are included, continue to communicate through traditional means and by printing and sending home hard copies of your Web site announcements and general e-mails.

Remember, some families may need these items in their home languages. You might choose to apply for funding from various public and private sources to secure laptop computers that families can check out for home use. For example, the following organizations award computer grants to schools serving pre-K through grade 12 students: (1) Computers for Learning, http://computersforlearning.gov; (2) Sun Microsystems Open Gateways Grant program, www.sun.com/aboutsun/comm_invest/giving/education.html; and (3) the HP Technology for Teaching Grant, www.hp.com/hpinfo/grants/us/programs/tech_teaching/kl2_main.html. In addition, the Teachers Network posts technology grant opportunities at www.teachersnetwork.org/Grants/grants_technology.htm. Computers acquired through grants can be placed in the family area of your center or school.

Resources for Creating a Web Site

Google sites
http://sites.google.com

Provides Web-based templates for creating Web pages and announcements, plus file cabinet (<10mb document upload), dashboard, and lists. Web pages can be modified easily by anyone who has editing privileges, and can include videos, Google docs, spreadsheets, presentations, photo slide shows, and calendars. The site manager designates members as owners, viewers, or collaborators. No advertisements.

webs (formerly freewebs)
www.webs.com

Template-driven Web site construction lets you create blogs, discussion forums, and calendars, and allow for comments. Share ideas, information, photos, and videos. Can accommodate group publishing, and can be set up for either public or member-only viewing. Web-based construction allows editing from any computer with Internet connectivity. Fee-based version does not contain advertisements.

Wikispaces
www.wikispaces.com

Classroom version features
www.wikispaces.com/site/for/teachers

Features include page editing, file and image uploads (including video), and links to Web pages. Allows unlimited members and discussion posts. RSS feeds can notify members of changes to the site. Free version for educators contains no advertisements.

9. **Provide opportunities for families to increase their technology skills.** In certain circumstances, technology-based solutions can produce an unintended communications gap. To ensure that families receive your communications, offer a brief orientation to your classroom Web site during Open House or parent-teacher conferences. Demonstrate how to access and navigate the site. Focus on teaching families how to use the interactive features (discussion board, e-mail response). Distribute information about computer availability at public libraries and any other local organizations that provide computer access.

Staff members could take turns becoming "experts" and train others in how to use the technology.

---

10. **Set aside time for technology-based communication.** Teachers need time for training, maintaining a Web site, keeping information current, and preparing regular communications. Seek professional development opportunities to learn how to use new technology, or consider contacting experts (or an older student) who can assist with the initial setup. Alternatively, access free online tutorials. Staff members could take turns becoming "experts" and train others in how to use the technology. Visit the Web site of the NAEYC Technology and Young Children Interest Forum, www.techandyoungchildren.org, for more information.

References

Abdal-Haqq, I. 2002. *Connecting schools and communities through technology.* Alexandria, VA: National School Boards Association.

Connell, C.M., & R.J. Prinz. 2002. The impact of childcare and parent-child interactions on school readiness and social skills development for low-income African American children. *Journal of School Psychology* 40 (2): 177–93.

Epstein, J.L. 2004. Foreword. In *Children's literacy development: Making it happen through school, family, and community involvement,* by P.A. Edwards, ix–xiv. Boston: Pearson Education.

Henderson, A.T., & K.L. Mapp. 2002. *A new wave of evidence: The impact of school, family, and community connections on student achievement.* Austin, TX: Southwest Educational Development Laboratory, National Center for Family & Community Connections with Schools.

McWayne, C., V. Hampton, J. Fantuzzo, H.L. Cohen, & Y. Sekino. 2004. A multivariate examination of parent involvement and the social and academic competencies of urban kindergarten children. *Psychology in the Schools* 41 (3): 363–77.

Sheldon, S.B. 2003. Linking school-family-community partnerships in urban elementary schools to student achievement on state tests. *Urban Review* 35 (2): 149–65.

Vazquez-Nuttall, E., C. Li, & J.P. Kaplan. 2006. Home-school partnerships with culturally diverse families: Challenges and solutions for school personnel. Special issue, *Journal of Applied School Psychology* 22 (2): 81–102.

Weiss, H., M. Caspe, & M.E. Lopez. 2006. Family involvement in early childhood education. *Family Involvement Makes a Difference* 1 (Spring). Cambridge, MA: Harvard Family Research Project, www.hfrp.org/publications-resources/browse-our-publications/family-involvement-in-early-childhood-education.

"Early Sprouts"

Establishing Healthy Food Choices for Young Children

KARRIE A. KALICH, DOTTIE BAUER, AND DEIRDRE MCPARTLIN

Four-year-old Tyler and 5-year-old Cole eagerly tear the shiny green leaves of rainbow chard into small pieces to use in today's recipe: Cheesy Chard Squares. Earlier in the week the children harvested some chard from the play-yard garden and cut up the stalks with scissors. They sampled each of the different colors and talked about the similarities and differences.

It is late in the harvest season, and while they work, Janet, their teacher, discusses plans for next year's garden with the children. Cole wants to plant tomatoes. Tyler suggests cucumbers. Both children agree they want to grow rainbow chard again. They mix together several eggs, grate the cheese, and combine the ingredients in preparation for baking. Tyler announces, "I'm going to eat these squares for dinner!"

The preschool years are a critical period for the development of food preferences and lifelong eating habits. Between the ages of 2 and 5, children become increasingly responsive to external cues, such as television commercials that use popular cartoon characters to advertise foods, candy in supermarket checkout aisles, and fast-food restaurants offering a free toy with the purchase of a kid's meal. These environmental messages influence children's decisions about what and how much they should eat (Birch & Fisher 1995; Fisher & Birch 1999; Rolls, Engell, & Birch 2000). By the age of 5, most children have lost their innate ability to eat primarily in response to hunger (Rolls, Engell, & Birch 2000; Haire-Joshu & Nanney 2002) and have learned to prefer calorie-rich foods (high fat and high sugar)—foods often used as a reward or for comfort in American society.

Some adults offer children healthy foods, such as fruits and vegetables, in a negative or coercive manner. But vegetables become less appealing if children must finish them prior to having dessert or leaving the dinner table (Birch & Fisher 1996). Using a positive approach to foster healthy eating behaviors helps young children develop lifelong habits that decrease the risk of obesity and other related chronic diseases.

Nutrition and Young Children

The current obesity epidemic in the United States is a fast-growing public health concern. For preschool-age children the prevalence of obesity has more than doubled in the past 30 years (CCOR 2006). Traditionally, early childhood educators have focused on the importance of meeting young children's nutritional requirements (Marotz 2009). With the increase in childhood obesity, there is a new call to early childhood educators to guide children and families in developing healthy eating and activity habits.

What we know now is that a diet rich in fruits and vegetables is recommended for achieving or maintaining a healthy body weight. The USDA (U.S. Department of Agriculture) recommends that preschool-age children eat 3 to 5 half-cup servings of vegetables and 2 to 4 half-cup servings of fruit daily (www.mypyramid.gov). However, on the average, preschool children consume approximately 2 servings of vegetables and 1.5 servings of fruit each day. Their diets are typically low in fruits, vegetables, and whole grains and high in saturated fat, sodium, and added sugar (Enns, Mickle, & Goldman 2002; Guenther et al. 2006). In fact, studies have consistently shown that the diets of U.S. children do not meet national dietary recommendations (Gleason & Suitor 2001; U.S. Department of Health and Human Services & U.S. Department of Agriculture 2005). While children ages 2 to 5 have somewhat better diets than older children, their diets still need improvement to meet the 2005 *Dietary Guidelines for Healthy Americans* (Fungwe et al. 2009).

Children's gardens provide an ideal setting for nutrition education by allowing children to observe and care for plants and develop a connection to the natural world.

Role of Early Education in Improving the Diets of Young Children

Early childhood educators have the opportunity to improve children's food choices because they interact with children daily (Birch & Fisher 1998). Family members and teachers can influence the food preferences of young children by providing healthy food choices, offering multiple opportunities to prepare and eat new foods, and serving as positive role models through their own food choices.

Children's preference for vegetables is among the strongest predictors of vegetable consumption (Birch 1979; Domel et al. 1996; Harvey-Berino et al. 1997; Morris & Zidenberg-Cherr 2002). Sullivan and Birch (1994) found that it takes 5 to 10 exposures to a new food for preschool children to become comfortable and familiar with its taste and texture. When children have repeated opportunities to taste a new food, they often change their food reactions from rejection to acceptance (Birch & Marlin 1982; Sullivan & Birch 1994).

Children's gardens provide an ideal setting for nutrition education by allowing children to observe and care for plants and develop a connection to the natural world (Subramaniam 2002; Lautenschlager & Smith 2007). Children exposed to homegrown produce tend to prefer those vegetables (Nanney et al. 2007). Some early childhood garden projects also focus on caring for the environment and science education (Perkins et al. 2005; Nimmo & Hallett 2008). Other nutrition education approaches for young children feature tasting exotic fruits and vegetables (Bellows & Anderson 2006). As more educators bring gardening and nutrition projects into their classrooms, there is a need for additional teacher support and curriculum development (Graham et al. 2005).

The Early Sprouts Program: An Overview

Early Sprouts is a research-based nutrition and gardening curriculum for the preschool years, created by Karrie Kalich and developed in collaboration with the Child Development Center at Keene State College in New Hampshire. We designed the curriculum to encourage children's food preferences for six selected vegetables (bell peppers, butternut squash, carrots, green beans, Swiss rainbow chard, and tomatoes) and increase their consumption of these vegetables (Kalich, Bauer, & McPartlin 2009). The program's scope includes planting raised organic garden beds, sensory and cooking lessons focused on the six vegetables, training and support for classroom teachers, and family involvement.

Through the curriculum we help children overcome an innate food neophobia (*fear of new foods*) through multiple exposures to the six vegetables. Additionally, the Early Sprouts model provides a "seed to table" experience by following the lifespan of the vegetables. The garden features six vegetables that represent a variety of colors and plant parts and are easy to grow in our region (New England), available at farmers' markets, and affordable and available year-round in supermarkets.

One project goal is to expose the children to the six vegetables multiple times over the course of the 24-week curriculum. In preparation for the project, we developed recipes for cooking snacks and meals using the vegetables. The Early Sprouts recipes include a variety of healthy ingredients: low-fat dairy products, healthy fats (canola and olive oils), whole grains (stone-ground cornmeal and whole wheat flours), and reduced amounts of sodium and sugar as compared to commercially available snack products.

Based on feedback from field-testing among teachers and children in our program, we chose 24 recipes (four per vegetable). We adapted the recipes for classroom use and for family use in the Family Recipe Kits component of the project. Each recipe has an accompanying sensory exploration activity that features the same vegetable and involves children in exploring the plant parts by using all of their senses.

We begin the Early Sprouts project at each site by building raised garden beds on the playground and filling them with alternating layers of compost, humus, and topsoil. To ensure children's health and safety, we practice organic gardening techniques, such as using only organic fertilizers and hand-picking garden pests. With the groundwork complete, teachers implement the healthy food curriculum in their preschool classrooms.

How the Early Sprouts Program Works

The program begins when children help plant seeds and seedlings in late May and early June. This is followed by watering, weeding, watching, and waiting. After months of anticipation, the children harvest the vegetables from July through early October; thus they observe the complete growing cycle. The children make many discoveries.

> The children are in the play-yard garden at harvest time. Janet, the preschool teacher, asks Rachel, age 4½, what she thinks the Swiss chard will taste like. Rachel pauses, then she speculates, "It will taste like nachos." She spontaneously takes a bite of the Swiss chard directly from the garden and then corrects herself, proclaiming, "It tastes more like celery!"

Each week the curriculum introduces one of the six vegetables. By the end of the entire curriculum, each vegetable has been featured four times. At the start of the week, the children use their senses to explore the vegetable. This exploration is followed by a cooking activity featuring an Early Sprouts recipe. At the end of the week, the children pack a Family Recipe Kit containing the recipe, tips for cooking with children, and many of the necessary ingredients to take home. The purpose of the kit is to help families reinforce the food preparation and healthy eating experience children have had at preschool. Here is one example:

> Cooper, a cautious 3½-year-old, is hesitant to try any of the Early Sprouts vegetables but thoroughly enjoys all of the sensory and cooking activities. He almost never misses an Early Sprouts activity and spends time in the garden almost daily. His interest in the vegetables continues throughout the 24-week experience, but so does his hesitancy to taste the vegetables. About five weeks before the end of the program, Cooper starts to cautiously lick the vegetables. Three weeks later, he tastes them. By the last two weeks, he has developed into a true vegetable lover. His family says that he requests and eats several vegetables a day.

Sensory Exploration

The sensory exploration experiences safely introduce children to each vegetable. Their familiarity increases as they smell each vegetable, feel the shape and texture, touch its leaves and stalks, shake it and listen for sounds, and notice how it looks before tasting the raw food or the results of the prepared recipe.

> Jackson, Caitlin, and José, all enrolled in an older preschool group, enthusiastically gather red, yellow, and green bell peppers. Janet, the teacher, guides each of the children in cutting open their peppers and exploring the seeds. José quickly asks if they can taste them. Each child cuts a piece of pepper and tastes it. Caitlin wants to taste the other colors. The children cut and share pieces of their peppers. Janet and the children discuss the various characteristics of the bell peppers, using vocabulary such as *crunchy, juicy,* and *smooth.* When they finish, the children describe the peppers' characteristics and agree they enjoy all the different colored peppers.

The sensory exploration experiences safely introduce children to each vegetable.

Cooking

After children explore and taste a vegetable in its raw form, most are eager and willing to participate in the cooking and tasting process. Teachers encourage the children to perform each step of the recipe preparation as is developmentally appropriate—measuring, cutting (with safe tools), mixing, and preparing the food for serving.

> Children eagerly join Janet at the table after washing their hands. Janet helps them identify all the ingredients for making muffins. They use child-size table knives to dice the peppers and plastic graters to grate the cheese. Janet watches 5-year-old Jermaine as he breaks and mixes the eggs, while guiding 3½-year-old Thomas and 4-year-old Jocelyn in measuring and mixing the dry ingredients. All the children count to 10 as they take turns mixing the wet and dry ingredients.

Cooking experiences connect the Early Sprouts project to other curriculum areas, such as math, science, literacy, and social skills development (Colker 2005).

> Two 5-year-olds, Annabelle and Carolyn, are deciding where to place the different colored pegs on the peg board. From across the room, Janet watches the children and admires their cooperative play. After a few minutes, she approaches and sees the girls using many colors. "We're planting a garden," they explain. The orange pegs are carrots; the green pegs are green beans; the red pegs are tomatoes. Janet asks them about the mixed-color assortment of pegs in one of the rows. The children look at her impatiently and exclaim, "Those are rainbow chard, silly!"

Family Involvement

Social modeling by family (as well as peers) plays a particularly large role in the early development of food preferences (Birch & Fisher 1996). The Early Sprouts program supports families in encouraging children to make healthy food choices at home. One parent reports that as a result of the program, her whole family is eating better, even her "I-don't-eat-anything-green" husband.

The Early Sprouts monthly newsletter keeps families well informed of our activities. We also invite families to participate in garden planting; classroom-based sensory and cooking activities; food-based special events, such as the Stone Soup luncheon (made from the Early Sprouts vegetables); and a family nutrition education program. One father comments, "I used to battle with my child about eating vegetables. Now he requests specific vegetables at the store and at mealtimes."

The weekly Family Recipe Kits, which children help to pack, promote family-oriented nutrition education. They contain all needed ingredients and instructions to re-create the week's featured recipe with their child at home. The family experience reinforces the classroom activity and provides another opportunity for the child to taste the vegetable. At the end of the year, families receive a cookbook containing all of the Early Sprouts recipes. Through our weekly program surveys, parents tell us their stories.

> Sydney, the mother of two Early Sprouts participants, writes, "On Friday we brought home this week's kit, and, as usual, my oldest child, Ava, excitedly asked about the contents. When I told her it was butternut squash pancakes, she wrinkled her nose and said she would not eat them. Of course Clay, the youngest and a finicky eater, turned his nose up too.

> Sunday morning the children begged for "normal pancakes" but I told them that we were making the Early Sprouts pancakes. Three-year-old Clay wanted to help but kept saying he would not eat the squash. As the pancakes were cooking, Ava came to the stove and asked to see what they looked like. I ate the first (Yummy!), put the second on Clay's plate, and kept cooking. Then Ava said she wanted some too. Both children ate the pancakes. Their only comments were, "How soon until the next one?" and "He (she) got more pancakes."

> Sydney described the pancakes as "delicious and so easy to make." She wrote, "I did not even serve them with syrup! My only complaint—they were so good I only got two pancakes! I feel good about serving them. I LOVE THIS PROGRAM! These are the only pancakes we will eat from now on!"

Cooking experiences connect the Early Sprouts project to other curriculum areas, such as math, science, literacy, and social skills development.

Involving Teachers and Staff

Training professional and volunteer staff is important to the ongoing success of the Early Sprouts project. Because some adults are unfamiliar with the six vegetables and unsure about how to introduce them to the children, we provide detailed background sheets for each vegetable. We post guidelines in the classrooms to encourage staff and volunteers to serve as positive role models during snack and mealtimes when serving the vegetables and presenting new recipes (see "Early Sprouts Tasting— Suggestions for Teachers and Volunteers"). One experienced teacher even commented, "I know it is important to teach our children about nutrition, but I was never really sure how to do that before Early Sprouts."

Early Sprouts: What We Have Learned

A strong research component supports the Early Sprouts program and has evaluated the impact of the curriculum on the eating habits of young children and their families. At the start, midpoint, and conclusion of the 24 weeks of sensory exploration and vegetable recipes, we measure children's preferences for the program's vegetables as well as dietary changes observed by families at home. At the conclusion of the program, children are more willing to taste the Early Sprouts vegetables and express a greater preference for the six vegetables highlighted. Teachers describe a greater personal confidence in guiding young children in the development of healthy eating behaviors.

Ways to Adapt Early Sprouts at Your Center

The Early Sprouts model can be easily adapted to other geographic regions. When selecting vegetables for your area, consider the available space, the length of the growing season, rainfall levels, and soil type. If outdoor space is limited, try container or window-box gardening, with dwarf cherry tomato plants, greens, or pole beans. Local greenhouses, community garden associations, community-supported agriculture programs, cooperative extension offices, and garden shops have information and are potential partners. There are many ways to engage children and families in a seed-to-table experience that is appropriate for your setting and location. Visit the Early Sprouts website (www.earlysprouts.org) for more information. We encourage you to be creative and innovative in your approach to using the Early Sprouts model. We change and grow ourselves!

> Janet has hosted a Stone Soup luncheon for 10 years with children and families during the harvest season. In the past, children brought vegetables from home to contribute to the soup. The luncheon is a great family event. But the downside has been that the children rarely would eat or even taste the soup.
>
> Now, with the Early Sprouts program, Janet notices that the children contribute many more vegetables and

---

Early Sprouts Tasting— Suggestions for Teachers and Volunteers

- Taste a portion of the Early Sprouts snack. Children will be more willing to try the new snack if you are eating with them and model how to try new foods.
- Invite children to serve themselves from a common bowl, first taking just one helping. Offer a second helping once the children have finished the first one.
- Be a positive role model and adventurous about trying new foods. The goal in providing recipes is to introduce foods creatively and engage all children in trying at least one bite.
- Share your enthusiasm and positive comments if you like the Early Sprouts snack. Even if you do not especially enjoy the snack, let your comments express that it sometimes takes multiple tries to become accustomed to a new food. Explain that we want to give ourselves and the food a chance.
- Compliment the children on their preparation of the snack. Many of them participated in the activity. Thank them for their work and for making delicious food.
- Ask the children to explain how they made the food (the ingredients needed, the stirring, measuring, and so on). They will be eager to talk about what they did to follow the recipe.
- Engage the children in a pleasant conversation about the things they did in cooking, surprises they may have had, and what they'd like to cook next. Discourage negative criticism but invite suggestions for ways to vary the recipe another time. Talk about why we want to respect the feelings of friends and teachers who prepared the food.

---

are especially focused on bringing in the Early Sprouts vegetables. Families have more interest because they feel involved in the cooking process. At the luncheon, almost all of the children eat the soup, and many request a second and even a third serving. They also eat up all the Confetti Corn Muffins baked to go with it.

References

Bellows, L., & J. Anderson. 2006. The food friends: Encouraging preschoolers to try new foods. *Young Children* 61 (3): 37–39.

Birch, L.L. 1979. Preschool children's food preferences and consumption patterns. *Journal of Nutrition Education* 11: 189–92.

Birch, L.L., & J.A. Fisher. 1995. Appetite and eating behavior in children. *Pediatric Clinical Nutrition America* 42: 931–53.

Birch, L.L., & J.A. Fisher. 1996. Experience and children's eating behaviors. In *Why we eat what we eat,* ed. E.D. Capaldi, 113–41. Washington, DC: American Psychological Association.

Birch L.L., & J.A. Fisher. 1998. Development of eating behaviors among children and adolescents. *Pediatrics* 101: 539–49.

Birch, L.L., & D.W. Marlin. 1982. I don't like it; I never tried it: Effects of exposure to food on two-year-old children's food preferences. *Appetite* 4: 353–60.

CCOR (Center for Childhood Obesity Research). 2006. Over the past 30 years, childhood obesity has doubled for preschool children. website home page at Pennsylvania State University, College of Health & Human Development. www.hhdev.psu.edu/ccor/index.html

Colker, L. 2005. *The cooking book: Fostering young children's learning and delight.* Washington, DC: NAEYC.

Domel, S.B., W.O. Thompson, H.C. Davis, T. Baranowski, S.B. Leonard, & J. Baranowski. 1996. Psychosocial predictors of fruit and vegetable consumption among elementary school children. *Health Education Research* 11 (3): 299–308.

Enns, C.W., S.J. Mickle, & J.D. Goldman. 2002. Trends in food and nutrient intake by children in the United States. *Family Economics and Nutrition Review* 14 (2): 56–69.

Fisher, J.O., & L.L. Birch. 1999. Restricting access to palatable foods affects children's behavioral response, food selection, and intake. *American Journal of Clinical Nutrition* 69: 1264–72.

Fungwe, T., P.M. Guenther, W.W. Juan, H. Hiza, & M. Lino. 2009. Nutrition Insight 43: The quality of children's diets in 2003–04 as measured by the Healthy Eating Index—2005. Alexandria, VA: U.S. Department of Agriculture Center for Nutrition Policy and Promotion.

Gleason, P.M., & C. Suitor. 2001. Children's diets in the mid-1990s: Dietary intake and its relationship with school meal participation. Report no. CN-01-CDI. Alexandria, VA: U.S. Department of Agriculture, Food and Nutrition Service.

Graham, H., D.L. Beall, M. Lussier, P. McLaughlin, & S. Zeidenberg-Cherr. 2005. Use of school gardens in academic instruction. *Journal of Nutrition Education and Behavior* 37 (3): 147–51.

Guenther, P.M., K.W. Dodd, J. Reedy, & S.M. Krebs-Smith. 2006. Most Americans eat much less than recommended amounts of fruits and vegetables. *Journal of the American Dietetic Association* 106 (9): 1371–79.

Haire-Joshu, D., & M.S. Nanney. 2002. Prevention of overweight and obesity in children: Influences on the food environment. *The Diabetes Educator* 28 (3): 415–22.

Harvey-Berino, J., V. Hood, J. Rourke, T. Terrance, A. Dorwaldt, & R. Secker-Walker. 1997. Food preferences predict eating behavior of very young Mohawk children. *Journal of the American Dietetic Association* 97 (7): 750–53.

Kalich, K., D. Bauer, & D. McPartlin. 2009. *Early Sprouts: Cultivating healthy food choices in young children.* St. Paul, MN: Redleaf Press.

Lautenschlager, L., & C. Smith. 2007. Beliefs, knowledge, and values held by inner-city youth about gardening, nutrition, and cooking. *Agriculture and Human Values* 24 (2): 245–58.

Marotz, L. 2009. *Health, safety, and nutrition for the young child.* 7th ed. Clifton Park, NY: Thomson Delmar Learning.

Morris, J., & S. Zidenberg-Cherr. 2002. Garden-enhanced nutrition curriculum improves fourth-grade school children's knowledge of nutrition and preferences for some vegetables. *Journal of the American Dietetic Association* 102 (1): 91–93.

Nanney, M.S., S. Johnson, M. Elliott, & D. Haire-Joshu. 2007. Frequency of eating homegrown produce is associated with higher intake among parents and their preschool-aged children in rural Missouri. *Journal of the American Dietetic Association* 107 (4): 577–84.

Nimmo, J., & B. Hallett. 2008. Childhood in the garden: A place to encounter natural and social diversity. *Young Children* 63 (1): 32–38.

Perkins, D., B. Hogan, B. Hallett, J. Nimmo, C. Esmel, L. Boyer, R. Freyre, & P. Fisher. 2005. *Growing a green generation: A curriculum of gardening activities for preschool and kindergarten children.* Durham: University of New Hampshire, Child Study and Development Center.

Rolls, B.J., D. Engell, & L.L. Birch 2000. Serving portion size influences 5-year-old but not 3-year-old children's food intake. *Journal of the American Dietetic Association* 100: 232–34.

Subramaniam, A. 2002. *Garden-based learning in basic education: A historical review.* 4-H Center for Youth Development Monograph, Summer. University of California, Davis. http://cyd.ucdavis.edu/publications/pubs/focus/pdf/ MO02V8N1.pdf

Sullivan, S.A., & L.L. Birch. 1994. Infant dietary experience and acceptance of solid foods. *Pediatrics* 9: 884–85.

U.S. Department of Health and Human Services & U.S. Department of Agriculture. 2005. *Dietary guidelines for healthy Americans.* 6th ed. Washington, DC: U.S. Government Printing Office.

Critical Thinking

1. Select several healthy food choices, in place of empty calorie foods, for young children.

2. Locate a place at your nearest preschool where children can grow foods.

3. Identify ways to get parents involved in selecting healthier children's foods.

KARRIE A. KALICH, PhD, RD, is an associate professor of health science and nutrition at Keene State College. Karrie has spent more than 14 years in community-based childhood obesity prevention. kkalich@keene.edu. **DOTTIE BAUER**, PhD, is a professor of early childhood education at Keene State College in Keene, New Hampshire. A former preschool teacher, Dottie now specializes in early childhood curriculum development and teacher preparation. dbauer@keene.edu. **DEIRDRE MCPARTLIN**, MEd, is the associate director at the Child Development Center, the early childhood demonstration site at Keene State College. Deirdre's experience in the field includes preschool and kindergarten teaching, child care administration, and preservice teacher training. dmcpartl@keene.edu. The authors expand the story of their Early Sprouts project in a new book from Redleaf Press, *Early Sprouts: Cultivating Healthy Food Choices in Young Children.*

UNIT 3

Development during Childhood: Cognition and Schooling

Unit Selections

Learning Outcomes

After reading this Unit you should be able to:

- Support the addition of more project-based creative activities to schools.

- Synthesize what is known about neuroenhancers and attention.

- Explain why Albert Einstein's and John Lennon's genius are considered similar.

- Contrast teacher-chosen tasks with student-selected projects.

- Formulate two changes in education which would increase students' motivation.

- Explain why a child's relationship with his/her teacher matters in education.

- Describe the changes Michelle Rhee wants to see in public schools.

- Design a rubric for rating teacher effectiveness which makes students matter.

- Appraise consequences for bullying: What will reduce the behavior?

Student Website
www.mhhe.com/cls

The mental process of knowing—cognition—includes aspects such as sensing, understanding, associating, and discriminating. Cognitive research has been hampered by the limitations of trying to understand what is happening inside the minds of living persons without doing harm. It has also been challenged by the problem of defining concepts such as intuition, unconsciousness, unawareness, implicit learning, incomprehension, and all the aspects of knowing present behind our sensations and perceptions (metacognition). Many kinds of achievement that require cognitive processes (awareness, perception, reasoning, judgment) cannot be measured with intelligence tests or with achievement tests.

Intelligence is the capacity to acquire and apply knowledge. It is usually assumed that intelligence can be measured. The ratio of tested mental age to chronological age is expressed as intelligence quotient (IQ). For years, schoolchildren have been classified by IQ scores. The links between IQ scores and school achievement are positive, but no significant correlations exist between IQ scores and life success. Consider, for example, the motor coordination and kinesthetic abilities of Hall of Fame baseball player Cal Ripken, Jr. He had a use of his body that surpassed the capacity of most other athletes and nonathletes. Is knowledge of kinesthetics a form of intelligence? Many people believe it is.

Some psychologists have suggested that uncovering more about how the brain processes various types of intelligences will soon be translated into new educational practices. Today's tests of intelligence only measure abilities in the logical/mathematical, spatial, and linguistic areas of intelligence, which is what schools now teach. Jean Piaget, the Swiss founder of cognitive psychology, was involved in the creation of the world's first intelligence test, the Binet-Simon Scale. He became disillusioned with trying to quantify how much children knew at different chronological ages. He was much more intrigued with what they did not know, what they knew incorrectly, and how they came to know the world as they did. He started the Centre for Genetic Epistemology in Geneva, Switzerland, where he began to study the nature, extent, and validity of children's knowledge. He discovered qualitative, rather than quantitative, differences in cognitive processes over the life span. Infants know the world through their senses and their motor responses. After language develops, toddlers and preschoolers know the world through their language/symbolic perspective. Piaget likened early childhood cognitive processes to bad thought, or thought akin to daydreams. By school age, children know things in concrete terms, which allows them to number, seriate, classify, conserve, think backward and forward, and think about their own thinking (metacognition). However, Piaget believed that children do not acquire the cognitive processes necessary to think abstractly and to use clear, consistent, logical patterns of thought until early adolescence. Their moral sense and personal philosophies of behavior are not completed until adulthood.

In the initial article in this unit Scott Sieder discusses the contribution of Multiple Intelligence theory and it increasing role as

© Bananastock/AGE Fotostock

a counterbalance to the current educational climate focused on high-stakes testing.

Cognitive scientists can study the brain in action today with functional magnetic resonance imaging (fMRI). The article "In Defense of Distraction" by Sam Anderson describes what fMRIs are revealing about multitasking and distraction. Rather than doing two things at once, our brains switch rapidly between two things. Too many distractions result in mistakes and inefficiency. We need to learn to allocate our attention and harness the power of distraction.

The fourth article of this unit explains, "What Really Motivates Kids." Many adults intuitively answer by naming some material reward (money, gifts, food), or by suggesting praise. The author points out that rewards reduce internal motivation and that praise can be toxic. Dana Truby interviews Daniel Pink, an expert on motivation, for answers on why this is so. He recommends student-chosen, student-led projects to really motivate kids.

Michelle Rhee, the author of the article "What I've Learned," believes that politics are hampering school reform. She believes good teachers are the key to good education. She has launched a national movement called Students First, to try to transform American educational policies. Instead of proceeding on the principle that the last hired should be the first fired, she wants effective teachers to be promoted and ineffective teachers to be let go.

The last article in this unit, "From Lockers to Lockup," asks the question: "Should cyberbullying be a crime?" There are many horror stories of how cyberbullying and other online aggressive acts have caused serious emotional harm and even suicidal deaths. What can teachers, parents, school administrators, and others do to prevent cyberbullying? How should adults respond to students who report that they have been harassed online?

Internet References

Children Now
www.childrennow.org

Council for Exceptional Children
www.cec.sped.org

Cyberbullying Research Center
www.cyberbullying.us/aboutus.php

Educational Resources Information Center (ERIC)
www.eric.ed.gov/

Federation of Behavioral, Psychological, and Cognitive Science
http://federation.apa.org

JumpStart Coalition for Personal Financial Literacy
www.jumpstart.org

Project Zero
http://pzweb.harvard.edu

Students First
www.studentsfirst.org

Teaching Technologies
www.inspiringteachers.com/bttindex.html

An Educator's Journey toward Multiple Intelligences

Scott Seider

During my first year as a high school English teacher, I got into the habit each Friday afternoon of sitting in the bleachers and grading papers while the players on the freshman football team squared off against their counterparts from nearby towns. I had been assigned four classes of rambunctious freshmen, and several of my most squirrelly students were football players. I hoped that demonstrating my interest in their gridiron pursuits might make them a bit easier to manage in the classroom.

My presence at their games unquestionably helped on the management front, but a second, unexpected benefit emerged as well. A couple of those freshmen—kids in my class who struggled mightily with subject-verb agreement and the function of a thesis statement—had clearly committed several dozen complex plays to memory. During one particularly impressive series of plays, I remember thinking, "These guys are really smart! I'm underestimating what they're capable of!" And over the course of my first year in the classroom, that same thought emerged several more times—at the school musical, visiting the graphic design class, and even just watching a couple of students do their math homework during study hall. Without my realizing it, my relationship with multiple-intelligences (MI) theory had begun.

Rethinking IQ

What has become a powerful force in the world of education all started in 1983, when Harvard University professor Howard Gardner began his book *Frames of Mind: The Theory of Multiple Intelligences* [1] with some simple but powerful questions: Are talented chess players, violinists, and athletes "intelligent" in their respective disciplines? Why are these and other abilities not accounted for on traditional IQ tests? Why is the term *intelligence* limited to such a narrow range of human endeavors?

From these questions emerged multiple-intelligences theory. Stated simply, it challenges psychology's definition of intelligence as a general ability that can be measured by a single IQ score. Instead, MI theory describes eight intelligences (see Howard Gardner's Eight Intelligences) that people use to solve problems and create products relevant to the societies in which they live.

MI theory asserts that individuals who have a high level of aptitude in one intelligence do not necessarily have a similar aptitude in another intelligence. For example, a young person who demonstrates an impressive level of musical intelligence may be far less skilled when it comes to bodily-kinesthetic or logical-mathematical intelligence. Perhaps that seems obvious, but it's important to recognize that this notion stands in sharp contrast to the traditional (and still dominant) view of intelligence as a general ability that can be measured along a single scale and summarized by a single number.

Multiple Misconceptions

During my eight years as a high school English teacher and an administrator, MI theory came up periodically. Colleagues shared assignments with me that sought to tap into the multiple intelligences. At parent-teacher conferences, I fielded questions about whether schools today are too focused (or, alternatively, not focused enough) on verbal-linguistic and logical-mathematical intelligences. In professional-development seminars, I was urged to keep multiple intelligences in mind while developing curriculum.

I also assured my students that everyone is gifted in at least one of the intelligences—a sentiment uttered with the best of intentions, but not entirely accurate.

Not only didn't I fully understand the theory, but when I began teaching at an urban public high school in Boston, I believed I had no time to concern myself with it. I was determined to help my students develop the tools they needed to make it into college: reading comprehension, writing skills, critical thinking, SAT vocabulary. I was certain there simply weren't enough hours in the day to foster students' musical intelligence or bodily-kinesthetic intelligence.

And, then, in 2004, my views began to change. I started working on my doctorate at Harvard University and asked Professor Howard Gardner to be my adviser. My interest in working with Gardner had more to do with his work on ethics than on MI theory, but over the next four years, MI theory was like fluoride in the water. There was a constant clamor from educators across the globe to hear from him about MI theory. Working each day about 20 yards away, I couldn't help overhearing the uproar and, amid that din, I started to pick up on my own misconceptions.

What MI Is—and Is Not

MI theory asserts that, barring cases of severe brain damage, everyone possesses all eight of the intelligences with varying levels of aptitude, giving each person a unique profile. And MI theory makes no claims about everyone being gifted in at least one of the intelligences.

I also discovered that neither Gardner nor MI theory has ever argued that educators should spend equal amounts of time teaching to the eight intelligences, or that every lesson should provide students with eight options for demonstrating their learning. In fact, MI theory offers neither a curriculum nor a goal toward which educators are expected to strive. Rather, MI theory is an *idea* about the concept of intelligence. A psychologist by training, Gardner left it to educators to decide how MI theory can be useful in the particular community and context in which they teach.

Nowadays, as a professor of education myself, when students or colleagues learn that I trained with Gardner, I am often asked facetiously, "How many intelligences is he up to now?" In truth, the original formulation of MI theory included seven intelligences, and Gardner has added just one (naturalistic intelligence) over the past 25 years.

Many other scholars and educators have proposed other intelligences—everything from moral intelligence to cooking intelligence to humor intelligence—but none have provided compelling evidence to justify an addition to the list. That said, advances in fields like neuroscience and genetics may well lead in coming years to the identification of new intelligences or the reorganization of existing intelligences. Ultimately, what is important about MI theory is not the number of identified intelligences, but, rather, its core premise that intelligence is better conceived of as multiple rather than general.

Far-Reaching Impact

Since its inception 26 years ago, thousands of schools, teachers, and researchers across the globe have drawn on MI theory to improve teaching and learning. There are Howard Gardner MI schools in Indiana, Pennsylvania, and Washington State and "multiple intelligences" schools in Bangalore, India, and Quezon City, Philippines. A 2002 conference on MI theory in Beijing attracted 2,500 educators from nine provinces and six neighboring countries. In 2005, a theme park opened in Nordborg, Denmark, that allows Danish children and adults to explore their aptitudes across the intelligences.

Some schools, like Indianapolis's *Key Learning Community*[2], aim to build all eight intelligences for each student. Others, like *New City School*[3], in St. Louis, focus on the two personal intelligences. Both schools are exemplary practitioners of MI theory.

It also happens that MI theory is used in ways that are neither educationally sound nor appropriate. Perhaps the most glaring example has been a state ministry in Australia that compiled a list of ethnic groups within the state as well as the particular intelligences that each group supposedly possessed and lacked—a practice Gardner has denounced as a perversion of his theory.

In Gardner's view, MI theory is used most effectively by educators who have a particular goal they are seeking to achieve and who conceive of the theory as a tool for achieving this goal. For instance, at the start of the school year, an elementary school teacher might want to identify students' strengths and weaknesses among the eight intelligences. That teacher might carefully observe the students' activities and interactions on the playground during recess or, alternatively, ask both students and parents to fill out a short survey identifying what they believe to be their (or their child's) strengths among the eight intelligences. Such information can facilitate lesson and unit planning down the road.

Or perhaps a school leader or department head seeks to improve communication among faculty about student achievement. For this objective, MI theory could serve as a framework or common language for discussing the strengths and challenges of individual students. In this instance, the concept of multiple intelligences may not even be raised directly with students, but, rather, may serve as a tool for fostering dialogue and collaboration among their teachers.

The irony of MI theory's tremendous impact on the educational community is that the theory was not developed with educators in mind. Rather, Gardner wrote his 1983 book, *Frames of Mind,* with the goal of inciting debate among psychologists about the nature of intelligence. By and large, such a debate did not occur. The psychology community has demonstrated relatively little interest in Gardner's theory, perhaps because, in sharp contrast to the traditional IQ test, it offers no easy scale for measuring aptitude across the various intelligences.

In what amounted to a sort of grassroots uprising, however, educators at all grade levels in many types of communities have embraced MI theory with a genuine passion. In describing this groundswell of support, Gardner has often speculated that MI theory provided empirical and conceptual support for what educators had known all along: that the notion of a single, general intelligence does not accurately depict the children that educators see in their classrooms each day.

Perhaps it is for this reason that the earliest groups of educators to embrace MI theory were teachers whose daily work entailed supporting students with learning disabilities. Even more so than their general-ed colleagues, special educators see firsthand that youth who struggle with, say, language can simultaneously possess a strong aptitude for numbers or music or graphic design, and vice-versa. These teachers knew intuitively that IQ tests were not measuring what they purported to measure.

A Broader View

Perhaps the greatest contribution of MI theory, I would argue, has been its role over the past decade as a counterbalance to an educational climate increasingly focused on high-stakes testing, such as the IQ test, the SAT, and the various state assessments that have emerged from the No Child Left Behind Act.

Howard Gardner's Eight Intelligences

- Verbal-linguistic intelligence refers to an individual's ability to analyze information and produce work that involves oral and written language, such as speeches, books, and memos.
- Logical-mathematical intelligence describes the ability to develop equations and proofs, make calculations, and solve abstract problems.
- Visual-spatial intelligence allows people to comprehend maps and other types of graphical information.
- Musical intelligence enables individuals to produce and make meaning of different types of sound.
- Naturalistic intelligence refers to the ability to identify and distinguish among different types of plants, animals, and weather formations found in the natural world.
- Bodily-kinesthetic intelligence entails using one's own body to create products or solve problems.
- Interpersonal intelligence reflects an ability to recognize and understand other people's moods, desires, motivations, and intentions.
- Intrapersonal intelligence refers to people's ability to recognize and assess those same characteristics within themselves.

Source URL: http://www.edutopia.org/multiple-intelligences-theory-teacher

rest—at the expense of art, music, theater, physical education, foreign language, and even science and social studies.

In the face of these powerful forces, MI theory has served as a reminder to educators to focus on the strengths and weaknesses of the individual child and has also offered conceptual support for educators seeking to prevent individual students from being stigmatized by a low score on one of these standardized tests. On a schoolwide scale, administrators contemplating eliminating or reducing funding for the subjects not covered by state assessments are likely to hear protests (from parents, teachers, students, and even internally) about neglecting children's multiple intelligences. I would argue that MI theory has offered an important check on the standards-based reform movement that has dominated American education for the past decade.

Or, put more simply, MI theory has helped facilitate in the heads of thousands of educators the same sort of appreciation I experienced while watching my students march down the football field: "These guys are really smart! I'm underestimating what they're capable of!" MI theory is neither a curriculum nor a goal nor an endpoint, but it remains, 26 years after its birth, a powerful tool for helping educators to teach more effectively and students to learn more deeply and enduringly.

Links

1. www.perseusbooksgroup.com/basic/book_detail.jsp?isbn=0465025102
2. www.616.ips.k12.in.us
3. www.newcityschool.org
4. www.ribasassociates.com/books.htm

Critical Thinking

1. Repeat Howard Gardner's eight intelligences.
2. Share reasons why some intelligences cannot be measured on IQ tests.
3. Recognize why multiple intelligence recognition supports students with learning disabilities.

SCOTT SEIDER, a former public school teacher, is an assistant professor of curriculum and teaching at Boston University. He is coauthor of *Instructional Practices That Maximize Student Achievement*[4].

Even if one believes that these assessments have contributions to offer to the practice of teaching and learning, it seems equally true that these tests have presented new challenges to the educational world as well. The IQ test and the SAT, two assessments unquestionably correlated with an individual's class status and schooling opportunities, have been utilized to declare some children intrinsically "smarter" than others and more deserving of seats in gifted-and-talented programs, magnet schools, and elite universities. Particularly in urban schools, the pressure from testing has narrowed the curriculum to focus on those subjects on which graduation and accreditation

In Defense of Distraction

Twitter, Adderall, lifehacking, mindful jogging, power browsing, Obama's BlackBerry, and the benefits of overstimulation.

SAM ANDERSON

I. The Poverty of Attention

I'm going to pause here, right at the beginning of my riveting article about attention, and ask you to please get all of your precious 21st-century distractions out of your system now. Check the score of the Mets game; text your sister that pun you just thought of about her roommate's new pet lizard ("iguana hold yr hand LOL get it like Beatles"); refresh your work e-mail, your home e-mail, your school e-mail; upload pictures of yourself reading this paragraph to your "me reading magazine articles" Flickr photostream; and alert the fellow citizens of whatever Twittertopia you happen to frequent that you will be suspending your digital presence for the next twenty minutes or so (I know that seems drastic: Tell them you're having an appendectomy or something and are about to lose consciousness). Good. Now: Count your breaths. Close your eyes. Do whatever it takes to get all of your neurons lined up in one direction. Above all, resist the urge to fixate on the picture, right over there, of that weird scrambled guy typing. Do not speculate on his ethnicity (German-Venezuelan?) or his backstory (Witness Protection Program?) or the size of his monitor. Go ahead and cover him with your hand if you need to. There. Doesn't that feel better? Now it's just you and me, tucked like fourteenth-century Zen masters into this sweet little nook of pure mental focus. (Seriously, stop looking at him. I'm over here.)

Over the last several years, the problem of attention has migrated right into the center of our cultural attention. We hunt it in neurology labs, lament its decline on op-ed pages, fetishize it in grassroots quality-of-life movements, diagnose its absence in more and more of our children every year, cultivate it in yoga class twice a week, harness it as the engine of self-help empires, and pump it up to superhuman levels with drugs originally intended to treat Alzheimer's and narcolepsy. Everyone still pays some form of attention all the time, of course—it's basically impossible for humans not to—but the currency in which we pay it, and the goods we get in exchange, have changed dramatically.

Back in 1971, when the web was still twenty years off and the smallest computers were the size of delivery vans, before the founders of Google had even managed to get themselves born, the polymath economist Herbert A. Simon wrote maybe the most concise possible description of our modern struggle: "What information consumes is rather obvious: It consumes the attention of its recipients. Hence a wealth of information creates a poverty of attention, and a need to allocate that attention efficiently among the overabundance of information sources that might consume it." As beneficiaries of the greatest information boom in the history of the world, we are suffering, by Simon's logic, a correspondingly serious poverty of attention.

If the pundits clogging my RSS reader can be trusted (the ones I check up on occasionally when I don't have any new e-mail), our attention crisis is already chewing its hyperactive way through the very foundations of Western civilization. Google is making us stupid, multitasking is draining our souls, and the "dumbest generation" is leading us into a "dark age" of bookless "power browsing." Adopting the Internet as the hub of our work, play, and commerce has been the intellectual equivalent of adopting corn syrup as the center of our national diet, and we've all become mentally obese. Formerly well-rounded adults are forced to MacGyver worldviews out of telegraphic blog posts, bits of YouTube videos, and the first nine words of *Times* editorials. Schoolkids spread their attention across 30 different programs at once and interact with each other mainly as sweatless avatars. (One recent study found that American teenagers spend an average of 6.5 hours a day focused on the electronic world, which strikes me as a little low; in South Korea, the most wired nation on earth, young adults have actually died from exhaustion after multiday online-gaming marathons.) We are, in short, terminally distracted. And *distracted,* the alarmists will remind you, was once a synonym for *insane.* (Shakespeare: "poverty hath distracted her.")

The most advanced Budhist monks become world-class multitaskers. Meditation might speed up their mental processes enough to handle information overload.

This doomsaying strikes me as silly for two reasons. First, conservative social critics have been blowing the apocalyptic bugle at every large-scale tech-driven social change since Socrates' famous complaint about the memory-destroying properties of that newfangled technology called "writing." (A complaint we remember, not incidentally, because it was written down.) And, more practically, the virtual horse has already left the digital barn. It's too late to just retreat to a quieter time. Our jobs depend on connectivity. Our pleasure-cycles—no trivial matter—are increasingly tied to it. Information rains down faster and thicker every day, and there are plenty of non-moronic reasons for it to do so. The question, now, is how successfully we can adapt.

Although attention is often described as an organ system, it's not the sort of thing you can pull out and study like a spleen. It's a complex process that shows up all over the brain, mingling inextricably with other quasi-mystical processes like emotion, memory, identity, will, motivation, and mood. Psychologists have always had to track attention second-hand. Before the sixties, they measured it through easy-to-monitor senses like vision and hearing (if you listen to one voice in your right ear and another in your left, how much information can you absorb from either side?), then eventually graduated to PET scans and EEGs and electrodes and monkey brains. Only in the last ten years—thanks to neuroscientists and their functional MRIs—have we been able to watch the attending human brain in action, with its coordinated storms of neural firing, rapid blood surges, and oxygen flows. This has yielded all kinds of fascinating insights—for instance, that when forced to multitask, the overloaded brain shifts its processing from the hippocampus (responsible for memory) to the striatum (responsible for rote tasks), making it hard to learn a task or even recall what you've been doing once you're done.

When I reach David Meyer, one of the world's reigning experts on multitasking, he is feeling alert against all reasonable odds. He has just returned from India, where he was discussing the nature of attention at a conference with the Dalai Lama (Meyer gave a keynote speech arguing that Buddhist monks multitask during meditation), and his trip home was hellish: a canceled flight, an overnight taxi on roads so rough it took thirteen hours to go 200 miles. This is his first full day back in his office at the University of Michigan, where he directs the Brain, Cognition, and Action Laboratory—a basement space in which finger-tapping, card-memorizing, tone-identifying subjects help Meyer pinpoint exactly how much information the human brain can handle at once. He's been up since 3 A.M. and has by now goosed his attention several times with liquid stimulants: a couple of cups of coffee, some tea. "It does wonders," he says.

My interaction with Meyer takes place entirely via the technology of distraction. We scheduled and rescheduled our appointment, several times, by e-mail. His voice is now projecting, tinnily, out of my cell phone's speaker and into the microphone of my digital recorder, from which I will download it, as soon as we're done, onto my laptop, which I currently have open on my desk in front of me, with several windows spread across the screen, each bearing nested tabs, on one of which I've been reading, before Meyer even had a chance to tell me about it, a blog all about his conference with the Dalai Lama, complete with RSS feed and audio commentary and embedded YouTube videos

and pictures of His Holiness. As Meyer and I talk, the universe tests us with a small battery of distractions. A maximum-volume fleet of emergency vehicles passes just outside my window; my phone chirps to tell us that my mother is calling on the other line, then beeps again to let us know she's left a message. There is, occasionally, a slight delay in the connection. Meyer ignores it all, speaking deliberately and at length, managing to coordinate tricky subject-verb agreements over the course of multi-clause sentences. I begin, a little sheepishly, with a question that strikes me as sensationalistic, nonscientific, and probably unanswerable by someone who's been professionally trained in the discipline of cautious objectivity: Are we living through a crisis of attention?

Before I even have a chance to apologize, Meyer responds with the air of an Old Testament prophet. "Yes," he says. "And I think it's going to get a lot worse than people expect." He sees our distraction as a full-blown epidemic—a cognitive plague that has the potential to wipe out an entire generation of focused and productive thought. He compares it, in fact, to smoking. "People aren't aware what's happening to their mental processes," he says, "in the same way that people years ago couldn't look into their lungs and see the residual deposits."

I ask him if, as the world's foremost expert on multitasking and distraction, he has found his own life negatively affected by the new world order of multitasking and distraction.

"Yep," he says immediately, then adds, with admirable (although slightly hurtful) bluntness: "I get calls all the time from people like you. Because of the way the Internet works, once you become visible, you're approached from left and right by people wanting to have interactions in ways that are extremely time-consuming. I could spend my whole day, my whole night, just answering e-mails. I just can't deal with it all. None of this happened even ten years ago. It was a lot calmer. There was a lot of opportunity for getting steady work done."

Over the last twenty years, Meyer and a host of other researchers have proved again and again that multitasking, at least as our culture has come to know and love and institutionalize it, is a myth. When you think you're doing two things at once, you're almost always just switching rapidly between them, leaking a little mental efficiency with every switch. Meyer says that this is because, to put it simply, the brain processes different kinds of information on a variety of separate "channels"—a language channel, a visual channel, an auditory channel, and so on—each of which can process only one stream of information at a time. If you overburden a channel, the brain becomes inefficient and mistake-prone. The classic example is driving while talking on a cell phone, two tasks that conflict across a range of obvious channels: Steering and dialing are both manual tasks, looking out the windshield and reading a phone screen are both visual, etc. Even talking on a hands-free phone can be dangerous, Meyer says. If the person on the other end of the phone is describing a visual scene—say, the layout of a room full of furniture—that conversation can actually occupy your visual channel enough to impair your ability to see what's around you on the road.

The only time multitasking does work efficiently, Meyer says, is when multiple simple tasks operate on entirely separate channels—for example, folding laundry (a visual-manual task) while listening to a stock report (a verbal task). But real-world scenarios that fit those specifications are very rare.

This is troubling news, obviously, for a culture of BlackBerrys and news crawls and Firefox tabs—tools that, critics argue, force us all into a kind of elective ADHD. The tech theorist Linda Stone famously coined the phrase "continuous partial attention" to describe our newly frazzled state of mind. American office workers don't stick with any single task for more than a few minutes at a time; if left uninterrupted, they will most likely interrupt themselves. Since every interruption costs around 25 minutes of productivity, we spend nearly a third of our day recovering from them. We keep an average of eight windows open on our computer screens at one time and skip between them every twenty seconds. When we read online, we hardly even read at all—our eyes run down the page in an *F* pattern, scanning for keywords. When you add up all the leaks from these constant little switches, soon you're hemorrhaging a dangerous amount of mental power. People who frequently check their e-mail have tested as less intelligent than people who are actually high on marijuana. Meyer guesses that the damage will take decades to understand, let alone fix. If Einstein were alive today, he says, he'd probably be forced to multitask so relentlessly in the Swiss patent office that he'd never get a chance to work out the theory of relativity.

II. The War on the Poverty of Attention

For Winifred Gallagher, the author of *Rapt,* a new book about the power of attention, it all comes down to the problem of jackhammers. A few minutes before I called, she tells me, a construction crew started jackhammering outside her apartment window. The noise immediately captured what's called her bottom-up attention—the broad involuntary awareness that roams the world constantly looking for danger and rewards: shiny objects, sudden movements, pungent smells. Instead of letting this distract her, however, she made a conscious choice to go into the next room and summon her top-down attention—the narrow, voluntary focus that allows us to isolate and enhance some little slice of the world while ruthlessly suppressing everything else.

This attentional self-control, which psychologists call executive function, is at the very center of our struggle with attention. It's what allows us to invest our focus wisely or poorly. Some of us, of course, have an easier time with it than others.

Gallagher admits that she's been blessed with a naturally strong executive function. "It sounds funny," she tells me, "but I've always thought of paying attention as a kind of sexy, visceral activity. Even as a kid, I enjoyed focusing. I could feel it in almost a mentally muscular way. I took a lot of pleasure in concentrating on things. I'm the sort of irritating person who can sit down to work at nine o'clock and look up at two o'clock and say, 'Oh, I thought it was around 10:30.'"

Gallagher became obsessed with the problem of attention five years ago, when she was diagnosed with advanced and aggressive breast cancer. She was devastated, naturally, but then realized, on her way out of the hospital, that even the cancer could be seen largely as a problem of focus—a terrifying, deadly, internal jackhammer. It made her realize, she says, that attention was "not just a latent ability, it was something you could marshal and use as a tool." By the time she reached her subway station, Gallagher had come up with a strategy: She would make all the big pressing cancer-related decisions as quickly as possible, then, in order to maximize whatever time she had left, consciously shift her attention to more positive, productive things.

One of the projects Gallagher worked on during her recovery (she is now cancer free) was *Rapt,* which is both a survey of recent attention research and a testimonial to the power of top-down focus. The ability to positively wield your attention comes off, in the book, as something of a panacea; Gallagher describes it as "the sine qua non of the quality of life and the key to improving virtually every aspect of your experience." It is, in other words, the Holy Grail of self-help: the key to relationships and parenting and mood disorders and weight problems. (You can apparently lose seven pounds in a year through the sheer force of paying attention to your food.)

"You can't be happy all the time," Gallagher tells me, "but you can pretty much focus all the time. That's about as good as it gets."

The most promising solution to our attention problem, in Gallagher's mind, is also the most ancient: meditation. Neuroscientists have become obsessed, in recent years, with Buddhists, whose attentional discipline can apparently confer all kinds of benefits even on non-Buddhists. (Some psychologists predict that, in the same way we go out for a jog now, in the future we'll all do daily 20- to 30-minute "secular attentional workouts.") Meditation can make your attention less "sticky," able to notice images flashing by in such quick succession that regular brains would miss them. It has also been shown to elevate your mood, which can then recursively stoke your attention: Research shows that positive emotions cause your visual field to expand. The brains of Buddhist monks asked to meditate on "unconditional loving-kindness and compassion" show instant and remarkable changes: Their left prefrontal cortices (responsible for positive emotions) go into overdrive, they produce gamma waves 30 times more powerful than novice meditators, and their wave activity is coordinated in a way often seen in patients under anesthesia.

Gallagher stresses that because attention is a limited resource—one psychologist has calculated that we can attend to only 110 bits of information per second, or 173 billion bits in an average lifetime—our moment-by-moment choice of attentional targets determines, in a very real sense, the shape of our lives. *Rapt's* epigraph comes from the psychologist and philosopher William James: "My experience is what I agree to attend to." For Gallagher, everything comes down to that one big choice: investing your attention wisely or not. The jackhammers are everywhere—iPhones, e-mail, cancer—and Western culture's attentional crisis is mainly a widespread failure to ignore them.

It's possible that we're evolving toward a new techno-cognitive nomadism, in which restlessness will be an advantage.

"Once you understand how attention works and how you can make the most productive use of it," she says, "if you continue to just jump in the air every time your phone rings or pounce on those buttons every time you get an instant message, that's not the machine's fault. That's your fault."

aking the responsible attention choice, however, is not always easy. Here is a partial list, because a complete one would fill the entire magazine, of the things I've been distracted by in the course of writing this article: my texting wife, a very loud seagull, my mother calling from Mexico to leave voice mails in terrible Spanish, a man shouting "Your weed-whacker fell off! Your weed-whacker fell off!" at a truck full of lawn equipment, my *Lost*-watching wife, another man singing some kind of Spanish ballad on the sidewalk under my window, streaming video of the NBA playoffs, dissertation-length blog breakdowns of the NBA playoffs, my toenail spontaneously detaching, my ice-cream-eating wife, the subtly shifting landscapes of my three different e-mail in-boxes, my Facebooking wife, infinite YouTube videos (a puffin attacking someone wearing a rubber boot, Paul McCartney talking about the death of John Lennon, a chimpanzee playing Pac-Man), and even more infinite, if that is possible, Wikipedia entries: puffins, *MacGyver,* Taylorism, the phrase "bleeding edge," the Boston Molasses Disaster. (If I were going to excuse you from reading this article for any single distraction, which I am not, it would be to read about the Boston Molasses Disaster.)

When the jackhammers fire up outside my window, in other words, I rarely ignore them—I throw the window open, watch for a while, bring the crew sandwiches on their lunch break, talk with them about the ins and outs of jackhammering, and then spend an hour or two trying to break up a little of the sidewalk myself. Some of my distractions were unavoidable. Some were necessary work-related evils that got out of hand. Others were pretty clearly inexcusable. (I consider it a victory for the integrity of pre-web human consciousness that I was able to successfully resist clicking on the first "related video" after the chimp, the evocatively titled "Guy shits himself in a judo exhibition.") In today's attentional landscape, it's hard to draw neat borders.

I'm not ready to blame my restless attention entirely on a faulty willpower. Some of it is pure impersonal behaviorism. The Internet is basically a Skinner box engineered to tap right into our deepest mechanisms of addiction. As B. F. Skinner's army of lever-pressing rats and pigeons taught us, the most irresistible reward schedule is not, counterintuitively, the one in which we're rewarded constantly but something called "variable ratio schedule," in which the rewards arrive at random. And that randomness is practically the Internet's defining feature: It dispenses its never-ending little shots of positivity—a life-changing e-mail here, a funny YouTube video there—in gloriously unpredictable cycles. It seems unrealistic to expect people to spend all day clicking reward bars—searching the web, scanning the relevant blogs, checking e-mail to see if a co-worker has updated a project—and then just leave those distractions behind, as soon as they're not strictly required, to engage in "healthy" things like books and ab crunches and undistracted deep conversations with neighbors. It would be like requiring employees to take a few hits of opium throughout the day, then being surprised when it becomes a problem. Last year, an editorial in the *American Journal of Psychiatry* raised the prospect of adding "Internet addiction" to the *DSM,* which would make it a disorder to be taken as seriously as schizophrenia.

A quintessentially Western solution to the attention problem—one that neatly circumvents the issue of willpower—is to simply dope our brains into focus. We've done so, over the centuries, with substances ranging from tea to tobacco to NoDoz to Benzedrine, and these days the tradition seems to be approaching some kind of zenith with the rise of neuroenhancers: drugs designed to treat ADHD (Ritalin, Adderall), Alzheimer's (Aricept), and narcolepsy (Provigil) that can produce, in healthy people, superhuman states of attention. A grad-school friend tells me that Adderall allowed him to squeeze his mind "like a muscle." Joshua Foer, writing in *Slate* after a weeklong experiment with Adderall, said the drug made him feel like he'd "been bitten by a radioactive spider"—he beat his unbeatable brother at Ping-Pong, solved anagrams, devoured dense books. "The part of my brain that makes me curious about whether I have new e-mails in my in-box apparently shut down," he wrote.

Although neuroenhancers are currently illegal to use without a prescription, they're popular among college students (on some campuses, up to 25 percent of students admitted to taking them) and—if endless anecdotes can be believed—among a wide spectrum of other professional focusers: journalists on deadline, doctors performing high-stakes surgeries, competitors in poker tournaments, researchers suffering through the grind of grant-writing. There has been controversy in the chess world recently about drug testing at tournaments.

In December, a group of scientists published a paper in *Nature* that argued for the legalization and mainstream acceptance of neuroenhancers, suggesting that the drugs are really no different from more traditional "cognitive enhancers" such as laptops, exercise, nutrition, private tutoring, reading, and sleep. It's not quite that simple, of course. Adderall users frequently complain that the drug stifles their creativity—that it's best for doing ultra-rational, structured tasks. (As Foer put it, "I had a nagging suspicion that I was thinking with blinders on.") One risk the scientists do acknowledge is the fascinating, horrifying prospect of "raising cognitive abilities beyond their species-typical upper bound." Ultimately, one might argue, neuroenhancers spring from the same source as the problem they're designed to correct: our lust for achievement in defiance of natural constraints. It's easy to imagine an endless attentional arms race in which new technologies colonize ever-bigger zones of our attention, new drugs expand the limits of that attention, and so on.

One of the most exciting—and confounding—solutions to the problem of attention lies right at the intersection of our willpower and our willpower-sapping technologies: the grassroots Internet movement known as "lifehacking." It began in 2003 when the British tech writer Danny O'Brien, frustrated by his own lack of focus, polled 70 of his most productive friends to see how they managed to get so much done; he found that they'd invented all kinds of clever little tricks—some high-tech, some very low-tech—to help shepherd their attention from moment to moment: ingenious script codes for to-do lists, software hacks for managing e-mail, rituals to avoid sinister time-wasting traps such as "yak shaving," the tendency to lose yourself in endless trivial tasks tangentially related to the one you really need to do. (O'Brien wrote a program that prompts him every ten minutes, when he's online, to ask if he's procrastinating.) Since then, lifehacking has snowballed into a massive self-help program, written and revised constantly by the online global hive mind, that seeks to help you allocate your attention efficiently. Tips range from time-management habits (the 90-second shower) to note-taking techniques (mind mapping) to software shortcuts (how to turn your Gmail into a to-do list) to delightfully retro tech solutions (turning an index card into a portable dry-erase board by covering it with packing tape).

When I call Merlin Mann, one of lifehacking's early adopters and breakout stars, he is running late, rushing back to his office, and yet he seems somehow to have attention to spare. He is by far the fastest-talking human I've ever interviewed, and it crosses my mind that this too might be a question of productivity—that maybe he's adopted a time-saving verbal lifehack from auctioneers. He talks in the snappy aphorisms of a professional speaker ("Priorities are like arms: If you have more than two of them, they're probably make-believe") and is always breaking ideas down into their atomic parts and reassessing the way they fit together: "What does it come down to?" "Here's the thing." "So why am I telling you this, and what does it have to do with lifehacks?"

Mann says he got into lifehacking at a moment of crisis, when he was "feeling really overwhelmed by the number of inputs in my life and managing it very badly." He founded one of the original lifehacking websites, 43folders.com (the name is a reference to David Allen's Getting Things Done, the legendarily complex productivity program in which Allen describes, among other things, how to build a kind of "three-dimensional calendar" out of 43 folders) and went on to invent such illustrious hacks as "in-box zero" (an e-mail-management technique) and the "hipster PDA" (a stack of three-by-five cards filled with jotted phone numbers and to-do lists, clipped together and tucked into your back pocket). Mann now makes a living speaking to companies as a kind of productivity guru. He Twitters, podcasts, and runs more than half a dozen websites.

Despite his robust web presence, Mann is skeptical about technology's impact on our lives. "Is it clear to you that the last fifteen years represent an enormous improvement in how everything operates?" he asks. "Picasso was somehow able to finish the *Desmoiselles of Avignon* even though he didn't have an application that let him tag his to-dos. If John Lennon had a BlackBerry, do you think he would have done everything he did with the Beatles in less than ten years?"

One of the weaknesses of lifehacking as a weapon in the war against distraction, Mann admits, is that it tends to become extremely distracting. You can spend solid days reading reviews of filing techniques and organizational software. "On the web, there's a certain kind of encouragement to never ask yourself how much information you really need," he says. "But when I get to the point where I'm seeking advice twelve hours a day on how to take a nap, or what kind of notebook to buy, I'm so far off the idea of lifehacks that it's indistinguishable from where we started. There are a lot of people out there that find this a very sticky idea, and there's very little advice right now to tell them that the only thing to do is action, and everything else is horseshit. My wife reminds me sometimes: 'You have all the information you need to do *something* right now.'"

For Mann, many of our attention problems are symptoms of larger existential issues: motivation, happiness, neurochemistry.

"I'm not a physician or a psychiatrist, but I'll tell you, I think a lot of it is some form of untreated ADHD or depression," he says. "Your mind is not getting the dopamine or the hugs that it needs to keep you focused on what you're doing. And any time your work gets a little bit too hard or a little bit too boring, you allow it to catch on to something that's more interesting to you." (Mann himself started getting treated for ADD a year ago; he says it's helped his focus quite a lot.)

Mann's advice can shade, occasionally, into Buddhist territory. "There's no shell script, there's no fancy pen, there's no notebook or nap or Firefox extension or hack that's gonna help you figure out why the fuck you're here," he tells me. "That's on you." This makes me sound like one of those people who swindled the Beatles, but if you are having attention problems, the best way to deal with it is by admitting it and then saying, 'From now on, I'm gonna be in the moment and more cognizant.' I said not long ago, I think on Twitter—God, I quote myself a lot, what an asshole—that really all self-help is Buddhism with a service mark.

"Where you allow your attention to go ultimately says more about you as a human being than anything that you put in your mission statement," he continues. "It's an indisputable receipt for your existence. And if you allow that to be squandered by other people who are as bored as you are, it's gonna say a lot about who you are as a person."

III. Embracing the Poverty of Attention

Sometimes I wonder if the time I'm wasting is actually being wasted. Isn't blowing a couple of hours on the Internet, in the end, just another way of following your attention? My life would be immeasurably poorer if I hadn't stumbled a few weeks ago across the Boston Molasses Disaster. (Okay, seriously, forget it: I hereby release you to go look up the Boston Molasses Disaster. A giant wave of molasses destroyed an entire Boston neighborhood 90 years ago, swallowing horses and throwing an elevated train off its track. It took months to scrub all the molasses out of the cobblestones! The harbor was brown until summer! The world is a stranger place than we will ever know.)

The prophets of total attentional melt-down sometimes invoke, as an example of the great culture we're going to lose as we succumb to e-thinking, the canonical French juggernaut Marcel Proust. And indeed, at seven volumes, several thousand pages, and 1.5 million words, *Á la Recherche du Temps Perdu* is in many ways the anti-Twitter. (It would take, by the way, exactly 68,636 tweets to reproduce.) It's important to remember, however, that the most famous moment in all of Proust, the moment that launches the entire monumental project, is a moment of pure distraction: when the narrator, Marcel, eats a spoonful of tea-soaked madeleine and finds himself instantly transported back to the world of his childhood. Proust makes it clear that conscious focus could never have yielded such profound magic: Marcel has to abandon the constraints of what he calls "voluntary memory"—the kind of narrow, purpose-driven attention that Adderall, say, might have allowed him to harness—in order to get to the deeper truths available only by distraction. That famous cookie is a kind of hyperlink: a little blip that launches an associative cascade of a million other subjects. This sort of free-associative wandering is essential to the creative process; one moment of judicious unmindfulness can inspire thousands of hours of mindfulness.

My favorite focusing exercise comes from William James: Draw a dot on a piece of paper, then pay attention to it for as long as you can. (Sitting in my office one afternoon, with my monkey mind swinging busily across the lush rain forest of online distractions, I tried this with the closest dot in the vicinity: the bright-red mouse-nipple at the center of my laptop's keyboard. I managed to stare at it for 30 minutes, with mixed results.) James argued that the human mind can't actually focus on the dot, or any unchanging object, for more than a few seconds at a time: It's too hungry for variety, surprise, the adventure of the unknown. It has to refresh its attention by continually finding new aspects of the dot to focus on: subtleties of its shape, its relationship to the edges of the paper, metaphorical associations (a fly, an eye, a hole). The exercise becomes a question less of pure unwavering focus than of your ability to organize distractions around a central point. The dot, in other words, becomes only the hub of your total dot-related distraction.

This is what the web-threatened punditry often fails to recognize: Focus is a paradox—it has distraction built into it. The two are symbiotic; they're the systole and diastole of consciousness. Attention comes from the Latin "to stretch out" or "reach toward," distraction from "to pull apart." We need both. In their extreme forms, focus and attention may even circle back around and bleed into one other. Meyer says there's a subset of Buddhists who believe that the most advanced monks become essentially "world-class multitaskers"—that all those years of meditation might actually speed up their mental processes enough to handle the kind of information overload the rest of us find crippling.

The truly wise mind will harness, rather than abandon, the power of distraction. Unwavering focus—the inability to be distracted—can actually be just as problematic as ADHD. Trouble with "attentional shift" is a feature common to a handful of mental illnesses, including schizophrenia and OCD. It's been hypothesized that ADHD might even be an advantage in certain change-rich environments. Researchers have discovered, for instance, that a brain receptor associated with ADHD is unusually common among certain nomads in Kenya, and that members who have the receptor are the best nourished in the group. It's possible that we're all evolving toward a new techno-cognitive nomadism, a rapidly shifting environment in which restlessness will be an advantage again. The deep focusers might even be hampered by having too much attention: Attention Surfeit Hypoactivity Disorder.

I keep returning to the parable of Einstein and Lennon—the great historical geniuses hypothetically ruined by modern distraction. What made both men's achievements so groundbreaking, though, was that they did something modern technology is getting increasingly better at allowing us to do: They very powerfully linked and synthesized things that had previously been unlinked—

Newtonian gravity and particle physics, rock and blues and folk and doo-wop and bubblegum pop and psychedelia. If Einstein and Lennon were growing up today, their natural genius might be so pumped up on the possibilities of the new technology they'd be doing even more dazzling things. Surely Lennon would find a way to manipulate his BlackBerry to his own ends, just like he did with all the new technology of the sixties—he'd harvest spam and text messages and web snippets and build them into a new kind of absurd poetry. The Beatles would make the best viral videos of all time, simultaneously addictive and artful, disposable and forever. All of those canonical songs, let's remember, were created entirely within a newfangled mass genre that was widely considered to be an assault on civilization and the sanctity of deep human thought. Standards change. They change because of great creations in formerly suspect media.

Which brings me, finally, to the next generation of attenders, the so-called "net-gen" or "digital natives," kids who've grown up with the Internet and other time-slicing technologies. There's been lots of hand-wringing about all the skills they might lack, mainly the ability to concentrate on a complex task from beginning to end, but surely they can already do things their elders can't—like conduct 34 conversations simultaneously across six different media, or pay attention to switching between attentional targets in a way that's been considered impossible. More than any other organ, the brain is designed to change based on experience, a feature called neuroplasticity. London taxi drivers, for instance, have enlarged hippocampi (the brain region for memory and spatial processing)—a neural reward for paying attention to the tangle of the city's streets. As we become more skilled at the 21st-century task Meyer calls "flitting," the wiring of the brain will inevitably change to deal more efficiently with more information. The neuroscientist Gary Small speculates that the human brain might be changing faster today than it has since the prehistoric discovery of tools. Research suggests we're already picking up new skills: better peripheral vision, the ability to sift information rapidly. We recently elected the first-ever BlackBerry president, able to flit between sixteen national crises while focusing at a world-class level. Kids growing up now might have an associative genius we don't—a sense of the way ten projects all dovetail into something totally new. They might be able to engage in seeming contradictions: mindful web-surfing, mindful Twittering. Maybe, in flights of irresponsible responsibility, they'll even manage to attain the paradoxical, Zenlike state of focused distraction.

Critical Thinking

1. Explain how a wealth of information creates a poverty of attention.

2. Identify simple tasks you can perform together where multitasking is efficient.

3. Defend meditation as a solution to our attention problems.

What Really Motivates Kids

It's time to give up the stickers, stars, and well-intentioned but gushing praise, says best-selling author Daniel Pink. Sound like your entire toolbox? It's not.

DANA TRUBY

A safe learning environment. An exciting lesson plan. Compassionate classmates and a dynamic and tuned-in teacher. It sounds like the perfect setup for a child's success. But every teacher knows there's one more essential—and sometimes elusive—ingredient. Motivation.

And so we make sticker charts, fill jars with jellybeans, and stock up on action-figure and sparkly-pencil prizes at the dollar store. We scour entire books devoted to the "magic words"—and we find ourselves blaming parents who aren't saying them.

While a teacher isn't the only factor playing into a child's desire to succeed—home life and individual personality play a major part—we rarely stop to think about whether we're going about it the right way. In his new book, *Drive: The Surprising Truth About What Motivates Us,* Daniel Pink argues that perhaps we aren't. We caught up with Pink a few weeks before the release of *Drive* to talk about motivation, the problem with the "carrot and stick" approach, and why it may be time to shake up the school day as we know it.

• Your new book takes a hard look at the science behind motivation.

We tend to think that the way to get people to perform is to punish the bad and reward the good. There's some logic to that, but, particularly as you ask people, even kids to do more complex, creative tasks, that sort of approach, that "carrot and stick" approach, simply doesn't work and actually causes all kinds of collateral damage.

• Don't we all value rewards?

What the science tells us is that contingent incentives, what I call "if-then" rewards—if you do this, then you get that—do work for simple, rule-based tasks. Routine tasks defined most of the 20th century. On the manufacturing line, gaining compliance worked just fine. But that was then.

• Now we're preparing kids for the jobs of the future.

Certainly, fewer of us have jobs that involve solving very simple problems by following a set of steps and getting a right answer.

The definitional tasks of 21st-century work are more complex, more creative. Solving complex problems requires an inquiring mind and the willingness to experiment one's way to a fresh solution. Where Motivation 2.0 sought compliance, Motivation 3.0 seeks engagement.

• How would you define Motivation 3.0?

Our basic nature is to be curious and self-directed. Have you ever seen a 1-year-old who's not curious and self-directed? Human beings want to learn, to make choices, to achieve. If we want higher-level work, the science shows us the better way to motivation is to build more on autonomy, our desire to be self-directed; on mastery, which is our desire to get better and better at something that matters; and on purpose, which is our desire to be part of something larger than ourselves.

Have you ever seen a 1-year-old who's not curious and self-directed?

• How do rewards work against intrinsic motivation?

When you say, "If you get an A on this test, I'll give you $5," that's a colossal mistake. What that says is the only purpose of getting an A on a test is to get a reward. It extinguishes intrinsic motivation to do well; it puts the focus on getting the reward and not on the work itself.

• What would you say to schools that claim to have found success by paying for grades?

In general, I opposed it, but I'm willing to reserve judgment for kids who have been so betrayed by the system, who have no real understanding of what learning is. If it takes a little bit of a bribe to get that kid to open up a book, then it's hard for me to argue that that's a bad idea. But, there's research being done in New York City and some other jurisdictions about whether those sorts of mechanisms are effective even for the most disadvantaged kids.

• **Can rewards ever be done well in school?**

For the vast majority of kids, contingent rewards are an abject disaster. At the same time, if your students do well on a test and you say, "Hey, you really worked hard. You really learned a lot. You mastered algebra, and to celebrate, let's have a pizza party," that's really not the same thing because it's not contingent on the performance. The danger, however, is if kids begin to think of that as an entitlement and say, "Every time I do well on a test I get a pizza party."

So I think that in general, rewards should be in the form of feedback and information and, to some extent, praise. But even praise can be toxic for kids. It needs to be deployed very carefully.

• **What would you consider toxic praise?**

Carol Dweck has done a lot of research on it. Praise is toxic when you don't give a child feedback on what he or she is doing, whether it's sports, school, or anything else, and only show a loving, praising type of attitude when they've done as well as you want them to. And so, the kid begins to say to herself, "The only reason to do well is to get praise and approval." Feedback is the way you get better at something, whether it's sports, art, or academics. If all your feedback is positive, you really don't have any sense of how you're doing.

• **Can you tell us a little more about Dweck's research?**

Sure. She says that people essentially have two different "self theories of intelligence." In one, you look at intelligence as an entity, or fixed supply. Therefore, everything you do is a measure of how much intelligence you have. The other way to think of it is a growth theory of intelligence, which says that intelligence is not a fixed amount. It's something that you can grow and develop.

What she's found is that kids who have this entity theory of intelligence are more likely to take shortcuts like cheating or to choose easier challenges because they don't want to be "proved" to be stupid. Whereas kids who have internalized growth theory often end up being more inspired and more honest in their approach to schoolwork. They take more challenging courses and they learn "grit," the habit of persistence, because they recognize that persistence is the way to get better at something.

• **Is it possible for teachers to change how a child views his or her own intelligence?**

Dweck shows that you can actually move people from one category to another fairly quickly. It goes back to praise. If you praise somebody for getting an answer right, and you say, "Oh, you got the answer right, you're so smart," that coincides with an entity theory of intelligence.

But if you praise by saying, "Wow, you got that problem right. Show me how you did it," and the kid shows you how she did it, and then you say, "Wow, that's a great strategy for solving that," then you're demonstrating a growth theory of intelligence. So I think it's how you talk to kids, the problems that we give to kids, and even how teachers themselves behave and view the world.

• **In the education world, the call is growing for greater autonomy and experimentation with the learning process in schools. At the same time, there is a push toward greater regimentation.**

The push toward regimentation, in my view, is far more prevalent. Yes, there are more and more innovative public and charter schools and a notable rise of homeschooling. But that said, the vast majority of kids are going to classrooms where high-stakes standardized testing sets the agenda.

• **Most schools are still operating on Motivation 2.0.?**

Yes, and that's a problem. There's a disconnect between how we prepare kids for work and how work actually operates: In school, problems almost always are clearly defined, confined to a single discipline, and have one right answer. But in the workplace, they're practically the opposite. Problems are usually poorly defined, multidisciplinary, and have several possible answers, none of them perfect.

---

5 Ideas to Help Our Kids

If we want to raise Type I kids, we need to help them move toward autonomy, mastery, and purpose. Here are some ways to start the journey, says Pink.

Rethink Assignments

Before assigning homework, ask yourself three questions: Am I offering students any autonomy over how and when they do it? Does this assignment promote mastery by offering an engaging task? Do my students understand the purpose of the assignment—that is, how it contributes to the larger enterprise the class is engaged in?

Try DIY Report Cards

At the beginning of the semester, ask kids to formulate their own learning goals. Then, at the end of the semester, ask kids to create their own report cards along with a 1–2 paragraph review of their progress. Once students have completed their report cards, share the teacher's report card and let the comparison of the two be the start of a conversation on how they are doing on the path to mastery.

Offer Praise the Right Way

Praise effort and strategy, not intelligence. Children who are praised for "being smart" often believe that every encounter is a test of whether they really are. Kids who understand that effort and hard work lead to mastery are often more willing to take on new or difficult tasks.

Help Kids See the Big Picture

Whatever your students are studying, be sure they can answer these questions: Why am I learning this? How is this relevant to the world I live in? Then get out of the classroom and apply what they are studying.

• **At the same time, there are amazing examples of innovative, inquiry-based schools out there.**

Absolutely, and I talk about some of them in *Drive*. The Big Picture Learning high school in Providence, Rhode Island, is a great example. The kids' interests dictate the curriculum. The students are assessed the way adults are—on work performance, individual presentation, effort, attitude, and behavior on the job. Big Picture kids, most of whom come from disadvantaged backgrounds, overall completely outperform their peers on standardized tests. They end up easily outperforming their peers on language arts because they're reading and writing about subjects that are relevant to them and that they're interested in.

• **So it's all individualized learning for every child?**

Here's an example. One student I met had a strong interest in martial arts, so they ended up building a curriculum around it. He works two days a week in a martial arts studio, so he's learning business skills. He uses martial arts in his physics and math projects. Not to mention this kid knows more about Japanese history than any non-academic Westerner I've ever met. I should say that a lot of work goes into helping students discover those "just-right" tasks, into helping them to find their paths. It's teaching of a different kind.

• **What about younger kids? How do we allow autonomy within reasonable learning requirements for a third grader?**

Even for younger learners, the more that you break down the barriers between school and the rest of the world, the better. Everybody, little kids included, wants to work on real-world problems that are relevant. A lot of schools are doing this.

• **The mandate of public schools is to educate every child. Do you think an individualized program like Big Picture Learning is reproducible on a large scale?**

I think that it's challenging, but not impossible. We are seeing a move now toward differentiated learning. The more we allow a kid's learning style to shape how the learning occurs, the more you're allowing that kid to be an autonomous learner.

• **This vision of a 21st-century education would very much change how educators work at every level.**

Definitely. Perhaps it would make the jobs of teachers and of education leaders more complicated and yet more satisfying at the same time.

• **If you could change three things about public education tomorrow, what would they be?**

Wow, that's a tough one. First, I would give teachers far greater autonomy, that is, unshackle them from standardized tests and allow them to teach what they want the way that they want. I think that would have a remarkable positive effect on 85 percent of the classrooms in this country.

The second thing would be—to the extent possible—to tear down the walls between disciplines, and between the school and the wider world. One of the strengths of primary school is that it doesn't segment math and science, and English and history.

By the time our kids get to about sixth grade, we frog-march them from one discipline to another and rarely point out the connections among those disciplines. The world itself is inherently multidisciplinary.

• **You have one more magic educational wish left.**

The third thing would be a FedEx day—I talk about that a lot in *Drive*—one school day set aside for student-chosen, student-led learning projects. In advance, help them collect the tools, information, and supplies they might need. The next morning, ask them to deliver—by reporting back to the class—on their discoveries and experiences. I think the neurons would be firing so rapidly that kids might just end up producing things that would blow the socks off all the adults in the room.

Critical Thinking

1. Indicate why internal motivation declines when tasks are rewarded.
2. Support the notion that unconditional praise is toxic.
3. Name an educational task that engaged you and enabled you to use your new knowledge.

The Truth about Kids and Money

**From bank cards to interest rates, how to teach the
real-life math skills all kids need to learn.**

PEG TYRE

Mary Sturgeon, a fifth-grade teacher at Vinton Elementary School in Lafayette, Indiana, knows many of her students' families are facing hard times. Parents have been laid off, and some are having trouble finding new jobs. A student recently moved to a new neighborhood in the same district after her parents lost their house to foreclosure. "Our community has been very affected by the financial downturn," says Sturgeon.

All of this inspires Sturgeon to throw her heart and soul into teaching her kids about financial literacy as part of her fifth-grade social studies curriculum. For a few weeks every year, she launches a mini-economy project robust enough to make U.S. Treasury Secretary Timothy Geithner proud. Her students apply for jobs such as attendance taker and blackboard cleaner, get paid in play dollars, learn how to calculate taxes, and explore the concept of compound interest when they save—or borrow—from the National Bank of Vinton Elementary. They divide up into three "factories" and, using PlayDoh as their raw material, churn out shirts, baskets of apples, hammers, or cup-and-saucer sets. Then, to experience the laws of supply and demand, they sell the goods to one another. At the end of the unit, Sturgeon auctions off a collection of trinkets—books, hats, elegant markers—and her students use the play money they've amassed to bid on them.

The economic lessons she's teaching her students, she says, are more vital now than ever before. "For a lot of my students, material things came easy," says Sturgeon. That era, it seems, is over, and Sturgeon wants to be sure her kids have the knowledge they'll need to survive and even thrive in the coming years.

The Teachable Moment

While the Great Recession drags on, children from all walks of life—from those attending poor schools in the Rust Belt to affluent schools in Fairfield County, Connecticut—are seeing the impact of the financial downturn writ large. Real estate prices have plunged. Homes are in foreclosure. Jobs have been lost or cut back, or are increasingly uncertain. Savings, including most college funds, have cratered. Financial well-being, which many kids have taken for granted in their short lives, is no longer assured. Some, like the students of Village Academy High School in Pomona, California, created a powerful YouTube video, "Is Anybody Listening?,"

in which they described the toll the country's financial woes had taken on them, their families, their inner lives, and their dreams for higher education. (It turns out President Barack Obama was listening. He visited the school in March of 2009 and promised to revamp policies to help right the economy.) For many kids, though, anxieties about the economy go unspoken.

Which doesn't mean teachers should ignore them. "It is a teachable moment," says Robert Duvall, former president of the Council for Economic Education. And schools disregard it at their peril. "Most of our current economic problems—the subprime meltdown and the hedge fund implosion, for instance, show you the high cost of financial illiteracy. We've failed at teaching people the basics. And now we are paying the price," says Duvall. Since the stock market took a dive last September, his group, which trains teachers to provide personal finance and economics instruction and supplies free K–12 lesson plans to teachers and schools, has been deluged by calls from educators hoping to find a way to make the younger generation more sophisticated about debt, mortgages, investing, and savings.

Start the Dialogue

A new study suggests that teachers have their work cut out for them. In the spring of 2008, researchers at the University of Arizona surveyed 2,000 college freshmen to probe their attitudes about money, financial-literacy education, and their own personal monetary habits. They found that nearly 73 percent of those students had resorted to at least one risky financial behavior, such as maxing out credit card limits or not paying bills on time. More alarming still: Nearly one in five of those surveyed had used some extreme strategy for meeting day-to-day financial needs, such as taking out a payday loan or using one credit card to pay another. Soyeon Shim, director of the John and Doris Norton School of Family and Consumer Sciences at the University of Arizona and the study's principal investigator, says she hopes to follow this cohort for 20 years. "We want to measure the impact of financial literacy on their life outcomes. Our question is this: Where do they learn their positive habits? And how can we maximize what they learn so that they can have a satisfying and happy life?" She's convinced that providing explicit financial literacy instruction will yield long-term benefits. And interest in learning to do more with

How to Talk to Kids About Money

It's not always easy to start the conversation. Here are some pointers from Jump$tart's Laura Levine and Janet Bodnar, editor of *Kiplinger's Personal Finance* and author of *Raising Money Smart Kids*.

Pre-K and Kindergarten

The chief lesson at this age is that money has value. Let them put coins in a piggy bank, play "store," or sort your change into pennies, nickels, dimes, and quarters. Remember: Children at this age don't do abstract. It's hard to explain to a preschooler that a dime is more valuable than a nickel. (Bigger seems better.) You can begin the important discussion about the difference between wants and needs but don't expect too much. You can talk about saving but don't expect them to participate. Planning ahead is usually a developing skill at this age. Keep it simple.

Early Elementary School

This is a good age to begin an allowance so children can toy with concepts like saving and budgeting. As part of the school curriculum, children will be learning to identify currency, name monetary value, and make change. It's a good idea to practice this with a child whenever it is practical. Now is the time for a child to observe adults talking about comparison shopping and learning, at least by osmosis, this essential lesson: Every day is not a treat day. There is a time to spend and a time to be budget conscious. Continue the discussion about wants and needs and how to delay gratification.

Later Elementary School

It's time for a field trip to the bank. You are going to have to do a lot of explaining: There is not much about banking that is intuitive. No, the back room of a bank is not filled with bags and bags of money. No, you don't get the same $10

back that you deposit. Introduce the concept of compound interest—both for savings and for loans—and how you can make money work for you. Also, suggest the concept of charitable donations, too, perhaps by raising money for a favorite cause. If you are saving for a car or a vacation, give them periodic updates on how your own savings plan is working out.

Middle School

This is the age where kids are targeted by The Great American Marketing Machine. Teachers: Help parents fight back. Middle schoolers ask for many things—some of them quite costly. At this age, they need to hear that some purchases—a designer purse or the latest cell phone—are beyond the reach of family budgets or [horrors!] outside what you think is appropriate for a preteen. You'll hear that "everyone has it!" This is not true. Make it clear that no 12-year-old needs a $170 phone. The $39 phone will do just fine. Start talking about the importance of saving—for a trip to an amusement park, for a particular item of clothing, and, at least partially, for college.

High School

Start talking to kids about good debt and bad debt, and warn them about the dangers of credit card interest. Some patents get their kids credit cards around now to "learn how to use credit responsibly." Others call that a terrible mistake. Whatever the social, climate, it is time to talk about how long it will take—and how much you will actually pay—if you only pay the minimum balance on a bill. Also, introduce kids to the stock market. They're old enough to understand that owning stock means being part owner—and sharing in the profits—of a company whose products or services they use. It is useful to know about other investment and savings tools, too, such as Roth IRAs, 401ks, bonds, and CDs.

---

less has rarely been higher. Even in the short time the study has been under way, Shim says, the changing financial outlook has altered the way her subjects are managing money.

Some states are already teaching at least components of financial literacy. Seventeen states require high schoolers to take an economics class (up from 13 in 1998). Twenty-eight states have some personal-finance knowledge woven into their standards (up from 14 in 1998). Seven states mandate that students take a personal-finance class as a requirement for graduation. Three more states—Virginia, New Jersey, and Arizona—will be making personal finance a graduation requirement in the 2009–10 school year. And financial literacy, points out Harlan Day, executive director of the Indiana Council for Economic Education, doesn't have to be a stand-alone class. "Teachers have come up with ways to teach economic concepts in geography, history, even through literature."

Many experts say instruction should begin in the home before children are even old enough for school. Laura Levine, executive director of the Jump$tart Coalition for Personal Financial Literacy, which advocates for more finance classes in schools, says parents are the first and best teachers. "Like all tricky issues—drugs,

sexuality, and money—parents need to talk to their kids early and often," she says. But where to start?

"The very youngest kids should know a few basic concepts, like the fact that money has value, why people should save, and the difference between wants and needs," says Levine. At that age, good lessons about finance come when parents take a child to the store and comparison shop as a way to discuss price and value. Early education teachers, she says, can focus on budgeting and planning, supply and demand, as well as savings and compound interest. At-risk students, she says, should get beefed-up instruction on careers and entrepreneurship—and be taught that income is an important part of the equation. In high school, lessons should touch upon savings, investing, credit, insurance, and identity theft.

Reality Check

In the 10 years that Sheila Miller has been teaching personal finance literacy, an elective for 11th and 12th graders at Newfound Regional High School in Bristol, New Hampshire, she's cleared up a lot of misconceptions about money. "This generation, they

Resources

Money coach Lynnette Khalfani-Cox offers her top financial-education resources for encouraging money-savvy kids.

Online:

councilforeconed.org

Council for Economic Education

aafcs.org

American Association of Family and Consumer Sciences

jumpstart.org

The Jump$tart Coalition for Personal Financial. Literacy teaches 12 financial principles all kids should know.

nefe.org

The National Endowment for Financial Education has a variety of resources and games to teach young people financial skills. NEFE also has a group of energetic volunteers who visit—free of charge—schools nationwide to introduce young teenagers to a range of financial-literacy topics, including budgeting, credit management, and financial goal-setting.

usmint.gov

The United States Mint offers parents and educators free materials and information on personal finance-education, ranging from lesson plans and newsletters to interactive challenges that help kids learn about money and how it's made.

msgen.com

The Money Savvy Generation teaches kids how to responsibly handle—throughout their lifetime—the four important uses for money: how to save, spend, invest, and donate it wisely.

handsonbanking.org

Sponsored by Wells Fargo, this program teaches money skills for kids, teens, young adults, and adults. The colorful curriculum is free and available in English and Spanish. It's designed for both self-paced, individual learning and classroom use, as it comes complete with instructor guides.

Books:

Alexander, Who Used to Be Rich Last Sunday, by Judith Viorst
If You Made a Million, by David M. Schwartz
Pigs Go to Market, by Amy Axelrod
The Millionaire Kids Club series, by Susan Beacham and Lynnette Khalfani-Cox

are used to having a lot," she says. Until they get their first jobs, her students often crave designer purses or expensive electronics—without a clue of how much money it takes to buy those luxury goods. The ones who get after-school jobs tend to be more grounded—they quickly learn what an iPod costs, and that they need to mentally subtract the cost of gas from their weekly net earnings. But Miller says even the ones with part-time jobs struggle when it comes to thinking long-term about their financial well-being. "A lot of times I hear, 'I'm not going to pay for car insurance.' Although it is not required in my state, I have to explain to them why they should at least have liability," she says.

> ## "This generation, they are used to having a lot."
>
> —Sheila Miller, *Personal Finance Teacher, Newfound Regional High School*

The most common myth she runs up against is how much a $10-an-hour wage buys in this day and age. "Many of my students have an idea that they can get out of school, get a $10-an-hour job, and actually live on their own, in an apartment with a car and a fancy cell phone. I tell them that even with one or two roommates, having your own apartment on that kind of salary can be really difficult." This year, as the For Sale signs proliferated in her community and news of foreclosures trickled in, the conversation in her class about budgets, good debt versus bad debt, mortgages, and income got increasingly serious.

Miller says that by talking about it now—when her students are 17—she's hoping she can save them some of the pain their parents are experiencing. She knows her message is getting through. "I'll see a student who has been out of school for a while, and that student will say, 'The course you taught me was the most useful thing I learned in school!' That feels pretty good!" she says with a laugh. Although enrollment in her class has been increasing steadily, she's been pushing to give all kids an opportunity to take it. Next year, she'll get her wish. District officials have made her class a graduation requirement. "I'm sorry that it's taken an economic downturn to give kids this opportunity," she says. But she's sure the class will provide lessons worth learning.

Critical Thinking

1. Identify ways in which financial literacy can be taught in school.

2. Discuss the need for children to have financial literacy in a recession.

3. Share a problem you encountered due to a lack of some financial knowledge.

PEG TYRE is a Spencer Fellow at Columbia University and a former senior writer at *Newsweek*. Her book *The Trouble With Boys* (Random House, 2008) is now available in paperback.

What I've Learned

We can't keep politics out of school reform. Why I'm launching a national movement to transform education.

MICHELLE RHEE

After my boss, Washington, D.C., mayor Adrian Fenty, lost his primary in September, I was stunned. I had never imagined he wouldn't win the contest, given the progress that was visible throughout the city—the new recreation centers, the turnaround of once struggling neighborhoods, and, yes, the improvements in the schools. Three and a half years ago, when I first met with Fenty about becoming chancellor of the D.C. public-school system, I had warned him that he wouldn't want to hire me. If we did the job right for the city's children, I told him, it would upset the status quo—I was sure I would be a political problem. But Fenty was adamant. He said he would back me—and my changes—100 percent. He never wavered, and I convinced myself the public would see the progress and want it to continue. But now I have no doubt this cost him the election.

The timing couldn't have been more ironic. The new movie *Waiting for Superman*—which aimed to generate public passion for school reform the way *An Inconvenient Truth* had for climate change—premiered in Washington the night after the election. The film championed the progress Fenty and I had been making in the District, and lamented the roadblocks we'd faced from the teachers' union. In the pro-reform crowd, you could feel the shock that voters had just rejected this mayor and, to some extent, the reforms in their schools.

When I started as chancellor in 2007, I never had any illusions about how tough it would be to turn around a failing system like D.C.'s; the city had gone through seven chancellors in the 10 years before me. While I had to make many structural changes—overhauling the system for evaluating teachers and principals, adopting new reading and math programs, making sure textbooks got delivered on time—I believed the hardest thing would be changing the culture. We had to raise the expectations that people had about what was possible for our kids.

I quickly announced a plan to close almost two dozen schools, which provoked community outrage. We cut the central office administration in half. And I also proposed a new contract for teachers that would increase their salaries dramatically if they abandoned the tenure system and agreed to be paid based on their effectiveness.

Though all of these actions caused turmoil in the district, they were long overdue and reaped benefits quickly. In my first two years in office, the D.C. schools went from being the worst performing on the National Assessment of Educational Progress examination, the national test, to leading the nation in gains at both the fourth and eighth grade in reading as well as math. By this school year we reversed a trend of declining enrollment and increased the number of families choosing District schools for the first time in 41 years.

Because of results like these, I have no regrets about moving so fast. So much needed to be fixed, and there were times when I know it must have felt overwhelming to the teachers because we were trying to fix everything at once. But from my point of view, waiting meant that another year was going by when kids were not getting the education they deserved.

My comments about ineffective teachers were often perceived as an attack on all teachers.

I know people say I wasn't good enough at building consensus, but I don't think consensus can be the goal. Take, for example, one of our early boiling points: school closures. We held dozens of community meetings about the issue. But would people really have been happier with the results if we had done it more slowly? I talked to someone from another district that spent a year and a half defining the criteria that outlined which schools would close. But when the results were announced, everyone went nuts. They had seen the criteria. What did they think was going to happen? That's when I realized there is no good way to close a school.

Still, I could have done a better job of communicating. I did a particularly bad job letting the many good teachers know that I considered them to be the most important part of the equation. I should have said to the effective teachers, "You don't have anything to worry about. My job is to make your life better, offer you more support, and pay you more." I totally fell down on doing that. As a result, my comments about ineffective teachers were often perceived as an attack on all teachers. I also underestimated how much teachers would be relying on the blogs, random rumors, and innuendo. Over the last 18 to 24 months, I held teacher-listening sessions a couple of times a week. But fear was already locked in. In the end, the changes that we needed to make meant that some teachers and principals would lose their jobs in a punishing economy. I don't know if there was any good way to do that.

Some people believed I had disdain for the public. I read a quote where a woman said it seemed like I was listening, but I didn't do what she told me to do. There's a big difference there. It's not that I wasn't listening; I just didn't agree and went in a different direction. There's no way you can please everyone.

But it's true that I didn't do enough to bring parents along, either. I saw a poll of people who live in a part of the city where the schools experienced a significant turnaround, and everyone agreed that they were overwhelmingly much better now. But when they were asked, did we need to fire the teachers to see this turnaround, they said no. We didn't connect the dots for them.

After the shock of Fenty's loss, it became clear to me that the best way to keep the reform going in the D.C. schools was for me to leave my job as chancellor. That was tough for me to accept. I called the decision heartbreaking, and I meant it, because there is a piece of my heart in every classroom, and always will be. To this day, I get mail from D.C. parents and kids who say, "Why did you leave us? The job wasn't done. Why did you give up on us?" Those kinds of letters are really hard to read and respond to. I loved that job. But I felt that Mayor-elect Vincent Gray should have the same ability that Fenty had to appoint his own chancellor. And I knew I had become a lightning rod and excuse for the anti-reformers to oppose the changes that had to be made.

After stepping down, I had a chance to reflect on the challenges facing our schools today and the possible solutions. The truth is that despite a handful of successful reforms, the state of American education is pitiful, and getting worse. Spending on schools has more than doubled in the last three decades, but the increased resources haven't produced better results. The U.S. is currently 21st, 23rd, and 25th among 30 developed nations in science, reading, and math, respectively. The children in our schools today will be the first generation of Americans who will be less educated than the previous generation.

When you think about how things happen in our country— how laws get passed or policies are made—they happen through the exertion of influence. From the National Rifle Association to the pharmaceutical industry to the tobacco lobby, powerful interests put pressure on our elected officials and government institutions to sway or stop change.

The truth is, the state of American education is pitiful, and it's getting worse.

Education is no different. We have text-book manufacturers, teachers' unions, and even food vendors that work hard to dictate and determine policy. The public-employee unions in D.C, including the teachers' union, spent huge sums of money to defeat Fenty. In fact, the new chapter president has said his No. 1 priority is job security for teachers, but there is no big organized interest group that defends and promotes the interests of children.

You can see the impact of this dynamic playing out every day. Policymakers, school-district administrators, and school boards who are beholden to special interests have created a bureaucracy that is focused on the adults instead of the students. Go to any public-school-board meeting in the country and you'll rarely hear the words "children," "students," or "kids" uttered. Instead, the focus remains on what jobs, contracts, and departments are getting which cuts, additions, or changes. The rationale for the decisions mostly rests on which grown-ups will be affected, instead of what will benefit or harm children.

The teachers' unions get the blame for much of this. Elected officials, parents, and administrators implore them to "embrace change" and "accept reform." But I don't think the unions can or should change. The purpose of the teachers' union is to protect the privileges, priorities, and pay of their members. And they're doing a great job of that.

What that means is that the reform community has to exert influence as well. That's why I've decided to start Students-First, a national movement to transform public education in our country. We need a new voice to change the balance of power in public education. Our mission is to defend and promote the interests of children so that America has the best education system in the world.

From the moment I resigned, I began hearing from citizens from across this country. I got e-mails, calls, and letters from parents, students, and teachers who said, "Don't give up. We need you to keep fighting!" Usually, they'd then share with me a story about how the education system in their community was not giving students what they need or deserve. I got one e-mail from two people who have been trying to open a charter school in Florida and have been stopped every step of the way by the school district. No voices have moved me more than those of teachers. So many great teachers in this country are frustrated with the schools they are working in, the bureaucratic rules that bind them, and the hostility to excellence that pervades our education system.

We're hoping to sign up 1 million StudentsFirst members and raise $1 billion in our first year.

The common thread in all of these communications was that these courageous people felt alone in battling the bureaucracy. They want help and advocates. There are enough people out there who understand and believe that kids deserve better, but until now, there has been no organization for them. We'll ask people across the country to join StudentsFirst—we're hoping to sign up 1 million members and raise $1 billion in our first year.

Studentsfirst will work so that great teachers can make a tremendous difference for students of every background. We believe every family can choose an excellent school—attending a great school should be a matter of fact, not luck. We'll fight against ineffective instructional programs and bureaucracy so that public dollars go where they make the biggest difference: to effective instructional programs. Parent and family involvement are key to increased student achievement, but the entire community must be engaged in the effort to improve our schools.

Though we'll be nonpartisan, we can't pretend that education reform isn't political. So we'll put pressure on elected officials and press for changes in legislation to make things better for kids. And we'll support and endorse school-board candidates and politicians—in city halls, statehouses, and the U.S. Congress—who want to enact policies around our legislative agenda. We'll support any candidate who's reform-minded, regardless of political party, so reform won't just be a few courageous politicians experimenting in isolated locations; it'll be a powerful, nationwide movement.

Lastly, we can't shy away from conflict. I was at Harvard the other day, and someone asked about a statement that Secretary of Education Arne Duncan and others have made that public-school reform is the civil-rights issue of our generation. Well, during the civil-rights movement they didn't work everything out by sitting down collaboratively and compromising. Conflict was necessary in order to move the agenda forward. There are some fundamental disagreements that exist right now about what kind of progress is possible and what strategies will be most effective. Right now, what we need to do is fight. We can be respectful about it. But this is the time to stand up and say what you believe, not sweep the issues under the rug so that we can feel good about getting along. There's nothing more worthwhile than fighting for children. And I'm not done fighting.

Critical Thinking

1. What role does politics play in public school education?
2. How do you feel about the "last hired, first fired" policy of unionized workers? Why?
3. Why is public school reform needed in the United States?

From Lockers to Lockup

School bullying in the digital age can have tragic consequences. But should it be a crime?

JESSICA BENNETT

It started with rumors, a love triangle, and a dirty look in a high-school bathroom. Soon jokes about an "Irish slut" cropped up on Facebook, and a girl's face was scribbled out of a class photo hanging up at school. One day, in the cafeteria, another girl marched in, pointed at her, and shouted "stay away from other people's men." A week later as the girl walked home, a car full of students crept close. One kid hurled a crumpled soda can out the window, followed closely by shrieks of "whore!" If your children had behaved like this, how would you want them punished? Certainly a proper grounding would be in order; computer privileges revoked. Detention, yes-maybe even suspension. Or what about 10 years in jail? Now what if we told you that the girl had gone home after the soda-can incident and killed herself-discovered by her little sister, hanging in a stairwell. Now which punishment fits the crime?

This is the conundrum of Phoebe Prince, the 15-year-old South Hadley, Mass., girl the media have already determined was "bullied to death." It's the crime of the moment, the blanket explanation slapped on cases from Texas to California, where two 13-year-old boys recently killed themselves after being tormented for being gay. One of the most shocking examples yet came last week, when Tyler Clementi, an 18-year-old New Jersey college student, threw himself off the George Washington Bridge after his roommate and a friend allegedly streamed a Webcam video of his tryst with a man. Cases like these are being invoked as potent symbols for why, in the digital age, schools need strong bullying policies and states need stronger legislation.

But do they? Is the notion of being bullied to death valid? It's one thing to hold bullies responsible for their own actions, but it's trickier to blame them for the chain of events that may follow. No one would deny that Clementi's roommate did the unconscionable-the alleged crime is all the more disturbing because of the specter of antigay bias. Yet they couldn't have known how badly the stunt would end. Now he and his friend face up to five years in prison for invasion of privacy. In the case of Phoebe Prince, the answer of who's to blame might change if you knew that she had tried to kill herself before the epithets,

was on medication for depression, and was struggling with her parents' separation. So where is the line now between behavior that's bad and behavior that's criminal? Does the definition of old-school bullying need to be rewritten for the new-media age?

In effect, it already has been. Forty-five states now have anti-bullying laws; in Massachusetts, which has one of the strictest, anti-bullying programs are mandated in schools, and criminal punishment is outlined in the text for even the youngest offenders. It's a good-will effort, to be sure-prevention programs have been shown to reduce school bullying by as much as 50 percent. With 1 in 5 students bullied each year-and an appalling 9 in 10 gay and lesbian students-that's good news: kids who are bullied are five times more likely to be depressed, and nearly 160,000 of them skip school each day, fearful of their peers. Bullies themselves don't fare well, either: one study, of middle-schoolboys, found that 60 percent of those deemed "bullies" would be convicted of at least one crime by the time they reached 24.

But forget, for the moment, the dozens of articles that have called bullying a "pandemic"—because the opposite is true. School bullying can be devastating, but social scientists say it is no more extreme, nor more prevalent, than it was a half century ago. In fact, says Dan Olweus, a leading bullying expert, new data shows rates of school bullying may have even gone down over the past decade. Today's world of cyberbullying is different, yes-far-reaching, more visually potent, and harder to wash away than comments scrawled on a bathroom wall. All of which can make it harder to combat. But it still happens a third less than traditional bullying, says Olweus.

The reality may be that while the incidence of bullying has remained relatively the same, it's our reaction to it that's changed: the helicopter parents who want to protect their kids from every stick and stone, the cable-news commentators who whip them into a frenzy, the insta-vigilantism of the Internet. When it comes down to it, bullying is not just a social ill; it's a "cottage industry," says Suffolk Law School's David Yamada—complete with commentators and prevention experts and a new breed of legal scholars, all preparing to take on an enemy that's always been there. None of this is to say that bullying is not a serious problem, or that tackling it is not important. But like a stereo with the volume turned too high, all the noise distorts the facts, making it nearly impossible to judge when a case is somehow criminal, or merely cruel.

To make sense of the punishment, of course, we must first understand the crime. Phoebe Prince's problems at South Hadley High School began around November of last year, when the freshman became involved with two senior boys—Austin Renaud and Sean Mulveyhill, the school's star football player—both of whom had girlfriends. According to their indictments, the boys, their girlfriends, and students Ashley Longe and Sharon Velasquez engaged in what the DA described as a "nearly three-month campaign" of verbal assault and physical threats against Phoebe. What appears to be the worst of the crimes involves a threat to "beat Phoebe up"; repeated taunts of "whore" and "Irish slut"; and, on the day of her death, the soda-can incident, which left Phoebe in tears. When Phoebe got home that afternoon, she texted a friend: "I can't do it anymore." Her sister found her body at 4:30 P.M.

Her death, understandably, sent South Hadley into a shame-and-blame spiral. The school principal opened an internal investigation, but allowed the then-unidentified bullies to remain in class. A community member sympathetic to Phoebe's story went to *The Boston Globe,* which published a column chastising school officials for allowing the "mean girls" to remain in school, "defiant, unscathed." A Facebook group with the headline "Expel the three girls who caused Phoebe Prince to commit suicide" suddenly had thousands of fans. School officials took to the press—defending how they could have let the bullying go on, asserting they had only learned of the problem the week before Phoebe's death. "I'm not naive [enough] to think we'll have zero bullying . . . but this was a complex tragedy," South Hadley principal Dan Smith tells Newsweek.

Enter District Attorney Elizabeth Scheibel, whose profile on the National District Attorneys Association Web site, until recently, detailed how, as a child, she beat up a schoolyard bully who was picking on her brother. On March 29, Scheibel released the names of six students she would indict on felony charges, whose "relentless activity," she said, was "designed to humiliate [Phoebe] and make it impossible for her to remain at school" Since there is no law explicitly making bullying a crime, Scheibel charged two of them with stalking, two with criminal harassment, and five with civil-rights violations resulting in bodily injury, alleging that Phoebe's ability to get an education had been made impossible. She also charged both of the boys with statutory rape, for allegedly having sex with Phoebe while she was underage—an offense punishable by up to three years in jail. The civil-rights violation carries a maximum of 10 years. (All six defendants have pleaded not guilty.)

The law (and the media) may assess the world in black or white, but the players in the case don't fit into neat categories. Phoebe suffered a terrible tragedy, but court filings have since revealed she had her own demons, too. She struggled with depression, self-mutilation, had been prescribed Seroquel (a medication to treat mood disorders), and had attempted suicide once before. By the same token, each of the students

charged with bullying Phoebe were in good academic standing, South Hadley's superintendent, Gus Sayer, told Newsweek. Does that in any way excuse their behavior? Not at all—and each has been out of school since March, suspended, indefinitely, until their case is resolved in court. Their trials are expected early next year. "These are not the troubled kids we sometimes deal with," says Sayer. "These are nice kids, regular kids. They come from nice families. They were headed to college. And now, in addition to losing Phoebe, we're losing [them] too." (Phoebe's father, Jeremy Prince, has said he would ask the court for leniency if the teens confessed and apologized.)

'Even if [these kids] are ultimately acquitted, they might never recover', says Velasquez's attorney, Colin Keefe.

Still, even if they are acquitted, it's clear the lives of the accused are forever altered. None completed school last year; Mulveyhill has already lost a football scholarship. Angeles Chanon, the mother of Sharon Velasquez, says her daughter is studying for her GED, but heartbroken that she can't return to class this fall. Since there aren't any other public high schools in South Hadley—and public schools in Massachusetts can deny entrance based on a felony charge—her options for continuing on a different campus are slim, and her mother, also a full-time student, can't afford a private school. In the mean-time, Sharon is still haunted by the tragedy of Phoebe's death. She sits at home most days, reading, watching TV—but scared to leave the house alone. Sharon's family has received death threats, prank calls, and a rock thrown through a second-story window, along with a stream of nasty unsigned letters delivered to her door. Some call for her to be "raped and killed"; others hurl insults and racial slurs. "I don't know if I can even describe what my family has been through," says Chanon, who agreed to speak to Newsweek with her lawyer, Colin Keefe, present. "The cameras in our faces, the harassment, the letters—I'd come home and people would be in the parking lot waiting for me."

The irony, of course, is that it all sounds a bit like the kind of torment Phoebe allegedly endured. But if these kids are bullies according to the law, what about the people around them? Massachusetts anti-bullying statute defines bullying as repeated behavior that, among other things, "causes emotional harm" or "creates a hostile environment" at school. If it were applied to the real world, wouldn't most of us be bullies? It's easy to see how the blossoming field of bullying law could ultimately criminalize the kind of behavior we engage in every day—not just in schoolyards, but in workplaces, in politics, at home. "You're not going to prevent a lot of this stuff," says former New York prosecutor Sam Goldberg, a Boston criminal attorney. "It may seem harsh, but to some degree, you're going to have to tell your kid, 'Sometimes people say mean things.'"

What most bullying experts and legal scholars agree on is that prosecution—in the Prince case, anyway—may be the worst possible scenario. There is longstanding research to show that law is not a deterrent to kids who respond emotionally to their surroundings; ultimately, labeling a group of raucous teens as "criminals" will only make it harder for them to engage with society when they return. Certainly, there is behavior that should be treated as a crime—the story of Clementi, the young Rutgers student who jumped off the bridge, is particularly hard to stomach. But many kids "just mess up," says Sameer Hinduja, a criminologist at Florida Atlantic University, and the codirector of the Cyberbullying Research Center. "They react emotionally, and most of them express a lot of remorse. I think most kids deserve another chance."

Critical Thinking

1. Relate your own personal experiences with bullying. Do you feel that a bully should be punished?
2. At what point should a bully be considered a criminal?
3. How can school administrators create a friendly environment at school that discourages bullying?

UNIT 4

Development during Childhood: Family and Culture

Unit Selections

Learning Outcomes

After reading this Unit you should be able to:

- Appraise reasons for role-reversal based on external criteria.
- Formulate ways to make family role-reversal more satisfactory and fair.
- Recognize the more subtle signs of passive-aggressive behavior.
- Explain why assertive expression of anger should be encouraged.
- Interpret the consequences on both boys and girls when young girls dress and act provocatively.
- Summarize ways in which parents can help young children dress and act like children.
- Contrast the effects of time-out discipline and spanking.
- Justify introducing talks about race and social class to young children.
- Choose activities for a week of summer camp to encourage acceptance of diversity.
- Discuss cost-effective strategies to improve the lives of at-risk children.
- Propose tactics to recruit at-risk families into compensatory programs.
- Explain what corpulence means and list behaviors that could curtail our culture of corpulence.

Student Website

www.mhhe.com/cls

Internet References

Harborview Injury Prevention and Research Center
http://depts.washington.edu/hiprc/

Families and Work Institute
www.familiesandwork.org/index.html

Optimal Weight for Life (OWL) Program
www.childrenshospital.org/clinicalservices/site1896

Parentsplace.com: Single Parenting
www.parentsplace.com/

Passive Aggressive Diaries
www.PassiveAggressiveDiaries.com

Families and cultures have substantial effects on child outcomes. How? New interpretations of behavioral genetic research suggest that genetically predetermined child behaviors may have substantial effects on how families parent, how children react, and how cultures evolve. Nature and nurture are very interactive. Is it possible that there is a genetic predisposition toward more warlike, aggressive, and violent behaviors in some children? Do some child-rearing practices suppress this genetic trait? Do others aggravate it? Are some children predisposed to care for others? The answers are not yet known.

If parents and societies have a significant impact on child outcomes, is there a set of universal family values? Does one culture have more success than another culture? Laypersons often assume that children's behaviors and personalities have a direct correlation with the behaviors and personality of the person or persons who provided their socialization during infancy and childhood.

Are you a mirror image of the person or persons who raised you? How many of their beliefs, preferences, and virtuous behaviors do you reflect? Did you learn their hatreds and vices as well? Do you model your family, your peers, your culture, all of them, or none of them? If you have a sibling, are you alike because the same person or persons raised you? What accounts for all the differences between people with similar genes, similar parenting, and the same cultural background? These and similar questions are fodder for future research.

During childhood, a person's family values are compared to and tested against the values of schools, community, and culture. Peers, schoolmates, teachers, neighbors, extracurricular activity leaders, religious leaders, and even shopkeepers play increasingly important roles. Culture influences children through holidays, styles of dress, music, television, the Internet, world events, movies, slang, games, parents' jobs, transportation, exposure to sex, drugs, and violence, and many other variables. The ecological theorist Urie Bronfenbrenner called these cultural variables exosystem and macrosystem influences. The developing personality of a child has multiple interwoven influences: from genetic potentialities through family values and socialization practices to community and cultural pressures for behaviors.

The first article in this unit, "Role Reversal," reveals that the current economic downturn has created many stay-at-home dads and breadwinner moms. Sara Eckel explains the psychological adjustments and job learning skills this requires. She gives suggestions for making a role-reversal more acceptable.

The second article in this unit, "The Angry Smile," suggests that having a passive resistance to demands and

© David Ashley/Corbis

a pervasive negative attitude is not only troubling and destructive in family interactions, but is also fairly common. It is not a behavior that is genetically preprogrammed. It is learned. It can be unlearned. The author, Signe Whitson, explains how parents can help their children learn assertive expression by both modeling it and encouraging assertion.

The third article, "Fast Times," discusses the pressures on very young girls to look and act like sex objects. Television, music videos and games encourage sexually provocative behaviors from both young girls and boys. The author, Deborah Swaney, gives many suggested activities for countering the sexually-charged kids' culture. She advises families to let children see what their bodies can do physically through exercise, sports, music, art, and non-sex-laden games.

Unit 4, subsection B (Culture), emphasizes socialization of our children in an increasingly diverse society. The first article in this section tells why we all should be "Engaging Young Children in Activities and Conversations about Race and Social Class." The mixture of races, religions, and economic situations in our neighborhoods and schools fosters friendships between groups. The authors suggest several positive activities (art, role-play, games, books) to reduce prejudice and discrimination.

The second article about children and culture addresses the needs of the poor and disadvantaged. Infants, school-age boys and girls, and adolescents are termed "at-risk" when their physical, cognitive, and social-emotional development is thwarted by lack of food, shelter, and/or a sense of belonging and love. Susan Neuman discusses what can help in "Use the Science of What Works to Change the Odds for Children at Risk."

The last selection for this unit, "Culture of Corpulence," evaluates the multitude of reasons why children are growing heavier, with much more bulk on their bodies. The health risks of this largeness include more diabetes, lower self-esteem, depression, and cardiovascular complications (high cholesterol, high blood pressure). The author reports on Michelle Obama's initiative to curb childhood obesity.

Role Reversal

Amid bruised egos, resentments and confusion, families are struggling to find their footing as they cope with the financial, emotional and who-does-the-dishes-now restructuring of their lives brought on by the recession.

Sara Eckel

On a cold, rainy November morning, Christine Fruehwirth's 5-year-old son showed up at preschool without a coat—or even a sweater. "The sweater was dirty," says Christine's husband, John. He also had taken their 7-year-old daughter out to run errands in the ballerina pajamas she'd slept in. "I didn't know. I thought it was an outfit," John says of the wardrobe mishap, one of several that have occurred since he took over many of the household and child-care duties two years ago. That's when he lost his job as the managing director of a Washington, DC, private equity firm. To support their family of five, Christine began working part-time as a career consultant for George Washington University in addition to the career-coaching business she was already running out of their home.

Like many families coping with the turmoil brought on by the recession, the Fruehwirths have been fumbling to find their footing now that the roles of family breadwinner and household caretaker have been shuffled around. Though Christine, 40, had planned to work while her three kids were young, she was thinking one job, not two. But now she says, "Maybe this was meant to be." She's appreciating the chance to further develop her professional life. And although John is adamant that he's *not* a stay-at-home dad—he's developing a private equity company he purchased with his severance pay—he's enjoying extra time with the kids now that he's the one taking them to and from school and helping them with homework.

With job loss comes heightened anxiety, as well as recast parental and household duties, causing a major upheaval in many families. Working moms are increasingly logging extra hours in the office—and spending more time away from their children—while more men are finding themselves without an office to go to. Getting the bills paid and cutting back on nonessential spending is a strain for sure. Yet for many, the greatest challenge hasn't been financial; it's been psychological. Amid all the changes, moms and dads are trying to adjust not only to new daily schedules but also to bruised egos and growing resentments. We talked to couples about how their families are coping with this shift—and learned what they're doing to keep the peace.

Shattered Self-esteem

After Stefania Sorace Smith's husband lost his security job last May, she landed a higher-paying position in her profession, as the residential programmer at a home for mentally disabled people. But she also doubled her commuting time, and her workweek soared to 60 hours from 40—a particular strain since she's now pregnant with the couple's second child. Even with her higher salary and the part-time work her husband, Darren, has secured, the Dingman's Ferry, PA, couple has not made up the lost income. Now charged with the family's financial security, Stefania, 26, is more stressed than ever. "Bills definitely get behind," she says, adding that she sometimes plays "Russian roulette" with her checkbook by alternating which bills she pays—and which she skips—each month. At home, Darren is doing more of the basic cleaning, and he makes their 2-year-old daughter breakfast and prepares dinner for the family—but the major scrub work still falls to Stefania because he "just doesn't do it the way I want it done," she says.

For Stefania, one of the biggest disparities in this new structure is free time. She spends most of her day working and commuting. Darren—while doing handyman work and pitching in with the household chores—still spends a fair amount of time playing Flight Simulator on his computer. "This transition has been tough," he says. "I started building houses when I was twelve. I'm used to working ninety hours a week. All I ever did was work." Though he's enjoying the time he spends with his daughter, he feels unproductive. "It's difficult to go from self-sufficient to depending on someone, but we're making it work," he says. "It is what it is."

The ego blow of job loss leaves many men unable to find fulfillment in their new role. In the months after Ron Mattocks was laid off two years ago, he admits, he had a tough time transitioning from his former life as a vice president of sales for a major homebuilder to Daddy Day Care. "I was an officer in the army and then an executive in the corporate world. Suddenly, I'm packing lunches and making sure the kids have everything in their backpacks. My entire self-image pretty much got shattered," says Ron, 37, from Houston. "I had to really rethink myself, and that's been a long, discouraging process."

Feeling the Pain

The loss of a husband's job can cause severe stress as some families move into smaller homes or scramble to secure health insurance. Here, a snapshot by the numbers.

- **75%** of the jobs lost during this recession were held by men. That has made the ever-growing share of women in the workforce even larger.
- **51%** of all workers on U.S. payrolls are women, compared with 33% in 1969.
- **31%** of working moms earned as much as or more than their husbands in 2008 vs. 11% in 1967. More women are now the primary breadwinner.

He misses the external validation he got through his work—the backslapping for a job well done—and is struggling to find that same sense of confidence internally. It has helped, however, to see his wife, Ashley, gain confidence in her career. "Though I don't bring value to the family the way I used to, my role is important," he says.

Why Men Don't Do Windows

Wives should be mindful of the fact that a recently unemployed husband is in a fragile emotional state, says Ellen Ostrow, PhD, a psychologist who works with professional women reentering the workforce. "The psychological impact is enormous," she says. This is one reason many men don't automatically start picking up the scrub brush after a job loss. According to the 2008 American Time Use Survey released by the U.S. Bureau of Labor Statistics, unemployed women spend almost six hours a day on child care and household chores like cleaning and cooking, while unemployed men spend only three hours a day on such tasks—and also spend more than four hours a day watching television.

Often men with a very traditional view of gender roles will refuse to do housework, as a way to gain control, says Stephanie Coontz, who teaches history and family studies at The Evergreen State College in Olympia, WA. "They think that they have to compensate for their loss of masculinity by asserting masculine privilege in other ways."

But the reasoning may be even more subtle than that. Jeremy Adam Smith, author of *The Daddy Shift,* suggests that most men simply don't see housework and child care as a vocation that could give them a sense of identity and pride, as many women do. "For a lot of women who lose their job, a pathway presents itself," he says. "They decide, 'I'm a stay-at-home mom. My job now is to take care of the home and kids, and I'm going to be good at that.' But for many fathers, that pathway doesn't exist in any well-developed way."

Teaching the Basics

However understandable this aversion to scouring bathtubs and laying out school clothes may be, the fact remains that the work needs to be done. Kelly Sons says her marriage became

Making Mr. Mom

Do you bring home the bacon—but he refuses to fry it up in a pan? Experts say there are ways to nudge even the most reluctant husband into doing his share.

Make a plan. Rather than give him piecemeal instructions or complaints about picking up dry cleaning, sit down with him and discuss what needs to be done—and decide who should do it. "It's quite likely that the husband doesn't *know* what Mom did. Everything just sort of happened," says Professor Joan C. Williams, JD, director of the Center for WorkLife Law at the University of California, Hastings.

Give up control. He may not do the laundry or load the dishwasher the way you do, but if the work is getting done, don't nitpick. "Wives do have this tendency to regard husbands as unskilled assistants, but that's the worst thing you can do to men who have had the ego blow of being laid off," says family historian Stephanie Coontz, author of *Marriage, a History: How Love Conquered Marriage.*

Show your appreciation. It doesn't matter if the pork chops overcooked—let him know how much you appreciate coming home to a hot meal. Coontz says that most families don't show enough gratitude, which is essential for marital harmony—and why, for example, men who do more housework also have more sex. One survey found that the more housework a man did, the happier he was with his sex life.

rocky two years ago when her husband's declining auto repair business forced her to support the family. The problem wasn't the *paying* work—Kelly gets tremendous satisfaction from her freelance writing—but rather her second shift as the primary caregiver to their six children. "He assumed that I would handle everything. I was incredibly stressed out," says Kelly, 40, of Morrison, TN.

Though working mothers have long grumbled that their spouses are slackers when it comes to housework in their dual-income homes, a husband's refusal to chip in often becomes intolerable when she's suddenly working longer hours and he's home all day. Kelly's very traditional husband, James, had to be schooled in the basics—like the fact that their sons' black clothes should not be washed with the bathroom towels—but he did gradually step up. Today, he runs the household with pride. "He does most of the housework and takes care of our children and actually brags about me to his friends," says Kelly.

Getting to that point was a long, painful process, says Kelly. Her breakthrough came when she realized that instead of fighting and nagging, she needed to make him a partner in finding the solution. "I told him we needed to figure this out—together." With each would-be housework war, she stopped taking on full responsibility and instead turned to him for an answer. "If our family wanted to go to the local aquarium, I'd say, 'I can't go

The Impact on Your Kids

Studies show that a drop in family income can have a negative effect on child development, particularly when parents become depressed, disengaged or argumentative. Kids can struggle with behavioral issues, anxiety or depression. To fend off problems:

Stay positive. Shield kids from any escalating fighting. Be honest but "use language that doesn't scare them," says Joshua Coleman, PhD, cochair of the Council on Contemporary Families. Say, "It's going to work out. Dad will find another job."

Reassure them. Assure kids that it's not their fault if Mom and Dad are feeling a bit down right now. "Children tend to personalize things," Dr. Coleman says. "If they can't make a parent happy, they think there is something wrong with them."

Enlist their help. Ask if they can think of ways the family can save money—like starting a garden or cutting back on soda. "Use it as a teaching experience that can show them that crisis is a part of life and this is how we deal with it," says Dr. Coleman.

until I have this work done and the house is clean, so how is that going to happen?'"

'Watching the Michael Keaton character in the movie *Mr. Mom* struggle with his new role and then master it had a big influence on my husband.'

Surprisingly, one of the most helpful influences came from an old movie. "It sounds crazy, but a lot of it had to do with *Mr. Mom*. Watching the Michael Keaton character struggle with his new role and then master it and eventually take pride in it had a big influence on James." Kelly has also made sure to recognize her husband's contribution—even though it was completely taken for granted when she was doing it. "That's what made it so hard at first. Nobody ever told me thank-you." Since James was sensitive to criticism, especially about his cooking, she always tried to find something positive to say and advises other women to do the same: "Find the good in it even if it's the worst thing you've ever eaten . . . Well, it smells good."

Making Inroads

While they may not do as much around the house as women, American men are doing substantially more than their fathers or grandfathers ever did. In 1980, 29 percent of wives reported that their husbands did absolutely no housework; 20 years later, that figure dropped to 16 percent. And today, a third of American wives report that their husbands do at least half or more of either the housework or the child care.

"The more attached a man is to the size of his paycheck, the more difficult the transition will be," says Coontz. "The good news is a lot of men have been discarding that kind of identity. They're seeing themselves less as workers and more as husbands and fathers."

Of course, it's not just men who have a hard time letting go of old roles. Many women have a difficult time seeing Dad do his job a little too well. Dara Turketsky Blaker, 42, a music educator from Coral Springs, FL, says her heart breaks when her daughter wakes up in the middle of the night and calls for Daddy. "At first it was all about Mommy, and then suddenly it wasn't."

The question remains: Once kids get used to spending more time with Dad, Mom learns to appreciate his quirky housekeeping and parents value each other's role, will it last when the economy rebounds? For the Fruehwirths, seeing how the other half lives has given them more empathy for each other. "We often laugh about it," says Christine. "I'll come home and say, 'That commute was an hour!' and he'll say, 'Yeah, I remember.' Or he'll say, 'The kids drove me crazy,' and I'll say, 'Yeah, been there.'" Whether or not roles revert back remains to be seen. But the growing empathy couples say they've experienced for one another cannot help but linger. They know firsthand that indeed the surest cure for judging another person is to walk a mile in their shoes.

Critical Thinking

1. Predict percentage of male homemaker, female breadwinner by 2015.
2. Identify factors that make a job loss psychologically traumatic.
3. Give advice for making role reversal more fulfilling for men and women.

From *Working Mother*, February/March 2010. Copyright © 2010 by PARS International Corp. Reprinted by permission.

The Angry Smile

Recognizing and responding to your child's passive aggressive behaviors.

SIGNE L. WHITSON

Amber had been giving her mother the silent treatment all week. She was angry about not being allowed to sleep over at a friend's house. Late Thursday night, she left a note on her mother's pillow, asking her mom to wash her uniform before Friday's soccer game. When Amber returned home from school on Friday, in a rush to pack her gear, she looked all over for her uniform. She finally found it in the washer—perfectly clean, as per her request—but still soaking wet! Amber was late for her game and forced to ride the bench.

When all was un-said and done, Amber's mother felt defeated. Having one-upped her daughter in the conflict, it was clear to her that she had lost by winning. As parents, most of us have been in situations where traveling the low road is irresistible and we become temporarily reckless in our driving. But anytime we mirror a child's poor behavior instead of modeling a healthier way to behave, our victories add up to long-term relationship damage and lasting hostilities.

So, what could Amber's mother have done differently in this hostile un-confrontation? What can any parent do to avoid the agony of victory and the defeat of healthy communication? The following guidelines offer parents strategies for maintaining their calm in a passive aggressive storm and responding in ways that lay the groundwork for less conflictual relationships with their children and adolescents.

1. Know What You Are Dealing With

Amber's silent treatment is a classic example of passive aggressive behavior, a deliberate and masked way of expressing feelings of anger. Common passive aggressive behaviors in young people include:

- Verbally denying feelings of anger (*"I'm fine. Whatever!"*)
- Verbally complying but behaviorally delaying (*"I'll clean my room after soccer."*)
- Shutting down conversations (*"Fine."* and *"Whatever."*)
- Intentional inefficiency (*"I did make my bed. I didn't know you meant all of the blankets had to be pulled up!"*)

- "Forgetting" or "misplacing" important items (*"I don't know where your car keys are."*)
- Avoiding responsibility for tasks (*"I didn't know you wanted me to do it. Putting away the clean dishes is his chore!"*)

Parents who are familiar with these typical patterns are able to respond directly to their children's underlying anger and to avoid misbehaving in counter-passive aggressive ways!

2. Consult the Mirror on the Wall

Passive aggressive persons master concealing their anger, and are expert at getting unsuspecting others to act it out in one of two ways. Many respond with an outburst of anger and frustration—yelling, finger wagging, threatening punishment—then feel guilty and embarrassed for having lost control. Others keep the tension low, but turn up the heat on the simmering conflict by mirroring the passive aggression. When Amber's mother purposely left the soccer uniform in the washer, she mirrored the anger that Amber had been feeling all week long. What's more, her counter-passive aggression ensured that the anger between mother and daughter would linger, fester, and grow more intense over time in its buried, unaddressed form! The second step in effectively confronting passive aggression is to refuse to act out the anger for the other person. Helping Amber learn to express her anger assertively is one of this mother's most valuable parenting opportunities!

3. Say Yes to Anger

Anger is a basic, spontaneous, neurophysiological part of the human condition. As such, it is neither good nor bad. It just is. Too often young people are held to an unrealistic social standard about what it takes to be "good." From a very early age, they begin to associate having angry feelings with being bad. Like Amber, our children perceive anger as taboo and take steps to suppress angry feelings.

When parents teach their children to say "yes" to the presence of anger and "no" to the expression of anger through aggressive or passive aggressive behaviors, they build a foundation for lifelong emotional intelligence and strong relationships.

4. Be the Change You Want to See

Each time passive aggressive behavior is answered with a mirrored counter-passive aggressive response, the hidden means of expressing anger is reinforced and an opportunity for direct emotional expression is lost. On the other hand, each time passive aggressive behavior is confronted assertively, the hidden anger is weakened.

The most effective way for our kids to learn to acknowledge and accept angry feelings is to role model this for them on a daily basis. As parents, this can be a real challenge since we, too, may have faced stringent socializing forces regarding the expression of our anger. It's never too late to learn to express anger in emotionally honest, direct ways, however, and the stakes have never been so high!

5. Allow It, Tolerate It, Encourage It, Even!

The final essential angle to confronting passive aggressive behavior in our kids is our willingness to receive their anger when they test out their new voice. If you are going to guide your child to be more open and direct with his anger, then you must also be willing to accept his anger when he expresses it. For many, this is truly difficult. But for lasting change to take hold for Amber and other young people, they must know that the assertive expression of their anger will be tolerated, respected and even honored!

Critical Thinking

1. Describe five common passive-aggressive behavior patterns.

2. Give an example of counter-passive aggression to express underlying anger.

3. Describe how anger can be expressed in an emotionally honest way.

SIGNE WHITSON is a co-author of the book, *"The Angry Smile: The Psychology of Passive Aggressive Behavior in Families, Schools, and Workplaces, 2nd edition."* She is also the creator of the website www .PassiveAggressiveDiaries.com. Signe is a licensed social worker and therapist who has developed and delivered numerous training programs around the country in areas related to child and adolescent mental health. Copies of *The Angry Smile,* as well as information on Angry Smile seminars, can be found at www.Isci.org.

Fast Times

When did 7 become the new 16? For today's young girls, the pressure to look and act hot is greater than ever. Here's help cooling things down.

Deborah Swaney

The job description for parent says you prep yourself for the dicey stuff kids are likely to ask for. So I was ready for the day my daughter would beg for a fashion doll of notoriously unrealistic proportions, or even for one of those skimpily dressed Bratz dolls. Instead, last fall my 7-year-old freaked me out a whole different way—by begging for a bra. "Two girls in my class have them," she argued.

Skeptical that she'd gotten her facts straight, I checked out a local children's store. Yikes! They had a whole assortment of flirty bras and panties perfectly sized for second-graders. Staring at those crazy underthings, and at the body-glitter tubes on the counter, something creepy dawned on me. Today's girls don't just want to *own* a hot-looking doll, they want to *be* one.

Maybe I shouldn't have been so shocked. After all, my daughter and her friends are more likely to worship teen heroes like Troy and Gabriella from the *High School Musical* movies than to expend energy adoring cuddly cartoon characters like the Care Bears. And these same kids are the ones shaking their little booties when the Pussycat Dolls come on the radio, singing, "Don'tcha wish your girlfriend was hot like me?"

Clearly, something's going on, so much so that the American Psychological Association (APA) recently convened a task force on girls' sexualization. "There's a real syndrome happening, and it's picking up speed," says Eileen L. Zurbriggen, PhD, who chaired the APA group. "Even little girls are now feeling they should look and act alluring." Her committee found that this is harmful to girls on several levels.

> **"The core issue is what girls feel valued for. It's as though factors like whether they're smart or kind or talented at something get erased."**
>
> —Eileen L. Zurbriggen

"The core issue is what they feel valued for," Zurbriggen explains. "It's as though factors like whether they're smart or funny or kind or talented at something like sports or art get erased." And their self-esteem suffers for it. "The images their idols present are so idealized, most girls can't attain them. That makes them feel bad about their own bodies, and this can eventually lead to anxiety and depression," Zurbriggen says. Preoccupation with their "hot-o-meter" score can even hurt their school performance. "A girl's mind becomes literally so full of worries about how she looks and what other people are thinking, she doesn't have enough energy left to focus on learning," says Zurbriggen.

How did things get that way, and what can parents do to counteract the situation? For answers, we have to look beyond the kiddie lingerie aisle.

Stay Tuned for Mature Content

The sexy-girl trend didn't start overnight. "I trace it to the mid-1980s, when children's television was deregulated, allowing TV shows to market products to kids," says Diane Levin, PhD, of Wheelock College in Boston and co-author of *So Sexy So Soon* (Ballantine Books). Companies noticed girls' love for ultra-feminine programs and their product tie-ins, and played it to the max. In the flush 1990s the media pushed harder, with the teen dial moving more toward sexy with sitcoms like *Saved by the Bell*.

Nowadays, "programs aimed at my daughter feature kids twice her age," complains Lisa Rinkus, of Newton, Massachusetts, mom of 9-year-old Elizabeth. "There's stuff like *Wizards of Waverly Place,* where girls dress up and go on dates." Even cartoons have become sexier. A recent study released by the Geena Davis Institute on Gender in Media found that female animated characters wear less clothing than male ones. And the current rash of reality TV shows like *America's Next Top Model* and *My Super Sweet 16* also fuel the fire.

The media onslaught extends to cyberspace as well, with an explosion of kids' interactive websites tied to TV shows like *iCarly* and *Hannah Montana.* "They push girls to further identify with these older, more mature girls," says Levin. And that's just the nice sites: One called "Miss Bimbo" gives girls a nearly naked doll to look after and urges them to score points redeemable for plastic surgery and skimpy clothes.

The Action behind the Scenes

Still, sex-tinged kids' TV has been around for a couple of decades. So why are girls today more precocious than just five years ago? Because a whole other pop culture avalanche has hit, experts say. For starters, we've got tons of teen idols now, including Miley Cyrus (the real-life Hannah Montana) and Demi Lovato, star of the Disney TV movie *Camp Rock.* "Even little kids look up to them," says M. Gigi Durham, author of *The Lolita Effect* (Overlook Press).

These teen stars and their characters may seem mild (say, compared with the Britneys, Lindsays and Jessicas in the headlines or even the adolescents on your block), but much of what they do and say is still over the top for tweens. "When younger girls watch them they see ways of behaving, looking, and feeling that would otherwise be outside their world," Levin says.

And now teen idols are also prime paparazzi fodder. As their personal slipups are relentlessly captured and widely publicized, even their littlest fan's consciousness is being raised in ways her parents hoped wouldn't happen for years. Donna Miller of Summit, New Jersey, faced this recently. Her daughter Lucie, 8, loves the show *Zoey 101,* whose star, Jamie Lynn Spears (Britney's sis), gave birth earlier this year at 17. "I tried to explain what was wrong with the whole situation," says Donna. "Lucie's answer was, 'But she and her boyfriend love each other, and you said love is important!' I think I communicated our family values about sex and babies in a way that didn't confuse Lucie. But she's so young. I'm not sure she understood all the nuances."

Parents are still the main influence on their daughters, but kids have got to be confused when bombarded with contradictory messages.

Certainly, fawning coverage of the birth didn't help clarify things for young fans. One tabloid cover featured a glowing picture of the teenage Spears cuddling with her daughter, calling motherhood "the best feeling in the world." Parents are still the main influence on their daughters, but kids have got to be confused when they're bombarded with contradictory messages.

Marketing Madness

If teen idols are a trap for young girls, it's partly because their princess obsession laid the groundwork. In 2007 sales of Disney princess products totaled $4 billion. "To parents, the princesses seem relatively wholesome," says Levin, "but they do convey the message that you should spend a lot of time, energy, and money on looking pretty." What's more insidious is the way girls use them. "Give a girl a princess-type doll and she often doesn't invent ways to play with it," says Levin. "Instead, she'll act out a fairy tale script, having learned that the princess should be beautiful and seductive and catch the prince." The more time a girl plays this way, the more she'll focus on looks and coquettish behavior, and the less time she'll spend doing the open-ended activities kids need. "It puts girls on a conveyor belt to early sexualization," Levin says.

And merchandizing linked to girls' idols doesn't stop with dolls. According to a report by the NPD Group, girls 8 to 12 years old now spend $500 million a year on beauty products of all kinds, including those endorsed by their idols. Then there are the flirty fashions. "Where are the age-appropriate clothes?" asks Marie Ortiz of San Antonio, mom of 8-year-old Karina. "Even the kids' fashions at mass retailers look like they're for mini Paris Hiltons." It's a coast-to-coast lament as mothers of girls shop among racks of child-size swimsuits with padded chests and slinky underwear for 8-year-olds.

Of course, when it comes to the 7-going-on-16 phenomenon, it's easy to point a finger of blame everywhere else, but we also have to take a hard look at ourselves. It's not that parents want to shirk being gatekeepers. "There's just so much sex around, it's easy to stop noticing and drawing the line," Durham explains. But we've got to try.

What's a Mom to Do?

Forget about overreacting. Sending your daughter to school in overalls, clutching your old prairie-skirted Holly Hobbie doll is like putting a giant "L" on her forehead and a "kick me" sign on her back. The idea is to help her live in the real world while preserving her innocence and honoring your family's morals. Try these tactics:

Cut back on the TV consumption. Her shows, your shows—just watch less. A 2005 Kaiser Family Foundation report found that the proportion of programs with sexual content rose from 54% to 70% between 1998 and 2005. And learn what the mysterious ratings at the start of kids' shows mean. Stuff tagged TV-Y or TV-G is the tamest. Other ratings require you to make a judgment call. You can get the scoop at fcc.gov/parents/parent_guide.html.

Teach your daughter how to think like a critic. When she does watch, try to join her. "That way when something questionable pops up, you can point it out," recommends

Where the Boys Are

While girls are getting trapped in a sexual pressure cooker, boys seem to steer clear of the worst of it. "I have 8-year-old boy-girl twins, and I see a huge difference," says Donna Miller of Summit, New Jersey. "My son doesn't feel the need to wear certain clothes like my daughter does." But there are some uncomfortable dynamics emerging. "I notice boys talking about girls being 'hot' earlier than they used to," says Richard Gallagher of the Parenting Institute of NYU. None of which, sadly, surprises him or other experts. "As girls are dressing provocatively at young ages, it's sparking the sexual inquisitiveness of younger boys," says Scott Haltzman, MD, a Brown University psychiatrist who specializes in gender issues.

Diane Levin, PhD, of Wheelock College, also sees negative sexual standards and messages in boys' toys and heroes. "The muscles on action toys have been getting bigger," she says. "It makes boys feel like they have to be rough instead of affectionate or tender. But those gentle qualities are what they'll need for developing good relationships in the future." Furthermore, says Gallagher, a sexually charged kids' culture can make it hard for a young boy to befriend a female classmate. "If he's afraid his buddies and the girl's friends are going to taunt them, saying, 'Ooh, what are you guys up to?' he often decides it's not worth it," he explains.

The solutions? They're not so different from what they are for girls. Tone down the sex-stereotype toys and be selective about what your sons watch on TV. "So many music videos show a guy surrounded by lots of girls, which sends boys the message that sexy equals cool," Haltzman says. And don't automatically assume your son would never hang out with a girl from his class. "At least suggest it and see what he says," advises Gallagher. It could help him like and respect girls as individuals.

Durham. Levin suggests regularly exposing the ridiculous or unrealistic sides of on-screen scenarios. For instance, you could try, "Don't you wonder how London gets her homework done when she spends so much time in front of the mirror?"

Monitor Web choices. Just because a website is linked to a TV show doesn't mean it's healthy or wholesome. Try bookmarking a few quality sites like pbskids.org or starfall.com, which are chockablock with fun learning games. "Be picky," says Maria Bailey, founder of bluesuitmom.com, an advice site for employed moms. "Thirty four percent of children will visit some kind of social networking or vitual-world website this year." One new option about to be launched is the Precious Girls Club social network, where girls can earn points for engaging in kind behavior (preciousgirlsclub.com).

Promote other kinds of idols. Show your daughter women she can admire for what they do, not for how they look, advises Richard Gallagher, PhD, director of the Parenting Institute at the Child Study Center of New York University. You could take her to a community musical and afterward meet the actress whose singing she loved. Or how about attending a local women's basketball game, where she can give the high-scorer postgame congratulations? And even if you aren't a fan of every female on the political scene, point out how cool it is that women are so prominent there.

Help her explore her talents and interests. Whether it's tennis or chess, being good at something gives girls confidence. "Sports especially are great," advises Levin. "They help girls value their bodies for what they're able to do, not for how pretty they look."

> "Sports especially are great. They help girls value their bodies for what they can do, not for how pretty they look."
> —Diane Levin

Hold the line on makeup and glittery clothes. "It's not enough to just say no," warns Levin. "Your daughter will be exposed to these things anyway, and if you clamp down entirely, it'll only set the stage for her to rebel later on." Instead she suggests moderation. If your daughter begs for a cropped top, for instance, layer it over a longer tee or tank, or let her wear it only at home.

Mix up her peer group. Invite over a kid from another class in her grade, or sign her up for an activity that isn't school-based (such as karate or art). Spending time with other kids, other ideas, other ways of doing things widens a girl's world and reduces the pressure on her to follow the crowd.

Guide the gift-giving. Tell grandparents and other relatives that you're trying to hold back on the sexy stuff, says Levin. Ideally, they'll shop more sensitively.

Personally, I'm taking all of this advice and using it with my daughter. I've been questioning what we're seeing on her favorite TV shows, as well as her fervent desire, sympathetic though I may feel, to emulate her fashion-forward classmates right down to their underwear.

And in case you're wondering whether I got her that bra, I'll admit I thought about it. But then I said no. "That's for when you're older," I told her. Then I took her to our community rec department and signed her up for our town's soccer league. Five weeks later I stood at the edge of a field, screaming like crazy as she scored her very first goal.

That, not a bra, is the kind of support young girls really need.

Critical Thinking

1. List some of the "props" sold to 7-year-old girls to make them look 16.

2. Discuss reasons why 7-year-olds should act and look their own age.

3. Identify ways to help children enjoy childhood while they have it.

Engaging Young Children in Activities and Conversations about Race and Social Class

While Philip is making a restaurant in the block area he boasts, "It's gonna cost $200 just to get in!" The teacher sitting near him holds up a few small dolls and asks in a quiet voice, "What about my family? They don't have any money." Philip hesitates and looks downcast for a few moments. Then he brightens up and says, "I know, We'll pay for them!"

REBEKKA LEE, PATRICIA G. RAMSEY, AND BARBARA SWEENEY

Conversations are a vital part of early childhood antibias and multicultural education because they enable children to connect with others and to begin to see the implications of certain assumptions, as Philip did when he realized that some people could not afford to eat at his expensive restaurant. However, engaging children in these conversations is not always easy. No matter what the question, children frequently resist answering adults, and for some, concerns about race and social class may seem distant or even irrelevant.

This article describes a project in which the authors observed kindergarten children's responses to specific antibias and multicultural activities to see which materials and teaching practices most frequently elicited meaningful conversations. We chose activities that focused on race and social class because many teachers find these issues difficult to address with young children and sometimes choose to work with "safer" topics, such as gender, disabilities, and culture (Ramsey 2006).

Because young children think in concrete terms and rely on their immediate experiences, many adults assume that young children are "color blind" to race and oblivious to economic disparities. However, studies spanning several decades have shown that children notice racial cues during infancy (Kelly et al. 2007) and that, by the age of 3 or 4, most children have a rudimentary concept of race (Katz 1976; Ramsey & Meyers 1990; Katz & Kofkin 1997; Van Ausdale & Feagin 2001; Katz 2003; Ramsey & Williams 2003). Many preschoolers also have learned that some people are "rich" and others are "poor" and associate concrete items such as certain types of clothing, homes, and possessions with each group (Leahy 1983; Ramsey 1991; Chafel 1997; Lee 2004). Children's relatively early cognitive development makes it difficult for them to discern between accurate depictions and stereotypes about race and social class prevalent in the media and in their communities (Aboud 1988; Van Ausdale & Feagin 2001; Katz 2003).

Reflecting this research, the NAEYC Early Childhood Program Standards and Accreditation Criteria (2005) advocate developmentally and culturally appropriate practices, which are supported by an abundance of suggested curricula in antibias/multicultural textbooks and programs. Unfortunately, there are very few systematic studies on the effects of these programs at any grade level, and those studies that have been conducted in early childhood settings have relied on anecdotal data.

These studies do, however, offer some insights into the effectiveness of various approaches. Some suggest that the "tourist approach"—simply exposing children to materials that represent different groups (such as diverse dolls, foods, clothing, and pictures)—does not stimulate substantive conversations or challenge children's attitudes (Day 1995; Aboud & Levy 2000; Lee & Lee 2001; Pfeifer, Brown, & Juvonen 2007). In contrast, other studies have shown that, when encouraged with meaningful activities and questions, children often do express, compare, and challenge their views and discuss social justice issues among themselves and with teachers (Marsh 1992; Levine 1993; Reeder, Douzenis, & Bergin 1997; de Marquez 2002; Chafel, Flint, Hammel, & Pomeroy 2007). These findings support a recurring theme in the NAEYC Early Childhood Program Standards that encourages teachers to engage children in explorations and discussions about many topics, including diversity (see accreditation criteria 1.D.01, 1.B. 15, 2.L.03, 2.L.06 [NAEYC 2005]).

Simulations in which children experience firsthand the effects of discrimination, such as Jane Elliott's well-known "Blue Eyes/Brown Eyes" exercise (Peters 1987), have elicited strong emotional reactions, intense conversations, and reevaluations of assumptions (McGregor 1993; Pfeifer, Brown, & Juvonen 2007). Despite the impact of such simulations, intensive role-playing activities have not been replicated in recent years, in part because current federal guidelines prohibit research projects that cause distress in children (Aboud & Levy 2000). However, shorter, lower intensity simulations that cause less discomfort are allowed and have the potential to stimulate conversations about the effects of stereotypes and inequities.

> **When encouraged with meaningful activities and questions, children often do express, compare, and challenge their views and discuss social justice issues among themselves and with teachers.**

Because conversations help uncover and challenge children's assumptions, it is important to systematically assess which activities are most likely to spark discussions about race and social class. To this end, we conducted a study in a kindergarten classroom. There were five girls and eight boys in the classroom. One child was Asian, one was biracial (African American and White), and 11 were White. Children were mostly middle class and lived in a suburban community. For this study, we implemented a series of antibias and multicultural activities (see "Materials and Activities") during the month of January and closely observed and reacted to children's responses. We increased the novelty of the relevant materials by removing some of them (skin-tone markers, for example) from the classroom for the month prior to the observation period. Then in January, two teachers introduced materials and activities while observing the children's initial reactions-including level of interest, aspects of the materials they seemed to notice, and the types of questions they asked. Based on the children's responses, the teachers modified the activities (when possible), added elements to make the activities more complex, and/or asked open-ended questions to encourage more meaningful discussion.

The teachers recorded field notes throughout each day. After each activity, they discussed their experiences and compiled a summary of the children's responses to the activities. Two trained undergraduate observers (who were not teaching) recorded detailed accounts of children's responses and their interactions with each other and the teachers. At the end of the month, the research team collated the observations and field notes into one chronological document with all the reports about each activity clustered together.

Next, the team categorized each activity by type: art, stories, puzzles and games, or role play. The first author and a fifth researcher (who did not participate in any of the teaching or observations and so had no preconceived ideas about the curriculum) read and coded the materials and identified which activities attracted and engaged children, triggered conversations related to race and social class, and/or helped children begin to express and challenge their assumptions.

Materials and Activities

Art

- Skin-tone crayons, markers, and paints provided in the art area
- Displays of contemporary and realistic images of children and adults from a range of racial groups
- Portraits of themselves and others
- Handprints
- Illustrations for a book about differences
- Family college

Stories

- Books and songs focusing on the themes of similarities and differences among people and families. Examples include
  - *Amazing Grace,* by Mary Hoffman
  - *Dear Juno,* by Soyung Pak
  - *The Talking Cloth,* by Rhonda Mitchell
  - *All the Colors of the Earth,* by Sheila Hamanaka
  - *Black, White, Just Right!* by Marguerite Davol

Puzzles and Games

- Concentration game with children's faces
- Life-size child puzzles
- Puzzles depicting a range of racial groups, families, occupations (some challenging gender roles)

Role Play

- 30 small multiracial, multiage dolls
- Play houses representing different levels of affluence (small, large, apartment style)
- Store simulation with unequal resources

Art Activities

During the observation period, the art area featured skin-tone markers and paints and color photographs of people from different racial groups. At first, the teachers simply added these new materials to the art area and observed children's comments and their choice of colors for free drawing activities. Then they encouraged children to use the materials to make portraits of themselves and others-often drawing children's attention to the displayed images.

> **Art activities can familiarize children with skin tones and help them begin to differentiate subtle distinctions in tone and hue.**

Over the course of the month, several children appeared to become more conscious of their own skin tones and the spectrum of skin colors, both among their peers and in the photographs. For example, at first, more than half of the White children chose orange, rather than more accurate peach and beige tones, to depict their skin. Others used their favorite colors, such as purple and green, regardless of their skin tones. In contrast, by the end of the observation period, children used the skin-tone markers more frequently and were able to determine what was (and was not) a skin color. At one point, Jake, looking at a commercially packaged box of "skin-tone" crayons that included white and black crayons, asked, "Why are all these colors together?" The teacher replied, "They all could be the colors of people's skin." Jake quickly answered, "The black and white ones don't belong."

At the end of the month we introduced a handprint activity, during which children identified paints that matched their own skin tone and those of children depicted in the images displayed in the classroom. The children then chose two skin-tone colors and painted them onto the palms of their hands, each child making two unique handprints. During this activity children readily differentiated subtle skin colors. For example, while closely comparing his hand with his teacher's, Silas remarked, "You have the same body color as me. Everybody has different body colors. My mom is peach."

Children's emotional reactions to the shades of brown also shifted. In the early days of the curriculum, several students avoided using brown tones during free art activities or indicated that they were less attractive than other colors. Jake said to Kyle, who was using a beige marker, "You can use a beautiful color instead," and pointed to a pink marker. Later in the month, children referred to the brown-hued paints in much more positive terms. Silas said, "I'm using caramel. I love caramel." Peter remarked, "It looks like cocoa . . . beautiful." Children also used the skin-tone colors more freely for a range of art projects. Sally made a rainbow using peach and two tones of brown.

These changes in children's reactions suggest that art activities can familiarize children with skin tones and help them begin to differentiate subtle distinctions in tone and hue. Moreover, this exposure can potentially counteract the aversion to darker colors that is prevalent in our society (for example, the common use of *black* and *dark* to describe negative objects, people, and events) and that children frequently express.

For another project, a teacher created several books that children could "write" according to their own interests and experiences. Each book contained the same outline of a story about a newcomer to the classroom who is different from her or his new classmates. Children then worked one-on-one with a teacher to adapt and illustrate the story. The children drew the requested pictures but did not seem very engaged and rarely added to the story or asked questions. In reviewing the observations of this activity, we concluded that it was too structured and didactic, thus stifling rather than engaging children's creativity and curiosity.

Books

During the observation month the teachers read several books with multicultural themes during circle time. After each story, the teachers asked the children open-ended questions about what they learned from the book. The impact of the books varied. In some cases (such as with *Dear Juno,* by Soyung Pak, and *All the Colors of the Earth,* by Sheila Hamanaka), children listened attentively but did not say much in the follow-up discussion beyond commenting on certain events or illustrations in the book. One book that did elicit a lively conversation was *Happy Birthday, Martin Luther King* (see "Discussing Martin Luther King Jr."). Since we read the book in January, the children had talked about Martin Luther King Jr. at school and, in some cases, at home, so the book related to ongoing discussions and activities. During their conversation about the book, children explored and refined their understanding of the events of the civil rights movement. Several children mentioned information they had learned from their families, illustrating the benefits of engaging children in discussions both at home and at school and using books to develop and support ongoing themes.

When considering why some books elicited more conversations than others, we noted that a clear story line and familiar themes or people (such as Martin Luther King Jr.) seemed to lead to more discussion. One way to spark conversations about books that, do not have a clear story line, such as *All the Colors of the Earth,* is to stop frequently, reread pages, and ask children to elaborate with their own images and words. Moreover, reading in small groups and encouraging children to take the lead in discussions (Cowhey 2006) and to connect the stories to their own lives and experiences (Chafel et al. 2007) may promote more in-depth conversations.

Puzzles and Games

Throughout the month of our study we introduced a number of puzzles featuring people in various occupations and children and adults of both genders from a range of racial and age groups. As with the art activities, teachers put out the materials and observed children's initial reactions. The children liked the puzzles but primarily focused on completing them rather than talking about the people depicted in them, even after the teachers asked questions about the content of the puzzles.

A Concentration-like game, which involved matching eight pairs of identical photographs of children representing different racial and gender groups, was more effective in sparking children's conversations and challenging their perceptions. The game drew children's attention to within-race differences and complemented the art activities that explored skin tones and faces. Initially, the White kindergartners matched the photographs of the White children easily but often erroneously paired different African American or Asian American children, suggesting they might see all children in those groups as identical.

When teachers observed children making these mistakes, they asked the children to look more closely. Usually the children identified the false match and corrected themselves. In contrast to his White peers, Nigel, the one biracial child in the class, made all of the matches correctly the first time and often pointed out the mistakes in others' matches. When one classmate started to pair two different African American girls, Nigel quickly corrected him, pointing to one of the pictures and saying, "No, she has browner skin."

Discussing Martin Luther King Jr.

Silas: I know who he was. Black people had to sit on the bus, so he had to stop the bad things that were happening.

Nigel [correcting Silas's account]: Black people had to sit in the back of the bus. Martin Luther King Jr. had to stop that.

Cassandra: The white-skinned people sat in the front, and the black-skinned people sat in the back.

Kyle: No, they [White people] sat wherever they wanted.

When the teacher read the part of the book describing how King was shot, the children made comments such as, "The bad person didn't want the rules to change" and "The bad man shot him because he did not like what he was saying." Several other children joined in, and others raised their hands . . .

This game appealed to children and helped them to differentiate among individuals in various racial groups. However, once children had learned to make the matches successfully, they stopped engaging in the activity. To maintain their interest, we could have added pictures and introduced children to an ever-widening range of physical differences to keep the game challenging.

Role play

During the first week of the observation period, the teachers placed 30 small rubber dolls (male and female of varying races and ages) near two identical wooden playhouses usually available in the classroom. They encouraged the children to play with the dolls in any way they wanted. Interestingly, almost all of the children formed multiracial families. (See "Playing with Dolls" for a teacher's description of two girls playing with the dolls.)

During the second week, the children painted three cardboard dwellings constructed by the teachers to represent different levels of affluence: an apartment house, a small single-family house, and a large single-family house. When the teachers moved the dolls over to these new houses, the children

Playing with Dolls

Both girls picked up many dolls—Black, Hispanic, White, and Asian, little and big—and added them to the house to eat dinner. Eva declared that a Black baby doll and a white little girl doll were sisters and also said that the Asian woman was the grandmother. All the dolls sat down and ate dinner together.

A Child's View of Poverty

Billy: He has no bed because he does not have enough cash to buy a bed.

Teacher: Why does he not have enough cash?

Billy: Because he is not a rich man . . . because he just got fired. That's the only job he liked. He has no money left. He used the money up and got all the food he can. He eats just one bite of everything. He only has $1 and they [the beds] are usually $25.

continued to form multiracial families and moved them in and out of the houses as they had before. None of the children's actions or comments suggested they were making any connection between race and social class. However, the houses did evoke a few conversations about economic disparities.

For example, Billy and the teacher talked about a man living in the small house (see "A Child's View of Poverty,"). For Billy, the variable sizes of the dwellings triggered a vision of what poverty entails. Because the teacher supported but did not lead the conversation, Billy could express his own ideas about the concrete effects of poverty-limited access to food, possessions, and jobs.

Not all children had such a sophisticated economic interpretation. One child simply focused on the sizes of the houses and put all the children in the smallest house because it was the "baby house." Other children's responses revealed the standard of affluence in this middle-class group (for example, pointing to the large house and saying, "I want that regular house"). Likewise, the children showed little experience with apartments, often turning the apartment house into a school or even into a jail. The house and family role-playing activity sparked only a few conversations about social class. We wondered, if we had involved the children in building the houses (perhaps providing different amounts of materials to construct them), rather than just inviting children to paint them, would the children have talked more about the concrete implications of having varying amounts of resources?

One child simply focused on the sizes of the houses and put all the children in the smallest house because it was the "baby house."

In an effort to draw children's attention more explicitly to the impact of economic disparities, the teachers set up a store in which items had specific prices. The children went shopping in small groups, and individuals received different amounts of play money for their purchases. It didn't take the children long to discover the consequences of having more or less money, and several announced that the situation was "not fair." During

Reflecting on Money

Kyle, Ashley, and Billy suggested sharing the food with the group after each shopping trip. Eva, Jake, and Corey argued that the group should redistribute the money more evenly. Jake was adamant on this point, saying, "Everyone should have two [dollars]" and "I want to play the fair and square way."

Recommendations for Activities and Teaching Practices

- Provide a wide variety of materials and activities that appeal to both boys and girls and to different interests and learning styles
- Balance familiarity and novelty to stimulate curiosity and questions
- Use active, hands-on experiences and open-ended activities to encourage children to express their own ideas
- Develop materials and simulations that elicit surprise, curiosity, and disequilibrium
- Encourage dialogue among children with novel materials and open-ended questions
- Observe children's responses closely, and continually modify activities and approaches to encourage their emerging interests and to challenge misinformation that they reveal
- Use small groups, rather than large circle times, for in-depth conversations
- Facilitate rather than direct discussion, and encourage free flowing conversations and interactions among peers
- Balance imparting values with encouraging exploration—avoid moralizing
- Develop themes that encompass books, songs, puzzles, and classroom displays
- Involve families in activities in order to mutually support home and school efforts.

small group follow-up discussions, the children expressed indignation and offered a number of solutions. (See "Reflecting on Money" for the teacher's field notes.)

More general discussions about economics and social class developed from the store activity as children shared their ideas and questions about where money comes from, how it relates to having a job, and what happens when someone has zero dollars.

Implications for Teaching

The children's responses to this antibias/multicultural curriculum support previous research findings; the children noticed differences and expressed a range of ideas about race and social class. The fact that their responses varied across situations suggests that specific activities and teaching practices induce different types of inquiry and learning. The visually oriented activities (such as the art projects and concentration game) led to the most conversations about physical attributes-including race-while the role-play activities (particularly the store) generated the most discussions about discrimination and inequity.

In a few cases, children did challenge the status quo (for example, questioning why the box of skin-tone crayons included black and white crayons, discussing the unfairness of the store activity). Not surprisingly, children talked more when actively engaged (for example, while drawing and painting, enacting roles, or playing games) than they did when they were in more passive roles (such as listening to a story in a large group). The observations also suggest that materials such as puzzles and books stimulate more discussion when they are connected to ongoing and familiar themes.

Gender seemed to play a role because the activities appealed more to girls than to boys. Girls more often volunteered to go to the areas with the art materials and dolls, whereas the boys had to be encouraged to participate. However, once boys became engaged in the activities, they tended to be more outspoken than the girls. This pattern may be a function of the individuals in this particular class, but it also suggests that the girls have begun to absorb the gender-typed role that females should "be polite" and not mention differences. Thus, a challenge for teachers is to develop activities that appeal to both boys and girls (such as building different types of dwellings) while simultaneously encouraging girls to be more forthcoming about their thoughts, feelings, and questions related to differences and inequities.

The level and type of teacher involvement was also critical. As found in previous research (for example, Day 1995;

Aboud & Levy 2000; Lee & Lee 2001), simply providing multicultural materials did not stimulate that much conversation or challenge children's ideas. Conversely, if teachers were too directive, then children were less engaged, as we saw in the book illustration project. The children explored issues in greater depth when the teachers created situations that evoked curiosity and/or disequilibrium and then facilitated, rather than directed, the discussions. Sometimes the teachers could not take advantage of teachable moments because, at the time, they were preoccupied with time constraints or logistics. They either did not see a particular question or, action or were not able to shift gears quickly enough to respond. Thus, one future priority is to organize activities so that teachers can closely observe children's behaviors and have the flexibility to pursue unexpected questions and comments.

Overall, this study shows that anti-bias and multicultural activities do have the potential to raise questions and stimulate meaningful conversations among children and teachers and that specific materials and teaching practices evoke different types of inquiry. Given the small size of this study, we cannot generalize these patterns to a wide range of children and classrooms. However, the study indicates that when teachers closely observe their particular children's interests and responses, they gain rich information to use in the development of meaningful activities. We hope this project will encourage teachers and researchers to collaborate to study the effects of particular anti-bias and multicultural activities and practices so they can plan and implement them in nuanced and effective ways.

References

Aboud, F.E. 1988. *Children and prejudice.* New York Blackwell.

Aboud, F.E., & S.R. Levy. 2000. Interventions to reduce prejudice and discrimination in children and adolescents. In *Reducing prejudice and discrimination,* ed. S. Oskamp, 269–94. Mahwah, NJ: Erlbaum.

Chafel, J.A. 1997. Children's views of poverty: A review of research and implications for teaching. *Educational Forum* 6l (4): 360–71.

Chafel, J.A, A.S. Flint, J. Hammel, & K.H. Pomeroy. 2007. Young children, social issues, and critical literacy: Stories of teachers and researchers. *Young Children* 62 (l): 73–81.

Cowhey, M. 2006. *Black ants and Buddhists: Thinking critically and teaching differently in the primary grodes.* Portland, ME: Stenhouse.

Day, J.A.E. 1995. Multicultural resources in preschool provision— An observational study. *Early Child Development and Care* 110 (June): 47–68.

de Marquez, T.M. 2002. Creating world peace, one classroom at a time. *Young Children* 57 (6): 90–93.

Katz, P.A. 1976. The acquisition of racial attitudes in children. In *Towards the elimination of racism,* ed. P.A. Katz, 125–154. New York: Pergamon.

Katz, P.A. 2003. Racists or tolerant multiculturalists? How do they begin? *American Psychologist* 58 (11): 897–909.

Katz, P.A., & J.A. Kofkin. 1997. Race, gender, and young children. In *Developmental perspectives on risk and pathology,* eds. S. Luthar, J. Burack, D. Cicchetti, & J. Weisz, 51–74. New York: Cambridge University Press.

Kelly, D.J., S. Liu, L. Ge, P.C. Quinn, A.M. Slater, K. Lee, Q. Liu, & O. Pascalis. 2007. Cross-race preferences for same-race faces extend beyond the African versus Caucasian contrast in 3-month-old infants. *Infancy* 11 (l): 87–95.

Leahy, R.L. 1983. The development of the conception of social class. In *The child's construction of social inequality,* ed. R.L. Leahy, 79–107. New York: Academic Press.

Lee, R. 2004. Developing measures to learn how multicultural activities affect children's attitudes about race and social class. Senior honors thesis. Mount Holyoke College.

Lee, C.E., & D. Lee. 2001. Kindergarten geography: Teaching diversity to young people. *Journal of Geography* 100 (5): 152–57.

Levine, L. 1993. "Who says?" Learning to value diversity in school. In *Celebrating diverse voices: Progressive education and equity,* eds. F. Pignatelli & S.W. Pflaum, 87–111. Newbury Park, CA: Corwin Press.

Marsh, M.M. 1992. Implementing antibias curriculum in the kindergarten classroom. In *Reconceptualizing the early childhood curriculum: Beginning the dialogue,* eds. S.A. Kessler & B.B. Swadener, 267–88. New York: Teachers College Press.

NAEYC. 2005. NAEYC Early Childhood Program Standards and Accreditation Criteria. www.naeyc.org/academy/standards

Peters, W. 1987. *A class divided: Then and now.* Exp. ed. New Haven, CT: Yale University Press.

Pfeifer, J.H., C.S. Brown, & J. Juvonen. 2007. Teaching tolerance in schools: Lessons learned since Brown v. Board of Education about the development and reduction of children's prejudice. *Social Policy Report* 2l (2):3–23.

Ramsey, P.G. 1991. Young children's awareness and understanding of social class differences. *Journal of Genetic Psychology* 152: 71–82.

Ramsey, P.G. 2006. Early childhood multicultural education. In *Handbook of research on the education of young children,* 2nd ed., eds. B. Spodek & O.N. Saracho, 279–301. Mahwah, NJ: Erlbaum.

Ramsey, P.G., & L.C. Meyers. 1990. Salience of race in young children's cognitive, affective, and behavioral responses to social environments. *Journal of Applied Developmental Psychology* 11: 49–67.

Ramsey, P.G., & L.R. Williams. 2003. *Multicultural education: A source book.* 2nd ed. New York: Routledge.

Reeder, J., C. Douzenis, & J.J. Bergin. 1997. The effects of small group counseling on the racial attitudes of second grade students. *Professional School Counseling* 1 (2):15–18.

Van Ausdale, D., & J.R. Feagin. 2001. *The first R: How children learn race and racism.* Lanham, MD: Rowman & Littlefield.

Critical Thinking

1. Identify reasons why young children should talk about race and social class.

2. Propose home and school activities which stimulate discussions about diversity.

3. Explain how political correctness/incorrectness affects children's behaviors.

Rebekka Lee, BA, is an MS candidate and research assistant in the Harvard School of Public Health's Department of Society, Human Development, and Health. She investigated the impact of antibias curriculum on young children's attitudes as part of her undergraduate thesis at Mount Holyoke College. rlee@mtholyoke.edu **Patricia G. Ramsey,** EdD, is a professor of psychology and education at Mount Holyoke College in South Hadley, Massachusetts. She has worked with children and teachers in developing early childhood multicultural curricula and practices and has published several articles and books in this area. pramsey@mtholyoke.edu **Barbara Sweeney,** MS, is associate director and kindergarten teacher at Gorse Child Study Center, the lab school for the Department of Psychology and Education at Mount Holyoke College. Barbara has participated in many student and faculty research projects in her classroom at the center.

An expanded version of this article is available online in Beyond the Journal, November 2008, at www.journal.naeyc.org/btj/200811.

Use the Science of What Works to Change the Odds for Children at Risk

The federal government should heed seven essential principles when it invests in breaking the cycle of disadvantage.

SUSAN B. NEUMAN

Dating back to President Lyndon Johnson's War on Poverty, Americans have relied on federal dollars to tackle our most intractable issues in education. For example, the federal government helped support school integration, recognize the needs of handicapped and challenged children, and provide for the "least restrictive environments" in classrooms. The federal push for early education led to Head Start, a program targeted to the preschool years. Federal funds also helped to defray the costs of college, allowing even the poorest student to get a high-quality college degree. In these and other cases, federal funds have provided a safety net, a kind of "emergency response system," a means of filling in the gaps when critical national priorities and needs arise that go beyond the means of individual states and local supports for education.

The federal government must once again step up to the challenge. Today, despite the great wealth for some in this nation, nearly one out of every five American children lives in poverty—one of the highest poverty rates in the developed world (Neuman 2008b). And even though our schools are in the midst of the most major and costly education reform in their history and are grappling with the federal mandates to leave no child behind, any influence a school might have is trumped by this reality. The single best determinant of a school's likely output is a single input—the characteristics of the entering children. The painful truth is that we have done almost nothing to raise or change the trajectory of achievement for our disadvantaged children.

The single best determinant of a school's likely output is a single input—the characteristics of the entering children.

The idea that schools, by themselves, can't cure educational inequity is hardly astonishing, but much of our political discourse is implicitly predicated on the notion that schools can do it alone. The national conversation has almost exclusively targeted schools as if they were the source of the problem, as well as the sole solution. The fact that 6.7% of our country's population lives in the very poorest and most vulnerable census tracts with higher proportions of very young children and higher rates of single parenting and less-educated adults, and that it is in these very same census tracts where schools supposedly are failing miserably to close the achievement gap has seemed to be lost in the ongoing conversation (Browning 2003). Expecting teachers to overcome a 30-million-word gap between high- and low-income children (Hart and Risley 2003) in kindergarten alone is beyond optimistic. It is nonsensical. Regardless of what political aisle you stand on, fixing schools has become the cure to everything but the common cold, erasing all debate about the devastating effects of entrenched poverty and what to do about it.

Good schools can go a long way toward helping poor children achieve more, but the fact remains that educational inequity is rooted in economic problems and social pathologies too deep to be overcome by school alone. Even as we work to reform schools as if there were no limits to their powers, our only hope to break the cycle of disadvantage lies outside their influence.

Ending the cycle of disadvantage requires prevention and early intervention programs that help families who are desperately struggling to do the best for their children. Childcare, family support, and community-based programs working in public settings and social service agencies are a critical part of the "closing the gap" equation. But they are not nearly enough. If we're truly serious about breaking cycles of poverty, inequality, and limited opportunity that place enormous constraints on our nation's resources, we need to recognize and appropriately support education whether it is delivered in clinics, childcare centers, community-based organizations, libraries, church basements, or storefronts. By using the science of what works, we can change the odds, helping create a more promising future for millions of children growing up in vulnerable circumstances.

Research over the last 30 years has pointed to seven essential principles for breaking the cycle of disadvantage:

- Target interventions to children who need help the most;
- Begin early;
- Engage highly trained professionals;
- Provide intensive interventions;
- Coordinate health, education, and social services;
- Provide compensatory instructional benefits; and
- Be accountable.

How We Can Change the Odds

There is the story of 86 young children growing up in a small rural town in the Southeast in the 1960s. The families were black and poor. Isolated both geographically and socially from the larger community and the beginning stirrings of the civil rights movement, these children were about to attend segregated schools. They seemed destined to follow in their parents' footsteps—a life of poverty, discrimination, and disadvantage.

But here the predictable trajectory for what we might expect for these children took on a different, more positive twist. By age 20, these children were neither on welfare nor delinquent or indigent. Instead, most had completed high school, and a few had gone on to college. Tracking their progress, Susan Gray and her colleagues (1982) tell the story of these children's lives, their schooling, and their experiences as participants in an early intervention program, a preschool program fashioned to help children advance through school with greater success.

During the turbulent years of the late 1950s and early 1960s, a group of academics, psychologists, and social scientists began to challenge the prevailing view that ability and achievement were immutable. Recognizing the all-too-consistent correlation between poverty and achievement, these researchers realized that intellectual development couldn't possibly relate solely to the child's inherent ability. Intellectual ability had to relate to the environment. To explore this notion of "intellectual plasticity," a series of experimental early intervention programs began throughout the country, all sharing the presumption that environmental factors must play an important role in children's cognitive and social-emotional development and that early intervention could have significant, positive, long-term effects.

Susan Gray and her colleagues at Vanderbilt University took up the challenge in what became known as the Early Training Project. Identifying characteristics of early experience that related to educability, she developed an intervention designed to offset the cumulative deficits for these three-year-olds, targeting language, concept development, and motivation. Setting up an intensive summer camp program, highly experienced expert teachers worked with children in small groups, supporting their perceptual and cognitive skills and attitudes related to achievement.

Nevertheless, soon it became clear that even 10 weeks in the highest quality program could hardly overcome the economic hardships that children had accumulated, even at three years old. So she developed a home visiting program, enlisting mature women with certified experience in early education to make weekly hour-long visits with the children and parents in an effort to bridge what had been learned from one summer to the next. These home visits weren't just about teaching, but about enlisting the mothers' emotional support for helping their children learn, explore, and communicate, with the goal of eventually meeting school requirements. Over the next 2½ years, children from ages 3 to 6 and their families participated in these summer programs and winter visits.

Yet the resolute Gray and her colleagues charted children's progress far beyond these years. In fact, at regular intervals, she continued to measure their development until they were 20 years old. And strikingly, many of the gains that Gray and her colleagues reported were enduring, some for long periods of time. Children were able to meet school requirements, fewer were placed in special education, fewer were likely to be retained or drop out of high school. Even those who became pregnant as teens were more likely to return to school. As one mother remarked, "I wasn't going to let a little old baby keep me from graduatin' from high school."

There is another story, this time in the heart of the Rust Belt—Ypsilanti, Michigan, home to automobile manufacturing—where local school administrators, despite entreaties from local families, refused to adjust the curriculum to better serve their high-risk children. With high special education referrals and high school dropout rates soaring, 123 of the poorest children in the neighborhood were about to enter these settings with all the odds against their success.

However, David Weikart and his special service staff took things into their own hands (Weikart, Bond, and McNeil 1978). Checking the local census for who might be entering from the Perry School neighborhood, Weikart and his team walked door-to-door, identifying children most likely at risk for school failure. He found them in crowded residences with over twice the number of people you might expect in a typical household, their children's intelligence bordering only on educability (79 I.Q.), the parents unskilled and too beaten down to provide much encouragement for learning. Working against all odds, Weikart was determined to change those odds by developing what was unheard of at the time, a daily preschool program starting with three-year-olds along with regular visits to their families in homes. Over a period of either one or two years, specialists in early childhood involved small groups of children—no more than five or six at a time—to actively learn, think, plan, and express their ideas in language. Recognizing that children learn best through hands-on activities, such as sand and water play, teachers encouraged them to experiment with materials and talk about what they'd learned. They would ask "why" questions, like "Why might the cork float in water?" helping the children to discover new concepts on their own. In addition to turning around these children's lives, the enormous return on investment would be hard for an economist to ignore: 65% of these children graduated from high school, compared to only 45% of those not in the program; 61% got good jobs, compared to just 38% in the nonprogram group. The findings have remained stable some 27 years later.

Garber recognized that risk is a caution and not a condemnation, essentially proving that early intervention had the power to change children's lives.

Then there is another story that completely blows away the myth of equal opportunity for all children. In this case, the story is about 20 infants in Milwaukee, Wisconsin, born to severely low-functioning mothers. Each family's poverty conditions only exacerbated any hope for stimulation or learning. Examining surveys that yielded the likely trajectory for these children, all evidence amassed by Herb Garber (1988) suggested that by the time they entered school, these children would likely succumb to what was described as "induced retardation," declining functioning and cognitive processing skills.

Recognizing, perhaps for the first time, that disorganized multi-risk families face a level of disadvantage far different from poor but stable working families, Garber devised a two-generation program, foreshadowing others that would come later. Starting at about three months, infant caregivers helped prepare mothers and children, first visiting them for three to five hours three times a week, then transitioning them to center-based care, where the infants received seven hours of stimulating activities each day until they were four years old. At the same time, caregivers helped mothers learn basic home-management skills and got them enrolled in vocational education programs so that they could get jobs and responsibly take care of their children.

Garber's intervention effectively stopped the decline in children's cognitive development. He prevented the intergenerational transfer of risk and disadvantage. In fact, all experimental children whose mothers were mentally retarded performed at least 20 points higher than their mothers and averaged 32 points higher than did their own mothers. By providing an intensive program designed to compensate for what children were lacking in the home, Garber was able to offset the negative influences of an impoverished learning environment. By focusing on the single most important environmental influence—the intimate interaction between child and caregiver—he was able to help severely at-risk children avoid significant cognitive delays. He recognized that risk is a caution and not a condemnation, essentially proving that early intervention had the power to change children's lives.

Despite differences in location, population, and risk categories, each of these stories—backed by the solid scientific evidence that accompanies them (Consortium for Longitudinal Studies 1983; Shonkoff and Phillips 2000)—share some striking commonalities. Each recognized the extraordinary role that environment plays in children's development. Acknowledging its malleability, each modified the environment to maximize children's potential. Involving the primary caregivers in their children's education, each regarded the family as a learning unit that is a critical part of the solution.

Weaving these accounts together, however, illuminates an even more powerful story. Across these richly detailed programs is a set of principles for what is required to make a difference in the lives of highly vulnerable children. Recognizing the sense of urgency, these programs *targeted their efforts to children and families at greatest risk*. They *began early* in the child's development, engaging *highly trained professionals* to provide *intensive interventions,* operationally defining intensity as more hours, longer-term, and greater focus according to the family's needs. Together, these programs reached children and families where they were located, both psychologically and physically, through *comprehensive services,* realizing that a child who is suffering from Otis media (ear infections) and other illnesses can't possibly be successful in learning without relief from continuing pain. Furthermore, they recognized that the problem was not children's ability to learn, but the opportunities to learn, so they provided *compensatory instructional benefits* to make up for the cognitively and socially stimulating activities that many of these children lacked. Finally, all were *accountable,* using tangible, quantitative evidence and evaluations to examine whether they were achieving desired effects, adjusting when necessary in order to make that happen.

In essence, evident throughout these programs, and subsequently validated through research over the last 30 years (Bowman, Donovan, and Burns 2000; Farren 2000; Shonkoff and Phillips 2000), are seven essential principles for breaking the cycle of disadvantage:

- Target interventions to children who need help the most;
- Begin early;
- Engage highly trained professionals;
- Provide intensive interventions;
- Coordinate health, education, and social services;
- Provide compensatory instructional benefits; and
- Be accountable.

These stories, each better known by their project names and illustrative leaders—Susan Gray's Early Learning Project, David Weikart's Perry Preschool Project, and Herb Garber's Milwaukee Project—were originally conceived as research and demonstration projects and, as such, designed to examine the extent to which interventions, given adequate resources, a fully engaged and highly talented staff, and continuous and ongoing monitoring of progress, might affect the cognitive and social development of disadvantaged children. Capturing the public's attention even more than skill achievements, however, were the real life measures used in these reports, such as employment histories and declines in delinquency that, when combined with cost-benefit analysis, led to dramatic claims that early intervention was a highly sound investment, saving citizens an average of $7 for every dollar spent.

Together, they set a benchmark for what was possible, making a compelling case in public policy for early intervention and for the ways in which resources might be allocated for improving achievement for highly disadvantaged children.

The science of intervention has come a long way since these projects. Yet the principles remain the same. Programs that serve our most vulnerable children are tied to seven essentials and have a coherent and self consistent vision of pedagogy, curriculum, and structure. Interventions like the Nurse-Family

Partnership, Early Head Start, and Avance provide critical parent supports early on; Reach Out and Read and Books Aloud give important access to books in community wide programs in libraries and clinics; Core Knowledge and Bright Beginnings have programs that help children develop content-rich learning in developmentally appropriate ways (Neuman 2008*a*).

These programs and others like them provide demonstrable evidence that we can remove some of the most significant risk factors through systematic intervention and support. And this new knowledge can become the foundation of a broader, bolder new effort in education to change the odds of our most at risk children, reorienting the federal role in education to become the emergency response system it was designed to be.

References

Bowman, Barbara, Suzanne Donovan, and M. Susan Burns. *Eager to Learn: Educating Our Preschoolers.* Washington D.C.: National Academy Press, 2000.

Browning, Lynnley. "U.S. Income Gap Widening." *New York Times,* September 25, 2003, p. 10.

Consortium for Longitudinal Studies. *As the Twig Is Bent.* Hillsdale, N.J.: Lawrence Erlbaum Associates, 1983.

Farren, Dale C. "Another Decade of Intervention for Children Who Are Low Income or Disabled: What Do We Do Now?" In *Handbook of Early Childhood Intervention,* ed. Jack P. Shonkoff and Sam Meisels. New York: Cambridge University Press, 2000.

Garber, Herb. *The Milwaukee Project.* Washington, D.C.: American Association on Mental Retardation, 1988.

Gray, Susan W., Barbara K. Ramsey, and Rupert A. Klaus. *From 3 to 20: The Early Training Project.* Baltimore, Md.: University Park Press, 1982.

Hart, Betty, and Todd Risley. "The Early Catastrophe." *American Educator* 27 (Spring 2003): 4, 6–9.

Neuman, Susan B. *Changing the Odds for Children at Risk: Seven Essential Principles of Educational Programs That Break the Cycle of Poverty.* Westport, Conn.: Praeger, 2008. a

Neuman, Susan B., ed. *Educating the Other America: Top Experts Tackle Poverty, Literacy, and Achievement in Our Schools.* Baltimore, Md.: Brookes, 2008. b

Shonkoff, Jack P., and Deborah Phillips, eds. *From Neurons to Neighborhoods.* Washington, D.C.: National Academy Press, 2000.

Weikart, David, James T. Bond, and J.T. McNeil. *The Ypsilanti Perry Preschool Project.* Ypsilanti, Mich.: High/Scope, 1978.

Critical Thinking

1. Give examples of activities of daily life for children living in poverty.
2. Explain why children at-risk affect the school achievement of all students.
3. Suggest research-based solutions for high-low income inequality.

SUSAN B. NEUMAN is a professor of educational studies at the University of Michigan, Ann Arbor, Michigan.

Culture of Corpulence

America is the world's preeminent fat-making machine.

CLAUDIA KALB

L ook around anywhere in America and the reality assaults you: we are simply too big. Nowhere is the evidence for this more striking than the Centers for Disease Control and Prevention's color-coded obesity map. Between 1990 and 2008 the country morphs from a sea of pleasant blue, representing an obese population of less than 19 percent, to an alarming patchwork of tan, orange, and maroon, where the stats range from 21 percent obese in Connecticut to 32.8 percent in Mississippi.

The epidemic is most alarming among American children: rates have tripled among kids ages 12 to 19 since 1980, with one third of America's youth now overweight or obese and almost 10 percent of infants and toddlers dangerously heavy. Obese kids, defined by a body-mass index at or above the 95th percentile for children of the same age and sex, are at risk for developing conditions in childhood once monopolized by adults: high blood pressure, high cholesterol, and type 2 diabetes. And many are stigmatized and suffer from low self-esteem, which can lead to depression. If current trends continue, nearly one in three kids born in 2000—and one in two minorities—will develop type 2 diabetes in their lifetime, according to the American Diabetes Association. The disease is linked to heart attack, stroke, blindness, amputation, and kidney disease. Indeed, a study published last month found that obese children are more than twice as likely to die prematurely as adults than kids on the lower end of the weight spectrum. In the U.S., new government data show an overall plateau of high BMIs in kids over the last 10 years—a hopeful sign. But "even without further increases in childhood obesity, the toll of the epidemic will mount for decades to come," says Harvard's Dr. David Ludwig, director of the Optimal Weight for Life program at Children's Hospital Boston.

This goes way beyond fitting into our jeans or airline seats: the estimated annual cost of obesity in the United States is $147 billion. The problem even threatens our national security—being overweight is the No. 1 reason recruits are turned away from the military. Not so long ago, a lack of personal willpower was blamed. Today, obesity is considered a public-health threat, the toll of a toxic environment that endangers the well-being of our children and their future.

It's not just us, either. "Globesity" has consumed much of the planet, with more than 1 billion adults overweight or obese. And while we're not the fattest—Nauru, Micronesia, and a handful of other countries beat us—we're very close to the top of the list. Urbanization, modernization, technology, and the globalization of food markets, which includes the exportation of Coke and burgers, has created a crisis of "epidemic proportions," in the words of the World Health Organization.

But it's America that has become the world's preeminent fat-making machine. To dismantle it we need a coordinated, comprehensive plan of attack, one that pairs individual responsibility with a social construct that fosters good nutrition and a healthy lifestyle. We need to be surrounded by food that makes us well, not sick. We need schools and workplaces that reward us for exercising our bodies, not just our brains. "If you want people to make the right choices, they need to have the right choices to make," says Dr. William Dietz, director of the CDC's Division of Nutrition, Physical Activity, and Obesity. We need forceful and well-enforced policies, a government that invests dollars in improving the diet of school kids and puts limitations on the advertising that targets them. We need Americans to perceive obesity as a personal threat to themselves and to their children, not as somebody else's problem. We have a long way to go.

When McDonald's opened in the 1950s, a soda weighed seven ounces; today, 7-Eleven's 44-ounce Super Big Gulp has its own fan club on Facebook.

We got here through multiple innovations, many of them meant to improve, not corrupt, our lifestyles. Fast food is a quick fix for hungry working families. Cars and buses get kids to school faster than sidewalks. We have grown used to a world order of speed and convenience.

But with our processed diets come fat, sugar, and calories. And a lot of it. When McDonald's opened in the 1950s, a soda weighed seven ounces, according to a study in the *Journal of the American Dietetic Association;* today, 7-Eleven serves a behemoth 44-ounce Super Big Gulp, which has its own fan club on Facebook. Burger King's signature Whopper packs almost 700 calories. And research shows that the more we're served, the more we eat.

High-calorie, low-nutrient foods are ubiquitous—at gas stations, at airports, and at school, where it matters most for kids. The National School Lunch Program, signed into law in 1946 by President Harry Truman, was designed to feed hungry children who needed extra calories. Today it serves 31 million kids, most of whom don't. School meals, which are subsidized by the government, are subject to nutritional standards, but that doesn't always translate to apples and cucumbers. Almost 42 percent of schools do not offer any fresh fruits or raw vegetables on a daily basis.

Kids supplement, and often substitute, their lunches with "competitive foods." Vending machines, some stocked with cookies and sodas, exist in 17 percent of elementary schools, 82 percent of middle schools, and 97 percent of high schools. Most states have extremely weak standards or none at all when it comes to competitive foods, says Margo Wootan, director of nutrition policy at the Center for Science in the Public Interest. Mary Story, director of the Robert Wood Johnson Foundation's Healthy Eating Research, asks a simple question: if the average school day is only about six hours, why do snack foods or beverages need to be sold at all? If they are, she says, they should come from the food groups lacking in children's diets today: fruits, vegetables, low-fat and nonfat dairy, and whole grains.

Calories are not the entire problem. Exercise used to be built into the day; today it is an elite privilege for too many kids. With a focus on standards of learning propelled by the reading- and math-focused No Child Left Behind Act, many schools cannot afford, financially or academically, to offer physical education—even though studies show exercise can improve academic performance. The surgeon general recommends at least 60 minutes of moderate physical activity a day most days of the week for kids; two thirds of high schoolers fail to get it. Too many boys and girls end up wired instead: 8- to

18-year-olds spend an average of seven and a half hours a day multitasking in front of TVs, videogames, or computers.

Our suburban designs, influenced by age-old zoning laws, also work against us. A century ago, residential neighborhoods were separated from workplace factories to spare people from breathing in soot. Fast-forward to 2010: we live in subdivisions and drive to shopping centers and office parks. Biking and walking have been "systematically taken out of our lives," says Jim Sallis, director of the RWJF's Active Living Research program.

Exercise used to be built into the day; now, kids spend 50-plus hours a week in front of TVs, videogames, and computers.

We've battled public-health crises before by collecting data, raising public awareness, and passing tough laws. Everybody must now wear seat belts, kids must be buckled into car seats, and drunken driving is an offense punishable by jail. Winning the war on obesity demands the same kind of big-think solution and the determination to take on and also collaborate with powerful interests. It will require time, money, and both individual and political will to undo or rework what got us here.

Aware that it has a public-relations problem, the food industry is taking steps to show it can be part of the solution without help from government regulators. "We have changed the recipes for more than 10,000 of our products to reduce fat, calories, sugar, and sodium," says Scott Faber of the Grocery Manufacturers Association. Salads are now routinely offered at fast-food chains; KFC introduced grilled chicken last year (one grilled wing, 80 calories; one extra-crispy fried, 190). Coke debuted a mini 7.5-ounce can in December. And the beverage industry has substituted high-calorie soft drinks with lower-calorie, more nutritious options in schools, resulting in an 88 percent reduction in calories since 2004.

But those efforts are still aimed more at healthy competition than healthy nutrition. The 100-calorie snack packs of

| 7 fl. oz. | 21 fl. oz. | 12 fl. oz. | 22 fl. oz. | 12 fl. oz. | 32 fl. oz. |
| 1955 | 2002 | 1954 | 2002 | 1973 | 2002 |

Our Cups Runneth Over Regular-size fast-food sodas had modest beginnings. But years later even "medium" drinks have grown to gargantuan proportions.

Source: journal of the american dietetic association, 2003

Doritos and Oreos are an attempt to merge both agendas, and while some pediatricians give these products a thumbs up—fewer calories is, after all, a good thing—purists like Dr. Sarah Armstrong, a pediatrician at Duke University Medical Center, want their patients to make better choices, not just eat smaller amounts of the bad stuff. Diet sodas are also double-edged. They save on calories, but they're far from nutritious.

Public-health advocates are taking on Big Food just as their predecessors took on Big Tobacco. Dr. David Kessler, the former head of the FDA, argues that the fattening of America has happened by design as food companies intentionally manufactured irresistible cocktails of sugar, fat, and salt. Manufacturers' efforts to do better don't assuage Kelly Brownell, head of Yale's Rudd Center for Food Policy and Obesity. "The country defaults to giving industry the benefit of the doubt," he says. "Industry says you don't need to regulate us; we'll police ourselves. The tobacco industry abused that with God knows how many lives as a consequence. To expect the food industry to be different may be wishful thinking."

Especially when laudatory efforts are entwined with deceptive information. Earlier this month, FDA Commissioner Margaret Hamburg sent an open letter to the food industry citing violations in food labeling that mislead consumers. Example: particular brands of coconut custard pie, fish fillets, and organic vegetable shortening are promoted as having no trans fat, but fail to disclose the fact that they are high in saturated fat and total fat.

And then there's rampant marketing. Food and drink advertising to children is a $1.6 billion annual effort. The food industry has made an effort to increase ads for healthy foods and reduce the not-so-healthy stuff. But parents and kids are still besieged. The least nutritious cereals are the ones most aggressively and frequently marketed to children, according to a recent Yale study. "I think it's a stretch to say that the First Amendment protects the right of a cereal manufacturer to advertise a sugary breakfast product to a 5-year-old," says Harvard's Ludwig. "These kinds of practices cry out for regulation."

Maybe it would help to adopt a more European approach, increasing our comfort level with government meddling that encourages healthier behavior. Sweden and Norway forbid advertising of any kind to children younger than 12 on commercial TV shows. The French removed more than 22,000 food and drink vending machines from schools and replaced them with water fountains. Denmark banned trans fatty acids in 2003 and plans a tax on saturated fat this year. New York City launched its own local revolution in the United States. As head of the city's Department of Health, Dr. Tom Frieden banned trans fats and forced calorie counts onto restaurant-chain menus. Whether or not this will change eating habits is unclear, but a new study out of Seattle found that parents will choose meals with 100 fewer calories for their kids when they see the numbers. Frieden's approach caught Obama's attention: he appointed him to head the CDC.

Now Frieden and others support a tax on sugar-sweetened beverages. Brownell's calculation: a penny per ounce on soda could reduce consumption by 23 percent, which would ultimately save about $50 billion over 10 years in health-care costs. A controversial federal soft-drink tax was considered as a way to help pay for health-care reform. Last fall President Obama said, "It's an idea that we should be exploring." But a coalition led by the beverage industry spent millions lobbying against it, arguing that it would burden working families. And, fearing the "food police," many constituents don't like it either. The idea may be gaining momentum at the local level, however; a handful of states have introduced soda-tax legislation and New York City Mayor Michael Bloomberg said it "makes sense" as a way to build state revenue.

Ludwig believes a tax would also level the playing field against government subsidies on abundant commodities like corn and soy. High-fructose corn syrup, synthesized from corn, is a main ingredient in a multitude of sweetened drinks and snacks. "We've got a cheap calorie environment, where a lot of the calories are coming from added fats and added sugars that are derived from these few crops," says Dr. David Wallinga of the Institute for Agriculture and Trade Policy in Minnesota. "What we don't have is a policy encouraging the production of fruits and vegetables and other healthy foods." Price does have some sway over the salivary glands: a new study out of the University of North Carolina at Chapel Hill, which followed participants over 20 years, finds that young adults eat less pizza and soda as the cost for these items goes up. And here's the really good news: their weight and risk for diabetes go down.

It took decades after the surgeon general's 1964 report on the hazards of tobacco for anti-smoking laws to go into effect. And there is, of course, one major and critical difference between tobacco and food: you can live without smoking, but you will die without eating. Which makes tackling childhood obesity such a complicated challenge.

An entire cultural shift is required, starting with nutrition education. Showing children the government's food pyramid is fine, but it's not enough. Kids need to learn which items to choose in the lunch line, says CSPI's Wootan, and someone needs to show them what a plate of colorful, nourishing food looks like. Schools must get the funding they need to fix ovens and buy mixers and salad bars so their meal staff can do more than reheat processed foods. Educators must figure out creative ways to incorporate exercise into the day, even if it means blasting music over the PA system for 10 minutes every morning and afternoon for all-school dance time.

Nutritionists and community organizations must team up to reinvent the way families cook, especially in poor and undernourished neighborhoods—the "food deserts," where corner bodegas sell candy bars and white bread. In her hometown Alabama shrimping village, Surgeon General Regina Benjamin taught people to shift from frying to broiling. Gumbo can be less greasy and "still taste very good," says Benjamin. Workplaces should offer an area for pumping or breast-feeding, which has been shown to reduce the risk of obesity, perhaps because breast-fed babies may be better at regulating how much they eat. Parents should eat with their kids as often as possible and set limits on TV, computer, and videogame use. Above all, they should demand healthful foods and environments for their children.

Obesity endangers our health-care budget and our national security: being overweight is the No. 1 reason recruits are turned away from the military.

First lady Michelle Obama is being careful not to alienate anyone—from the food lobby to beleaguered parents trying their best. She's investing $400 million in the eradication of food deserts, but she isn't giving anybody a pass on individual responsibility. She's growing fresh fruits and veggies on the White House lawn, but isn't banning the occasional burger and fries. Will her approach be aggressive enough? It's hard to know. But it is ambitious.

With her initiative comes the president's executive order for a Task Force on Childhood Obesity, which requires government departments that have often been at cross-purposes to work together. The president's appointments signal a seriousness about public health. And his higher-ups are not afraid to concede their personal fat demons. Benjamin has acknowledged her own weight struggle, which she told Newsweek, started in her 40s. So has Agriculture Secretary Tom Vilsack. He says he can't forget the cartoon his mother put on the fridge to discourage him from snacking when he was an overweight child: a heavyset kid wearing a beanie cap, busting out of his britches. "Every time I opened the refrigerator door, I had to look at that guy," he told a crowd at the National Press Club.

Now he's calling on Congress to increase meal-reimbursement rates so that schools can buy higher-priced healthier foods, including whole grains, fruits, and vegetables. He's asking for a stronger link between local farmers and cafeterias, and the authority to set standards on competitive foods. The American Academy of Pediatrics, partnering with the first lady, is urging its doctors to write exercise and eating "prescriptions" for their patients. "Just as we give immunizations," says AAP president Judith Palfrey, "we're going to give healthy eating and exercise advice at every visit." Benjamin says she is planning to travel the country to educate schools and communities about nutrition and physical activity "anywhere we can get the message out." Americans are trying—the multibillion-dollar diet industry attests to that—but they need help, she says. Her personal goal: a hike to the top of Mount Kilimanjaro by 2011.

Talk about a steep climb. Childhood obesity is so vast, so complex, so entrenched. We must all join the journey. "When we come together as a nation and really commit ourselves, we can do it," says Robert Wood Johnson Foundation CEO Risa Lavizzo-Mourey. "If we can get that kind of resolve, we'll be able to create a legacy of healthy children and a healthier nation." Our future depends on it.

Critical Thinking

1. Why do children become corpulent (large, bulky, fat, portly)?

2. What are some health risks of obesity in childhood?

3. How does technology (TVs, videography, computers) contribute to the culture of corpulence? What else contributes?

UNIT 5

Development during Adolescence and Young Adulthood

Unit Selections

Learning Objectives

After reading this Unit you should be able to:

- Explain why many young adults are making critical decisions without parental guidance.

- Explain how trait aggressiveness can be influenced by playing violent video games.

- Summarize the effects of attending a high school with a GSA.

- Distinguish between normal-eating thin persons and anorexic thin persons.

- Evaluate Bem's evidence that ESP exists.

- Explain the factors that lead to the termination of new hires in the workplace.

- Defend "less is more" when it applies to decisionmaking.

- Explain why women and men are not equal in the workplace.

- Contrast unemployment of white, college-educated, and older men in 1983 and in 2011 and tell why changes occurred.

- Judge how early experiences (e.g., love, loss, lies, success) affect you today.

- Explain why children tend to reduce marital happiness.

Student Website

www.mhhe.com/cls

The term "adolescence" was coined in 1904 by G. Stanley Hall, one of the world's first psychologists. He saw adolescence as a discrete stage of life that bridges the gap between sexual maturity (puberty) and socioemotional and cognitive maturity. He believed it to be characterized by "storm and stress." At the beginning of the twentieth century, it was typical for young men to begin working in middle childhood (there were no child labor laws), and for young women to work as wives and mothers as soon as they were fertile and/or spoken for. At the turn of the twenty-first century, the beginning of adolescence was marked by the desire to be independent of parental control. The end of adolescence, which once coincided with the age of legal maturity (usually 16 or 18, depending on local laws), has now been extended upwards. Although legal maturity is now 18 (voting, enlisting in the armed services, owning property, marrying without permission), the social norm is to consider persons in their late teens as adolescents, not adults. The years between 18 and 21 are often problematic for youth tethered between adult and not-adult status. They can be married, with children, living in homes of their own, running their own businesses, yet not be able to drive their cars in certain places or at certain times. They can go to college and participate in social activities, but they cannot legally drink. Often the twenty-first birthday is viewed as a rite of passage into adulthood in the United States because it signals the legal right to buy and drink alcoholic beverages. "Maturity" is usually reserved for those who have achieved full economic as well as socioemotional independence as adults.

Erik Erikson, the personality theorist, marked the passage from adolescence to young adulthood by a change in the nuclear conflicts of two life stages: identity versus role confusion and intimacy versus isolation. Adolescents struggle to answer the question, "Who am I?" Young adults struggle to find a place within the existing social order where they can feel intimacy rather than isolation. In the 1960s, Erikson wrote that females resolved both their conflicts of identity and intimacy by living vicariously through their husbands, an unacceptable idea to many females today.

As adolescence has been extended, so too has young adulthood. One hundred years ago, life expectancy did not extend too far beyond menopause for women and retirement for men. Young adulthood began when adolescents finished puberty. Parents of teenagers were middle-aged, between 35 and 55. Later marriages and delayed childbearing have redefined the line between young adulthood and middle age. Many people today consider themselves young adults well into their 40s.

Jean Piaget, the cognitive theorist, marked the end of the development of mental processes with the end of adolescence. Once full physical maturity, including brain maturity, was achieved, one reached the acme of his or her abilities to assimilate, accommodate, organize, and adapt to sensations, perceptions, associations, and discriminations. Piaget did not feel cognitive processing of information ceased with adulthood. He believed, however, that cognitive judgments would not reach a stage higher than the abstract, hypothetical, logical reasoning of formal operations. Today, many cognitive theorists believe post-formal operations are possible.

© Purestock/SuperStock

The first article, "Foresight Conquers Fear of the Future," discusses the difficulty adolescents have selecting and preparing for jobs previously unknown. Parental guidance is nil. The skill of foresight (knowledge or insight of the future) can be acquired and practiced. The author recommends realistic, creative thinking about long-term benefits of future readiness for change.

The third selection for Adolescence, "Offsetting Risks," deals with high schools that have Gay-Straight Alliance (GSA) clubs. The presence of such clubs make hate messages and victimization of sexual minority students less common, and the school environment safer.

The fourth article, "Portrait of a Hunger Artist," describes the beginning, middle, and end of the author's obsessive need to control what she ate. Emily Troscianko provides an insightful look at the thought processes of adolescents with eating disorders. She dismisses four common myths about anorexia. She translates her own real experiences into helpful advice for others struggling to eat normally.

The last article in the Adolescent portion of this unit, "53.1% of You Already Know What This Story's About, or Do You?," suggests that precognition may exist. Students will be interested to learn why the author believes this.

The first Young Adulthood selection, "How to 'Ace' Your Freshman Year in the Workplace with C's: Culture, Competence, and Consequences," discusses the differences between educational goals and employment goals. The author lists skills and qualities which employers desire from employees. He also indicates common reasons for job termination and characteristics that lead to promotions and new assignments.

The second article about Young Adults, "I Can't Think!," illustrates how technology aides (twittering, instant messaging, texting, Facebook, smart phones, etc.) give us non-stop information. The author contends that too many choices leave us in a blur, resulting in a total failure to decide or in making unwise judgments.

The selection entitled, "Are We There Yet?," analyzes 40 years of women's struggles for equal rights in the workplace. Despite many gains, women across all professions are paid 20% less (on the average) than their male counterparts. Why are women afraid to fight for what they deserve? The authors explain some of the reasons.

The next selection, by Jay Dixit, describes "Heartbreak and Home Runs: The Power of First Experiences." Some adult behaviors are shaped by how they experience first love, first loss, first lies, and early success or failure at work. Rather than dwelling on early experiences as defining moments, young adults can choose to move forward and make future experiences different and better.

In the last article in Unit 5, Jennifer Senior asks us to consider "All Joy and No Fun: Why Parents Hate Parenting." Couples expect that their relationships will be improved when children arrive. While there is tremendous joy in having children, it is often experienced when watching them sleep, looking at their photos, and/or reminiscing about past activities. Day-to-day child care responsibilities reduce marital happiness. They are very tiring duties with few immediate rewards.

All of the selections on Adolescence and Young Adulthood will engage students and lead to dynamic discussions.

Internet References

Alcohol & Drug Addiction Resource Center
www.addict-help.com/

ADOL: Adolescent Directory On-Line
http://site.educ.indiana.edu/aboutus/
AdolescenceDirectoryonLineADOL/tabid/4785/Default.aspx

AMA—Adolescent Health On-Line
www.ama-assn.org/ama/pub/category/1947.html

American Academy of Child and Adolescent Psychiatry
www.aacap.org/

Depression
www.depression-primarycare.org

Foresight Conquers Fear of the Future

Today's youth are growing up in the midst of radical social and economic transformations. Now is the time to develop the most critical skill for effectively managing their careers and personal lives: Foresight.

EDWARD CORNISH

"I'm scared," the young man confessed. "I'm starting my eighteenth year in a world that makes no sense to me. All I know is that this world I'm living in is a shambles and I don't know how to put it together."

The young man bared his soul to an invisible audience during a radio call-in show. Other callers agreed with his dismal assessment of the state of the world. Nobody offered an answer for his fears.

Bill Moyers, the TV interviewer, happened to be listening that night and was profoundly affected by what he heard.

"Such lamentations," Moyers commented later, "are deep currents running throughout the liberal West today. Our secular and scientific societies are besieged by violence, moral anarchy, and purposelessness that have displaced any mobilizing vision of the future except hedonism and consumerism."

Moyers put his finger on what may be a key challenge faced by many young people today: their inability to think realistically, creatively, and hopefully about the future. Instead, these young people suffer from what can be described as "futurephobia."

Some futurephobes have an acute version of this malady, like the young man described by Moyers, but most futurephobes simply focus on their immediate circumstances and drift into the future without thinking much about it at all. Either way, they may drift into financial or other kinds of trouble.

The connection between poor foresight and serious problems is widely recognized by psychologists and sociologists. Yale sociologist Wendell Bell asserts that some authorities "go so far as to claim that all forms of deviant, criminal, and reckless behavior have the same fundamental cause: the tendency to pursue immediate benefits without concern for long-term costs, a disregard for inevitable and undesirable future consequences."

Successful self-management, says Bell, requires understanding and giving appropriate value to the likely consequences of your actions. If you have little or no foresight, you cannot think realistically and creatively about your future, so you cannot steer your career and personal life toward long-term success.

Poor foresight can threaten not just the careers of emerging adults, but even their lives. Young people lacking foresight are prone to act recklessly—drive too fast, use drugs, play with guns, commit crimes, and even kill themselves (or others).

On the other hand, when young people do manage to develop good foresight, they can think realistically, creatively, and hopefully about the future. So empowered, they can aim their careers toward achievable goals and cheerfully accept the burdens of responsibility and self-discipline required for success. Barack Obama is a recent example of foresight-empowered success.

The New Urgency of Foresight

Older people are prone to dismiss the problems of youth as just a normal part of growing up, but the fact is that today's youth are coming of age in a world undergoing an unprecedented transformation powered by multiple technological revolutions. These technological advances, all occurring simultaneously, are overturning the world's economies and undermining long-established institutions, careers, and lifestyles.

Amid such turbulence, making a good decision concerning one's career or private life can be highly problematic, and the demographic group most acutely affected are young people moving into adulthood. These emerging adults have entered a time of life when parents and teachers have diminished power to guide them, so young people must make critical decisions by themselves at a time when their experience of the world is limited and their brains are still immature. (Foresight, scientists say, is largely a function of the brain's prefrontal cortex, which does not reach maturity until about age 25.)

Adding to the challenge of making appropriate decisions in today's world is the fact that knowledgeable and trustworthy advisors are now less available to emerging adults. In bygone days, most young people lived in villages or small towns where people got to know each other well, enabling the elders to offer wise counsel for a young person trying to find a suitable job or marriage partner.

In today's highly mobile mass society, young people roam the world and can choose among thousands of potential careers and mates in countless different locations. In principle, the abundance of choice offers wonderful opportunities, but it can pose a baffling conundrum for an emerging adult with little experience of the world.

Making matters worse for many young people, technological advances have eliminated most of the jobs that could be learned quickly and paid enough for an 18-year-old to live on and maybe support a family. Now, getting a decent job is likely to require years of training at a college or university during which time the student earns little or no money and may go heavily into debt.

Improving Youth Foresight

Ironically, it was fear of the future that led to some of our most useful foresight tools.

Relatively little was done to create a science of foresight until after World War II, which had led to the development of rockets and atomic bombs. Frightened that the Soviet Union might use the new superweapons, the U.S. Air Force established the RAND Corporation in Santa Monica, California, as a "think factory." The main task of RAND's scientists and scholars was to think about future wars—how to fight and win them.

To fulfill their mission, the RAND scientists had to think seriously about the future, and in the process they developed a variety of methods for thinking more scientifically about the future than had ever been done before. Mathematician Olaf Helmer and his RAND colleague Norman Dalkey developed the Delphi technique, a way to refine and synthesize scientists' forecasts of future technological developments. In addition, Herman Kahn developed his scenario technique for exploring the implications of possible future events. The scenario method is now widely used in government and business.

Meanwhile, Arnold Brown, Edie Weiner, and others refined ways for identifying and analyzing social trends. Today trend analysis is widely recognized as one of the most useful ways for identifying significant developments in technology and society and anticipating outcomes.

Many of the methods developed since World War II can now be used in simplified forms by young people and by teachers or others trying to help young people gain a practical understanding of what is happening in the world now, where things are going, and the opportunities that young people have to make valuable contributions to human welfare as well as succeed in their chosen careers and personal lives.

The task now is to make foresight into a recognized life skill that can empower young people to think more clearly, constructively, and hopefully about the future. The World Future Society has already initiated several projects for improving youth foresight, and more are under development.

Young people interested in participating in a Society conference now can attend at a reduced rate of $125 ($150 on site) and many members have been donating funds to cover one or more full scholarships for young people.

In addition, the Society recently sponsored a High School Essay Contest, and the first group of winners was announced in July. Other programs will be instituted as funding becomes available.

If we can equip today's young people with good foresight, we can all be much more optimistic about their future and ours.

Critical Thinking

1. Indicate forces which are transforming our social and economic worlds.
2. Identify jobs that have been eliminated by modern technology.
3. Provide a rationale for foresight and the need to practice it.

EDWARD CORNISH, founder of the World Future Society, is editor of The Futurist and a member of the Society's Board. His book *Futuring: The Exploration of the Future* provides a readable description of the futures field, including many of the methods now in use. It may be ordered from the World Future Society for $19.95 (member's price $17.95). Go to www.wfs.org/futuring.htm.

Interview with Dr. Craig Anderson
Video Game Violence

Dr. Craig Anderson, a leader in the research on the effects of exposure to violent video games on aggressive behavior, was invited to speak at Nebraska Wesleyan University. A group of Nebraska Wesleyan University students interviewed Dr. Anderson. We explored his interest and experiences in this research area.

SARAH HOWE, JENNIFER STIGGE, AND BROOKE SIXTA

Since 1997, Nebraska Wesleyan University (NE) has held an endowed lecture to honor the 40-year career of Dr. Clifford Fawl. The FAWL Lecture Series brings distinguished psychologists to the Wesleyan campus to present their research and interact with undergraduate psychology students. On March 22, 2007, we welcomed Dr. Craig Anderson as the FAWL lecturer to speak on *Violent Video Games: Theory, Research, and Public Policy.*

Dr. Craig Anderson received his bachelors degree at Butler University (IN) in 1976. He earned a masters degree (1978) and PhD (1980) in psychology at Stanford University (CA). He currently is a distinguished professor of psychology at Iowa State University and is widely regarded as the leader in research on the effects of violent video games and other forms of media violence. He has published widely on depression, loneliness, and shyness; attribution processes; social judgment; and human aggression. He has earned recognition as the second most highly cited scholar in social psychology textbooks. He has testified before the U.S. Senate Committee on Commerce, Science and Transportation's hearing on "The Impact of Interactive Violence on Children" and has served on the Media Violence Expert Panel for the Surgeon General.

Dr. Anderson started his visit by discussing the importance of good methodology to a research methods class. He was then interviewed by a small group of Wesleyan students concerning his work on violence and video games.

Student: What was your motivation for starting research on media violence and video games?

Anderson: It originally had to do with working on the General Aggression Model and learning about the media violence literature. There were literally hundreds of studies, but there were still gaps and unanswered questions. I had some students looking for research topics that were interesting and publishable, and then they identified gaps in the research.

That was the initial reason. Later they basically extended the research using video games to test some aspects of the General Aggression Model. Next, my research team looked at priming issues, which prior to our work, had never been used in the context of media violence effects. After talking to some colleagues in cognitive psychology and debating about which method to use, we thought of using some cognitive measures such as a modified Stroop test but we chose a reading reaction time task.

Student: Looking back on many of your articles, we noticed you first did a study on video games in 1987 and another in 1995, but the majority of your studies have been since 1999. Did this more recent increase in research on the effects of video games have anything to do with Columbine and other school shootings?

Anderson: No, it had to do with an internal grant I received about 1996. It funded three graduate students and enabled us to start doing research on the effects of violent video games. I had been writing grant proposals on the topic for some time, but this was the first time I had the opportunity to do some of those studies. Then, Columbine came along.

Student: Were you asked to help with any of the Columbine research?

Anderson: No, although I was asked to testify in the U.S. Senate hearing about violent video games some time after the shooting.

Student: What group of people do you think are the most susceptible to the effects of violent video games, and why?

Anderson: Many researchers in the field of media violence think that people who are high on what you would call trait aggression (especially children and adolescents) are going to be more influenced by exposure to media violence than people who are low on trait aggression. In other words, many scholars believe that highly aggressive people are more susceptible to the harmful effects of media violence than are nonaggressive people. However, I think that the research evidence over the years doesn't bear that out, yet. Some studies show this heightened susceptibility of highly aggressive people, but some studies show the opposite including one of my studies (Anderson, 1997). That study found that people who are lowest on trait aggression showed the biggest effect of a violent movie manipulation. Those data yielded a significant interaction between measures of trait aggression and measures of media violence exposure. The nonaggressive people who watched a violent movie clip displayed more aggressive thoughts than nonaggressive people who saw the nonviolent clip, but highly aggressive people were relatively unaffected by the movie clip manipulation. Other researchers have found the opposite type of interaction. For example, in some studies those who score high on trait aggressiveness and have been exposed to a lot of violent media are the ones who are most likely to have, at some time in their lives, been arrested for assault. Well, is that because the media violence effect only operates on high trait-aggressive people? Perhaps low traitaggressive people are equally affected, but because their general level of aggression is low, media violence can't increase their willingness to aggress enough to rise to the level of assaulting someone.

Student: From where do you recruit your participants?

Anderson: Well, very often, it's a convenience sample. However, the present grant research that my colleagues/students and I have been doing allows us to pay participants. So we are able to pay kids to play video games, which they think is great (laughter). Some try to come in two or three times, and we have to tell them they cannot. In these situations, we have to select samples to fit the particular research question or issue.

Student: In your experimental research, how do you account for the participants who regularly play video games from those who have little to no experience?

Anderson: We usually give the participants questionnaires that tell us how much the individuals have played and what kinds of games they play. Prior experience with video games can then figure into the data analysis. We seldom find any kind of difference in our experimental studies between those participants with a lot of experience and those without. The one difference we do find is that participants with a lot of gaming experience really like being in the violent video game condition. Typically, we do not find much of a statistically reliable effect of gaming experience on aggressive thought processes and behavior.

Student: Do you feel that your research has or will have an impact on the video game industry? If so, what impact do you think it will have?

Anderson: Our research has probably had a bigger impact in countries other than in the United States. Almost every other modern country has legal restrictions on violent media including video games. Many of them ban some of the games outright and most have age-based restrictions. Certainly the research that my students and I have done over the years has been used by child advocacy groups and others in these countries to make sure that these ratings are enforced. The research certainly has increased the awareness of the issue in the United States. However, there are no U.S. laws regarding violent video games. I have never said publicly whether I support a legislative solution, because my political opinion is not relevant to what I regard as my scientific expertise. Even in the court cases with which I have been involved, I say upfront that I will not comment on what I think about the law under judicial review. I will talk about what the science says or what it cannot say. The work and interviews that we've done concerning violence in video games is used to get the word out to parents about the effect of violent video games. Our research has had a big impact on parents, but not as big as it needs to be. There are still people teaching their 2- or 3-year-olds how to shoot a gun in these video games.

Student: What are some of the stronger arguments against your research? How do you counter those arguments?

Anderson: One of the best arguments, until recently, is that there are no longitudinal studies, but we have now published one (Anderson, Gentile, & Buckley, 2007). Previously in my various talks, I had described the lack of longitudinal data on the effects of video games. The paucity of these studies was due to the lack of government support for longitudinal research. The support for the longitudinal study I just mentioned came from non-governmental sources. More recently, we finally got the funding needed to perform a larger, longer term longitudinal study after being turned down six or seven times. There really aren't any long-term longitudinal studies such as when you follow the group of individuals and see where these participants end up after several years. Some participants may end up in jail, juvenile detention facilities, or kicked out of school, which makes this an important field of interest. A response to this criticism about the lack of longitudinal studies on violent video games is that such studies have already been done pertaining to television violence, which is the same phenomenon, but some individuals fail to see the similarities between violence on television and violence in video games. People used this lack of a longitudinal study, focusing on violent video games, as a criticism for the evidence found between increased aggression and exposure to violent video games. Of course, they can no longer do this.

Student: Do you have any plans for the future implementation of your research? How should your research be applied to schools, home, everyday life, etc.?

Anderson: We haven't been thinking much about intervention studies, mainly because I don't do intervention studies. There is a group at Iowa State University that does intervention studies, but most of their work focuses on drug use and intervention to reduce kids' use of alcohol, tobacco, and various illegal substances. There have been some TV/video game interventions done in school systems, but intervention as a whole is done by another group of researchers.

Student: Where do you think video game research will go from here?

Anderson: There are two related issues that are going to be big soon. One is the identification of video game addiction or Internet addiction, including text messaging, as a true addiction in need of clinical intervention for some individuals. The other has to do with attention deficit disorders, executive control, and impulse control. There is potential long-term damage in those brain systems due to extensive viewing of media that flash across the screen and demand constantly shifting attention. Some evidence indicates that extensive use of screening media, whether it is violent or not, leads to attention deficit disorder, especially in very young children who see a lot of TV.

References

Anderson, C. A. (1997). Effects of violent movies and trait irritability on hostile feelings and aggressive thoughts. *Aggressive Behavior, 23,* 161–178.

Anderson, C. A., Gentile, D. A., & Buckley, K. E. (2007). *Violent video game effects on children and adolescents.* New York: Oxford University Press.

Critical Thinking

1. Identify youth who are more susceptible to the harmful effects of video violence.
2. Suggest reasons why the United States has not restricted video violence like other countries.
3. Support or refute the idea that Internet addiction is a true addiction.

SARAH HOWE, a junior at Nebraska Wesleyan University, is a psychology major with a minor in health and human performance. Following graduation, she plans to attend graduate school in counseling. JENNIFER STIGGE, also a junior at Nebraska Wesleyan University, is an industrial-organizational psychology (I/O psychology) major with a business administration minor. She plans to begin graduate school in the fall of 2009 in I/O psychology. BROOKE SIXTA graduated from Nebraska Wesleyan University in December of 2007 with a bachelor's degree in psychology and a minor in business administration. She is currently working; however, plans to also attend I/O psychology graduate school beginning at the fall of 2008.

Author's note—We would like to thank Dr. Anderson for visiting with Nebraska Wesleyan students and faculty, and presenting his research regarding violence and video games. We would also like to give a special thanks to Dr. Marilyn Petro, Dr. Michael Tagler, Allyson Bell, and Amanda Holmgren for their assistance with the process of this interview.

Offsetting Risks: High School Gay-Straight Alliances and Lesbian, Gay, Bisexual, and Transgender (LGBT) Youth

Nicholas C. Heck, Annesa Flentje, and Bryan N. Cochran

Studies of lesbian, gay, bisexual, and transgender (LGBT)[1] youth have consistently found that this population is at-risk for experiencing psychological distress. Specifically, lesbian, gay, and bisexual (LGB) youth have been found to report more challenges related to depression (D'Augelli, 2002; Fergusson, Horwood, & Beautrais, 1999), suicidality (Faulkner & Cranstron, 1998; Jiang, Perry, & Hesser, 2010; Russell & Joyner, 2001; Silenzio, Pena, Duberstein, Cerel, & Knox, 2007; Zhao, Montoro, Igartua, & Thombs, 2010), and problematic substance use (Bontempo & D'Augelli, 2002; Corliss, Rosario, Wypij, Wylie, Frazier, & Austin, 2010; Faulkner & Cranstron, 1998; Russell, Driscoll, & Truong, 2002) when compared to heterosexual youth. According to McGuire, Anderson, Toomey, and Russell (2010), "the cumulative literature suggests that some transgender youth face significantly more mental health difficulties, such as depression, anxiety, and self harming behaviors . . . than their gender conforming peers" (p. 1175). This body of literature has grown to the point where meta-analytic evidence suggests that LGB youth are at higher risk for substance misuse when compared to heterosexual youth (Marshal et al., 2008).

Research indicates that others' reactions to an individual's sexual orientation may be a key factor in identifying elevated risk. For example, LGB youth who experience parental rejection upon disclosure of their minority statuses appear to be at an increased risk for using illegal drugs, developing depressive symptoms, and for attempting suicide (D'Augelli et al., 2001; Ryan, Huebner, Dias, & Sanchez, 2009), while parental support has been shown to mediate the relationship between sexual orientation and depression and sexual orientation and suicidal thoughts in the transition to young adulthood (Needham & Austin, 2010).

Abuse and Victimization among LGBT Youth

According to the gay-related stress hypothesis, growing up in a stigmatizing, heterosexist society leads to an increase in substance use and psychological distress among people who identify as LGBT (Rosario, Schrimshaw, Hunter, & Gwadz, 2002; also see Meyer, 1995). Consistent with this hypothesis, LGBT persons report experiencing victimization and abuse at higher rates than heterosexuals. LGB youth have been found to experience more abuse perpetrated by family members when compared to heterosexual youth (Balsam, Rothblum, & Beauchaine, 2005; Corliss, Cochran, & Mays, 2002; Saewyc, Skay, Petingell, Reis, Bearinger, Resnick, & Combs, 2006; Temeo, Templer, Anderson, & Kotler, 2001), while experiencing parental verbal and physical abuse is a factor related to suicide attempts among transgender youth (Grossman & D'Augelli, 2007).

Saewyc and colleagues (2006) combined data from seven population-based surveys and found that LGB youth, relative to heterosexual youth, were more likely to report histories of physical and sexual abuse. Using data from a sample of 168 homeless adolescents, Cochran, Stewart, Ginzler, and Cauce (2002) found that LGBT youth were more likely to have left home as a result of physical abuse when compared to a matched sample of homeless, heterosexual youth. Failing to conform to gender-norms also appears to be related to childhood abuse experiences among LGBT youth (D'Augelli, Grossman, & Starks, 2006; Grossman, D'Augelli, Howell, & Hubbard, 2006).

Evidence from population-based studies demonstrates that experiencing verbal, physical, and sexual abuse in childhood is associated with a number of negative health outcomes (Chartier, Walker, & Naimark, 2009; Springer, Sheridan, Kuo,

& Carnes, 2007). Additional evidence suggests that the association between childhood abuse and negative health outcomes also extends to LGBT people. For example Robohm, Litzenberger, and Pearlman (2003) found that lesbian and bisexual women with a history of childhood sexual abuse (CSA) were more likely to experience a number of emotional and behavioral challenges, when compared to lesbian women without a history of CSA. Wilsnack et al. (2008) reported higher rates of problematic drinking and experiences of CSA among lesbian and bisexual women when compared to exclusively heterosexual women. Similar associations between childhood abuse and health risk behaviors, especially unsafe sexual practices, have been reported for gay and bisexual males (Lenderking, Wold, Mayer, Goldstein, Losina, & Seage, 1997; Neisen & Sandall, 1990; Rosario, Schrimshaw, & Hunter, 2006; Saewyc, Skay, Richens, Reis, Poon, & Murphy, 2006).

The victimization of youth at school is a factor associated with negative mental health outcomes for LGBT individuals. Prior research indicates that LGBT youth report experiencing significantly more at-school victimization than their heterosexual peers. Bontempo and D'Augelli (2002) used data collected from 9,188 high school students who completed the Youth Risk Behavior Survey in Massachusetts and Vermont and found that LGB youth reported higher levels of at-school victimization when compared to heterosexual youth. Furthermore, when the entire sample was classified as either experiencing high or low levels of at-school victimization, high victimization LGB youth reported significantly more challenges related to substance use and suicidality than high victimization heterosexual and low victimization LGB youth.

Using a community sample of 97 sexual minority high school students and a matched comparison sample of heterosexual students, Williams, Connolly, Pepler, and Craig, (2005) found more reports of bullying, harassment, and depression among LGBT youth. Victimization at school and social support were found to mediate the associations between sexual orientation and psychological distress; these findings highlight how the school environment can relate to both positive and negative mental health outcomes.

D'Augelli, Pilkington, and Hershberger (2002), collected data from 350 LGB youth and young adults ages 14–21 and found that high school victimization experiences were associated with current mental health problems. Specifically, 9% of the variance in mental health symptoms was accounted for by at-school victimization, while 92% of the sample was between the ages of 18 and 20, suggesting that the effects of at-school victimization may extend beyond the high school years and impact psychosocial adjustment.

According to the Gay, Lesbian, and Straight Education Network's (GLSEN) National School Climate Study, which consisted of more than 6,000 sexual minority high school students, 86% reported being verbally harassed at school within the past year, 44% reported being physically harassed, and 22% reported being physically assaulted (Kosciw & Diaz, 2006). The GLSEN (2008) sampled 1,580 public school principals and found that approximately 30% of principals reported that their teachers were either "fair" or "poor" at being able to address the bullying of sexual minority students. Additionally, 95% of principals reported that students are harassed based upon gender expression and 92% reported harassment based upon sexual orientation. Overall, at-school victimization disproportionally impacts LGBT youth and has been shown to be related to lower levels of school belonging, feeling unsafe at school, poorer academic performance, more substance use, and more depressive symptomatology.

Gay-Straight Alliances (GSAs)

Gay-straight alliances are usually student led, school-based clubs that exist in middle and high schools whose goals involve improving the school climate for LGBT youth and educating the school community about sexual minority issues (GLSEN, 2007). Such school-based organizations can be a place for LGBT youth to spend time with peers and may increase social support for sexual minority youth (Jordan, 2000). Fetner and Kush (2008) found that GSAs were more likely to form in liberal urban and suburban areas, in larger school districts with greater financial resources, and in communities with existing support groups for LGBT youth. There is a limited amount of research available regarding school-based interventions for sexual minority youth; however, promising data exists to suggest that GSAs are related to more favorable psychosocial outcomes for this population (Hansen, 2007). The GLSEN has highlighted key findings that depict the positive benefits related to attending a high school with a GSA.

First, the presence of GSAs in schools may contribute to a safer atmosphere for LGBT youth by sending a message that hate speech and victimization will not be tolerated (GLSEN, 2007). This finding is supported by research conducted by Szalacha (2003), who found that students attending a high school with a GSA were less likely to hear homophobic comments in school when compared to youth attending a school without a GSA. Lee (2002) conducted qualitative interviews with seven high school students who reported that they felt safer and harassed less because of their involvement with the GSA, a finding that has been consistently supported by research related to attending high schools with GSAs (see Kosciw & Diaz, 2006; Walls, Kane, & Wisneski, 2010). Using data from the Massachusetts Youth Risk Behavior Survey, Goodenow, Szalacha, and Westheimer (2006) found that GSAs were associated with less at-school victimization and lower risk for past-year suicide attempts among LGB youth. At-school victimization was found to significantly predict suicidality, while perceived teacher and staff support was found to offset suicide risk (Goodenow et al., 2006).

Second, by having a GSA in a school, the school may be viewed as a place where LGBT youth feel they belong and are supported (GLSEN, 2007). Research conducted by Kosciw and Diaz (2006) and Walls et al. (2010) found that LGBT youth attending a school with a GSA appear less likely to miss school because of concerns for their physical safety when compared to peers who attend a school without a GSA. Attending a high school with a GSA has also been associated with hearing teachers make positive statements about LGBT people (Szalacha, 2003).

Finally, GSAs may help LGBT youth identify school teachers and staff who are supportive, which is shown to positively impact the academic achievement and experiences of LGBT youth (GLSEN, 2007). LGBT youth attending a high school with a GSA report having more supportive school teachers and staff members; these youth also appear to have higher GPAs and a greater sense of belonging to their schools, when compared to LGBT youth attending a high school without a GSA (Kosciw & Diaz, 2006; Szalacha, 2003; Walls et al., 2010).

At the same time, many LGBT youth in the U.S. still do not have access to a GSA or another type of high school club that provides support (GLSEN, 2007). Lee (2002) pointed out that GSAs are important because they offer support to LGBT youth, but they can also be of benefit to heterosexual youth. GSAs may provide a space where heterosexual youth can be come educated about LGBT issues, and they may also provide support to children of same-sex parents.

No studies to date have examined whether attending a high school with a GSA is related to lower levels of problematic drinking and other forms of psychopathology. Therefore, the purpose of this study is to replicate and extend the research base related to the potential benefits of attending a high school with a GSA. Specifically, it is hypothesized that LGBT youth who have attended a high school with a GSA (GSA +) will report significantly more school belonging and less at-school victimization, problematic alcohol use, depression, and general psychological distress when they are compared to LGBT peers who attended a high school without a GSA (GSA −). Furthermore, it is predicted that these significant differences will exist while controlling for abuse (including physical, sexual, and emotional abuse) during childhood, and other important demographic or environmental factors that might distinguish GSA + and GSA − youth.

Method
Participants
To be included in this study, participants had to identify as LGBT, be between the ages of 18 and 20, and have completed 12 or more years of education. We selected this age range to improve the accuracy of participants' reporting of experiences in high school and to ensure that none of the participants were of legal age to consume alcohol, (i.e., including participants of age 21 + would introduce a confound of legal vs. illegal alcohol consumption). Initially, 153 potential participants were considered for inclusion in the study. Four participants did not meet the inclusion criteria because they self-identified as heterosexual and four participants were excluded because of their age and/or education level. Thus, data from 145 subjects is analyzed for this study and comprise our sample.

Seventy-nine participants indicated that they attended a high school with a GSA, while 66 indicated that they had not. In terms of ethnicity, 102 (70.8%) participants identified as White, while 14 (9.7%) identified as African American, 8 (5.6%) identified as Asian American, 7 (4.9%) identified as Hispanic or Chicano, one (0.7%) identified as Native American, 12 (8.3%) selected "other" to represent their ethnicities, and 1 participant failed to provide a response to the ethnicity item.

Measures
The survey contained standard demographic questions including age, gender, ethnicity, relationship status, years of education, and the population of the city or town where participants attended high school. The Outness Inventory (OI; Mohr & Fassinger, 2000) was administered to measure how open participants were about their sexual orientation with various individuals (e.g., parents, siblings, extended family members). Participants reported their current levels of outness using a scale from 1, "person definitely does not know about your sexual orientation status" to 7, "person definitely knows about your sexual orientation, and it is openly talked about" (an option to enter 0, "does not apply" was also provided).

Participants also completed two items that assessed the climate for LGBT youth in their high schools and their communities. Response options for these items ranged from 1–5 and included the following descriptors: (1) "Extremely safe and accepting," (2) "Safe and accepting," (3) "Neutral," (4) "Unsafe and not accepting," and (5) "Extremely unsafe and not accepting." For the purposes of this study, LGBT status was verified by asking participants to select the option that best described their sexual orientation. The options included: gay, lesbian, or homosexual; bisexual; heterosexual; and not sure. Sexual orientation was also assessed using a continuous scale from 1: "Exclusively Heterosexual" to 7: "Exclusively Homosexual" and additional domains of sexual orientation (behavioral and affective) were also assessed but not analyzed for this study.

At-school victimization (while in high school) was assessed using nine questions taken from the Olweus' Bullying and Victimization Scale (Olweus, 1994). An additional item that assessed hearing homophobic jokes and comments was also included. The 10 items were revised so they could be answered retrospectively (e.g., "In high school, I was called mean names, made fun of, or teased in a hurtful way by other students") and so that participants could indicate whether they felt the victimization was related to their sexual orientation. Researchers studying bullying have often relied on retrospective self-reports, and the accurate reporting of bullying experiences by victims has been demonstrated (Olweus, 1993).

For each item, participants indicated how often they experienced each form of at-school victimization using a Likert scale ranging from 0 (this never happened to me in high school) to 4 (this happened to me several times each week). For an item to count toward the total victimization score, participants also had to indicate that they felt the victimization experience was because of their sexual orientation. Thus, the total score is one that is comprised of victimization experiences that are uniquely linked to sexual orientation and not other factors that may also put youth at-risk for experiencing victimization.

The Alcohol Use Disorders Identification Test (AUDIT; Saunders, Aasland, Babor, de la Fuente, & Grant, 1993) was used to measure problematic alcohol use. The AUDIT contains 10 items that assess the frequency of alcohol consumption, potential alcohol dependence, and harmful aspects of alcohol use. The AUDIT is scored on a scale from 0–40, with higher scores indicating more problematic alcohol use. The AUDIT has demonstrated sound psychometric qualities across a number of empirical investigations (Meneses-Gaya, Zuardi, Loureiro, & Crippa, 2009). The Beck Depression Inventory-II (BDI-II; Beck, Steer, Ball, & Ranieri, 1996) was used to assess depressive symptoms. The BDI-II is a 21-item self-report measure that assesses depressive symptomatology using a 4-point scale for each item; total scores on the BDI-II range from 0 to 63 with greater scores indicating higher levels of reported depressive symptoms. The Brief Symptom Inventory (BSI; Derogatis, 1993), which contains 53-items that assess how often over the past week participants experienced general psychological distress in relation to specific problems (e.g., feeling lonely, feeling blue) on a scale from 0 "not at all" to 4 "extremely," was also administered. The BSI has been used to assess psychological distress among sexual minority youth in a number of previous studies and has demonstrated excellent reliability with alphas ranging from .70 to .95 (D'Augelli et al., 2002). The Childhood Trauma Questionnaire, Short Form (CTQ-Short Form; Bernstein et al., 2003) was used to assess childhood abuse. The CTQ-SF contains 24-items that assess experiences of emotional, physical, and sexual abuse during childhood and adolescence; the measure has demonstrated internal consistency coefficients ranging from .80 to .95 for the three abuse categories (Bernstein et al., 2003). A total score to quantify abuse was calculated by adding the scores from the emotional, physical, and sexual abuse subscales. Finally, to measure high school belonging, four items from Rostosky, Owens, Zimmerman, and Riggle, (2003) were used. These items measure high school belonging using a 5-point Likert scale where participants indicate their degree of agreement or disagreement. These items are: "I was happy to be at school," "I felt safe at school," "The teachers at my school treated me fairly," and "I felt like I fit in at school." An additional item, "I attended or was involved in some kind of school related activity or school function," was also added.

Procedures

Participants were recruited from college and university LGBT student organizations between April and July of 2009. A total of 152 colleges and universities were identified as having one or more student organizations for sexual minorities. A recruitment e-mail that included information about the purpose of the study was sent to faculty advisors and/or student leaders of such organizations. Potential participants were informed that this study sought to understand their experiences in high school, and how those experiences shaped their development. Student organizations distributed the recruitment e-mail with a link to the survey to their members via e-mail distribution lists and/or by posting the recruitment information on a social networking website.

The recruitment e-mail requested that faculty advisors and/or student leaders inform the researcher if or when the study information was distributed. The recruitment e-mail suggested that the researcher be blind carbon copied (BCCed) on e-mails sent to student distribution lists; 59 universities were determined to have participated based on this information. As an incentive for their participation, participants could elect to enter into a raffle to win 1 of 10, 10-dollar gift certificates for an online merchant.

Analyses

To examine our hypotheses, a total of seven individual analyses of covariance (ANCOVAs) were calculated using the presence or absence of a GSA as our independent variable. For each analysis, childhood abuse scores (from the CTQ-SF) were entered as a covariate. This covariate was selected a priori and based upon the multiple studies that demonstrate that LGBT youth are often the victims of childhood abuse. As childhood abuse is associated with a number of negative psychosocial outcomes, we sought to minimize the influence of childhood abuse on our dependent variables of interest.

Additionally, some preexisting differences were found between GSA + and GSA − groups. Chi-square analyses revealed that more GSA + youth identified as bisexual in comparison to GSA − youth, and more GSA + youth attended high schools in cities or towns with larger populations. Significant differences in community climate and sexual orientation were detected between GSA + and GSA − youth using independent samples t tests; GSA − youth reported significantly higher scores on the continuous measure of sexual orientation, while GSA + youth reported attending high school in safer and more accepting communities. Given these differences, sexual orientation, population, and community climate were also included as covariates. A significant difference in current levels of outness was not detected.

Results

Cronbach's alpha was calculated for each measure corresponding to a dependent variable: .672 (Victimization), .770 (AUDIT), .815 (school belonging), .920 (BDI-II), and .960 (BSI).

High School Experiences: School Belonging and At-School Victimization

As predicted, GSA + youth reported significantly higher ratings of school belonging compared to GSA − youth when controlling for the effects of the four covariates $F(1, 135) = 9.04$, $p = .003$, $\eta^2_p = .062$. The overall adjusted R^2 for the model was .195. Community climate was a significant predictor of school belonging in the model, while population and sexual orientation, were not significant at the $p < .05$ level. A trend toward statistical significance was observed for childhood abuse. In addition, GSA + youth reported significantly less at-school victimization because of their sexual orientation, $F(1, 137) = 4.39$, $p = .038$, $\eta^2_p = .031$. The overall adjusted R^2 for this model was .287. Childhood abuse and community climate were significant predictors in the model, while population and sexual orientation were not.

Problematic Alcohol Use

As predicted, GSA + youth reported more favorable outcomes related to their alcohol use behaviors. Specifically, GSA + youth endorsed significantly lower total AUDIT scores compared to their GSA − peers when controlling for the covariates, $F(1, 135) = 16.93$, $p = .001$, $\eta_p^2 = .111$. The overall adjusted R^2 for the model was .087. None of the covariates were significant predictors of total AUDIT scores.

In examining AUDIT Dependence scores, GSA + youth reported significantly lower scores when controlling for the effects of the covariates, $F(1, 136) = 12.44$, $p = .001$, $\eta_p^2 = .084$. The overall adjusted R^2 for the model was .090. Population and childhood abuse approached significance in the model, while community climate and sexual orientation were not significant predictors of AUDIT Dependence scores. Additionally, GSA + youth reported significantly lower AUDIT Consumption scores when controlling for the influence of the covariates, $F(1, 137) = 10.09$, $p = .002$, $\eta_p^2 = .069$. The overall adjusted R^2 for this model was .039, and none of the covariates were significant predictors of AUDIT Consumption scores.

Depression and General Psychological Distress

As predicted, GSA + youth had more positive outcomes related to depression and general psychological distress when compared to GSA − youth. Specifically, GSA + youth reported significantly lower scores on the BDI-II when controlling for the covariates, $F(1, 137) = 4.83$, $p = .030$, $\eta_p^2 = .034$. The overall adjusted R^2 for the model was .128. Childhood abuse was a significant predictor of depression in this model, while population, community climate, and sexual orientation were not. A significant difference was also found on the BSI with GSA + youth reporting significantly lower scores, $F(1, 129) = 5.83$, $p = .017$, $\eta_p^2 = .043$. The overall adjusted R^2 for this model was .112. Childhood abuse and sexual orientation were significant predictors of total BSI scores.

Discussion

As predicted, GSA + youth reported more school belonging and less at-school victimization because of their sexual orientation when compared to GSA − youth. These findings, along with those of Goodenow et al. (2006); Kosciw and Diaz (2006); Szalacha, (2003), and Walls et al. (2010) again highlight the benefits of attending a high school with a GSA for LGBT youth. Additionally, GSA + youth reported more favorable outcomes related to alcohol use, depression, and general psychological distress. These findings extend previous research examining GSAs and may hold implications for considering a high school GSA as a protective factor that offsets some risk for developing problematic substance use, depression, and psychological distress among LGBT youth as they enter into young adulthood. GSAs may offset these risks by reducing experiences of at-school victimization, while increasing feelings of connectedness to the school environment for LGBT youth.

An interesting and unexpected result, which was not the focus of this study, was the absence of a relationship between childhood abuse and problematic alcohol use. A substantial body of research has consistently reported this association. At the same time, Rosario, Schrimshaw, and Hunter (2004) failed to find an association between CSA and problematic drinking among LGB youth. Rosario and colleagues argued that periods of time during an individual's identity development are potentially risky for experiencing increased substance use. Identity development experiences may be partially related to the aforementioned differences in substance use. However, the absence of a difference in outness scores between the GSA + and GSA − youth may suggest that the influence of high school and college experiences has a greater impact on the current alcohol use behaviors of our participants relative to childhood abuse experiences and identity development processes.

Implications for School Psychologists

School psychologists possess a unique training that blends research, assessment, counseling/intervention/prevention knowledge, and an appreciation for culture and diversity (National Association of School Psychologists; NASP, 2008). In turn, school psychologists may be best suited to identify potential solutions to reduce the risks that LGBT youth experience at school and to intervene at various levels within the dynamic and multifaceted school system (Graybill, Varjas, Meyers, & Watson, 2009; NASP, 2003). Specific recommendations for how to improve the school climate for sexual minority youth may involve: (1) establishing and publicizing an anti-bullying policy that specifically prohibits bullying and bullying based upon factors such as sexual orientation, gender, and gender identity; (2) training teachers to recognize and intervene when students engage in behaviors that are homophobic or transphobic in nature; (3) supporting the establishment of GSAs or similar student organizations; (4) working to integrate information about sexual orientation and gender identity into educational curricula and modern conceptualizations of diversity (Russell, McGuire, Laub, & Manke, 2006).

A school psychologist's role may include advocating for changes in policies through brief conversations and suggestions with teachers, staff, and administrators; this process may be effective in shaping the school climate toward acceptance of LGBT youth. School psychologists may also consider working with teachers and administrators to help these individuals decide how to effectively prevent homophobic slurs and bullying (e.g., by having teachers discuss the topic at the beginning of each semester and/or incorporating anti-discrimination policies into syllabi). They may also recommend self-disclosure on the part of the teachers and staff members by encouraging these individuals to express offense to homophobic language. School psychologists can also assist teachers in developing appropriate disciplinary actions in an effort to foster a supportive and affirming atmosphere (Graybill et al., 2009; NASP, 2003). They may also be helpful in the process of forming GSAs by identifying teachers who might be willing to sponsor such club; factors related to motivation to become a GSA advisor include having a protective attitude toward LGBT youth and having a personal connection to LGBT people (Valenti & Campbell, 2009).

Overall, the results of this study are important because they suggest that the high school environment may be related to experiences of psychological distress and problematic substance use as LGBT youth enter young adulthood. School psychologists are valuable assets within the school environment and may help to promote a safe and affirming school climate for LGBT youth by assisting in the development of policies and interventions that protect this population, and by helping teachers and administrators prevent and respond to homophobia and transphobia within the school context.

Limitations

There are a number of limitations that clearly limit the generalizability of the results and prevent causal inferences from being drawn. First, because participants were not randomly assigned to schools with and without GSAs, causality cannot be inferred with regard to the relationship between GSA status and any of the outcome variables of the study. Rather, GSAs should be viewed as indicative of an environment that may be conducive to healthy development for LGBT youth. Though we did attempt to control for the acceptance of and safety for LGBT people in the communities that participants attended high school, some of the benefits detected in this study may still stem from living in a community where the climate for sexual minorities is quite positive. These communities are more likely to have schools with a GSA and other resources, compared to communities where the climate for LGBT people is less than desirable (Fetner & Kush, 2008).

Second, our participants were reporting on experiences and behaviors within the context of communities and states that are likely to have varying levels of systemic and/or institutionalized homophobia that can give rise to varying degrees of psychopathology (Hatzenbuehler, Keyes, & Hasin, 2009). Statistical control over these state and community level systemic factors was not obtained, though they are likely to differentially influence the experiences of the LGBT youth.

A third limitation of this study involves the generalizability of the findings because of the homogeneous sample of college-age participants who elected to participate in the study. Because this study utilized a convenience sample of participants who were self-selected, the participation rate for the study cannot be determined and we cannot know if the findings are applicable to those individuals who were targeted by our recruitment efforts but decided not to complete the survey. Additionally, the results may not generalize to LGBT individuals who are older, who "come out" later in life, who do not seek higher education, who do not join a college LGBT organization, and who are ethnic minorities. In addition, LGBT youth who are most "at-risk," such as youth who dropped out of high school, were not targeted by our recruitment method. If GSAs enhance school belonging and reduce at-school victimization, youth who dropped out of high school may be more likely to have been attending schools without a GSA, and if they had been included, the group differences reported herein might actually be larger than reported.

A fourth limitation involves the sample size. Had the sample been larger, additional analyses could have examined whether the findings are consistent with respect to gender and behavioral and affective domains of sexual orientation. Recent findings highlight the importance of considering both gender and multiple domains of sexual orientation when evaluating risks for developing substance use disorders and psychopathology (Bostwick, Boyd, Hughes, & McCabe, 2009; McCabe, Hughes, Bostwick, West, & Boyd, 2009).

Finally, the retrospective nature of this study may have influenced the accuracy of data obtained in relation to at-school victimization, school belonging, childhood abuse, and community climate, in particular. Though the results consistently demonstrated more positive outcomes among GSA + youth, future research that is conducted longitudinally would eliminate concerns about retrospective reporting and could resolve a number of the limitations noted in this study.

Future Directions

In the future, longitudinal studies with larger samples that can account for genetic factors, systemic/institutionalized homophobia, community climate, school climate, family environment, as well as the role of GSAs, may be able to illuminate the contributions of these factors in the development of problematic substance use and other mental health outcomes. Future research could begin by studying LGBT youth who live in the same state and same city or town, but attend high schools with and without GSAs. Additionally, recruiting heterosexual siblings of these youth could provide some controls for genetic factors and family environment. Though random assignment may not be feasible, additional control over these factors may allow researchers to examine the unique variance that can be accounted for by GSAs in relation to various outcome variables of interest.

Future research must also attempt to understand the possible effects of attending a high school with a GSA on heterosexual youth. If LGBT youth are viewed as being at-risk for experiencing at-school victimization, then the question of "Who are the victimizers, and what affect does attending a school with a GSA have upon them?" will require evaluation. In addition, researchers should attempt to study youth who display gender-nonconforming behaviors, regardless of sexual orientation. Longitudinal studies that incorporate teacher, student, and peer ratings could be used to understand how GSAs might benefit youth who defy gender norms.

Though school psychologists might engage in any of the above efforts, they might also serve as program evaluators to monitor the impact that establishing a GSA has on the school environment. Assessment could include student and staff perceptions of the safety for and acceptance of LGBT youth in schools, the attendance and performance of LGBT youth, and the frequency with which LGBT youth are involved in behaviors that require disciplinary actions. Programmatic research that identifies aspects of GSAs that are effective in fostering a safe school environment would not only be valuable to the scientific community, but could also be used on a community level to determine best practices within school systems.

In the end, if GSAs are a source of protection for LGBT youth, future research with this population can, and must, be guided to better maximize this protectiveness while advancing theories that seek to explain why LGBT youth are an at-risk population in the first place. Collaboration among students, teachers, administrators, and school psychologists practicing in schools and school psychologists in academia alike must occur so that programs that encourage education, awareness, prevention, and intervention in an integrative manner will be developed and implemented to produce positive changes that will better the lives of all youth.

Note

1. LGBT is a commonly used acronym in the literature that combines aspects of sexual orientation (i.e., lesbian, gay, and bisexual identities) with gender identity (i.e., transgender). *Sexual minority* as a term is also frequently used to describe LGBT people. Though neither categorization can capture the complexities of sexual orientation and gender identity accurately, we use the term LGBT more often throughout this paper, as it best reflects the identities of the participants in this study. As the previous research is reviewed, we have attempted to use the terminology that best reflects the samples under study

Critical Thinking

1. Why do gay-straight alliances in high schools reduce the bullying and victimization of LGBT students?

2. Would you join a gay-straight alliance? Why or why not?

3. What can school psychologists, and other school administrators, do to help prevent harassment of culturally diverse students?

This article was published Online First May 2, 2011.

NICHOLAS C. HECK, ANNESA FLENTJE, AND BRYAN N. COCHRAN Department of Psychology, The University of Montana.

Correspondence concerning this article should be addressed to NICHOLAS C. HECK, Department of Psychology, The University of Montana, Skaggs Building Room 143, Missoula, MT 59812. E-mail: heck.nicholas@gmail.com

Portrait of a Hunger Artist

The anorexia began innocently enough, until eating became the point of living. Precisely because it was so special, it had to be made more perfect by hunger.

EMILY TROSCIANKO

"You are welcome in our new home, but your anorexia isn't," my mother said to me one day in April 2008. How dare she imply that there was any distinction between "me" and "my anorexia"?

I couldn't imagine my life without it, nor did I want to. It dictated everything I did and was, from going to bed almost when other people were getting up, to the solitude of my existence on a boat in Oxford, studying and starving, to my absolutely nonnegotiable daily bike rides and my constantly being cold—and my incomparable pleasure in the plate of bread and low-fat margarine and boiled vegetables in bed last thing at night, followed by cereal with skimmed milk diluted with water to go further, and finally mouthfuls of creamy chocolate to send me to sleep without hunger.

That was life; that was me. How to say "I" could come to their new house, and "it" couldn't? Her words made me so angry, so upset—and so scared. I was 26, and for 10 years I and my anorexia had grown ever more inseparable.

But my mother and her partner were moving and they told me they couldn't face the idea of me and my illness coming like a black shadow over their new home. He couldn't bear my cooking for the family and never eating, sitting there and watching them eat, or my nocturnalism; she couldn't bear any of it, least of all how it threatened their relationship, too.

I wept. But a few months after that conversation, I did make the decision to start to eat more. And it felt like I was bidding good-bye to my closest, most loyal friend.

That friendship began so innocuously I'm not sure I can identify a proper beginning. I do remember the end of a family ski holiday in France. I'd had one too many vodka-and-Cokes in the hotel bar. The après-ski haze of warm fires and hilarity ended at the hotel toilets. The next morning the others got in some last skiing while I sat in the car feeling ill. Then the queasy hairpin bends all the way down the mountain, and in the evening all I could stomach were a few salty crisps.

The next day, on motorways and the ferry, I had a few more crisps, but I felt a weakness that at once demanded more food and made "more" too much effort. It was a new weakness that mutated into an almost-strength, which was no longer physical but manifested itself in ways like this: "You sure you don't want any dinner?" "Yeah, still don't feel very hungry, I'll get myself something later." And then I wouldn't.

Looking back over my diaries, though, I realize that wasn't really the beginning, but rather a stepping-stone along the way to starvation: learning how exhilarating hunger can be. The power to keep on deferring eating felt like a true triumph, even as the hunger itself became more oppressive.

Deferring food was proof of strength, so it was a victory always to be a little later than yesterday. There was always a perverse pleasure in staying hungrier longer. So the day's single meal would be at two or three or four or five in the morning.

One winter it went all the way around the clock, several times, so for a week or so I'd be going to bed at 9 or 10 in the morning, and then soon bedtime would be back around to 10 at night. This does not make for a good mood or many social opportunities. Waking up to a wintry sunset is one of the most depressing things in the world, especially when you must now have a bike ride and work eight hours or so before eating.

Starvation was the very thing that made food so sublime. I couldn't imagine any pleasure that could replace that of chocolate in bed at dawn. I knew that the sense of power, self-control, and superiority was all just my entrapment in the rigid mind-set of the starved and frail. I knew that the purity I idealized was every night belied by the feverish inspection of my stools, and by the demeaning obsessive-compulsive habits of counting and checking and memorizing and tidying that were infiltrating my brain and dragging me further into exhaustion. Yet understanding simply could not translate into action.

Starvation was the very thing that made food so sublime. And the purity I idealized was every night belied by the feverish inspection of my stools.

As to the causes of it all, there are the usual nature-nurture suspects: my parents' genes (my father stopped eating at age four in protest over his parents' arguments; my mother inherited her mother's debilitating penchant for guilt) and all the ethereal cheekboned catwalk girls. But the thread woven through the years was a line I found much earlier in my diary: "the flat stomach I've always wanted."

Through the years of my increasing starvation, I would look in the mirror and see the curves of my thighs and breasts gradually give way to sharp outcrops of hips, ribs, and sternum, and elbows become wider than the arms they held together. But I really only cared about one thing: my tummy. Right from the beginning, I'd turn this way and that, in light and shadow, pressing it in, breathing in—imagining, in the early days, being the person I was when I breathed in, and imagining staying that person when I breathed out.

I imagined being the person I was when I breathed in, and imagined staying that person when I breathed out.

Eventually, I did become the image of my imaginings. But by then I had become someone quite different. The almost-flatness of the tummy was a perpetual torment: One can always breathe in more, make it flatter still, or concave; one can never quite become the person in whom breathing out and breathing in make no difference. After a decade of losing weight so gradually that I hardly noticed, maybe I finally did reach the impossible concavity of the tummy that isn't, that doesn't contain or speak of past contents, past consumption, but simply declaims, right now, its perfection.

As my tummy withered, all sorts of things became untenable. The cold—it started at the fingertips and worked its way inwards, so that throughout the Winter, and the end of the autumn and the beginning of the spring, there was an awful core of cold, which knew that warmth comes from movement but which wanted only to curl up into itself; which turned walking and sitting and lying into variations on huddling; which kept muscles taut with resistance against the outside; which saw in every activity, every location, only sources of heat or threats of cold.

It, or the fear of it, or the attempt to preempt it, was always there. A room would be reduced to its radiators, an evening outing refused for the frosty distances between bedroom and bar.

My trousers began to settle on my protruding hips instead of at my waist, and so trailed below the heels, as if my body's shrinkage had been in height as well as width. Tops began to hang shapeless, and bras became superfluous. But while all these things became too big, they were at the same time too small: They offered too little protection against the eyes of other people—who saw only bones—and against the cold.

While my clothes became too big, they were at the same time too small; they offered too little protection against the eyes of other people and against the cold.

My wardrobe now filled up with cardigans and trousers. Where once one layer was enough, now I needed two or three. Having done so much to denude the body of its padding, this body, so overly "purified," now had to be encumbered with layers of external insulation far less efficient than fat. And then even when summer came, I couldn't embrace it with open arms; I feared that all the energy hitherto expended in the attempt to keep warm might now be converted back into the fat that could warm me so much better.

Along with coldness, tiredness, and hunger came solitude. Social contact dwindled firstly because it can't be separated from food and drink, and then doubly so due to the gulf of mental separation. At first, I found it hard to talk at all about food and eating, or not eating: It was so private, so shameful, so glorifying—but simply unspeakable. An evening in a bar or a friend's family dinner—simple past pleasures—demanded excuses for not eating, which multiplied in inventive excess.

Even the seemingly unthreatening walk or shopping trip or cinema outing was precluded by a brain that counted hours not working as hours lost that had to be made up. A tangle of emotions grew between old friends. There was envy—of thinness on the one hand, and of carelessness on the other. There was resentment—of just this thinness and this carelessness. And scorn—of fatness or absence of control, which amounted to the same thing. Ultimately, I envied, scorned, and resented other people's inability to comprehend me, and made every effort to prevent their comprehending.

With my family it was even worse. On and off over the years, my father tried to persuade me to eat, with what I saw as emotional blackmail that swung between tears and rage, pity and fear. He feigned indifference—"I don't care if you eat it but it's there if you want it"—while silently screaming how he was being destroyed, and sometimes screaming it aloud: "I'm not going to let you kill yourself without a fight, it's a crisis point, you have to eat some dinner." There were moments of pure paternal tenderness—the unreserved will to help, to protect—and unreserved daughterly love and gratitude. But when the immediate danger was past these moments would fade. Gradually there was nothing but distance between us.

With my mother it was less dramatic and, for a longtime, far more intimate. She never tried to force anything as he did, and I relied more and more upon her patience in letting me stay at home, not sending me away as he thought I should be. She, more than anyone, made deep and sincere attempts to understand. Together we would pick apart the pseudo-logic, uncover hidden paths of obsessive reasoning. And every time she would be ready to hug and hold and support me when the excavations brought tears and shameful despair at the exposed absurdities.

And so when she told me "it" wasn't welcome, I was devastated. Somehow, though, I needed to know this more and more deeply until the blackness and the narrowness became unmitigated. The thought of infertility and bones breaking with brittleness in my old age had to surface once more, hauntingly. I needed the obsessive compulsions to feel ever more like madness and the weakness to make just one more flight of stairs feel insurmountable. I needed a moment in a dressing room, seeing myself like a corpse sticking out of a silk dress I could never

Four Big Myths about Anorexia

1. Anorexics don't feel hungry.

Of course they do. Hunger is the point, after a while: It's the great tormentor and the great addictive high.

2. Anorexics don't like food.

In general, anorexics love eating as much as they love being hungry. The eating, too, becomes the point: Eating can only be as perfect as it should be if you're hungry enough, if it's late enough, if you've prepared the food meticulously according to your own immutable rules.

3. Anorexics look in the mirror and see a fat person.

Of course they don't. They're not stupid. You look in the mirror and see your ribs with their thinly stretched coating of papery skin. But what you care about is some tiny, specific aspect of your body that has always to be more and more pared away: inner thighs that must be more

and more fleshless, or wrists that can be encompassed with the other hand with more and more space to spare. Anorexia isn't body dysmorphia.

4. Being thin is all that matters to an anorexic.

Being thin is in fact often only a minor matter compared to everything else that drives you. Control is probably at the center of it all. Control of food and eating might be the most obvious anorexic behavior, but the control illusion stretches its tentacles into all the rest of life—how much you work, how much you spend, how many people you spend time with—until going out for a drink on a Saturday night is as impossible as not having the next day and week and month planned into nothingness. Control equals strength, strength equals denial, denial equals simplicity, simplicity equals purity, purity equals perfection, perfection equals perfect control. It's the ultimate illusion; simplicity and perfection are equally inhuman.

---

wear. And one more compulsive half hour in a supermarket, not being able to stop myself from checking every package I saw for nutrition information when all I'd come for was a loaf of bread. I needed my mother to tell me I could come to her new house, but not laden with all this.

Even when, at last, I decided this all must go, and my friends took matters into their own hands and found me an eating disorders clinic, I didn't believe it could. Eating was the point of living, of getting through the next interminably long day; precisely because it was so special, it had to be waited for, made more and more perfect by the hunger that would grow deeper and deeper so that nothing else mattered.

Rather than trying to visualize some unimaginable end point, I simply had to decide to eat 500 calories more every single day, without fail. I didn't really believe anything would happen. Yes, I might put on a few kilos, and although that terrified me it wouldn't change who I was. Food would still be the ultimate point and pleasure of life, made perfect by infinitely deferring, restricting, and meticulously, secretively orchestrating the eating of it.

But then emotions came back, and I fell in love, and one night there was the first night without chocolate last thing. Funny that learning to do without food should in any sense be part of the recovery from anorexia. But it is; the most terrifying and thrilling thing I've learned in this last year since I began to eat again is that food is the means and not the end, a part rather than the whole, and that life cannot be as simple as simply longing for another day of hunger to be over.

Not long ago, I was sitting in a high-ceilinged apartment in Berlin with a cup of tea and my laptop, my boyfriend lying on the bed reading, interrupting me now and then with talk of where we might go and eat the next night, our last evening before we flew back to England. We had eaten at a restaurant the night before, too, and did so almost every night we were in Berlin. It was a holiday, after all, and we were treating ourselves.

I still get overcome with how miraculous it is: the repeated miracle of eating with other people, at a normal time of day, and of having eaten thus for days and weeks and months now. Sometimes it still feels unreal. But gradually, now, it's my old anorexic self who feels like she never really existed.

Critical Thinking

1. Support the idea that a non-living thing can be viewed as a friend.

2. Review the activities of daily life of a person with anorexia nervosa.

3. Identify the forces that helped the author recover normal eating patterns.

EMILY TROSCIANKO is a lecturer in German at Jesus College, University of Oxford, and just completed a doctoral thesis on Franz Kafka. She writes the *PT* blog A Hunger Artist.

53.1% of You Already Know What This Story's About. Or do You?

Need a Hint? It's about Professor Daryl Bem and his cheerful case for ESP.

DAN KOIS

I stare at the two curtains side by side on my computer screen. I try to focus on the task at hand: *Which image has a photo hidden behind it?* And what might it be? The alpine lake at sunset? The loving husband embracing his wife?

I choose the curtain on the left. Behind it are a naked man and woman, fucking.

The pair's sleek, airbrushed bodies flash on my monitor for precisely two seconds, long enough for me to wonder: Did they know? When these two posed, could they guess that one day this Jpeg would wind up on a Mac Mini in a lab at Cornell University? Did he know that from his depilated testicles might be launched the first salvo in the war against the ESP skeptics? Did she know her O-face might change the face of science? Could they see the future?

Maybe so, if you believe the research of Daryl Bem. According to "Feeling the Future," a peer-reviewed paper the APA's *Journal of Personality and Social Psychology* will publish this month, Bem has found evidence supporting the existence of precognition. The experiment I'm trying, one of nine Bem cites in his study, asks me to guess which of two curtains hides a photograph. (Some of the images are erotic, some neutral, in an attempt to see if different kinds of photos have different effects.) If mere chance governed each guess, I'd be right 50 percent of the time. Naturally, I'd guess correctly more like 100 percent of the time if you showed me where the photo was before I chose.

But what about if you showed me the photo's location immediately *after* I chose? Perhaps, if I had ESP, I could peek into the future and improve my guesswork, even just a little bit. Over seven years, Bem tested more than 1,000 subjects in this very room, and he believes he's demonstrated that some mysterious force gives humans just the slightest leg up on chance.

Responses to Bem's paper by the scientific community have ranged from arch disdain to frothing rejection. And in a rebuttal—which, uncommonly, is being published in the same issue of *JPSP* as Bem's article—another scientist suggests that not only is this study seriously flawed, but it also foregrounds a crisis in psychology itself.

The scourge of responsible psychological research stands behind me, wearing a red cardigan and an expression of great interest. "How were your results?" Bem asks. He points out that I scored better predicting the location of erotic photos—in Bem's hypothesis, more arousing images are more likely to inspire ESP—than I did boring old landscapes and portraits. In this dingy lab in the basement of an Ivy League psych department, is the future now?

Even before Daryl Bem, 72, began studying ESP, he was a mind reader—or rather, a mentalist, who performed Kreskin-style magic acts for students and friends. He knew how easily audiences could be tricked, so he was a skeptic about parapsychology, or PSI. "Like most psychologists," he says, sitting on an elderly couch in his townhouse two miles from Cornell's campus in Ithaca, "I knew all the ways in which people could fool themselves and interpret coincidences as premonitions." But reading the existing PSI research changed his opinion about how the brain works. Years ago, he says, "the model of the brain we had was more of a switchboard: stimulus in, response out. Now we have a richer metaphor for thinking about the brain: the computer." His hands trace a flourish in the air, as if to say *Presto!* "Short-term and long-term memory have analogs in the computer. There's stuff in ram that'll disappear when you turn the computer off, and there's stuff you've saved to disk. The computer does an enormous amount of unconscious processing—that is, stuff that does not appear on the screen, if you think of the screen as the consciousness."

Over seven years, Bem measured what he considers statistically significant results in eight of his nine studies. In the experiment I tried, the average hit rate among 100 Cornell undergraduates for erotic photos was 53.1 percent. (Neutral photos showed no effect.) That doesn't seem like much, but as Bem points out, it's about the same as the house's advantage in roulette.

Thinking counterintuitively about ESP appealed to him. "My career has been characterized," he says, "by trying to solve conundrums where I just don't believe the conventional explanation." More than 40 years ago, Bem's doctoral dissertation challenged the dominant paradigm of social psychology, Leon Festinger's concept of cognitive dissonance. Bem's groundbreaking "self-perception theory" suggests that rather than possessing an ironclad sense of self, we define our own emotions and attitudes using the same haphazard external cues (*If I bite my nails, I must be nervous*) that others use when observing us. "It's a clever theory," Bem says, "but what made me rich and famous is that I called the article 'Self-Perception Theory: An Alternative to Cognitive Dissonance.'"

Still, precognition seems a little too counterintuitive—and easily counterargued. For example, wouldn't I notice if I had ESP? Also, why do I always lose at roulette?

To science-writing eminence Douglas Hofstadter, the publication of work like Bem's has the potential to unleash, and legitimize, other "crackpot ideas." In *The New York Times,* the University of Oregon's Ray Hyman used the words "an embarrassment for the entire field." Some critics protest that the article can't explain what mechanism might be behind precognition. ("We almost always have the phenomenon before we have the explanation," Bem says.) Others just scoff: Why limit yourself to one kind of pseudoscience? As York University's James Alcock points out in *Skeptical Inquirer,* that 53 percent might as well be proof of the power of prayer.

"It shouldn't be difficult to do one proper experiment and not nine crappy experiments," the University of Amsterdam's Eric-Jan Wagenmakers tells me. He's the co-author of the rebuttal that accompanies Bem's article in *JPSP.* Wagenmakers uses Bayesian analysis—a statistical method meant to enforce the notion that extraordinary claims require extraordinary evidence—to argue that Bem's results are indistinguishable from chance. In essence, he explains, 53 percent of a bunch of Cornell sophomores, in unmonitored experiments conducted by a pro-PSI professor, shouldn't really move the needle, considering how deeply unlikely the existence of precognition actually is. The paper, says Wagenmakers, never should have made it through peer review, and the fact that it did is representative of a larger crisis in the field: The methods and statistics used in psychology, he writes, are "too weak, too malleable, and offer far too many opportunities for researchers to befuddle themselves and their peers."

In a statement printed in the March issue, *JPSP*'s editors admit that they find Bem's results "extremely puzzling." Nevertheless, they write, "our obligation as journal editors is not to endorse particular hypotheses, but to advance and stimulate science through a rigorous review process." One of the article's four peer reviewers, Jonathan Schooler of UC Santa Barbara, says he approved the study for publication because, simply, "I truly believe that this kind of finding from a well-respected, careful researcher deserves public airing." (Schooler is currently engaged in PSI research; the *JPSP* would not divulge the identities of any of the peer reviewers.) He agrees with Wagenmakers's objections to a point, but protests that "if you hold the bar too high, you'll never be able to get the data out there for scrutiny."

And boy, has the data gotten out there; Bem even made a lively appearance on *The Colbert Report.* Which means that if

his study fails to replicate and is discredited, it'll be just another widely reported "breakthrough" that turned out to be wrong—like vaccines and autism, except this time it's ESP. "When I look at the results in high-impact journals, I have to laugh, the ridiculous things that are in there. And it's your fault as well," Wagenmakers tells me. "The media presents these spectacular findings, like, if you eat a certain species of tomato, you're 12 percent less likely to develop cancer. Well, how on earth could you design an experiment to prove that?"

Daryl Bem's mother, Sylvia, was the bowling pioneer of Denver, running the local leagues when the game was still considered unsuitable for ladies. "She always had a gleam in her eye about the fact the neighbors disapproved," Bem remembers. "Being out of step with the rest of the world just never bothered her any."

Nor him. Bem dismisses detractors like Ray Hyman as "not worth listening to, because they haven't come up with any alternative." But he insists he takes serious critics—"who take the time to read the research thoroughly"—seriously. He praises Wagenmakers's rebuttal, and with the help of two statisticians, he has written a rebuttal to the rebuttal, currently in peer review at *JPSP.* "I think I've pretty well covered my ass." (I later send a copy to Wagenmakers; he comments, "There's nothing new there. I'm not convinced at all.")

Bem's gone against the grain his whole life; sometimes, he's been right. He was arrested at civil-rights sit-ins in Michigan in the sixties and testified with his wife before the FCC in the seventies to force AT&T to change its discriminatory hiring practices toward women. Daryl Bem, Ph.D., and Sandra Lipsitz Bem, Ph.D., were even interviewed in the first issue of *Ms.* magazine about their egalitarian, gender-liberated marriage.

The Drs. Bem lectured together for years, giving three-hour seminars to packed houses about a partnership in which housework was split evenly and careers were equally important. Though both are now professors emeriti at Cornell, they don't share a home; neither divorced nor legally separated, they've been apart for eighteen years.

"I always loved living alone," Bem says. "And then the other thing is, I identify as gay." He tucks his white-socked feet under a couch cushion and remembers an early date with Sandra. "I said, 'Well, I'm from Colorado, and I'm a stage magician, and I'm predominantly homoerotic.' And she said, 'I don't think I've ever known anyone from Colorado before.'" He chuckles at his well-practiced joke.

Bem and his partner, Bruce Henderson, a professor of communication studies at Ithaca College, just celebrated their fifteenth anniversary. They've never lived together. "He's a total slob," Bem confides. "His place looks like somewhere you'd find a body amid all the junk and the cats." (Insists Henderson: "I have what seems like 100 cats but is in reality only one very old one.") Bem's home, by contrast, is tidy. Decorative owl knickknacks perch attentively atop the window seat, flanking a doll of Edna Mode, the fashion designer from *The Incredibles.*

Despite "a certain irreverence toward the academy," as Henderson puts it, Bem never senses any resentment from inside Cornell. "The faculty all have the property of being sufficiently arrogant," Bem explains, "that it doesn't trouble them to have a flake in their midst. They value the kind of non-conformity that leads you to new things. That's why they're here rather than at the University of Mexico, or whatever."

Thomas Gilovich, Bem's department head, agrees: "You have to be a very solid university to have the luxury of having someone like Daryl around." Before retiring to emeritus status, Bem taught a variety of classes, including a seminar on the culture wars. "My purpose every week," he says, "was to give them an *aha!* experience, where they say, 'I've never thought of an issue in that way.'" He publishes less than other academics of his stature. "It's not embarrassingly low, but in pure publication terms, you'd probably be surprised," says Gilovich. But when he does publish, it's a showstopper. As Gilovich puts it, "His impact factor is high."

Still, Cornell's grad students never assist with Bem's ESP studies, at Bem's insistence, to avoid possible career-hampering stigma. "I tell students, 'Only undergraduates and tenured professors should study this stuff,'" he says. Bem got tenure "in 1968, 1969, or 1970, I'm not sure which," well before he ever started studying PSI. Because he can't get grants, he pays for his research himself.

Gilovich has known Bem for 33 years. ("Daryl and Sandy taught us how to play bridge.") He has an unforced affection for his colleague, and he's dubious of warnings that science might suffer if Bem's research turns out to be bunk. "I feel like science is strong enough," he says. "It's a very corrective discipline. If an idea is boringly wrong, it'll be forgotten. If it's excitingly wrong, other people will do research and will find out."

I ask him about Bem's research plans for the spring semester: to recruit students in Gilovich's Intro to Social Psych class and feed them answers after they've taken the multiple-choice quizzes. If Bem's results are positive, would that be a violation of Cornell's Code of Academic Integrity?

Gilovich laughs. As long as everyone in the class has the same opportunity, he says, it should be okay. "Look, there are a lot of skeptics who say, 'Oh, the world's interesting enough.' Yeah, it is, but if there were other, you know, realms, dimensions, whatever, that we don't know about—that would be even

better." He's quiet for a moment. "It would be cool if it's true. I'm just . . . I'd bet a lot of money it's not."

Before PSI, Bem made his biggest splash in the nonacademic world with a politically incorrect but weirdly compelling theory of sexual orientation. In 1996, he published "Exotic Becomes Erotic" in *Psychological Review,* arguing that neither gays nor straights are "born that way"—they're born a *certain* way, and that's what eventually determines their sexual preference.

"I think what the genes code for is not sexual orientation but rather a type of personality," he explains. According to the EBE theory, if your genes make you a traditionally "male" little boy, a lover of sports and sticks, you'll fit in with other boys, so what will be exotic to you—and, eventually, erotic—are females. On the other hand, if you're sensitive, flamboyant, performative, you'll be alienated from other boys, so you'll gravitate sexually toward your exotic—males.

EBE is not exactly universally accepted. "The evidence is overwhelming that sexuality is constitutionally based," Glenn Wilson, a professor at London's Gresham College and the co-author of a book on the psychobiology of sexual orientation, tells me in an e-mail. "Bem's theory has no merit. It does not specify why one individual would be affected by 'alienation' rather than another."

Bem seems unconcerned. "Colleagues of mine, especially those in biological science, say, 'Daryl, your theory is beautifully written and well argued and almost certainly wrong.' Which is fine!" He laughs. He's moved on in search of other magic tricks—more *aha!* moments to rile, and perhaps expand, the world of research psychology. "I'm perfectly happy to be wrong."

Critical Thinking

1. What is precognition? Do you believe in its existence?

2. Describe Daryl Bem's controversial theories prior to his arguing for the existence of precognition.

3. Is a 53.1% success rate statistically significant? What percentage of correct responses would you require to believe in precognition if your answer to the first part of the question was no?

How to "Ace" Your Freshman Year in the Workplace with C's

Culture, Competence, and Consequences

PAUL HETTICH

When you start to feel comfortable and confident as juniors and seniors often do, having declared the best academic major in school, established solid friendships, mastered multiple-choice tests, and "psyched-out" the tough teachers, it is time to think about becoming a freshman again.

Graduates seeking a career with a bachelor's degree in psychology and fortunate enough to obtain a full-time job or better part-time employment (either a truly challenging position or a mind-numbing white collar assembly-line job) will enter a new organizational culture with new responsibilities, new relationships, and new challenges at a critical and long-anticipated life transition often characterized by high expectations, uncertainties, and self-doubt. You *will be* a humble freshman again but one now armed with a college education. Do not expect miracles from that degree during your first few years in the workplace but do expect life to be different from college. As you read, count the times *expect* or *expectation* appears; understanding how these terms apply may be critical to your success.

There are several important issues involved in the college-to-workplace transition, especially in an economic climate when bright, motivated graduates enter a poor job market carrying high loan debt and equally high hopes. Space does not permit me to address career planning, psychosocial and cognitive development, or managing finances. Instead, I will focus on three important but often ignored practical topics: **culture** (the customs, practices, and expectations of your new organization), **competence** (skills and qualities your employer expects you to use), and **consequences** (promotion, discipline, or termination which are based on your behaviors). If you have held full-time or several significant part-time jobs, you may know what I am talking about; if you have not, be ready to adjust your expectations and attitudes about the workplace even if you are a revered campus leader with a magna cum laude GPA. Organizations differ vastly, so many of my remarks are generalizations that may or may not apply to your particular situation as a student or a new employee.

Culture

One of the best insights I can share was articulated by Holton and Naquin (2001) who maintain that college and work are essentially different.

> The *knowledge* you acquired in college will be critical to your success, but the process of succeeding in school is very different from the process of succeeding at work. Certain aspects of your education may have prepared you to be a professional, but evidence from the workplace indicates that this is not enough for professional success (p. 7).

The knowledge you acquired in college will be critical to your success, but the process of succeeding in school is very different from the process of succeeding at work.

Several processes they refer to are embedded in your new organization's culture and practices. In college you can choose to do "B" or "C" level work in some courses, but your supervisor will expect "A" level work continuously (and don't look for "make-up" or "extra credit" assignments). In college you expect detailed syllabi; in your job expect less structure and more uncertainty. Your course grades are based primarily on individual effort, but teamwork is very common in the workplace. You can sit passively through most courses and earn "C" or better grades; in the workplace your supervisor and coworkers expect you to be an active participant and problem-solver (After all, you *are* a college graduate as are most of them). Perhaps most important, in college you focus *on your* development (intellectual, personal, moral, and social); in the workplace you concentrate on productivity and making your boss look good.

> **. . . in college you focus on your development (intellectual, personal, moral, and social); in the workplace you concentrate on productivity and making your boss look good.**

How do these comparisons apply to your current job? Will you be able to adapt quickly to specific practices that challenge you? Adaptability is a quality employers seek in new hires. I have encountered some graduates who adapted well and others, having entered with limited experience and unrealistic expectations, who described their experience as "a slap in the face" or "hitting a brick wall." Be ready to quickly extinguish many habits and expectations to which you were conditioned since grammar school and rapidly substitute new behaviors.

Competence

The most revered measure of success in college is grades. Grades are an important criterion to over half of the companies participating in the annual NACE (National Association of Colleges and Employers) survey, and a GPA of 3.0 is the typical cut-off (NACE, 2009). Do not be surprised, however, if recruiters (sometimes called Talent Sourcers) show more interest in your ability to identify your specific competencies and apply them to their organization's needs. Anticipate interviewers' questions such as: "What would you do in the following situation?" Table 1 lists in descending order of importance the top 10 skills and qualities employers seek (NACE, 2009). Although you may not think of these everyday behaviors as transferable skills, you should be developing them directly or indirectly in your coursework, cocurricular activities, jobs, and interactions with others. Because syllabi and assignments in most schools seldom articulate competencies, your challenge is to identify particular situations in which such qualities are cultivated and subsequently translate them to resumes and job requirements. Fortunately, a strong correspondence exists between the NACE list and the benchmarks recommended for undergraduate psychology programs (Dunn, McCarthy, Baker, Halonen, & Hill, 2007). I encourage you to read the Dunn et al. article and compare the five student-related benchmarks to the NACE skills.

Ironically, although communications is regularly listed as the most important skill set in the NACE survey, employers report that new hires enter the workplace deficient in face-to-face communication, writing, teamwork, presentation, and overall interpersonal skills. Other deficiencies include the absence of a work ethic, time management, multi-tasking, realistic expectations, loyalty, maturity, and business etiquette (NACE, 2009). Review Table 1 and critically examine your coursework, job, and nonacademic experiences in which these qualities and competencies can be strengthened or are absent. Also, log on to the NACE student website at www.jobweb.com/studentarticles.aspx?id=2121 and explore these and other job-related issues. To rephrase a popular political slogan: It's the skills, stupid (not just your GPA)!

Table 1 Skills & Qualities Employers Seek

1. Communication skills
2. Strong work ethic
3. Teamwork skills (works well with others)
4. Initiative
5. Analytical skills
6. Computer skills
7. Flexibility/adaptability
8. Interpersonal skills (relates well to others)
9. Problem-solving skills
10. Technical skills

Note: Reprinted from *Job Outlook 2009* with permission of the National Association of Colleges and Employers (copyright holder) retrieved from www.jobweb.com/studentarticles.aspx?id = 2121.

Consequences

As a workplace freshman you are excited about your new challenges and relationships, but the bottom line will be the consequences of your actions (i.e., what you should do to avoid costly mistakes and earn promotion). Among the questions contained in his annual survey of employer hiring practices, Gardner (2007) inquired about factors that lead to the disciplining, firing, and promotion of college graduates. Table 2 presents the top 10 reasons why new employees are disciplined, ranked in order by mean score and listing the corresponding percentage at the high end of the scale. All 10 behaviors are an integral part of the overall college experience (e.g., work ethic/commitment; avoiding unethical behavior; inappropriate use of technology) or coursework and nonacademic activities.

In short, the behaviors that get new hires disciplined are those they should have avoided during college. The situations may differ and some differences are critical. For example, recall from Table 1 that in college you focus on your personal development. If as a student you lack commitment, fail to follow instructions, fail to take initiative, miss deadlines, communicate ineffectively, and are late for class or work, the consequences of your actions usually affect you alone. The same behaviors when exhibited in the workplace, however, can have negative consequences for your supervisor, coworkers, department, and possibly the whole organization—as well as your family who may depend on you. No wonder these behaviors are causes for discipline! If your first job is mind-numbing, you might respond as you did in college to that mind-numbing course. If you reacted in a negative manner think twice before you respond similarly in the workplace. Your job and a bad start to your career may be at stake.

Note that six of the causes for discipline (Table 2) are the same reasons new hires are terminated. Are there counterparts to these behaviors in college? Depending on the situation(s), perseverance of the behaviors, and other factors, such acts may

Table 2 Factors That Influence the Disciplining and Termination of New Hires

Reasons for Discipline	Occurrence: Fairly—Very Often (%)	Mean Score
Lack of work ethic/ commitment	52	3.46
Unethical behavior	46	3.22
Failure to follow instructions	41	3.21
Ineffective in teams	41	3.19
Failure to take initiative	26	3.10
Missing assignments/ deadlines	33	2.98
Unable to communicate effectively—verbally	32	2.97
Inappropriate use of technology	34	2.90
Being late for work	28	2.83
Unable to communicate effectively—writing	28	2.81

Note: Occurrence: Percentage at the high end of the scale.

Mean Score: 5 = highest

Behaviors in boldface are also reasons for terminating new hires

Note: From *Moving Up or Moving Out of the Company? Factors That Influence the Promoting or Firing of New College Hires* (Research Brief 1-2007) by P. Gardner, 2007, retrieved from Michigan State University Collegiate Employment Research Institute website: www.ceri.msu.edu. Adapted with permission.

contribute to low grades, academic probation, and even expulsion. Students who strive to develop the positive habits opposite those negative behaviors will be rewarded in many ways.

Students who habitually exhibit the negative behaviors throughout college may ultimately receive their degree but their diploma (a piece of paper) does not transform them into responsible, capable employees.

On the positive side, Table 3 presents a cluster of qualities Gardner compiled from employer responses that lead new hires to promotions and new assignments. If you log on to www.ceri.msu.edu, link to Publications, and locate the Gardner (2007) study (see references), additional information is available, including specific definitions for many terms contained in Table 3. That list should not surprise you because these characteristics contribute to your success in the classroom, your job, cocurricular activities, and your relationships. Finally, search for the overlap between Table 2 and Table 3 behaviors and their positive or negative counterparts on the

Table 3 Characteristics That Lead to Promotions and New Assignments

Characteristic	Frequency as listed by employer (%)
Taking initiative	16
Self-management (e.g., prioritizing, time & stress mgt.)	13
Personal attributes	9
Commitment	9
Leadership	8
"Show and tell" (presenting ideas persuasively)	7
Technical competence	7
Organizational savvy	5
Learning	5
Critical thinking	5

Note: From *Moving Up or Moving Out of the Company? Factors That Influence the Promoting or Firing of New College Hires* (Research Brief 1-2007) by P. Gardner, 2007, retrieved from Michigan State University Collegiate Employment Research Institute website: www.ceri.msu.edu. Adapted with permission.

Table 1 skills list. Informally compare these tables to the expectations your teachers and your employer have of you. What do you conclude?

Concluding Comments

How many times did the words *expect* and *expectation* occur in this article? Like your next boss, I'll let you find the answer. I have met several employers who consistently report that for most new graduates, their unrealistic expectations pose a major problem.

You *can* succeed during your freshman year in the workplace with C's. Your corporate *culture* will differ from your college environment in numerous ways that you must become aware of and adapt to quickly. *Competencies* and skills replace GPA as the measure of your success; several of these you acquire during college and are very similar to the ones employers are seeking in their candidates. Finally, many *consequences* of positive and negative behaviors exhibited in college and workplace are identical, so continue to accentuate the positive habits, attitudes, and competencies; eliminate the negatives; and enjoy the journey into the next chapter in your life.

References

Dunn, D. S., McCarthy, M. A., Baker, S., Halonen, J. S., & Hill, G. W., IV. (2007). Quality benchmarks in undergraduate programs. *American Psychologist, 62*, 650–670.

Gardner, P. (2007). *Moving up or moving out of the company? Factors that influence the promoting or firing of new college hires* (Research Brief 1-2007). Retrieved from Michigan State University Collegiate Employment Research Institute website: www.ceri.msu.edu

How to Improve Your Workplace Readiness

Most of the following suggestions emerge directly or indirectly from the three Cs; others are derived from broad life experiences.

1. **Critically examine your current job,** even if the work is boring. Try to strengthen transferable skills such as those contained in the NACE list. Examine your attitudes toward your tasks and the people you work with. For example, to what extent can you: a) deal effectively with unstructured situations? b) work with people you do not like? c) respond maturely to criticism? d) work productively under stress and boredom? e) succeed in an organizational culture you may not like? Recognize that even the best jobs can be frustrating at times; you must learn to be effective under all conditions. If for one reason or another you have not held even a part-time job, get one—soon.

2. Seek internships, work, or research opportunities where you can **develop *real-world* experiences** and apply course concepts where possible.

3. Enroll in **courses that focus on process or organizational aspects of the workplace,** such as organizational behavior, small group communications, social psychology, public speaking, leadership, business writing, business or science technology, and others. Consider pursuing a business minor or at least courses in management, marketing, economics, accounting, business ethics, and human resources. Do you want to enter the contemporary business world illiterate in its most basic concepts?

4. **Join campus organizations and activities that promote collaboration, competition, and leadership;** focus on growth and change processes not just the activities—your Psi Chi chapter can be a wonderful choice for gaining valuable leadership experience. Join no later than your junior year with the goal of holding a major leadership position your senior year. You might not use leadership skills in your first couple of jobs, but they become invaluable as you advance.

5. By your junior year, **work with a career counselor** (in addition to your advisor) and create a plan that identifies your interests, goals, strengths, weaknesses, and potential career fields. Develop job-search and interview skills, create a computer-based skills portfolio of your achievements with your career counselor. Network!

6. **Search for campus workshops** and other opportunities that focus on self-development, conflict management, team building, time and stress management, leadership, and similar generic professional skills. Become a resident hall assistant if that position interests you.

7. Do not expect teachers and advisors to provide all the answers because they do not know them. There are, however, numerous **helpful resources** such as Psi Chi, APA, and others listed in the "Additional Resources."

8. Establish realistic expectations about the workplace by **avoiding the "entitlement mentality,"** (i.e., believing your degree entitles you to challenging work, good salary, and rapid advancement); embrace ambiguity and uncertainty as your constant companions.

9. **Develop a strong work ethic,** create meaning in your life; find value in what you do. Establish good habits of physical and mental health and solid relationships.

10. Try to **think and act positively** especially during the "bad" days and reduce self-doubts. You are not alone. You will become a senior again.

Hettich, P. I., & Helkowski, C. (2005). *Connect college to career: A student's guide to work and life transitions*. Belmont, CA: Thomson/Wadsworth Publishers.

Holton, E. F., III. (1998). Preparing students for life beyond the classroom. In J. N. Gardner, G. Van der Veer, & Associates *The senior year experience: Facilitating integration, reflection, closure, and transition* (pp. 95–115). San Francisco, CA: Jossey-Bass.

Holton, E. F., III., & Naquin, S. S. (2001). *How to succeed in your first job: Tips for new college graduates*. San Francisco, CA: Berrett-Koehler Publishers, Inc.

National Association Colleges and Employers (NACE). (2009). *Job outlook 2009—How you fit into the tight job market*. Retrieved from www.jobweb.com/studentarticles.aspx?id=2121

Additional Resources

Arnett, J. J., & Tanner, J.L. (Eds.). (2006). *Emerging adults in America: Coming of age in the 21st century*. Washington, DC: American Psychological Association.

Carducci, B. J. (2000). The successfully shy worker. In *Shyness: A bold new approach* (pp. 308–337). New York, NY: Quill/Harper Collins.

Fisher, S. Y., & Shelly, S. (2005). *The complete idiot's guide to personal finance in your 20's and 30's* (3rd Ed.). New York, NY: Penguin Group.

Furman, E. (2005). *Boomerang nation. How to survive living with your parents . . . the second time around*. New York, NY: Fireside.

Landrum, R. E. (2009). *Finding jobs with a psychology bachelor's degree: Expert advice for launching your career*. Washington, DC: American Psychological Association.

Levit, A. (2009). *They don't teach corporate in college: A twenty-something's guide to the business world* (2nd Ed.). Franklin Lakes, NJ: Career Press.

Peterson, C., Park, N., Hall, N., & Seligman, M. E. P. (2009). Zest and work. *Journal of Organizational Behavior*, 13, 161–172. doi: 10,1002/job.584

Robbins, A., & Wilner, A. (2001). *Quarterlife crisis: The unique challenges of life in your twenties*. New York, NY: Penguin Press.

Smith, W. S. (2008). *Decoding generational differences: Fact, fiction . . . or should we just get back to work?* Retrieved from Deloitte Development LLC website: www.deloitte.com/view/en_US/us/article/5abf899a961fb110VgnVCM100000ba42f00aRCRD.htm

Wilner, A., & Stocker, C. (2005). *Quarterlifer's companion: How to get on the right career path, control your finances, and find the support network you need to thrive.* Retrieved from www.quarterlifecrisis.com/about_qlc.shtml

Critical Thinking

1. Describe ways that school and work are essentially different.

2. List the major skills and competencies which employers seek.

3. Infer why lack of work ethic is the number one reason for job termination.

PAUL HETTICH, PHD, Professor Emeritus at DePaul University (IL), was an Army personnel psychologist, program evaluator in an education R&D lab, and a corporate applied scientist—positions that created a "real world" foundation for his career in college teaching and administration. He was inspired to coauthor *Connect College to Career: A Student Guide to Work and Life Transitions* (2005) by graduates and employers who revealed a major disconnect between university and workplace expectations, cultures, and practices.

I Can't Think!

The Twitterization of our culture has revolutionized our lives, but with an unintended consequence—our overloaded brains freeze when we have to make decisions.

Sharon Begley

Imagine the most mind-numbing choice you've faced lately, one in which the possibilities almost paralyzed you: buying a car, choosing a health-care plan, figuring out what to do with your 401(k). The anxiety you felt might have been just the well-known consequence of information overload, but Angelika Dimoka, director of the Center for Neural Decision Making at Temple University, suspects that a more complicated biological phenomenon is at work. To confirm it, she needed to find a problem that overtaxes people's decision-making abilities, so she joined forces with economists and computer scientists who study "combinatorial auctions," bidding wars that bear almost no resemblance to the eBay version. Bidders consider a dizzying number of items that can be bought either alone or bundled, such as airport landing slots. The challenge is to buy the combination you want at the lowest price—a diabolical puzzle if you're considering, say, 100 landing slots at LAX. As the number of items and combinations explodes, so does the quantity of information bidders must juggle: passenger load, weather, connecting flights. Even experts become anxious and mentally exhausted. In fact, the more information they try to absorb, the fewer of the desired items they get and the more they overpay or make critical errors.

This is where Dimoka comes in. She recruited volunteers to try their hand at combinatorial auctions, and as they did she measured their brain activity with fMRI. As the information load increased, she found, so did activity in the dorsolateral prefrontal cortex, a region behind the forehead that is responsible for decision making and control of emotions. But as the researchers gave the bidders more and more information, activity in the dorsolateral PFC suddenly fell off, as if a circuit breaker had popped. "The bidders reach cognitive and information overload," says Dimoka. They start making stupid mistakes and bad choices because the brain region responsible for smart decision making has essentially left the premises. For the same reason, their frustration and anxiety soar: the brain's emotion regions— previously held in check by the dorsolateral PFC—run as wild as toddlers on a sugar high. The two effects build on one another. "With too much information," says Dimoka, "people's decisions make less and less sense."

So much for the ideal of making well-informed decisions. For earlier generations, that meant simply the due diligence of looking things up in a reference book. Today, with Twitter and Facebook and countless apps fed into our smart phones, the flow of facts and opinion never stops. That can be a good thing, as when information empowers workers and consumers, not to mention whistle-blowers and revolutionaries. You can find out a used car's accident history, a doctor's malpractice record, a restaurant's health-inspection results. Yet research like Dimoka's is showing that a surfeit of information is changing the way we think, not always for the better. Maybe you consulted scores of travel websites to pick a vacation spot—only to be so overwhelmed with information that you opted for a staycation. Maybe you were *this close* to choosing a college, when suddenly older friends swamped your inbox with all the reasons to go somewhere else—which made you completely forget why you'd chosen the other school. Maybe you had the Date From Hell after being so inundated with information on "matches" that you chose at random. If so, then you are a victim of info-paralysis.

The research so far should give pause to anyone addicted to incoming texts and tweets. More information can lead to objectively poorer choices, and to choices that people quickly regret

The problem has been creeping up on us for a long time. In the 17th century Leibniz bemoaned the "horrible mass of books which keeps on growing," and in 1729 Alexander Pope warned of "a deluge of authors cover[ing] the land," as James Gleick describes in his new book, *The Information*. But the consequences were thought to be emotional and psychological, chiefly anxiety out being unable to absorb even a small fraction of what's out ere. Indeed, the Oxford English Dictionary added "information tigue" in 2009. But as information finds more ways to reach , more often, more insistently than ever before, another conse- ence is becoming alarmingly clear: trying to drink from a fire- ose of information has harmful cognitive effects. And nowhere e those effects clearer, and more worrying, than in our ability to ake smart, creative, successful decisions.

The research should give pause to anyone addicted to incom- g texts and tweets. The booming science of decision making as shown that more information can lead to objectively poorer oices, and to choices that people come to regret. It has shown at an unconscious system guides many of our decisions, and at it can be sidelined by too much information. And it has own that decisions requiring creativity benefit from letting e problem incubate below the level of awareness—something at becomes ever-more difficult when information never stops riving.

Decision science has only begun to incorporate research on ow the brain processes information, but the need for answers as urgent as the stakes are high. During the BP oil-well blow- ut last year, Coast Guard Adm. Thad Allen, the incident com- ander, estimates that he got **300** to **400** *pages* of emails, texts, ports, and other messages every day. It's impossible to know hether less information, more calmly evaluated, would have t officials figure out sooner how to cap the well, but Allen lls Newsweek's Daniel Stone that the torrent of data might ave contributed to what he calls the mistake of failing to close ff air space above the gulf on day one. (There were eight ear mid-air collisions.) A comparable barrage of information ssailed administration officials before the overthrow of the gyptian government, possibly producing at least one misstep: IA Director Leon Panetta told Congress that Hosni Mubarak as about to announce he was stepping down—right before the gyptian president delivered a defiant, rambling speech say- g he wasn't going anywhere. "You always think afterwards out what you could have done better, but there isn't time in e moment to second-guess," said White House Communica- ons Director Dan Pfeifler. "You have to make your decision nd go execute." As scientists probe how the flow of informa- on affects decision making, they've spotted several patterns. mong them:

otal Failure to Decide

very bit of incoming information presents a choice: whether pay attention, whether to reply, whether to factor it into an npending decision. But decision science has shown that peo- le faced with a plethora of choices are apt to make no decision t all. The clearest example of this comes from studies of finan- ial decisions. In a 2004 study, Sheena Iyengar of Columbia niversity and colleagues found that the more information peo- le confronted about a 401(k) plan, the more participation fell: rom 75 percent to 70 percent as the number of choices rose rom two to 11, and to 61 percent when there were 59 options. eople felt overwhelmed and opted out. Those who participated hose lower-return options—worse choices. Similarly, when

people are given information about 50 rather than 10 options in an online store, they choose lower-quality options. Although we say we prefer more information, in fact more can be "debili- tating," argues Iyengar, whose 2010 book *The Art of Choosing* comes out in paperback in March. "When we make decisions, we compare bundles of information. So a decision is harder if the amount of information you have to juggle is greater." In recent years, businesses have offered more and more choices to cater to individual tastes. For mustard or socks, this may not be a problem, but the proliferation of choices can create paralysis when the stakes are high and the information complex.

Many Diminishing Returns

If we manage to make a decision despite info-deluge, it often comes back to haunt us. The more information we try to assimi- late, the more we tend to regret the many forgone options. In a 2006 study, Iyengar and colleagues analyzed job searches by college students. The more sources and kinds of information (about a company, an industry, a city, pay, benefits, corporate culture) they collected, the less satisfied they were with their decision. They knew so much, consciously or unconsciously, they could easily imagine why a job not taken would have been better. In a world of limitless information, regret over the deci- sions we make becomes more common. We chafe at the fact that identifying the best feels impossible. "Even if you made an objectively better choice, you tend to be less satisfied with it," says Iyengar.

A key reason for information's diminishing or even negative returns is the limited capacity of the brain's working memory. It can hold roughly seven items (which is why seven-digit phone numbers were a great idea). Anything more must be processed into long-term memory. That takes conscious effort, as when you study for an exam. When more than seven units of infor- mation land in our brain's inbox, argues psychologist Joanne Cantor, author of the 2009 book *Conquer Cyber Overload* and an emerita professor at the University of Wisconsin, the brain struggles to figure out what to keep and what to disre- gard. Ignoring the repetitious and the useless requires cognitive resources and vigilance, a harder task when there is so much information.

It isn't only the quantity of information that knocks the brain for a loop; it's the rate. The ceaseless influx trains us to respond instantly, sacrificing accuracy and thoughtfulness to the false god of immediacy. "We're being trained to prefer an immedi- ate decision even if it's bad to a later decision that's better," says psychologist Clifford Nass of Stanford University. "In business, we're seeing a preference for the quick over the right, in large part because so many decisions have to be made. The notion that the quick decision is better is becoming normative."

'Recency' Trumps Quality

The brain is wired to notice change over stasis. An arriving email that pops to the top of your BlackBerry qualifies as a change; so does a new Facebook post. We are conditioned to give greater weight in our decision-making machinery to

---

DECISION: Where Should I Get My News?

CHOICES: Print versus online. Blog versus old-media site. Drudge Report versus Huffington Post RSS feeds versus Twitter.

NOISE: Can you trust what you read in newspapers? Can you trust what you read on the Internet? Are liberals more or less trustworthy than conservatives? Do you want to know a lot about one thing or a little about everything?

BEST STRATEGY: Mix it up. Read the top story in *The New York Times*—and then let the bloggers tell you what it missed.

DECISION: Which Jeans Should I buy?

CHOICES: Low-rise versus high-waisted. Boot-cut versus straight-legged. Regular out versus painter's pants with a hammer loop.

NOISE: Input from fashion blogs, celebrity photos, store employees, and your hips.

BEST STRATEGY: Find a pair that fits. Buy 20 of them.

DECISION: Should I Run for President?

CHOICES: A posh gig on cable versus leader of the free world. Millions in greasy lobbying dollars versus a flat rate of $400,000 per year. An ounce of privacy versus endless questions about your place of birth.

NOISE: Input from political pros, pundits, your spouse, your spiritual adviser, and Ohio-based plumbers.

BEST STRATEGY: Write a book. If you run out of material before you hit page 200, forget it.

DECISION: Which Coffee Drink Should I Order?

CHOICES: Dunkin' Donuts versus Starbucks. Fattening frappe versus low-cal. Venti versus grands. Fair trade versus cruel exploitation of Low-wage workers.

NOISE: Input from TV ads, liberal bloggers, Dr. Atkins, and your nagging caffeine headache.

BEST STRATEGY: Find a cup that meets at least two of your requirements. Buy it till the end of time.

---

what is latest, not what is more important or more interesting. "There is a powerful 'recency' effect in decision making," says behavioral economist George Loewenstein of Carnegie Mellon University. "We pay a lot of attention to the most recent information, discounting what came earlier." Getting 30 texts per hour up to the moment when you make a decision means that most of them make all the impression of a feather on a brick wall, whereas Nos. 29 and 30 assume outsize importance, regardless of their validity. "We're fooled by immediacy and quantity and think it's quality," says Eric Kessler, a management expert at Pace University's Lubin School of Business. "What starts driving decisions is the urgent rather than the important."

Part of the problem is that the brain is really bad at giving only a little weight to a piece of information. When psychologist Eric Stone of Wake Forest University had subjects evaluate the vocabulary skills of a hypothetical person, he gave them salient information (the person's education level) and less predictive information (how often they read a newspaper). People give the less predictive info more weight than it deserves. "Our cognitive systems," says Stone, "just aren't designed to take information into account only a little."

The Neglected Unconscious

Creative decisions are more likely to bubble up from a brain that applies unconscious thought to a problem, rather than going at it in a full-frontal, analytical assault. So while we're likely to think creative thoughts in the shower, it's much harder if we're under a virtual deluge of data. "If you let things come at you all the time, you can't use additional information to

make a creative leap or a wise judgment," says Cantor. "You need to pull back from the constant influx and take a break." That allows the brain to subconsciously integrate new information with existing knowledge and thereby make novel connections and see hidden patterns. In contrast, a constant focus on the new makes it harder for information to percolate just below conscious awareness, where it can combine in ways that spark smart decisions.

One of the greatest surprises in decision science is the discovery that some of our best decisions are made through unconscious processes. When subjects in one study evaluated what psychologist Ap Dijksterhuis of the Radboud University of Nijmegen in the Netherlands calls a "rather daunting amount of information" about four hypothetical apartments for rent—size, location, friendliness of the landlord, price, and eight other features—those who decided unconsciously which to rent did better. ("Better" meant they chose the one that had objectively better features.) The scientists made sure the decision was unconscious by having the subjects do a memory and attention task, which tied up their brains enough that they couldn't contemplate, say, square footage.

There are at least two ways an info-glut can impair the unconscious system of decision making. First, when people see that there is a lot of complex information relevant to a decision, "they default to the conscious system," says psychologist Maarten Bos of Radboud. "That causes them to make poorer choices." Second, the unconscious system works best when it ignores some information about a complex decision. But here's the rub: in an info tsunami, our minds struggle to decide if we can ignore this piece ... or that one ... but how about that one? "Especially online," says Cantor, "it is so much easier to look for more and more information than sit back and think about how it fits together."

Even experience-based decision making, in which you use a rule of thumb rather than analyze pros and cons, can go off the rails with too much information. "This kind of intuitive decision making relies on distilled expertise," says Kessler. "More information, by overwhelming and distracting the brain, can make it harder to tap into just the core information you need." In one experiment, M.B.A. students choosing a (make-believe) stock portfolio were divided into two groups, one that was inundated with information from analysts and the financial press, and another that saw only stock-price changes. The latter reaped more than twice the returns of the info-deluged group, whose analytical capabilities were hijacked by too much information and wound up buying and selling on every rumor and tip—a surefire way to lose money in the market. The more data they got, the more they struggled to separate wheat from chaff.

Which brings us back to the experimental subjects Angelika Dimoka has put in an fMRI scanner. The prefrontal cortex that waves a white flag under an onslaught of information plays a key role in your gut-level, emotional decision-making system. It hooks up feelings about various choices with the output of the rational brain. If emotions are shut out of the decision-making process, we're likely to overthink a decision, and that has been shown to produce worse outcomes on even the simplest tasks. In one classic experiment, when volunteers focused on the attributes of various strawberry jams they had just rated, it completely scrambled their preferences, and they wound up giving a high rating to a jam they disliked and a low rating to one they had found delicious.

How can you protect yourself from having your decisions warped by excess information? Experts advise dealing with emails and texts in batches, rather than in real time; that should let your unconscious decision-making system kick in. Avoid the trap of thinking that a decision, requiring you to assess a lot of complex information is best made methodically and consciously; you will do better, and regret less, if you let your unconscious turn it over by removing yourself from the info influx. Set priorities: if a choice turns on only a few criteria, focus consciously on those. Some people are better than others at ignoring extra information. These "sufficers" are able to say enough: they channel-surf until they find an acceptable show and then stop, whereas "maximizers" never stop surfing, devouring information, and so struggle to make a decision and move on. If you think you're a maximizer, the best prescription for you might be the "off" switch on your smart phone.

Critical Thinking

1. Recognize moments in your life when too many options prevented you from making a good decision. How did you feel after the fact? Would fewer options, or more time, have helped?

2. Select some creative venture in which you were involved. Did the creativity require "time to jell" or was it instantaneous?

3. How do you rate technology in your life? Is it something that makes you more efficient? Or less efficient?

Are We There Yet?

In 1970, 46 women filed a landmark gender-discrimination case. Their employer was Newsweek. Forty years later, their contemporary counterparts question how much has actually changed.

JESSICA BENNETT, JESSE ELLISON, AND SARAH BALL

They were an archetype: independent, determined young graduates of Seven Sisters colleges, fresh-faced, new to the big city, full of aspiration. Privately, they burned with the kind of ambition that New York encourages so well. Yet they were told in job interviews that women could never get to the top, or even the middle. They accepted positions anyway—sorting mail, collecting newspaper clippings, delivering coffee. Clad in short skirts and dark-rimmed glasses, they'd click around in heels, currying favor with the all-male management, smiling softly when the bosses called them "dollies." That's just the way the world worked then. Though each quietly believed she'd be the one to break through, ambition, in any real sense, wasn't something a woman could talk about out loud. But by 1969, as the women's movement gathered force around them, the dollies got restless. They began meeting in secret, whispering in the ladies' room or huddling around a colleague's desk. To talk freely they'd head to the Women's Exchange, a 19th-century relic where they could chat discreetly on their lunch break. At first there were just three, then nine, then ultimately 46—women who would become the first group of media professionals to sue for employment discrimination based on gender under Title VII of the Civil Rights Act. Their employer was Newsweek magazine.

Until six months ago, when sex- and gender-discrimination scandals hit ESPN, David Letterman's *Late Show,* and the *New York Post,* the three of us—all young Newsweek writers—knew virtually nothing of these women's struggle. Over time, it seemed, their story had faded from the collective conversation. Eventually we got our hands on a worn copy of *In Our Time,* a memoir written by a former Newsweek researcher, Susan Brownmiller, which had a chapter on the uprising. With a crumpled Post-it marking the page, we passed it around, mesmerized by descriptions that showed just how much has changed, and how much hasn't.

Forty years after Newsweek's women rose up, there's no denying our cohort of young women is unlike even the half-generation before us. We are post–Title IX women, taught that the fight for equality was history; that we could do, or be,

anything. The three of us were valedictorians and state-champion athletes; we got scholarships and were the first to raise our hands in class. As young professionals, we cheered the third female Supreme Court justice and, nearly, the first female president. We've watched as women became the majority of American workers, prompting a Maria Shriver–backed survey on gender, released late last year, to proclaim that "the battle of the sexes is over."

The problem is, for women like us, the victory dance feels premature. Youthful impatience? Maybe. But consider this: U.S. Department of Education data show that a year out of school, despite having earned higher college GPAs in every subject, young women will take home, on average across all professions, just 80 percent of what their male colleagues do. Even at the top end, female M.B.A.s make $4,600 less per year in their first job out of business school, according to a new Catalyst study. Motherhood has long been the explanation for the persistent pay gap, yet a decade out of college, full-time working women who *haven't* had children still make 77 cents on the male dollar. As women increasingly become the breadwinners in this recession, bringing home 23 percent less bacon hurts families more deeply than ever before. "The last decade was supposed to be the 'promised one,' and it turns out it wasn't," says James Turley, the CEO of Ernst & Young, a funder of the recent M.B.A. study. "This is a wake-up call."

In countless small ways, each of us has felt frustrated over the years, as if something was amiss. But as products of a system in which we learned that the fight for equality had been won, we didn't identify those feelings as gender-related. It seemed like a cop-out, a weakness, to suggest that the problem was anybody's fault but our own. It sounds naive—we know—especially since our own boss Ann McDaniel climbed the ranks to become Newsweek's managing director, overseeing all aspects of the company. Compared with the Newsweek dollies, what did we have to complain about? "If we judge by what we see in the media, it looks like women have it made," says author Susan Douglas. "And if women have it made, why would you be so ungrateful to point to something and call it sexism?"

Yet the more we talked to our friends and colleagues, the more we heard the same stories of disillusionment, regardless of profession. No one would dare say today that "women don't write here," as the Newsweek women were told 40 years ago. But men wrote all but six of Newsweek's 49 cover stories last year—and two of those used the headline "The Thinking Man." In 1970, 25 percent of Newsweek's editorial masthead was female; today that number is 39 percent. Better? Yes. But it's hardly equality. (Overall, 49 percent of the entire company, the business and editorial sides, is female.) "Contemporary young women enter the workplace full of enthusiasm, only to see their hopes dashed," says historian Barbara J. Berg. "Because for the first time they're slammed up against gender bias."

We should add that we are proud to work at Newsweek. (Really, boss, we are!) We write about our magazine not because we feel it's worse here, but because Newsweek was once ground zero for a movement that was supposed to break at least one glass ceiling. Just as our predecessors' 1970 case didn't happen in a vacuum, Newsweek today is neither unique nor unusual. Female bylines at major magazines are still outnumbered seven to one; women are just 3 percent of Fortune 500 CEOs and less than a quarter of law partners and politicians. That imbalance even applies to the Web, where the founder of a popular copywriting Web site, Men With Pens, revealed late last year that "he" was actually a she. "I assumed if I chose a male name [I'd] be viewed as somebody who runs a company, not a mom sitting at home with a child hanging off her leg," the woman says. It worked: her business doubled once she joined the boys' club.

We know what you're thinking: we're young and entitled, whiny and humorless—to use a single, dirty word, feminists! But just as the first black president hasn't wiped out racism, a female at the top of a company doesn't eradicate sexism. In fact, those contradictory signs of progress—high-profile successes that mask persistent inequality—are precisely the problem. Douglas describes those mixed messages as "enlightened sexism": the idea that because of all the gains women have made, biases that once would have been deemed sexist now get brushed off. Young women, consequently, are left in a bind: they worry they'll never be taken as seriously as the guys, yet when they're given the opportunity to run the show, they balk. A recent Girl Scouts study revealed that young women avoid leadership roles for fear they'll be labeled "bossy"; another survey found they are four times less likely than men to negotiate a first salary. As it turns out, that's for good reason: a Harvard study found that women who demand higher starting salaries are perceived as "less nice," and thus less likely to be hired. "This generation has had it ingrained in them that they must thrive within a 'yes, but' framework: Yes, be a go-getter, but don't come on too strong. Yes, accomplish, but don't brag about it," says Rachel Simmons, author of *The Curse of the Good Girl*. "The result is that young women hold themselves back, saying, 'I shouldn't say this, ask for this, do this—it will make me unlikable, a bitch, or an outcast.'"

Somewhere along the road to equality, young women like us lost our voices. So when we marched into the workforce and the fog of subtle gender discrimination, it was baffling and alien. Without a movement behind us, we had neither the language to describe it nor the confidence to call it what it was. "It's so much easier when you're the generation that gets to fight against [specific] laws than it is to deal with these more complicated issues," says Gail Collins, the *New York Times* columnist. In a highly sexualized, post-PC world, navigating gender roles at work is more confusing than ever. The sad truth is that when we do see women rise to the top, we wonder: was it purely their abilities, or did it have something to do with their looks? If a man takes an interest in our work, we can't help but think about the male superior who advised "using our sexuality" to get ahead, or the manager who winkingly asked one of us, apropos of nothing, to "bake me cookies." One young colleague recalls being teased about the older male boss who lingered near her desk. "What am I supposed to do with that? Assume that's the explanation for any accomplishments? Assume my work isn't valuable?" she asks. "It gets in your head, which is the most insidious part."

Recognizing that sexism still exists despite its subtlety is one of the challenges of the new generation—though it doesn't hold a candle to what the dollies of 1970 pulled off. When they filed their legal complaint, the bottom tiers of the Newsweek masthead were filled almost exclusively by women. "It was a nice place—especially if you were a man," says Nora Ephron, a Newsweek "mail girl" in 1962. The women reported on the murder of a colleague, the State Department, and the 1968 campaign. But when it came to writing, they were forced to hand over their reporting to their male colleagues. "It was a very hopeless time," remembers Brownmiller. "After a while you really did start to lose your confidence. You started to think, 'Writing is what the men do.'"

Over dinner one night, a young researcher poured out her frustration to a lawyer friend, who ordered her to call the Equal Employment Opportunity Commission. She did, and slowly her colleagues signed on to a class-action suit. They found a fiery young lawyer—now D.C. Congresswoman Eleanor Holmes Norton—and they waited, nervously, until the time was right. "We were very staid, ladylike, not guerrilla-theater types," says Pat Lynden, one of the group's early organizers, who wrote cover stories for *The Atlantic Monthly* and *The New York Times Magazine* even while she wasn't allowed to write for Newsweek. "But eventually we just couldn't take it anymore."

A year later, as the national women's movement gathered steam, Newsweek's all-male management decided to put feminism on their cover. Oblivious to the rebellion brewing at home, they looked past the legions of Newsweek women and went outside the building for a writer—to the wife of one of their top brass, whom they would ultimately describe, in an editor's note, as "a top-flight journalist who is also a woman." It was the final straw. The night before the issue hit newsstands, the Newsweek women sent a memo announcing a press conference. They pooled their money to fly a colleague to Washington to present a copy to Katharine Graham, the magazine's owner, who later asked, "Which side am I supposed to be on?" Then on Monday, March 16, 1970, the Newsweek women did what journalists do best: they took their story public. Crowded into a makeshift conference room at the ACLU, Newsweek's "news hens" (as a local tabloid called them) held up a copy of their magazine, whose bright yellow cover told their own story: "Women in Revolt." Two days later the women of *The Ladies' Home Journal* would stage their own sit-in; others were soon to follow.

Despite earning higher GPAs, one year out of college, young women will already take home just 80 percent of what their male colleagues do.

It was a moment of hope, one that set the stage for a wave of progress that continued rapidly through the 1990s. Twenty years after the Newsweek dollies rose up, mothers were entering the workforce in unprecedented numbers, women's organizations such as NOW saw surges in membership, and expanded affirmative-action programs ensured that girls had equal access to education. "Girl power" became the new female mantra, and young women's empowerment groups sprang up at YWCAs. By 2000, when the female employment rate peaked, many women thought the job was done.

In the 1960s, Nora Ephron was an aspiring writer at Newsweek. 'It was a nice place—especially if you were a man,' she says today.

In the years since, there has been what Douglas describes as "a subtle, insidious backlash." In the face of 9/11, two wars, and now the Great Recession, gender equality—and stereotyping—became a secondary concern. Feminism was no longer a label to be worn with pride; Britney Spears and Paris Hilton now dominated airwaves. But the changes were more than cultural. The Global Gender Gap Index—a ranking of women's educational, health, political, and financial standing by the World Economic Forum—found that from 2006 to 2009 the United States had fallen from 23rd to 31st, behind Cuba and just above Namibia. Companies may have incorporated policies aimed at helping women, but they haven't helped as much as you'd think. "The U.S. always scores abysmally in terms of work-life balance," says the WEF's Kevin Steinberg. "But even here, [women] still rank 'masculine or patriarchal corporate culture' as the highest impediment to success." Exhibit A: the four most common female professions today are secretary, registered nurse, teacher, and cashier—low-paying, "pink collar" jobs that employ 43 percent of all women. Swap "domestic help" for nurse and you'd be looking at the top female jobs from 1960, back when want ads were segregated by gender.

The women of Newsweek thought, or hoped, they'd begun to solve these problems four decades ago. Yet here we are. "It's sad," says Lynden, now 72. "Because we fought for all that." There's no denying that we're enjoying many of the spoils of those women's victories. We are no longer huddled in secret; we're reporting for a national magazine, and we're the ones doing the writing. We have a president whose first act in office was to sign a law that promises equal pay for equal work. Yet the fact that such a law is necessary makes the point: equality is still a myth. "We've got the entire weight of human history behind us, making us feel like we're kind of lucky to have jobs," says writer Ariel Levy. "And I think it takes a lot of fearlessness to think, 'F—k it, go ahead and yell at me, I'm going to fight for what I deserve.'" We've come a long way, baby. But there's still a long way to go.

Critical Thinking

1. Do you believe women have achieved equal status with men?

2. Why do women still earn less than men for the same jobs?

3. Identify reasons why females often choose "pink collar" jobs such as secretary, nurse, and cashier.

With SAM REGISTER *and* TONY SKAGGS

Heartbreak and Home Runs: The Power of First Experiences

From winning the science fair to losing a first boyfriend, certain youthful experiences cast a long shadow, revealing character and at times actually shaping it.

Jay Dixit

Patricia was a 15-year-old high school cheerleader in her 10th year of Catholic school.

Chuck was a basketball star, a senior from the rough side of town.

One night after a high school mixer where everyone danced to jukebox music, Chuck and a friend offered Patricia a ride home. Chuck held Patricia's hand in the back seat, and when they got to her house, he walked her to the door. "Then he put both arms around me and kissed me gently on the lips," recalls Patricia. "I thought for a fleeting moment that I was floating with angels in heaven."

The next instant, their bubble was burst when Patricia's father turned on the porch light.

"It was 49 years ago and I still remember nearly all the details," says Patricia. "I was suddenly desirable," she explains. "I was kissworthy—and oh my goodness, that was enough self-esteem to propel me into a lifetime of feeling good about myself."

Beginning in our late teenage years and early 20s, we develop and internalize a broad, autobiographical narrative about our lives, spelling out who we were, are, and might be in the future, says Dan McAdams, a psychologist at Northwestern and author of *The Redemptive Self: Stories Americans Live By.* The story is peppered with key scenes—high points, low points, and turning points—and a first experience can be any of these. "These experiences give us natural ways to divide up the stories of our lives—episodic markers that help us make sense of how our life has developed over time," McAdams explains.

Part of why firsts affect us so powerfully is that they're seared into our psyches with a vividness and clarity that doesn't fade as other memories do. You may not remember the 4th real kiss you ever had, or the 20th—but you almost certainly remember your first. This is known as the primacy effect.

When people are asked to recall memories from college, 25 percent of what they come up with draws from the first two or three months of their freshman year, says David Pillamer, a psychologist at the University of New Hampshire. What people remember most vividly are events like saying goodbye to their parents, meeting their roommates for the first time, and their first college class.

In fact, when psychologists ask older people to recall the events of their lives, the ones they most often name are those that occurred in their late teens and early 20s. We're also better at recalling the world events, music, books, and movies—as well as the cultural events such as the Academy Awards or the World Series—that happened during the early parts of our lives. This "early-life memory bump" occurs because that's when we have the most first experiences, explains Jefferson Singer, a psychologist at Connecticut College who studies autobiographical memory.

Consider a first kiss or sexual encounter. These can generate sensations so new and unfamiliar that the experience feels almost unreal. "Someone can be a primitive neophyte when it comes to writing, but when you get them to talk about their first kiss, you see eloquence, poetry, metaphor, synecdoche, and hyperbole," says John Bohannon III, a psychologist at Butler University who studies first kisses. That sensation of disembodiment—pleasurable during a kiss, aversive when you first suffer the death of a loved one—is common in first experiences, as are feelings of heightened reality or unreality.

Intense emotional sensations etch first experiences deeply into memory, creating what psychologists call "flash-bulb memories." Memories like our first kiss or tryst, our first glimpse of the ocean, our first day of school, or the birth of a first child engage all our senses simultaneously.

Besides emotional engagement, these experiences also pack a heavy dose of novelty. "Novelty drives up dopamine and norepinephrine, brain systems associated with focus and paying attention and rewards," explains anthropologist Helen Fisher, author of *Why Him? Why Her?*

A first romantic relationship has one critical novel element: "It's the only time you're ever in love where you've never had your heart broken," says Laura Carpenter, a sociologist at Vanderbilt University and author of *Virginity Lost: An Intimate Portrait of First Sexual Experiences.* "You can have better relationships after that, but there's never again one where you've never been hurt."

"Powerful first relationships can stamp a template in your mind that gets activated in later interactions," says Susan Andersen, a psychologist at NYU who studies mental representations of significant others. If you meet someone who reminds you even a little of an ex—whether it's a physical resemblance or a similarity in attitudes, gestures, voice, word choice, or interests—it may engage the representation you have in your memory, says Andersen. The effect is called transference. And since your first love, by virtue of its novelty and emotional significance, is potentially your most salient, it may well be the representation that's summoned when you meet someone new, forging the lens through which you see new relationships.

It's not just a person's qualities that get transferred in your mind—your old feelings, motivations, and expectations are also reactivated. If someone new reminds you of an ex you still love, Andersen's studies show, you'll like that new person more, want to be close to them, and even start repeating the behaviors you engaged in with your ex. "The behaviors I'm engaging in will lead this new person, temporarily at least, to actually confirm my expectations," says Andersen. "By interacting in a particular way, I will draw out of this new person behaviors my ex used to engage in. That's expectation becoming reality."

In Vladimir Nabokov's *Lolita,* the tormented antihero Humbert Humbert describes Annabel, a childhood neighbor who loves him passionately for one summer, then dies of typhus. "I leaf again and again through these miserable memories," writes Humbert, "and keep asking myself, was it then, in the glitter of that remote summer, that the rift in my life began?"

First loss differs qualitatively from later losses because it submerges us in the icy reality that we're in constant danger of losing the people we love most—a concept we grasp intellectually at a certain age, but which doesn't feel real until it actually happens to us.

"We're wired for attachment in a world of impermanence," says Robert Neimeyer, a psychologist at the University of Memphis who studies how people draw meaning from loss and grief. "How we negotiate that tension shapes who we become."

Early loss can poison your ability to trust or feel safe, or give yourself fully in subsequent relationships, explains Singer. There's a strong link between early loss and depression, and early loss is also associated with diminished ability to form later attachments.

Loss: Only after the first loss of a loved one do we truly understand the finality of death. We're wired for attachment in a world of impermanence, and that tension shapes us.

Setup For a Self-Fulfilling Prophecy

Expectations about how an experience "should" feel can prime you for a lifetime of disappointment.

A negative first relationship can doom people to get trapped over and over again in self-destructive relationships. The reverse effect applies also. If your first relationship is healthy and positive, you may expect new people to be similarly friendly and safe—causing you to feel fondly, disclose your emotions, and build intimacy with that new person.

Losing one's virginity is an experience often subject to self-fulfilling expectations. People who consider their first sexual encounter to be a momentous turning point and find that it is indeed positive tend to wait for another loving relationship before they have sex again, says Laura Carpenter, a sociologist at Vanderbilt University and author of *Virginity Lost: An Intimate Portrait of First Sexual Experiences.* But if they're rejected by their partner, such people feel worthless—as if they've lost a special part of themselves. "A number of them felt they didn't have the right to say no to future sexual partners because they were already 'soiled' and 'ruined,'" says Carpenter. "They get involved in relationships they don't want and feel they have to have sex because they've already had sex. It's a spiral."

As with other first experiences, the loss of virginity can be a rite of passage—an irreversible transition from a state of ignorance to a state of knowledge. "Like a teenager learning to drive or a surgeon mastering her craft, you're knifing off the old self and building this new self," says Carpenter. "Whether it's what sex is about, a body of knowledge about religious mysteries, or medical skills, you've gained this special knowledge and you can never go back."

Love & Sex: Your first love may come to define what love means for you, and any subsequent relationships you have will be influenced by this first experience whether you realize it or not.

But many people find that after surviving a painful loss, they emerge more resilient. Optimistic people take loss better than less optimistic people, as do people who grow up with strong, secure attachment to their caregivers.

But the biggest predictor of resilience in the face of loss is "sense-making," weaving the experience into a larger narrative about who we are and what our lives are about, says Mary-Frances O'Connor, a behavioral scientist at UCLA who studies grief. Robert Neimeyer's father committed suicide when Robert was a child, for instance, and he dedicated his life to studying how people draw meaning from grief.

Getting Past the Past

You can't change the past, but you can look at it differently. Here's how.

Make a choice.

Decide to stop dwelling, suggests Susan Nolen-Hoeksema. List the pros and cons of dwelling—an exercise that will feel absurd, since cons will vastly exceed the pros. Say to yourself, "I know it's hard, but I choose to move forward."

Contain your rumination.

Schedule limited blocks of time to wallow—say, 15 minutes twice a day. You're compartmentalizing your grief—and you'll soon get bored of it and move on.

Do a reality check.

Maybe you find yourself thinking, "I'll never be happy again." Stop. True, nothing will ever be exactly the same. But there's no reason you can't find happiness in the present and future, with new people and new experiences.

Do not confuse the path with the destination.

May be you lost a youthful love and can't let go. Maybe you got fired and you feel like a failure. Clarify your values—creativity? Love? Recognize that you don't need that particular job to do creative work. You don't need that particular partner to have a loving relationship. Continue on your path.

Get present.

Join a gym, take up a hobby, find a cause, and schedule time with friends. "The best way to break free of living in the past is to get focused on the present and the future," says psychologist Jefferson Singer. "Take risks and do concrete things to create new experiences for yourself in the here and now."

People struck by loss or trauma at an early age—such as victims of crime or abuse—are at risk of drawing unwarranted conclusions about the world and their own place in it. Maybe your first boyfriend abused you. You may mistakenly infer that you're not careful enough—when the truth is that it could have happened to anybody.

That's the catch with first experiences. Because they're memorable, they come readily to mind and we overgeneralize when drawing conclusions about what kind of person we are. Positive first experiences can inspire us for a lifetime, but negative ones can be hard to get past.

So if you're overly focused on a negative event as a turning point in your life, ask yourself: Is what happened truly a reflection of who you are? Or would others have made the same choices given the same circumstances? "In repeated experiences, we understand the situational factors outside ourselves," says Singer. "But the first time, we don't have the context, so we're more likely to see it as a reflection on our own character."

Two women recounted the story of their first lie to Bella DePaulo, a psychologist at the University of California at Santa Barbara who studies deception. The first one told a story about how she wanted to go out one night as a child but was barred from doing so by her father. So she went anyway and lied to him about where she'd been. When he cluelessly swallowed the whole story, she realized she had a new talent. She lied freely from that moment on.

The other woman told a story about how, as a girl, she was very curious about her sister's boyfriend. One night she snuck into a room with a phone extension and listened in on their conversation. When her father walked in and caught her *in flagrante delicto,* she panicked, blurting, "I was just cleaning the phone!" Guilt-stricken over the lie, she immediately confessed and apologized, resolving never to lie again.

A first lie crosses a line. You recognize a capacity you didn't realize you had. For the extremely honest or the extremely dishonest, the lie may reveal character: a decision never to repeat the act, or the realization that this is a new way to behave. But for many people between these two poles, the consequences of a first lie depend on one's reaction to it, says DePaulo. If we do something we shouldn't—say, shoplifting—and get caught and punished, we're likely to internalize the lesson that stealing is wrong, incorporating it into our value system. But if no one finds out, we may decide it's no big deal.

"First experiences tell you something about yourself and what you're like in a new situation," explains DePaulo. "It's testing the social environment and seeing how other people react, but it's also testing who you are, how you think of yourself, and whether you want to be that person."

If you get a thrill out of lying, it's easier to cross that line the next time.

"It's called the abstinence violation effect," explains Singer. "If I'm willing to make that first slip, then what's the point in holding on? Now that I'm no longer a dieter, I might as well have another cookie." The principle applies not only to straying from a diet but also to major transgressions. If you're a soldier, your first kill may force you to reflect on death and morality. But killing someone may not feel like such a big deal the second time around.

Lies: Your first lie crosses a line, making it easier to go through with it the next time. And the outcome—whether you get away with it or not—can shape your patterns later in life.

With transgressions, as with other first experiences, it's important to remember that one action doesn't define you. "When counselors treat addicts who have fallen off the wagon, they tell them, 'Look, you haven't relapsed, you've had a slip,'" explains Singer. "If you use the fallacy of saying, 'Oh, well, it's over now,' then you can easily rationalize taking the next drink and the next and the next and it will be a relapse. But a slip can be corrected."

In 1982, before Michael Jordan was Michael Jordan, he was a student at the University of North Carolina. He played good basketball, but as a 19-year-old freshman, he was constantly overshadowed by upper-classmen. When North Carolina entered the NCAA championship game against Georgetown, though, something changed in Jordan's play. In the first three quarters of the game, he scored 14 points and grabbed nine rebounds.

It wasn't enough. Georgetown, led by freshman superstar and future NBA powerhouse Patrick Ewing, was winning 62 to 61, with only 17 seconds left in the game. Then, when it looked like the game was over, Jordan made one of the most famous shots in basketball history: a 16-foot jump shot that won the game and earned North Carolina the championship.

That first game-winning shot was a turning point, Jordan recalled in later years. It gave him the confidence that he could come through in a clutch. For the rest of his career, especially when he needed to muster the intense concentration and Zen calm necessary to shoot free throws, he would summon up that moment to bring him into a winning state of mind. "He used that shot, performing in that pressure situation, as the foundation for his confidence in taking other big shots," says Richard Ginsburg, an athletic coach and author of *Whose Game Is It, Anyway?* "He'd tell himself, 'I've done this before, I can do it again.'"

Game-winning shots and home runs—as well as the times you ace an exam, nail a job interview, or win a standing ovation—provide potent fodder for your sense of identity as a successful person. "You think, 'I succeeded in this clutch situation, now I know I'm a clutch player,'" explains Singer. "It's revealing something in your character that wasn't clear before, telling you, 'This is something I can do. This is who I am.'"

"I remember the time I first won a tennis match against my father," says Tim Gallwey, author of the classic book *The Inner Game of Tennis.* Gallwey's father had promised him a new racket if he won. Gallwey was 13 at the time, and had been playing in state tournaments. During the match, he was torn between wanting to win a new racket and not wanting to beat his father. When he won, he felt regret and compassion for his dad, who'd just been defeated by his own son, but was also elated by victory, glowing with a sense that his abilities had reached a new height. "That sense of self-worth is very precious," says Gallwey.

Of course, first failures can be as memorable as first successes. If you flunk a test or miss an easy pop fly, you may start to feel like a loser. And failure is always a possibility. But what separates world-class performers from the rest of us is the ability to put negative experiences behind them (see "Getting Past the Past").

Success: A single victory can transform your sense of self. By telling yourself, "I've done this before, I can do it again," you realize your ability to come through when it counts.

"Once you can see yourself doing something—once you can experience it and feel what it's like—it changes you," explains Ginsburg. "The best performers are good at forgiving themselves, dropping failure from their mental bandwidth quickly so that they can focus on the positive." If you can do that, you may strike out many times, but you'll always be the person who hit that grand slam—which in turn will breed further success.

First successes often take the form of "redemption sequences," wherein a bad event suddenly turns good, says McAdams—like when you defy the odds in a basketball game you're losing by sinking a winning buzzer-beater with seconds left on the clock. "The construction of redemption sequences in life is a very common narrative strategy," he adds, "and one that seems to bring with it a certain sense of resilience."

A single win may not be sufficient to boost your confidence permanently. True confidence comes from the gradual accumulation of self-efficacy over a long period of successes. But a dramatic first triumph can inspire and motivate you and transform your self-conception from "I'm a loser" to "I'm the kind of person who hits grand slams."

And a first success can also uncover abilities you didn't realize you had. Days before he died, I interviewed George Carlin. Toward the end of our conversation, I asked him about the first time he made his mother laugh. "I noticed the moment something had happened," Carlin immediately recalled. "This was when I was very young. My mother laughed fairly frequently. But I knew the difference between her social laugh and her really spontaneous laugh when she was caught off guard and amused—I saw that in her and it registered with me. It meant I had said something witty. It was a little mark along the way, a little badge of honor."

Critical Thinking

1. Provide two reasons why first experiences have more power than later events.

2. Give an example of transference of a mental representation.

3. Suggest ways to look at your past experiences in a new light.

All Joy and No Fun
Why Parents Hate Parenting

JENNIFER SENIOR

There was a day a few weeks ago when I found my 2½-year-old son sitting on our building doorstep, waiting for me to come home. He spotted me as I was rounding the corner, and the scene that followed was one of inexpressible loveliness, right out of the movie I'd played to myself before actually having a child, with him popping out of his babysitter's arms and barreling down the street to greet me. This happy moment, though, was about to be cut short, and in retrospect felt more like a tranquil lull in a slasher film. When I opened our apartment door, I discovered that my son had broken part of the wooden parking garage I'd spent about an hour assembling that morning. This wouldn't have been a problem per se, except that as I attempted to fix it, he grew impatient and began throwing its various parts at the walls, with one plank very narrowly missing my eye. I recited the rules of the house (no throwing, no hitting). He picked up another large wooden plank. I ducked. He reached for the screwdriver. The scene ended with a time-out in his crib.

As I shuffled back to the living room, I thought of something a friend once said about the Children's Museum of Manhattan—"a nice place, but what it *really* needs is a bar"—and mused how, at that moment, the same thing could be said of my apartment. Two hundred and 40 seconds earlier, I'd been in a state of pair-bonded bliss; now I was guided by nerves, trawling the cabinets for alcohol. My emotional life looks a lot like this these days. I suspect it does for many parents—a high-amplitude, high-frequency sine curve along which we get the privilege of doing hourly surfs. Yet it's something most of us choose. Indeed, it's something most of us would say we'd be miserable without.

From the perspective of the species, it's perfectly unmysterious why people have children. From the perspective of the individual, however, it's more of a mystery than one might think. Most people assume that having children will make them happier. Yet a wide variety of academic research shows that parents are not happier than their childless peers, and in many cases are less so. This finding is surprisingly consistent, showing up across a range of disciplines. Perhaps the most oft-cited datum comes from a 2004 study by Daniel Kahneman, a Nobel Prize–winning behavioral economist, who

surveyed 909 working Texas women and found that child care ranked sixteenth in pleasurability out of nineteen activities. (Among the endeavors they preferred: preparing food, watching TV, exercising, talking on the phone, napping, shopping, *housework.*) This result also shows up regularly in relationship research, with children invariably reducing marital satisfaction. The economist Andrew Oswald, who's compared tens of thousands of Britons with children to those without, is at least inclined to view his data in a more positive light: "The broad message is not that children make you less happy; it's just that children don't make you *more* happy." That is, he tells me, unless you have more than one. "Then the studies show a more negative impact." As a rule, most studies show that mothers are less happy than fathers, that single parents are less happy still, that babies and toddlers are the hardest, and that each successive child produces diminishing returns. But some of the studies are grimmer than others. Robin Simon, a sociologist at Wake Forest University, says parents are more depressed than nonparents no matter what their circumstances—whether they're single or married, whether they have one child or four.

Mothers are less happy than fathers, single parents are less happy still.

The idea that parents are less happy than nonparents has become so commonplace in academia that it was big news last year when the *Journal of Happiness Studies* published a Scottish paper declaring the opposite was true. "Contrary to much of the literature," said the introduction, "our results are consistent with an effect of children on life satisfaction that is positive, large and increasing in the number of children." Alas, the euphoria was short-lived. A few months later, the poor author discovered a coding error in his data, and the publication ran an erratum. "After correcting the problem," it read, "the main results of the paper no longer hold. The effect of children on the life satisfaction of married individuals is small, often negative, and never statistically significant."

Yet one can see why people were rooting for that paper. The results of almost all the others violate a parent's deepest intuition. Daniel Gilbert, the Harvard psychologist and host of *This Emotional Life* on PBS, wrote fewer than three pages about compromised parental well-being in *Stumbling on Happiness*. But whenever he goes on the lecture circuit, skeptical questions about those pages come up more frequently than anything else. "I've never met anyone who didn't argue with me about this," he says. "Even people who believe the data say they feel sorry for those for whom it's true."

So what, precisely, is going on here? Why is this finding duplicated over and over again despite the fact that most parents believe it to be wrong?

One answer could simply be that parents are deluded, in the grip of some false consciousness that's good for mankind but not for men and women in particular. Gilbert, a proud father and grandfather, would argue as much. He's made a name for himself showing that we humans are pretty sorry predictors of what will make us happy, and to his mind, the yearning for children, the literal mother of all aspirations for so many, is a very good case in point—what children *really* do, he suspects, is offer moments of transcendence, not an overall improvement in well-being.

Perhaps. But there are less fatalistic explanations, too. And high among them is the possibility that parents don't much enjoy parenting because the experience of raising children has fundamentally changed.

"I'm going to count to three."

It's a weekday evening, and the mother in this video-tape, a trim brunette with her hair in a bun and glasses propped up on her head, has already worked a full day and made dinner. Now she is approaching her 8-year-old son, the oldest of two, who's seated at the computer in the den, absorbed in a movie. At issue is his homework, which he still hasn't done.

"One. Two . . ."

This clip is from a study conducted by UCLA's Center on Everyday Lives of Families, which earned a front-page story in the Sunday *Times* this May and generated plenty of discussion among parents. In it, researchers collected 1,540 hours of footage of 32 middle-class, dual-earner families with at least two children, all of them going about their regular business in their Los Angeles homes. The intention of this study was in no way to make the case that parents were unhappy. But one of the postdoctoral fellows who worked on it, himself a father of two, nevertheless described the video data to the *Times* as "the very purest form of birth control ever devised. Ever."

"I have to get it to the part and then pause it," says the boy.

"No," says his mother. "You do that *after* you do your homework."

Tamar Kremer-Sadlik, the director of research in this study, has watched this scene many times. The reason she believes it's so powerful is because it shows how painfully parents experience the pressure of making their children do their schoolwork. They seem to feel this pressure even more acutely than their children feel it themselves.

The boy starts to shout. "It's not going to take that long!"

His mother stops the movie. "I'm telling you no," she says. "You're not hearing me. I will *not* let you watch this now."

He starts up the movie again.

"No," she repeats, her voice rising. She places her hand firml[y] under her son's arm and starts to yank. "I *will not* have this—"

Before urbanization, children were viewed as economi[c] assets to their parents. If you had a farm, they toiled alongsid[e] you to maintain its upkeep; if you had a family business, th[e] kids helped mind the store. But all of this dramatically change[d] with the moral and technological revolutions of modernit[y.] As we gained in prosperity, childhood came increasingly t[o] be viewed as a protected, privileged time, and once colleg[e] degrees became essential to getting ahead, children became n[ot] only a great expense but subjects to be sculpted, stimulate[d,] instructed, groomed. (The Princeton sociologist Viviana Zelize[r] describes this transformation of a child's value in five ruthles[s] words: "Economically worthless but emotionally priceless." Kids, in short, went from being our staffs to being our bosses[.])

"Did you see *Babies*?" asks Lois Nachamie, a couples coun[-] selor who for years has run parenting workshops and suppo[rt] groups on the Upper West Side. She's referring to the rece[nt] documentary that compares the lives of four newborns—one i[n] Japan, one in Namibia, one in Mongolia, and one in the Unite[d] States (San Francisco). "I don't mean to idealize the lives of th[e] Namibian women," she says. "But it was hard not to notice ho[w] *calm* they were. They were beading their children's ankles an[d] decorating them with sienna, clearly enjoying just sitting an[d] playing with them, and we're here often thinking of all of thi[s] stuff as labor."

This is especially true in middle- and upper-income fami[-] lies, which are far more apt than their working-class counter[-] parts to see their children as projects to be perfected. (Childre[n] of women with bachelor degrees spend almost five hours o[n] "organized activities" per week, as opposed to children of hig[h] school dropouts, who spend two.) Annette Lareau, the sociolo[-] gist who coined the term "concerted cultivation" to describe th[e] aggressive nurturing of economically advantaged children, put[s] it this way: "Middle-class parents spend much more time talk[-] ing to children, answering questions with questions, and treat[-] ing each child's thought as a special contribution. And this i[s] very tiring *work*." Yet it's work few parents feel that they can i[n] good conscience neglect, says Lareau, "lest they put their chil[-] dren at risk by not giving them every advantage."

But the intensification of family time is not confined to th[e] privileged classes alone. According to *Changing Rhythms o[f] American Family Life*—a compendium of data about tim[e] use and family statistics, compiled by a trio of sociologist[s] named Suzanne M. Bianchi, John P. Robinson, and Melissa A[.] Milkie—*all* parents spend more time today with their childre[n] than they did in 1975, including mothers, in spite of the grea[t] rush of women into the American workforce. Today's marrie[d] mothers also have less leisure time (5.4 fewer hours per week[)] 71 percent say they crave more time for themselves (as d[o] 57 percent of married fathers). Yet 85 percent of all parents still[—] still!—think they don't spend enough time with their children.

These self-contradictory statistics reminded me of a conver[-] sation I had with a woman who had been in one of Nachamie['s] parenting groups, a professional who had her children late[r] in life. "I have two really great kids"—ages 9 and 11—"an[d] I enjoy doing a lot of things with them," she told me. "It's th[e] drudgery that's so hard: *Crap, you don't have any pants that fit?* There are just So. Many. Chores." This woman, it should be said, is divorced. But even if her responsibilities were shared with a partner, the churn of school and gymnastics and piano and sports and homework would still require an awful lot of administration. "The crazy thing," she continues, "is that by New York standards, I'm not even overscheduling them."

I ask what she does on the weekends her ex-husband has custody. "I work," she replies. "And get my nails done."

A few generations ago, people weren't stopping to contemplate whether having a child would make them happy. Having children was simply what you did. And we are lucky, today, to have choices about these matters. But the abundance of choices—whether to have kids, when, how many—may be one of the reasons parents are less happy.

That was at least partly the conclusion of psychologists W. Keith Campbell and Jean Twenge, who, in 2003, did a meta-analysis of 97 children-and-marital-satisfaction studies stretching back to the seventies. Not only did they find that couples' overall marital satisfaction went down if they had kids; they found that every successive generation was more put out by having them than the last—our current one most of all. Even more surprisingly, they found that parents' dissatisfaction only grew the more money they had, even though they had the purchasing power to buy more child care. "And my hypothesis about why this is, in both cases, is the same," says Twenge. "They become parents later in life. There's a loss of freedom, a loss of autonomy. It's totally different from going from your parents' house to immediately having a baby. Now you know what you're giving up." (Or, as a fellow psychologist told Gilbert when he finally got around to having a child: "They're a huge source of joy, but they turn every other source of joy to shit.")

Studies have found that parents' dissatisfaction only grew the more money they had, even though they could buy more child care.

It wouldn't be a particularly bold inference to say that the longer we put off having kids, the greater our expectations. "There's all this buildup—as soon as I get this done, I'm going to have a baby, and it's going to be a great reward!" says Ada Calhoun, the author of *Instinctive Parenting* and founding editor-in-chief of Babble, the online parenting site. "And then you're like, Wait, *this* is my reward? This nineteen-year grind?'"

When people wait to have children, they're also bringing different sensibilities to the enterprise. They've spent their adult lives as professionals, believing there's a right way and a wrong way of doing things; now they're applying the same logic to the family-expansion business, and they're surrounded by a marketplace that only affirms and reinforces this idea. "And what's confusing about that," says Alex Barzvi, a professor of child and adolescent psychiatry at NYU medical school, "is that there *are* a lot of things that parents can do to nurture social and cognitive development. There *are* right and wrong ways to discipline a

child. But you can't fall into the trap of comparing yourself to others and constantly concluding you're doing the wrong thing."

Yet that's precisely what modern parents do. "It was especially bad in the beginning," said a woman who recently attended a parents' group led by Barzvi at the 92nd Street Y. "When I'd hear other moms saying, 'Oh, so-and-so sleeps for twelve hours and naps for three,' I'd think, *Oh, shit, I screwed up the sleep training.*" Her parents—immigrants from huge families—couldn't exactly relate to her distress. "They had no academic reference books for *sleeping,*" she says. (She's read three.) "To my parents, it is what it is."

So how do they explain your anguish? I ask.

"They just think that Americans are a little too complicated about everything."

One hates TO invoke Scandinavia in stories about child-rearing, but it can't be an accident that the one superbly designed study that said, unambiguously, that having kids makes you happier was done with Danish subjects. The researcher, Hans-Peter Kohler, a sociology professor at the University of Pennsylvania, says he originally studied this question because he was intrigued by the declining fertility rates in Europe. One of the things he noticed is that countries with stronger welfare systems produce more children—and happier parents.

Of course, this should not be a surprise. If you are no longer fretting about spending too little time with your children after they're born (because you have a year of paid maternity leave), if you're no longer anxious about finding affordable child care once you go back to work (because the state subsidizes it), if you're no longer wondering how to pay for your children's education and health care (because they're free)—well, it stands to reason that your own mental health would improve. When Kahneman and his colleagues did another version of his survey of working women, this time comparing those in Columbus, Ohio, to those in Rennes, France, the French sample enjoyed child care a good deal more than its American counterpart. "We've put all this energy into being perfect parents," says Judith Warner, author of *Perfect Madness: Motherhood in the Age of Anxiety,* "instead of political change that would make family life better."

MOMS: Ever feel alone in how you perceive this role? I swear I feel like I'm surrounded by women who were once smart & interesting but have become zombies who only talk about soccer and coupons.

This was an opening gambit on UrbanBaby this past April. It could have devolved into a sanctimommy pile-on. It didn't.

I totally feel this way.

I am a f/t wohm—Work Outside the Home Mom—*have a career, and I don't feel smart or interesting anymore! I don't talk about soccer or coupons, but just feel too tired to talk about anything that interesting.*

I freely admit that I have gained "more" than I have lost by becoming a parent, but I still miss aspects of my old life.

More generous government policies, a sounder economy, a less pressured culture that values good rather than perfect kids—all of these would certainly make parents happier. But even under the most favorable circumstances, parenting is an extraordinary activity, in both senses of the word *extra:* beyond ordinary and *especially* ordinary. While children deepen your emotional life, they shrink your outer world to the size of a teacup, at least for a while. ("All joy and no fun," as an old friend with two young kids likes to say.) Lori Leibovich, the executive editor of Babble and the anthology *Maybe Baby,* a collection of 28 essays by writers debating whether to have children, says she was particularly struck by the female contributors who'd made the deliberate choice to remain childless. It enabled them to travel or live abroad for their work; to take physical risks; to, in the case of a novelist, inhabit her fictional characters without being pulled away by the demands of a real one. "There was a richness and texture to their work lives that was so, so enviable," she says. (Leibovich has two children.)

Fathers, it turns out, feel like they've made some serious compromises too, though of a different sort. They feel like they don't see their kids *enough.* "In our studies, it's the men, by a long shot, who have more work-life conflict than women," says Ellen Galinsky, president of the Families and Work Institute. "They don't want to be stick figures in their children's lives."

And couples probably pay the dearest price of all. Healthy relationships definitely make people happier. But children adversely affect relationships. As Thomas Bradbury, a father of two and professor of psychology at UCLA, likes to say: "Being in a good relationship is a risk factor for becoming a parent." He directs me to one of the more inspired studies in the field, by psychologists Lauren Papp and E. Mark Cummings. They asked 100 long-married couples to spend two weeks meticulously documenting their disagreements. Nearly 40 percent of them were about their kids.

"And that 40 percent is merely the number that was explicitly about kids, I'm guessing, right?" This is a former patient of Nachamie's, an entrepreneur and father of two. "How many other arguments were those couples having because everyone was on a short fuse, or tired, or stressed out?" This man is very frank about the strain his children put on his marriage, especially his firstborn. "I already felt neglected," he says. "In my mind, anyway. And once we had the kid, it became so pronounced; it went from zero to negative 50. And I was like, *I can deal with zero. But not negative 50.*"

This is the brutal reality about children—they're such powerful stressors that small perforations in relationships can turn into deep fault lines. "And my wife became more demanding," he continues. "'You don't do this, you don't do that.' There was this idea we had about how things were supposed to be: *The family should be dot dot dot, the man should be dot dot dot the woman should be dot dot dot.*"

This is another brutal reality about children: They expose the gulf between our fantasies about family and its spikier realities. They also mean parting with an old way of life, one with more freewheeling rhythms and richer opportunities for romance. "There's nothing sexy or intimate between us, based on the old model," he says. "The new model, which I've certainly come to adopt, is that our energy has shifted toward the kids. One of the reasons I love being with my wife is because I love the family we have."

Most studies show that marriages improve once children enter latency, or the ages between 6 and 12, though they take another sharp dive during the war zone of adolescence. (As a friend with grown children once told me: "Teenagers can be casually brutal.") But one of the most sobering declines documented in *Changing Rhythms of American Family Life* is the amount of time married parents spend alone together each week: Nine hours today versus twelve in 1975. Bradbury, who was involved in the UCLA study of those 32 families, says the husbands and wives spent less than 10 percent of their home time alone together. "And do you think they were saying, "Gee honey, you look lovely. I just wanted to pick up on that fascinating conversation we were having earlier about the Obama administration'?" he asks. "Nope. They were exhausted and staring at the television."

"I'M NOT WATCHING it," insists the boy. We're back to the videotape now, and that den in Los Angeles. Mother and son are still arguing—tensely, angrily—and she's still pulling on his arm. The boy reaches for the keyboard. "I'm putting it on pause!"

"I want you to do your homework," his mother repeats. "You are not—"

"I know," the son whines. "I'm going to pause it!"

His mother's not buying it. What she sees is him stalling. She pulls him off the chair.

"No, you're *not,*" says his mother. "You're still not listening!"

"*Yes I am!*"

"No, you're not!"

Children may provide unrivaled moments of joy. But they also provide unrivaled moments of frustration, tedium, anxiety, heartbreak. This scene, which isn't even all that awful or uncommon, makes it perfectly clear why parenting may be regarded as less fun than having dinner with friends or baking a cake. Loving one's children and loving the act of parenting are not the same thing.

Yet that's where things get tricky. Obviously, this clip shows how difficult and unpleasant parenting can be. What it doesn't show is the love this mother feels for her son, which we can pretty much bet has no equal. Nor does it convey that this unpleasant task she's undertaking is part of a larger project, one that pays off in subtler dividends than simply having fun. Kremer-Sadlik says that she and her fellow researchers were highly conscious of these missing pieces when they gathered each week to discuss their data collection. "We'd all remember the negative things," she says. "Whereas everything else was between the lines. So it became our moral dilemma: How can we talk about the good moments?" She pauses, and then asks the question that, to a parent (she herself has two children), is probably most relevant of all: "And why were the good moments so elusive?"

The answer to that may hinge on how we define "good." Or more to the point, "happy." Is happiness something you *experience?* Or is it something you *think?*

When Kahneman surveyed those Texas women, he was measuring moment-to-moment happiness. It was a feeling, a mood, a state. The technique he pioneered for measuring it—the Daily Reconstruction Method—was designed to make people reexperience their feelings over the course of a day. Oswald, when looking at British households, was looking at a condensed version of the General Health Questionnaire, which is best described as a basic gauge of mood: *Have you recently felt you could not overcome your difficulties? Felt constantly under strain? Lost much sleep over worry?* (What parent hasn't answered, yes, yes, and God yes to these questions?) As a matter of mood, there does seem to be little question that kids make our lives more stressful.

But when studies take into consideration how *rewarding* parenting is, the outcomes tend to be different. Last year, Mathew P. White and Paul Dolan, professors at the University of Plymouth and Imperial College, London, respectively, designed a study that tried to untangle these two different ideas. They asked participants to rate their daily activities both in terms of pleasure and in terms of reward, then plotted the results on a four-quadrant graph. What emerged was a much more commonsense map of our feelings. In the quadrant of things people found both pleasurable *and* rewarding, people chose volunteering first, prayer second, and time with children third (though time with children barely made it into the "pleasurable" category). Work was the most rewarding not-so-pleasurable activity. Everyone thought commuting was both unrewarding and unfun. And watching television was considered one of the most pleasurable unrewarding activities, as was eating, though the least rewarding of all was plain old "relaxing." (Which probably says something about the abiding power of the Protestant work ethic.)

Seven years ago, the sociologists Kei Nomaguchi and Melissa A. Milkie did a study in which they followed couples for five to seven years, some of whom had children and some of whom did not. And what they found was that, yes, those couples who became parents did more housework and felt less in control and quarreled more (actually, only the women thought they quarreled more, but anyway). On the other hand, the married women were *less depressed* after they'd had kids than their childless peers. And perhaps this is because the study sought to understand not just the moment-to-moment moods of its participants, but more existential matters, like how connected they felt, and how motivated, and how much despair they were in (as opposed to how much stress they were under): *Do you not feel like eating? Do you feel like you can't shake the blues? Do you feel lonely? Like you can't get going?* Parents, who live in a clamorous, perpetual-forward-motion machine almost all of the time, seemed to have different answers than their childless cohorts.

The authors also found that the most depressed people were single fathers, and Milkie speculates that perhaps it's because they wanted to be involved in their children's lives but weren't. Robin Simon finds something similar: The least depressed parents are those whose underage children are in the house, and the most are those whose aren't.

This finding seems significant. Technically, if parenting makes you unhappy, you should feel *better* if you're spared the

task of doing it. But if happiness is measured by our own sense of agency and meaning, then noncustodial parents lose. They're robbed of something that gives purpose and reward.

When I mention this to Daniel Gilbert, he hardly disputes that meaning is important. But he does wonder how prominently it should figure into people's decisions to have kids. "When you pause to *think* what children mean to you, of course they make you feel good," he says. "The problem is, 95 percent of the time, you're not thinking about what they mean to you. You're thinking that you have to take them to piano lessons. So you have to think about which kind of happiness you'll be consuming most often. Do you want to maximize the one you experience almost all the time"—moment-to-moment happiness—"or the one you experience rarely?"

Which is fair enough. But for many of us, purpose *is* happiness—particularly those of us who find moment-to-moment happiness a bit elusive to begin with. Martin Seligman, the positive-psychology pioneer who is, famously, not a natural optimist, has always taken the view that happiness is best defined in the ancient Greek sense: leading a productive, purposeful life. And the way we take stock of that life, in the end, isn't by how much fun we had, but what we did with it. (Seligman has seven children.)

About twenty years ago, Tom Gilovich, a psychologist at Cornell, made a striking contribution to the field of psychology, showing that people are far more apt to regret things they *haven't* done than things they have. In one instance, he followed up on the men and women from the Terman study, the famous collection of high-IQ students from California who were singled out in 1921 for a life of greatness. Not one told him of regretting having children, but ten told him they regretted not having a family.

"I think this boils down to a philosophical question, rather than a psychological one," says Gilovich. "Should you value moment-to-moment happiness more than retrospective evaluations of your life?" He says he has no answer for this, but the example he offers suggests a bias. He recalls watching TV with his children at three in the morning when they were sick. "I wouldn't have said it was too fun at the time," he says. "But now I look back on it and say, 'Ah, remember the time we used to wake up and watch cartoons?'" The very things that in the moment dampen our moods can later be sources of intense gratification, nostalgia, delight.

It's a lovely magic trick of the memory, this gilding of hard times. Perhaps it's just the necessary alchemy we need to keep the species going. But for parents, this sleight of the mind and spell on the heart is the very definition of enchantment.

Critical Thinking

1. Identify several factors that make child care an emotional roller coaster.

2. Report which of the following make parenting easier: money, age of parent, age of children, being single, knowledge of child development.

UNIT 6

Development during Middle and Late Adulthood

Unit Selections

Learning Objectives

After reading this Unit you should be able to:

- Explain why each person with depression is different from all others.
- Evaluate "Magic" Johnson's long survival with HIV and how he has used it to help others.
- Examine how "learning to hope" can prolong the lives of cancer patients.
- Describe the type of genotyping that can reduce cancer. Why is it not used?
- Summarize the known ways to improve our brains and select the best method.
- Appraise the difference between men's lib and women's lib, and support men's lib.
- Analyze the reasons why men die earlier. Explain how men can lengthen their lifespans.
- Break down the secrets of longevity of the people of Ikaria.

Student Website

www.mhhe.com/cls

Internet References

Alzheimer's Disease Research Center
    http://alzheimer.wustl.edu/
American Association of Retired Persons
    www.aarp.org
Lifestyle Factors Affecting Late Adulthood
    www.school-for-champions.com/health/lifestyle_elderly.htm
National Aging Information and Referral Support Center
    www.nausa.org/informationandreferral/index-ir.php
Department of Health and Human Services—Aging
    www.hhs.gov/aging/index.html

Joseph Campbell, a twentieth-century sage, said that the privilege of a lifetime is being who you are. This ego-confidence often arrives during middle and late adulthood, even as physical confidence declines. There is a gradual slowing of the rate of mitosis of cells of all the organ systems with age. This gradual slowing of mitosis translates into a slowed rate of repair of cells of all organs. By the 40s, signs of aging can be seen in skin, skeleton, vision, hearing, smell, taste, balance, coordination, heart, blood vessels, lungs, liver, kidneys, digestive tract, immune response, endocrine functioning, and ability to reproduce. To some extent, moderate use of any body part (as opposed to disuse or misuse) helps retain its strength, stamina, and repairability. However, by middle and late adulthood persons become increasingly aware of the effects of aging organ systems on their total physical fitness. A loss of height occurs as spinal disks and connective tissues diminish and settle. Demineralization, especially loss of calcium, causes weakening of bones. Muscles atrophy, and the slowing of cardiovascular and respiratory responses creates a loss of stamina for exercise. All of this may seem cruel, but it occurs very gradually and need not adversely affect a person's enjoyment of life.

Healthful aging, at least in part, seems to be genetically pre-programmed. The females of many species, including humans, outlive the males. The sex hormones of females may protect them from some early aging effects. Males, in particular, experience earlier declines in their cardiovascular system. Diet and exercise can ward off many of the deleterious effects of aging. A reduction in saturated fat (low density lipid) intake coupled with regular aerobic exercise contributes to less bone demineralization, less plaque in the arteries, stronger muscles (including heart and lung muscles), and a general increase in stamina and vitality. An adequate intake of complex carbohydrates, fibrous foods, fresh fruits, fresh vegetables, unsaturated fats (high density lipids), and water also enhances good health.

Cognitive abilities do not appreciably decline with age in healthy adults. Research suggests that the speed with which the brain carries out problems involving abstract (fluid) reasoning may slow but not cease. Complex problems may simply require more time to solve with age. On the other hand, research suggests that the memory banks of older people may have more crystallized (accumulated and stored) knowledge and more insight. Creativity also frequently spurts after age 50. One's ken (range of knowledge) and practical skills (common sense) grow with age and experience. Older human beings also become expert at the cognitive tasks they frequently do. Many cultures celebrate these abilities as the "wisdom of age."

© Tetra Images/Getty Images

The first article, "Good Morning, Heartache," discusses the common cold of psychiatry, depression. The author, Kathleen McGowan, points out that each unique individual experiences depression differently. Because causes and symptoms vary, treatments must be tailored to each individual. Many therapies are available and healing is possible.

The second selection, "I Survived," details the unexpected long-term survival of "Magic" Johnson, a former NBA star with the HIV virus. Even with the newest cocktail of drugs, he did not expect to live 20 years after his diagnosis. He has used his longevity to teach others about AIDS and AIDS prevention.

The next article about middle adulthood, "The New Survivors," deals with cancer. It is no longer the death threat it once was. Many persons who have survived malignancies find that their lives have been changed by the experience. The close brush with death focuses living on positive values such as forgiveness, gratitude, humor, and kindness.

The article about "Curing Cancer" highlights many of the scientific breakthroughs that may lead to cancer prevention, and cancer cure. Some ways to identify early cancers are known, but the technology is not widely used.

"Can You Build a Better Brain?" may surprise readers. While a diet rich in antioxidants, physical exercise, and mental exercise (e.g., crossword puzzles) helps, they are not the most important factor in brain stimulation. Learning something new is the best way to increase synaptic connections.

The first article for Part B of this Unit dealing with Late Adulthood is entitled "Why Do Men Die Earlier?" Bridget Murray-Law gives many reasons and explains why the personality trait of self-reliance can help extend one's lifespan.

The next selection for Late Adulthood, "More Good Years," highlights secrets from the Greek island of Ikaria. There many people reach age 100 in good health. They eat a Mediterranean diet and seem to have endless optimism. Dan Buettner lists thirteen likely contributors to Ikarian longevity.

The next Late Adulthood article, "This Is Your Brain. Aging.," gives good news about old age. Sharon Begley dispels the notion that old age brings forgetfulness and dementia. Most elders have increased emotional intelligence, social skills, and self-control. Memory for things known for years does not disappear. Learning and remembering new things declines somewhat. Mental activity can improve brain fitness.

Good Morning, Heartache

For millions, depression is a daily reality against which they must struggle to function. The many strategies now available provide what we all might envy—the knowledge that it's possible to get through the worst of times.

KATHLEEN McGOWAN

Last summer, Pata Suyemoto rode her bike from Boston to Cape Cod, 125 miles in one day. An educator who has taught everything from art to English to Reiki, she's funny, she's intense, and she's passionate. Never a jock, three years ago she became a relentless road warrior, riding more than 6,000 miles the first year she took up cycling.

But she would not say that she has conquered depression. Instead, like many people who experience major depression—and there are roughly 15 million Americans who do—she has achieved a kind of delicate détente with it. She manages to live with the disorder, or in spite of it. She thinks of her depression as a recurrent illness; getting it under control demands time, creativity, and an open mind. It keeps her on her toes.

Untamed, her depression is truly ferocious. Suyemoto, 47, has been in and out of psychiatric hospitals since age 17. Ten years ago, there came a time she now refers to as the bottom of the abyss. She could hardly do her job. Mustering the energy to stand in front of a class took all her strength. After class, she'd shut the door to her office and crawl under her desk. She had a young daughter, and she was trying to write her dissertation. Then, her mother died. "I'd write a page, and cry for an hour, then write another page, and cry for another hour," she says now.

Eventually she found cracks of light in the darkness. Antidepressants didn't help much. Glimmers of hope came more from things she did. She wrote in a journal daily, even when she had to prop herself up in bed to do it. She finally found a therapist who knew how to deal with severe depression and trauma. "It was gradual, working things into my life," she says. "It was like weaving a net."

A decade later, she now cherishes a whole a list of things that help, her own personal portfolio of antidepressants. Artistic self-expression in the form of collage gives her a way to communicate the darkest feelings without getting stuck in them. Acupuncture—as often as five times a week—helps. She finally found a medication that works. She volunteers with the Massachusetts group Families for Depression Awareness, leveraging her own experience to help other people who are struggling with depression. Self-help books and tapes offer a reality check, as does a sense of spirituality that puts her troubles in context.

And then there's the bike. It's not just good exercise. It's also a way to test limits and learn when to push herself and when to play it cool.

Is she cured? No. But she has her life back.

"I still have dark times, but they don't consume me in the same way," says Suyemoto. She expects that she may have other bad times; for her as for many people, major depression comes in cycles. She is ready for it. "It's not that I'm free and clear," she says. "But in doing all these things, and weaving them into my life, I've created a much stronger net."

A lot of the news about depression these days is good: An arsenal of treatments now available allows many to lead a normal life in spite of the disorder. The best estimate is that 80 percent of people find substantial relief from their worst symptoms, which typically include persistent sadness, guilt or irritability, sleep and appetite disruption, and the absence of pleasure. "People do recover from depression," says Michael Yapko, a clinical psychologist in California who specializes in treating depression. "There are many pathways in, and there are many pathways out."

Getting there, however, is rarely easy. Few people find simple cures. Instead, they patch together many measures. "I hate it when people say, 'Just go exercise.' Or, 'Just take medication,' or 'Just' anything," says Suyemoto. "Everybody has to find their own path, Healing from depression is a not a universal thing. Everybody's going to be different."

Major depression is so common because a lot of different biological and psychological roads lead to the same place. A variety of switches get tripped—whether by genetic vulnerability, trauma in early life, chronic stress, disturbance of neurochemistry, or guilt-prone tendencies—and the end result is depression.

To successfully cope with depression, most people stumble onto their own combination of lifestyle adaptations, therapeutic techniques, medications, and mental adjustments.

Combination Therapy Still Best

Finding the best treatment for depression today means wading through lots of options. There are 39 antidepressant drugs on the market. And for some people, cognitive therapy works just as well, or better. Other treatments range from light therapy to the implantation of electrodes in the brain.

A major test of drugs and talk therapy, the 2006 STAR*D trial, treated 4,000 participants who are highly typical of patients with major depression: Their disorder had not responded to the first drug they took, and most also had anxiety or an eating disorder.

The study found that no one drug or therapy was clearly best. Adding either a second drug or cognitive therapy worked equally well. Only about a third of subjects saw symptoms vanish with the first drug tried. But most—67 percent—eventually found substantial relief. The bottom line: Hang in there. It may take time to find the right treatments.

"The combination with psychotherapy is very useful," says psychiatrist Dennis Charney. "It's like hand and glove." Psychotherapy can take longer to start working, but it may have the edge in preventing relapses.

What causes depression is still basically a mystery. The altered brain chemistry goes far beyond serotonin, the neurotransmitter targeted by many antidepressant drugs. Dopamine-sensitive brain circuits, which influence pleasure and reward, are off-kilter and may underlie feelings of numbness or despair. Such circuits also influence mood, which may be why people prone to depression struggle to prevent disappointments and setbacks from spiraling into full-blown depressive episodes.

Stress also plays a role, especially in early life. Prolonged childhood stress, such as neglect or abuse, may influence neurochemistry and the responsiveness of the body's alarm system, setting the stage for depression in adulthood.

No one gene causes depression, and only about one-third of the risk of depression is inherited. But genetics might one day improve upon the current trial-and-error process of choosing a drug. A gene scan may predict which antidepressant will work best for you.

For the time being, the best approach is to seek out a depression specialist. Most people rely on their family doctor. But a depression expert has more experience with the range of options—and many more tricks up his or her sleeve.

Given the diversity of causes, antidepressant medications alone are rarely enough. To successfully cope with depression, most people stumble onto their own idiosyncratic combination of lifestyle adaptations, therapeutic techniques, medications and mental adjustments. But the most successful approaches for the long term, says Yapko, all encourage you to take action in the face of a disorder that saps your resolve. "Eventually, if you're persistent, there's a high probability you'll find something."

The most successful approaches for the long term all encourage you to take action in the face of a disorder that saps your resolve.

First, It's Physical

For many people the process of gaining control over depression begins with physical changes. Researchers now know that depression is not just a mental disorder. It affects the immune system, the heart, and basic body functions such as sleep and appetite as well. So it only makes sense that a lot of people who successfully manage their depression are careful about what they eat and drink, how much they sleep, and how active they are.

Former Massachusetts state senator and attorney Bob Antonioni, for example, always makes time for hockey, bike riding, or swimming. "In the past if I was struggling I'd curl up on the couch—that's not good, because you become more isolated, and the isolation feeds the depression," he says. "Very often I find, if I go out and exercise, I'm better for it."

Now 50, he's been dealing with depression since his mid-30s. After his brother's suicide in 1999, it got worse. He was profoundly sad, and the depression also settled into his body. His chest constantly ached. Sometimes it seemed like his body was going into panic mode. At the same time, as a politician, he had a public image to maintain. "I'm supposed to be out and about, smiling," he says now. "I just wasn't able to. I'd go into withdrawal."

He now has a comprehensive strategy; Antonioni goes for regular therapy and takes an antidepressant. But other physical interventions are equally important. He doesn't drink anymore, except on rare occasions—not that he ever had a drinking problem, but the depressant effects of alcohol worsened his symptoms.

Sleep is his number one secret weapon. "Sleep makes all the difference in the world to me," he says. It's not always easy to explain to his aides and colleagues why he won't arrange early-morning meetings. So be it. "The adjustments come," he adds. "People are a lot more willing to be flexible than I might originally have given them credit for."

Mood and sleep share basic biological mechanisms, and, according to Yapko, the single most common symptom of depression is some form of sleep disturbance. Getting lots of sleep is crucial. The challenge is in admitting that you just may not be able to do as much as you want to—and then sticking to your guns, even when life throws drama or excitement your way.

Getting Through Despair

"I've found that I have to be careful or I crash," says Kathryn Goetzke, a 37-year-old entrepreneur who battles major depression. "You have to be pretty disciplined about it," Goetzke has her own business, Mood-Lites, which develops decorative lighting. She also founded a nonprofit, the International Foundation for Research and Education on Depression (iFred). Then her husband ran for Congress in 2006. Of course, she got involved in the campaign. "I thought I had it all under control," she says now. "I just took on way, way, way too much."

He lost, and for maybe six months afterward she struggled to do anything at all. The marriage ended, and sometimes money was very tight—two other major sources of stress. "I learned the hard way," she says. "I have to listen to my body. I can't be ashamed. The consequences are much worse, in the long run, if I ignore it."

Goetzke reached out to her mother and brothers, who "moved mountains" to help her through the worst times. When she was closest to the brink, they pulled her back. She found a good therapist and, when she couldn't afford therapy, she turned to support groups, augmented by long walks outside.

Now, she says, she feels pretty good. "I'm happy to be around" is how she puts it. But it still takes a lot of work. She quit drinking entirely, avoids eating too much sugar, gets plenty of sleep, and hikes, plays tennis, does yoga, or bikes almost every day. She relies on her dogs, and the encouragement of a weekly women's support group. She, too, takes medication.

What might have made the biggest difference, though, was inside her own head—a major psychological shift. Before she started grappling with depression, Goetzke was an escapist. Her father, also depressed, committed suicide when she was in college, and she was eventually diagnosed with posttraumatic stress disorder. She drank, and she had an eating disorder, two ways of blunting the bleakness that only made things worse.

Finally, in her 30s, she began to confront how bad she felt and actually learned to live with her feelings of despair. "I sit through my feelings of awfulness," she says. "I let myself fully experience the bad feelings, and then move it toward something positive." Mindfulness meditation, which derails the obsessive thinking that typically intensifies negative feelings, is also useful. In these ways, she has learned to accept herself—and that includes accepting the sorrow.

Being able to withstand feeling lousy has been important to her success. As a businesswoman, she has to endure constant rejection. Once, the head of product development for a major lighting company told her that she would never get her product into a store. Her Mood-Lites are now on the shelves of hundreds of Wal-Marts, as well as in spas and chiropractors' offices across the country.

Cognitive tricks and techniques may seem insubstantial against such a formidable foe as depression, but they work. Cognitive behavioral therapy and interpersonal therapy both focus on the future, teaching mental and emotional skills that challenge negative thought patterns and counteract feelings of helplessness and self-loathing.

"Psychotherapy gives you a toolbox of approaches to handle stress, which can elicit depression," says noted mood disorder researcher Dennis Charney, dean of the Mt. Sinai School of Medicine in New York. "Part of it is getting the right treatment, the right doctor, the right psychotherapist." The important question to ask a therapist, says Charney, is whether she or he is experienced in teaching techniques that work.

'The Narcissism of Depression'

Learning how to step away from your own thoughts and see them objectively is a technique that can short-circuit the downward spiral of despair. In her 20s, Gina Barreca was drowning in sadness and emotional turmoil. Small setbacks and difficulties regularly turned into huge cataclysms that took over her life. She cried constantly, for just about any reason. "I really think of myself in those early days as somebody blindfolded, walking underneath an emotional piñata with a bat," she says now.

Now a professor of English at the University of Connecticut, Barreca, too, eventually found a medication that helped. But she got better mostly because she learned to stop torturing herself. She fills up journals with feelings of self-loathing and misery—but that is where they stay. Over time, with the help of a smart, committed therapist, she figured out how to step around emotional chaos rather than stir it up.

Barreca rejects what she calls "the narcissism of depression," the mental habit of taking wretched feelings seriously and burrowing into them. Instead, she thinks of depression and sorrow as familiar demons who arrive as unwelcome visitors. They're nasty, and they wreck the place, but eventually they move on. Enduring them is part of life. "The hardest thing in the world to learn is a sense of humility in the face of this, that these things are going to pass," says Barreca.

Now 52, she doesn't sink into sadness, but she doesn't shy away from it, either. "I'm not bubble-wrapped," she says. "I still get furious. I still get incredibly sad." But when the tormented feelings well up, she does her best to go on with her life. She shops. She talks to friends. She goes for coffee or has a nice meal. "I do those things that actually make me feel better," she says.

Barreca has written seven humor books; her latest, *It's Not That I'm Bitter,* will be out this month. She is a brilliant and witty writer. That's actually not as unlikely as it might seem. Finding the humor in things requires seeing them from an unexpected angle, a cognitive trick that is key to dispelling depression. "Pain plus time equals humor," says Barreca. "I've had both pain and time."

Making Light of the Darkness

There are many routes out of the isolation of depression. Both Bob Antonioni and Kathryn Goetzke turn to advocacy, going public to reach out to others and to cast off the shame. Pata Suyemoto creates artworks that express her emotional tumult. But there's something especially powerful about humor. It can connect through the terrifying darkness of the disorder, not in spite of it. Humor creates sparks of instantaneous intimacy, a rare gift for anyone—but particularly for those who feel hopelessly alone.

This unique power is the fuel for Victoria Maxwell's one-woman shows, *Crazy for Life and Funny, You Don't Look*

Crazy. In her performances, often to mental health workers, psychiatrists, and patients, she tells the epic story of her experiences with bipolar disorder. The details are hair-raising. But in her telling, they are also hilarious.

Maxwell's bouts of depression began shortly after she graduated from college, although at first neither she nor her therapist realized quite what they were dealing with. She was binge eating and oversleeping, had trouble concentrating, and was consumed with self-hatred.

At the same time, she embarked upon a spiritual quest. On a three-day meditation retreat, a lack of sleep and food, combined with the silence and stillness, pitched her into mania. During a manic episode, some people become aggressive and others feel unstoppable; her euphoria took on a powerfully spiritual tone. She felt rapturous, like a limitless being composed only of love. But when, convinced she had transcended her earthly body, she began having visions of her grave, her parents took her to the hospital.

Maxwell left with a prescription, but soon quit taking her pills. She thought she was having a spiritual struggle, not mentally ill. During the next couple of years, she went through several more manic episodes, interspersed with horrendous depressions. Finally, one night she went running through the streets of Vancouver naked, looking for God, and got picked up by the police. A wise psychiatric nurse who recognized both Maxwell's spiritual hunger and her mental illness introduced her to a sympathetic psychiatrist who finally convinced her to seek help.

Medication quickly tamed her manic upswings, but the depressions took much longer to manage. At the age of 42, Maxwell now feels pretty stable. She is careful to sleep at least eight hours a night. Intense workouts kick-start her body when she feels slow. And she practices a version of the same technique that Barreca and Goetzke use. Following Buddhist writer Pema Chodron's counsel, she treats her depressions with "compassionate witnessing": recognition and tolerance. "I'm comfortable enough to invite those demons to come in," she says. "I don't resist them."

Performing also helps. She can connect with strangers, rather than feel ashamed of her mental illness. And the sense of love and joy that she felt during her manias still resonates. "It's really liberating to tell people you ran down the street naked, and were tied to a gurney," she says. "At the time, it was terrifying. But to be able to say that to an audience is freeing. To have people laugh with you because they relate is really powerful."

Maxwell considers her bipolar disorder "in remission," but she doesn't take her health for granted. If she's overwhelmed, she takes a day off. She still sees her psychiatrist. But it's no longer a constant struggle: "My life is more about my life than my illness, which is a godsend."

Barreca, Suyemoto, and Maxwell all say they wouldn't wish what they've been through on anyone else. But they're not altogether sorry it happened. Depression required them to learn what many people, depressed or not, never find out: the knowledge that they can get through the worst of times. And after the worst times were over, they found out, it is possible to have a sense of perspective about it all—even to laugh. "Laughter is survival," says Barreca. "It's not because life is easy. It's something you wring out of life. You make joy."

Critical Thinking

1. Identify how depressed persons get through the worst of times.
2. Review the different types of therapy for depression.
3. Explain why most people differ in terms of what relieves their depression.

KATHLEEN MCGOWAN is a freelance writer in New York.

I Survived

When Magic Johnson famously announced he had HIV, it wasn't clear how long he'd live. Twenty years later, he tells of his struggles, fears, and triumphs.

ALLISON SAMUELS

Earvin "Magic" Johnson isn't the reflective type. He tends not to dwell on the past or even second-guess the decision he made 10 minutes ago. So when asked if he often thinks about that chilly November morning in 1991 when he stood onstage at the Great Western Forum in Los Angeles and announced to the world that he'd contracted HIV, the former point guard flashes his signature smile and shakes his head: no. "I don't look back that much at all, and I don't spend a lot of time on regrets," says Johnson. "I do regret putting my family and my wife, Cookie, through that entire experience and having to deal with certain things. But that's really the only regret I have."

Instead, the basketball legend turned business executive keeps his mind focused on one, profound thought: living. To the fame he earned as a Los Angeles Laker has been added the triumph of the survivor who beat the odds, and it may be the greater legacy of the two.

Up at 4 a.m. each workday, Johnson jogs five miles to his office in Beverly Hills, where he oversees Magic Johnson Enterprises, which operates movie theaters, Starbucks stores, and other businesses in long-neglected urban neighborhoods. Meanwhile, he's actively involved in his namesake foundation's efforts around HIV/AIDS and education, and works closely with the Obama administration on community-development issues. And when he finally gets home from the office after a brisk walk, he takes more business calls until 9 p.m.

And that's Johnson dialed back. "For a long time, I'd work until 10 or 11," until his wife laid down the law, he says. "When I work, I'm on. I'm 'Magic.' I love it, but it takes a lot out of me."

It's a pace that would challenge almost any 51-year-old—let alone someone who's spent every day for the past 20 years contending with HIV. "I'll hear people say every so often that having HIV must not be so bad—just look at Magic and how well he's doing," says Johnson, who has remained AIDS-free. "I'm blessed that the medicine I take really worked well with my body and makeup. It doesn't work like that for everyone. A lot of people haven't been as fortunate as I have."

It was June 5, 1981, when the U.S. Centers for Disease Control issued a report about a strange and lethal pneumonia discovered in five gay men in Los Angeles. By the time Johnson was diagnosed with HIV as part of a routine NBA preseason physical, more Americans had died of AIDS than in all the conflicts after World War II. With fatalities rising each year and few therapies on hand to fight the disease, the question in 1991 wasn't whether those infected with the virus could live full and productive lives but rather how long it would be before they died. Along the way, a cascade of opportunistic infections mottled the sufferers' skin with strange purple lesions, covered their lungs in a yeastlike fungus, and left them looking like the walking dead of Birkenau.

'I was never going to run from this . . . This happened for a reason, and I know it was to help someone else.'

Facing this prospect, and surrounded by Los Angeles Lakers team owner Jerry Buss, former Lakers star Kareem Abdul Jabbar, and NBA commissioner David Stern, Johnson appeared calm, even confident that morning in 1991. For those 15 excruciating minutes in front of the TV cameras, he put on his best game face. "I was never going to run and hide from this— I couldn't," he says. And yet, in walking off the stage he was walking away, at 32, from an astonishing career and driving passion and into the frightening unknown. What were his chances, and what would become of his young family?

Only months earlier, Johnson had married Earlitha "Cookie" Kelly, and she was now two months pregnant. An immediate concern was her health and the health of their unborn child (neither was infected). Beyond that was the indelicate question of how Johnson had contracted the virus (ultimately, he explained that he'd had sexual encounters with multiple female partners in the 1980s).

Initially, Cookie Johnson tried to talk her husband out of immediately going public with the news. "As soon as he found out he had HIV, he was ready to tell the world," she recalls. "I was afraid of what people would say, how people would treat us, and what it would mean—because we didn't know what it meant at that point. I just wanted him to wait."

At the time, AIDS was still widely perceived as targeting only the gay community, despite the fact that women, children, the elderly—and heterosexual men—were also at risk. People were still reluctant to admit to having the disease. The iconic African-American choreographer Alvin Ailey, who succumbed to AIDS in 1989, asked his doctors to announce that he'd died of a blood disease. The tennis legend Arthur Ashe, who contracted the virus via a blood transfusion in 1988, didn't announce he had AIDS until shortly before his death five years later.

But Johnson was determined to fight his battle out in the open. "This happened to me for a reason, and I know it was for me to help someone else" is how he puts it now.

While Johnson worked to raise public consciousness from Los Angeles, Andre, his 10-year-old son from a previous relationship, struggled to deal with the fallout from Lansing, Mich., where he lived with his mother. After the surprising announcement, Andre—who is now 30 and works for his father—recalls enduring hurtful remarks from fellow elementary-school children and their parents.

"My dad told me not to worry about him and not to worry about what people said. He knew that so many people didn't understand HIV or AIDS and that kids can be cruel."

Adults can be cruel, too: when Johnson returned to the hardwood with his doctors' approval in 1992, he experienced the ostracism that so many HIV-positive people encountered. Some of his teammates publicly contested his presence out of fear they could be infected if he were injured and bled during a game.

"I would say hands down, the first five years were the most difficult for me," he says. "That was before advances in medicine, and I was still struggling with my career. It wasn't the way I wanted things to go. It took me a while to figure out I needed closure to get unstuck. I was just stuck," he continues. "There were those moments when thoughts came like 'What if I don't make it?' But they were fleeting, or at least I tried to make them that way. I couldn't let myself stay there for long."

As Johnson fought his doubts, his doctors battled the killer that had infected him. Dr. David Ho had begun experimenting with a promising new weapon: a cocktail of antiretroviral medications that seemed to keep HIV in check and prevent patients from developing full-blown AIDS. And so, in 1994—about a year and a half before the new drug regimen was introduced to the general public—Ho put Johnson on it. "Since we pioneered that therapy, we were able to include Mr. Johnson early, and it made a major difference in his health and overall being," says Ho from his offices at the Aaron Diamond AIDS Research Center in New York. "In the beginning there were many pills he had to take several times a day. That's changed a great deal now, so he doesn't take but a few, and with fewer side effects." Johnson's drug regimen includes the pharmaceuticals Trizivir and Kaletra.

Ho says most of his conversations with Johnson these days are to make sure his patient is taking his medicine at the same time each day—a must for anyone with HIV. "That's the challenge for Mr. Johnson because he is such a busy man all the time," says Ho. "We work a lot on making that easier for him, but he understands how key the medicine is to his well-being. He's the poster child of success for living with HIV, because he understands what it takes to fight this virus, and he does it."

It troubles Johnson that 30 years into this epidemic, the battle against HIV is nowhere near ending. AIDS has claimed some 25 million lives worldwide, and more than 33 million people are living with HIV. In the United States, the incidence of HIV and AIDS cases in the African-American community has increased in recent years. Women account for about 25 percent of new HIV/AIDS cases in the U.S.; of those, two out of three are African-American women. In 2006, the rate of HIV infections for black women was 15 times as high as that for white women and four times as high as for Latina women. The majority of infected women reported contracting the virus through unprotected sex.

Do You Believe in Magic?

Earvin Johnson Jr. earned his nickname on the team of Everett High School in Lansing, Mich. And ever since—whether it's in basketball, in business, or in battling HIV—he has played to win.

1979

Johnson is selected first overall in the NBA draft by the Lakers and leads them to the championship in his rookie season.

1988

The Lakers beat the Detroit Pistons to claim their fifth NBA championship since Johnson joined the team.

1991

At 32, Johnson discovers he has HIV and announces his retirement. His wife and unborn son test negative.

1992

Back on the court, he wins the All-Star MVP, but retires again after protests from fellow players.

1994

Dr. David Ho puts Johnson on an experimental cocktail of antiretroviral drugs to help fight his HIV.

1995

Opens his first Magic Johnson movie theater in LA.'s Crenshaw district, part of an effort to revive inner-city neighborhoods.

2011

He acquires a stake in the company that owns *Vibe* magazine and is rumored as a possible buyer for the Los Angeles Dodgers.

"Those numbers really break my heart," says Johnson. "Because there is no reason for it."

He points out that "the gay community has done such a great job of getting their message across, and it's worked, But there is still such a stigma with the virus in our community, and that prevents any progress, because we won't talk about it with our kids or our families. What can change without talking? That's what I'm fighting to change with the foundation."

By contrast, Magic recalls how his family, most of whom still live in Michigan, handled the news of his illness 20 years ago. "My mom hung up the phone with me and got on a plane to come out here, my dad got on a plane, my brothers and sisters got on a plane to come be with me. My aunts, my cousins—they all were getting on a plane. That's love, that's support, and that makes a world of difference in how well you fight the virus. I know that's a large part of why I'm still here today."

For a man who doesn't spend a lot of time on reflection, Johnson seems a bit overwhelmed as he considers the enormity of what he's accomplished: he has shown the world what it means to live—fully—with HIV. "My son Andre, his wife and baby girl were over to the house on Easter," he says, his smile now widening as he recalls the day. "It was such a special moment, to be able to hold and play with my granddaughter and see my son actually become this great husband and father. Man, you don't know—I had to stop myself from tearing up, because who knew? Who really knew?"

Critical Thinking

1. Recall how early Magic Johnson was put on a cocktail of antiretroviral medications, before they were available to the general public.

2. Approximately how many people worldwide are HIV positive?

3. Summarize the amount of work Magic Johnson spends on community development and education.

The New Survivors

For over 11 million Americans, cancer is no longer a definite death sentence. The dreaded disease has instead become a crucible, often remaking personality and endowing survivors with qualities not even they knew they had.

PAMELA WEINTRAUB

Jasan Zimmerman WAS 6 months old when he was diagnosed with neuroblastoma of the left neck in 1976. First the cancer was surgically removed, then he was treated with radiation. Perhaps it was exposure to all that radiation that caused the thyroid cancer when he was 15. More surgery, more radiation. But this time, old enough to grasp the situation, he was terrified. "I didn't want to die" recalls Zimmerman, who grit his teeth through the grueling treatment. Almost as difficult was the aftermath: Traumatized by the experience, he spent his teen years sullen and depressed, without quite knowing why.

He tried to put it all out of his mind—until cancer appeared for a third time in 1997. He was 21 and had just graduated from college. Again Zimmerman was successfully treated. He pursued life goals, including a master's degree in microbiology, but his inner turmoil remained.

The literature on survivorship indicates that between 30 and 90 percent of patients became hardier and more upbeat after the diagnosis of cancer was made.

For 11 more years, he went for checkups, always fearing a return of the dread disease. "I'd get road rage on the way to the doctor. Even the smell of clinical antiseptic could piss me off," he reports. Despite some scares, the cancer never came back, but living with his history itself became a burden. How soon into a new relationship would he need to confess his medical past? Would he ever be free of the threat? By 2003, he was so angry that he punched a wall and broke his hand.

Today, Zimmerman is able to turn his back on the ordeal. He's done it only by embracing his role as a survivor and speaking out to many of the 1.4 million Americans diagnosed with the disease each year. His message is about the ability to *overcome,* and he openly describes his own experience.

"Each time I share my story people feel hopeful," he says And he does, too. "I was living under a thundercloud. It's taken me decades to grow from the experience, but the ability to inspire people has turned a negative into a positive and opened me up."

In the past, the very word *cancer* summoned images of hopelessness, pain, and death; little thought was given to life after cancer because it was considered brief. The cancer "victim" was seen as the passive recipient of ill fate and terrible luck. No more.

Survivorship is increasingly common; some 11.4 million Americans are alive today after treatment and are ever more vocal about their experiences. Emboldened by effective diagnosis and treatment strategies, celebrities such as Melissa Etheridge and Fran Drescher have made public disclosure of the disease increasingly routine and the fight definitely important and profound. Tour de France champion Lance Armstrong, determined to train for the world-class athletic event on the heels of treatment for advanced testicular cancer, turned his achievement into advocacy through his LiveStrong movement.

Many cancer survivors are travelers to a highly intense edge world where they battle death and return transformed. They leave as ordinary and burdened mortals and come back empowered and invigorated. In coming closer to fear, risk, and death than most of us, they wind up marshaling qualifies not even they knew they had.

As more patients have lived longer, a body of research on their experiences has developed. It demonstrates that many cancer patients muster enormous grit for highly aggressive treatments and endure considerable pain to accrue small gains in the fight for survival. Despite therapies that weaken them physically, they can be especially psychologically hardy, harnessing and growing from their stress. Even the most narrow-minded or inflexible people may come to love art, beauty, and philosophical truth as a way of getting through the ordeal. Those who survive often come out of the experience with bravery, uriosity, fairness, forgiveness, gratitude, humor, kindness, and n enhanced sense of meaning.

Is there something about cancer itself that is transformative nd growth-inspiring? Do we literally need to face death to go eyond the often petty limits of our workaday lives? William reitbart, chief of the psychiatry service at Memorial Sloan-ettering Cancer Center in New York City and an international eader in psycho-ontology, says we just might.

"It is in our nature to transcend our limitations, but too often e get distracted by everyday life. If life is always smooth, e're never challenged," he says. "Suffering is probably neces-ary to make us grow." The ultimate tool may be a brush with eath. "The need to find meaning is a primary force," adds Bre-bart, himself a cancer survivor, "but we may need to be con-ronted with our own mortality for that to occur." In the school f hard knocks, cancer amounts to earning a Ph.D.

Learning to Hope

arol Farran, an eldercare expert from Rush University Medi-al Center in Chicago, sought to understand why some nursing ome residents thrived despite adversity and isolation while oth-rs just withered away. The difference between the two groups, he found, was hope—not the blind or rigid optimism that usu-lly passes for hope, but an open sense of possibility, acceptance f risk, and a willingness to work things out. Hopeful people ace reality in a clear-eyed fashion, doing the best they can. ne woman too sick to go outdoors, for instance, maintained n upbeat attitude by remembering the emotional riches of her ast. "The hopeful person looked at reality and then arrived at olutions. If a hoped-for outcome became impossible, the hope-ul person would find something else to hope for," Farran found.

The role of hope in cancer has also come under scrutiny. sychologists at the Royal Marsden Hospital in London and utton studied women with early-stage breast cancer and found hat risk of recurrence or death increased significantly among hose who lacked hope. There was nothing mysterious or mysti-al about it: Hopeful patients managed their illness themselves nstead of letting outsiders pull the strings. They often chose he most aggressive treatments. And envisioning the light at the nd of the tunnel helped provide the strength they needed to get hrough each difficult day.

Yet hope was not a given for them; it was an attitude they wrested from despair. Despite being an expert on hope, Far-an could not muster any when she herself was diagnosed with reast cancer. She met the news with anger, grief, and fear of death. Panic propelled her through treatment, in a total daze. nly when she went in for breast reconstruction was a wise urse able to penetrate her panic: "A year from now you'll be where you want to be, but there is no way to get there except by oing through this experience, now."

As despair loosened its hold on Farran, she tried to embrace the flexibility she had studied in others. "I told myself to get a grip." she says. Finally she thought of her love of playing piano and decided to buy a metronome, a symbol of what she called "slow ime" It was a palpable reminder to calm down, confront her fear

of death, and think things through. "You can start in despair but arrive at hope," says Farran, 18 years later. Hope can be learned.

True Grit

Once empowered by hope, cancer patients have been known to search out cures in the face of daunting odds. Jerome Groop-man, a Harvard cancer specialist and author of *Anatomy of Hope,* tells the story of a patient, a pathologist with advanced metastatic stomach cancer that was considered fatal. Soon word spread around the hospital that the pathologist intended to do something "mad." Without any evidence that his cancer was survivable, he insisted on doses of chemotherapy and radiation so toxic they were, by themselves, probably lethal. To Groop-man and other cancer doctors on staff at the time, the effort seemed "like a desperate, wrongheaded, ultimately futile effort to resist the inevitable." Surely the treatment would deprive the pathologist of a peaceful end at home. Indeed, Groopman, stop-ping by the man's bedside, found him bleeding as tissues were literally burned away by the strong treatment he had engineered.

Twenty-five years later, while researching his book on hope, Groopman found that the pathologist was still going strong. "If I'd been treating him, I wouldn't have authorized the therapy and he would have died."

Similar tenacity gripped Sean Patrick, a business strategist and extreme sports enthusiast from Aspen, Colorado, whose rare form of ovarian cancer was diagnosed in 1998. Instead of simply agreeing to follow her doctor's treatment advice, she hired a research firm to comb the scientific literature and come up with a list of experts studying her specific disease. She quickly learned that her doctor had recommended the wrong treatment and if she followed through she might not survive the year.

So she fired her oncologist and hired a medical team known for experimental use of drugs. The side effects of her radical treatment were devastating. "Flu symptoms magnified a thou-sand times," Patrick said. There was nausea, vomiting, dis-abling body aches, extreme weakness, chills, and diarrhea. "I would shake so hard my teeth would knock and then have a fever so high I would sweat through my clothes." She nick-named the side effects "shake and bake." Still, she persisted, at one point even electing a surgery so risky she was not expected to wake up. "If I hadn't taken the risk, I wouldn't be here today," she said in 2006. Her grit gave her a full decade more than anyone expected; she died just before this article went to press, in 2009.

Most people don't have the financial resources to seek such customized or experimental options, but even patients depen-dent on treatment approvals by an insurance company can choose the most aggressive courses that might confer even a slight survival edge. That explains why so many women with stage-one breast cancer opt for removal of both breasts instead of the watch-and-wait approach. It also explains why ovarian cancer patients subject themselves to multiple rounds of che-motherapy, often rejecting studies contending the treatment will fail.

"Even if it is a long shot, someone is going to fall at the end of the bell curve," notes Groopman.

Soldiering On

Research shows that, even while dealing with the disease, large numbers of cancer patients deploy their tenacity in other realms of life, as well. Take Elizabeth Cowie, 44, a career sergeant in the Army who was headed to Iraq with her troops. There was only one problem: Months before deployment, in a routine Army physical, Cowie was diagnosed with early-stage breast cancer. Instead of going home to attend to treatment, Cowie poured her energy into finding a way to get to Iraq along with the soldiers she'd trained. She forsook the more extreme course of mastectomy for circumscribed lumpectomy, dramatically shortening surgical recovery, and decided against weeks of radiation therapy in favor of a new technique she learned of, called Mammasite, which delivers radiation directly to the tumor over the course of days. She underwent the procedures quietly, without telling the soldiers reporting to her until she was declared cancer-free, and went on with her deployment, gritting her teeth only when her vest chafed the still-healing surgical wound. Cowie endured the heat of Iraq while still recovering, all the while watching over and counseling the soldiers she'd become so close to.

"There were days I was so sore and the heat was so oppressive and it was so exhausting," Cowie recalls. "But I had a commitment to the people I was with. The soldiers counted on me being there. Just knowing that made me stronger, and I couldn't let them down. I put one foot in front of the other; that is how I saw my mission through."

Cowie's can-do attitude is a trait common among the new survivors. According to University of Utah psychologist Lisa Aspinwall, a sense of purpose and positivity is adaptive in cancer's midst. In reviewing the literature on survivorship, Aspinwall found that 30 to 90 percent of patients reported benefits, from increased optimism to better relationships, *after* diagnosis was made. At first it seemed counterintuitive. But the positive, active mind-set "is likely to help patients manage what they need to do next," she explains. "Those in treatment must make dozens of decisions. To hold things together, you need to pay attention to options. Just think about it—negative emotions orient us to threats, but they also narrow our attention. That's not the best state for navigating a complex and changing situation, just what cancer is."

Post-Traumatic Growth

The benefits seen during the trauma, however, may pale against those reaped later, after survivors have had the chance to reflect. "It's hard to grow much when you are in the middle of a war," says psychologist Lad Wenzel of the University of California at Irvine, who works with women surviving gynecologic cancer at least five years. "Instead, strength and meaning unfold for survivors as they retell their stories, again and again."

There is nothing mystical about the power of hope. Hopeful patients managed their own illness instead of letting outsiders do it. They often chose the most aggressive treatments.

University of Connecticut psychologist Keith Bellizzi say the life event is so intense that some people use it to reconstruct their lives; they don't return to the same level of functioning but to a greater level. "Post-traumatic growth is above and beyond resilience," he says. "Life after cancer means finding a new normal, but for many the new normal is better than the old normal."

Bellizzi, 39, speaks from direct experience. He was a well-paid marketing professional when, at age 25, he was diagnosed with stage-three testicular cancer so advanced it had spread to his lymph nodes and lungs. A few months later, a CAT scan revealed a golf-ball-size mass in his kidney. Almost as upsetting as the cancer was the news that he might never have biological children of his own. "It was an opportunity to reflect on my life and face my mortality," says Bellizzi.

Following several surgeries, including removal of a kidney, along with aggressive chemotherapy, he made a vow: "If I survived, I would dedicate my life to the fight against cancer." Bellizzi kept his vow. He quit his lucrative job and went back to school, earning masters degrees in public health and in psychology and a Ph.D. in human development and family studies. In 2005, he was one of 24 cyclists chosen to ride with Lance Armstrong on the Bristol-Myers Squibb Tour of Hope to heighten awareness of cancer research. He also has three daughters—and is a leading researcher in the field of post-traumatic growth.

Bellizzi's sense of purpose is just one type of growth that survivors report. Julia Rowland, head of the Office of Cancer Survivorship at the National Cancer Institute, points to enhanced and altered relationships. "You learn who's going to be there for you and who is not—you learn who your friends are," she says. Some friends, upset by the prospect of loss, may detach temporarily or even permanently. As some friendships fade, others may be forged, especially within the community of survivors. "You also learn to empathize," says Rowland, explaining how survivors acquire new depths of feeling.

Pleasures become more meaningful, too. As a team at the University of Pennsylvania found, those suffering chronic illness end up more immersed in art, music, and books. "Appreciation is often enhanced," points out Bellizzi. Many survivors literally stop to smell the roses even if they didn't before.

Not everyone diagnosed with cancer finds a new sense of purpose. "Some people have a glimpse of the possibilities but do not change. Cancer is just wasted on them."

The sense of self is often enhanced too. "Some survivors discover an inner strength they didn't realize they had," says Bellizzi. "A situation that might have seemed daunting before cancer may, after cancer, seem like something easily handled."

In one important study, Bellizzi looked at generativity—concerns, often arising at midlife, about the legacy one is likely to leave behind. Generativity can be expressed in many ways—making the planet a better place, giving children the love they need, being creative in work or intimate with family and friends. Midlifers surveying the past may vow to do more with the time they have left. But no matter an individual's age, Bellizzi found, cancer was a catalyst for generativity.

While cancer generally sparked more generativity in women than in men, all the survivors Bellizzi studied were more likely than those without cancer to forge a new life path reflecting their core values. Those reporting the most altered perspective "expressed an increased awareness of the fragility of life and the value of loved ones," he reports. "They also said they had learned not to worry about little annoyances." A patient with colorectal cancer said her disease had convinced her to put an end to meaningless pursuits; she resigned from her management position and spent time with her friends.

A Spiritual Dimension

Cancer can also promote a sense of inner meaning and add a spiritual dimension to life. Lisa Benaron, an internist and pediatrician from Chico, California, learned she had cancer in the midst of other traumas. Her sister-in-law, a dear friend, had just died of breast cancer. And her marriage was falling apart. Six months after her sister-in-law died, Benaron, too, was diagnosed with breast cancer. Although in stage one, her cancer was a particularly aggressive kind; further, she had the gene that signals ongoing risk.

Energized by her situation, Benaron focused on researching the best treatment options and chose the most aggressive course, to gain a few points of survival advantage. The chemo was debilitating, but she still recalls fondly the days after those sessions. They were, she insists, "great times. I didn't usually get enough time off to garden, or do yoga." She did then.

She made an effort to pursue the things she loved: kayaking, walks in nature, spending time with her daughter, Molly, then 7. "I took Molly to the Galapagos Islands on Easter break in 2004," Benaron recalls. "You could sit on the beach and the seals and iguanas would be right there within arms reach.

Having cancer made me aware of how fortunate I was and how much beauty was in the world."

Her own journey wasn't complete, though, until a friend she met in the local cancer community, Theresa Marcis, sought her help to travel to Abadiania, Brazil, to see a healer named John of God. "When she was first diagnosed, Theresa had a large mass and stage-three cancer; the prognosis wasn't good," says Benaron. "But she was full of hope. She wrote the word HEAL in big burgundy letters on her kitchen walls."

Under ordinary circumstances, the logical, driven doctor would have had little in common with the free-spirited Marcis, a college English teacher. But under the influence of cancer, they became a team. Benaron helped Marcis navigate the mainstream medical minefield, and Marcis exposed Benaron to acupuncture, sound therapy, and other alternative techniques. "They were enjoyable and peaceful," Benaron recalls.

In 2008, doctors found that Marcis's cancer had spread to every bone in her body. Instead of conceding defeat, she journeyed with a colleague to Brazil to see John of God. Though her conditioned later worsened, she spoke of going back. When she was too sick to travel, Benaron went in her stead, "to give Theresa peace."

Still very much the logical physician, Benaron doesn't believe that John's interventions can cure. But she loved taking the trip as proxy for her gentle friend, who died hoping that John's powers would stretch from central Brazil to her home in California. "I came to realize through her that every person has their own path through life; she tapped into every good feeling within herself and threw herself into being spiritual. It helped me to see the importance of love and openness to others," Benaron says.

The California physician remembers meditating in Abadiania with a huge thunderstorm whipping up around her. "It was this gorgeous experience," she reports. "But I realized I didn't have to go across the world or down a dirt road to find it. You can be in the moment wherever you are."

Tyranny vs. Transformation

The idea that cancer can be uplifting or transformative has become controversial in the cancer community itself. Posttraumatic growth, while common, does not define all survivors. Young people, whose disease may be more challenging, often grow more emotionally from the experience than older people. "It's very disruptive to have cancer while raising your family and climbing in your career," explains Bellizzi, "and it's the intensity of the experience and the realization that life is finite that forges change."

Not everyone diagnosed with cancer transcends the past, finds a new sense of purpose, or becomes more spiritual. And in the midst of a deadly disease, the pressure to remake oneself can feel harsh. "It's wrong to pressure people to be optimistic or change their lives," says Utah's Lisa Aspinwall.

"Some will not be able to take advantage of having had cancer," says Breitbart of Memorial Sloan-Kettering. "Some people with poor prognoses just want to hasten death. Some have a glimpse of the possibilities but do not change. Cancer is just wasted on some people."

Still, cancer patients have undeniably entered a new era in which long lives are very much a reality, and they are changed by having looked death in the eye and beaten it back. The experience has made them stronger and forced them to reevaluate the very foundations of their lives. "The bottom line for me is I finally realized that I want to turn the negative experiences of having cancer into a positive," says Jasan Zimmerman, "and the more I do, the more I want to do. I don't want to miss out on anything."

Critical Thinking

1. Paraphrase the following: "Suffering is necessary to make us grow."

2. Label some of the qualities "discovered" by people with cancer.

3. Relate how a battle with death can transform a person.

PAMELA WEINTRAUB is a writer in New York.

Curing Cancer

What treatable tumors can teach us about improving the odds in the deadliest cases.

SHARON BEGLEY

Given a choice, no one would opt to get cancer. And it's cruelly insensitive to tell patients how fortunate they are to have a particular cancer. Yet there is no question that the 33-year-old man who walked into oncologist George Bosl's office at Memorial Sloan—Kettering Cancer Center in New York in 2001 was lucky. He had testicular cancer.

He was lucky because the vast majority of such men are cured, sometimes with surgery alone, sometimes with radiation or chemotherapy as well. By "cured," we don't mean that a patient has cancer cells scattered throughout his body that will need to be kept in check by a lifetime of chemotherapy. We mean *cured:* the cancer is gone. Even men whose testicular cancer has metastasized—in the case of Bosl's patient, it had spread to the lungs and abdomen—have at least a 70 percent chance of being rid of their cancer forever, which is what this man has every reason to expect: nine years after testicular surgery, 12 weeks of treatment with the chemotherapy agents cisplatin and etoposide (both of which are decades old, not new miracle drugs), and an operation to remove the metastases in his lungs and abdomen, he remains free of cancer. "No matter how widespread testicular cancer is at the time of diagnosis, a patient has some chance of being cured," says Bosl. "The cure rate for men diagnosed in 2010 will be 90 to 95 percent," and even if a patient relapses twice, which usually means the cancer has returned in a form resistant to treatment, he has a fighting chance.

"Cured" is not a word you hear much from oncologists. Indeed, the hoary phrase "a cure for cancer" now sounds bitterly ironic, since scientists discovered no such thing after President Nixon declared war on the disease in 1971. Metastatic melanoma, lung cancer, pancreatic cancer, and esophageal cancer are often death sentences, with the result that cancer will kill 569,490 people in

the United States this year, projects the American Cancer Society. But there is a glimmer of hope in this bleak picture.

Some cancers are curable. Almost 90 percent of children with the most common form of pediatric leukemia will be cured; women whose estrogen-receptor-positive cancer responds to tamoxifen or aromatase inhibitors will often be truly rid of their disease, as will women with HER2-positive breast cancer, which responds to herceptin. Other cancers are treatable, in the sense that although patients have to take drugs for the rest of their lives (as diabetics must take insulin forever), at least they're alive and healthy. The best example of a treatable cancer is CML (chronic myelogenous leukemia), which can be held in check by Gleevec and related drugs. And now, says Bosl, cancer researchers are asking, "Can we use information about what makes some cancers curable to design treatments for the others?" The answer is an emphatic yes, says his Sloan-Kettering colleague Charles Sawyers, whose research was instrumental in developing Gleevec: "I feel like I've seen the future."

Pediatric oncologists saw it first. Although the search for a cancer cure has long centered on discovering new drugs, astonishing advances in pediatric leukemia have come with drugs that were developed from the 1950s to the 1970s. In the 1960s, the cure rate for ALL (acute lymphoblastic leukemia, the most common childhood form) was 5 percent, says oncologist Ching-Hon Pui of St. Jude Children's Research Hospital in Memphis. The reason it is now 90 percent lies in how those drugs are given and how patients are cared for.

Put simply, the kids are blasted with the highest doses of the most chemotherapy drugs they can stand—steroids and vinca alkaloids, asparaginase and anthracyclines and more. They are almost all treated at academic medical centers that specialize in pediatric cancer, not at community hospitals that set broken bones. At the former, oncologists take samples of leukemic cells from bone marrow to identify the genetic abnormalities, customizing treatment to the specific form of ALL a child has. "The lesson is that you need to precisely characterize the cancer cells," says Pui. "We apply personalized therapy to these kids; we don't treat them all the same." And unlike adults who might miss a chemo or radiation treatment, kids are 100 percent compliant. "You can damn well bet that Mom will get that kid to the chemo appointment and make sure he takes his pills," says oncologist Daniel DeAngelo of the Dana-Farber Cancer Institute in Boston.

All this make a difference. Adults with ALL—the same disease as in kids—are less likely to be cured (only 30 to 40 percent survive five years), in large part because they are not treated with the same intensive chemo and do not get the full-bore supportive care that children do to keep them from dying of complications, says oncologist James Downing of St. Jude. The life-or-death importance of that approach shows up starkly in adolescents and young adults. Some 16- to 20-year-olds are treated by a pediatric oncologist; others, by an adult oncologist. Seven years after diagnosis, scientists led by Wendy Stock of the University of Chicago Cancer Research Center reported in a 2008 study, 67 percent of those treated by a pediatric oncologist were alive; 46 percent of those treated as adults were. "They got the same drugs, but the doses were higher," says DeAngelo. "It shows what you can do with intense dosing."

How intense? When a 12-year-old boy from Illinois with ALL arrived at St. Jude in 2001, Pui administered everything but the kitchen sink: the drugs prednisone, vincristine, daunorubicin, and asparaginase, followed by cyclophosphamide, cytarabine, and mercaptopurine. Six weeks later, he gave the boy four courses of high-dose methotrexate, daily mercaptopurine, and four triple-drug treatments into the spinal fluid. For the next 20 weeks he got five more drugs, followed by two and a half years of treatment with three rotating drug pairs. It worked. The boy has been in remission ever since, and just started law school.

"In the past, we used one drug at a time," says Pui. "When one failed, we moved to another. But we learned that that just induces resistance, so now we hit the cancer with many drugs simultaneously. And we also used to use lower doses. But that also causes resistance to develop." High doses are less likely to. Now oncologists are studying whether slamming a cancer with multiple chemo agents will have the same success in adults, including preventing the development of resistance.

The other big object lesson in curing cancer comes from Gleevec, which is singlehandedly responsible for increasing the number of CML patients who survive at least eight years, from 20 percent in the past to 80 percent today. Gleevec must be taken forever, and so in that sense is a treatment more than a cure. (About 5 percent of CML patients per year develop resistance to Gleevec, but scientists figured out why, and developed two similar drugs that take the place of Gleevec when that happens.) Gleevec targets the single genetic change that causes CML, a "translocation" in which two pieces of DNA swap places and leave one gene stuck in the "on" position. The stuck gene makes a molecule called a kinase that, after a cascade of biochemical reactions, tells cells to divide or proliferate. Gleevec locks onto the kinase, incapacitating it. "The future," says Sawyers, "is about identifying such mutations in a tumor so we can offer individualized therapy. The lesson we learned from Gleevec should apply to other cancers that depend on kinases, including lung and melanoma."

That lesson—target the cancer-causing mutation—comes with a corollary, however. It is crucial to target not just any old mutation in a tumor, which can have hundreds, but to disable what are called "driver" mutations. Those are DNA changes that cause the malignancy, rather than "passenger" mutations, which are just along for the ride. It is also crucial that the cancer cells either not have a backup plan—that is, another way to proliferate out of control—or that drugs cripple that pathway, too. "To kill the cancer, you not only need a driver mutation, but the cancer cell also has to be truly addicted to it," says oncologist David Weinstock of Dana-Farber. Since 2008, he and colleagues have been searching for the driver mutations in individual tumor specimens. "We're asking, is there something the cancer is addicted to, like the translocation in CML?" he says.

It's the kind of high-risk, huge-payoff quest that the National Institutes of Health rarely funds; Weinstock got a $750,000 grant from Stand Up to Cancer, the two-year-old entertainment-industry initiative that has allotted $83.5 million for innovative research. (Its next star-packed telethon airs on Sept. 10 in 195 countries.) Weinstock started with cases of adult ALL, in which no such Achilles' heel had been discovered, and hit pay dirt: an obscure gene called $CRLF_2$ drives some 10 percent of ALLs. His team has identified drugs that target the deadly, cancer-driving product of this gene, and plans to launch clinical trials next year.

The recognition that different tumors are powered by, and even addicted to, specific mutations is triggering a revolutionary change in how cancers are classified and treated. Treatment will be based not on the organ where the cancer began, such as the breast or colon or lung, but on the driver mutation—with luck, its Achilles' heel. For instance, lung cancer is actually many different diseases with different molecular drivers, explains Sawyers. The alphabet soup of drivers includes EGFR, BRAF, MEK, and HER2. The good news is that all these are kinases, like Gleevec's target. He estimates that some 200 drugs targeting driver mutations are in the pipeline. The bad news is "we don't routinely profile lung tumors to identify the genetic alteration that's driving them," says Sawyers. "It should be malpractice not to genotype cancer patients."

Genotyping is not even routine in the clinical trials that test experimental drugs. As a result, says Sawyers, "the development of kinase inhibitors for lung cancer has been a 10-year saga of missteps." For instance, a drug that cripples EGFR cancers was tested on patients whose cancer was not driven by that mutation. Although one EGFR inhibitor, Iressa, was approved in 2003, it was a close call, and the drug was almost pulled from the market when it failed to help most lung-cancer patients—those without the EGFR mutation, who should never have gotten it in the first place. The lesson of Gleevec and herceptin—identify the driver mutation and cripple it—is still being ignored, keeping what could be effective drugs from reaching the market. "You would be shocked at how primitive the molecular characterization of cancer is," says cancer researcher Tyler Jacks of MIT. "Companies run big dumb trials" rather than test drugs only on patients whose cancer is driven by the mutation the drug targets. "There has to be a complete reassessment of how we do this."

That's finally happening, with the result that drug companies are seeing hints of success against some of the worst cancers. Metastatic melanoma is one. It seems to shrug off standard chemotherapy, repairing the DNA damage the drugs cause and continuing to multiply. As a result, half the patients with metastatic melanoma—which has seen no therapeutic advances in the last 20 years—die within six months. But in 2002, scientists discovered that about half of melanomas are driven by a mutation in a gene called BRAF (pronounced bee-raff). A biotechnology company, Plexxikon, developed an oral drug that targets the product of that mutation. In a study published last month in *The New England Journal of Medicine,* scientists reported that the drug shrank the metastases (in bone, liver, and bowel) of 80 percent of patients with metastatic melanoma; in two of 32 patients, the cancer vanished. An 80 percent response rate in a solid tumor is unheard of. If the drug is approved by the FDA, it might do for metastatic melanoma what Gleevec did for CML.

Unfortunately, most of the patients relapse within a year. It's not clear why. Maybe other mutations kick in, keeping the drug from binding to BRAF, or the melanoma

switches to a different driver mutation. If so, scientists will have to find backup drugs to keep the cancer in check after it becomes resistant to a drug. With CML, they have: the drugs Sprycel and Tasigna attack leukemic cells that become resistant to Gleevec. With melanoma, they're trying: a clinical trial now underway is testing a one-two punch: a drug that targets BRAF and one that targets a backup pathway. With pancreatic cancer, it may be a lost cause. These tumors are so rife with mutations, says Daniel Von Hoff of the Translational Genomics Research Institute, that "24 patients have 63 genetic changes, and the cancer probably has six or seven different drivers." (He is working on attacking pancreatic cancer by cutting off its fuel supply instead.) With other cancers, scientists haven't found these backup drugs, with the result that when lung and other recalcitrant cancers are hit with one drug they switch drivers as smoothly as a flight from L.A. to Sydney switches pilots over the Pacific. And go on proliferating as insidiously as ever.

In these cases, oncologists believe that combinations of several kinase-targeting drugs, covering all known resistance mutations and backup pathways, "could shut off all mechanisms of escape," says Sawyers. That would be applying the lesson of pediatric leukemia, where success comes from hitting a cancer with everything you've got, upfront, before resistant cells run amok. In that vein, oncologist Dennis Slamon of UCLA's Jonsson Comprehensive Cancer Center is studying whether treating breast cancers with herceptin (which is based on his discoveries), as well as a drug targeting a pathway that makes tumors resistant to herceptin, might save more women. "I don't think we'll be treating patients with 12 drugs," he says, "but it might be three. It's going to be hand-to-hand combat."

Kinase hunters are also seeing glimmers of hope against a form of lung cancer. In 2007 Japanese researchers discovered that about 3 to 5 percent of lung cancers are driven by a mutation in the ALK gene. An oral drug called crizotinib, from Pfizer, shrinks or stabilizes the tumor in 90 percent of patients, the company reported in June. Pfizer hopes to submit the drug for FDA approval next year. The success of another kinase-targeting drug "spurred us to think there are a lot more kinase mutations in cancers that haven't been found, especially in solid tumors," says William Pao of Vanderbilt University, who is using a $750,000 Stand Up to Cancer grant to search for them.

At a recent biology meeting, Jim Watson, codiscoverer of the double-helix structure of DNA, chided MIT's Jacks for saying the revolution in identifying driver mutations and tailoring drugs against them would yield results in 10 to 20 years. It simply has to be faster than that, Watson said: "People need miracles, and we're the only ones who can give it to them." Kids with leukemia, men with testicular cancer, and patients who are alive because of Gleevec or herceptin have their miracles. For the first time, people with cancers that have long outwitted science have a realistic chance of getting a miracle, too.

Critical Thinking

1. Discuss the role of genetic mutations in the development of cancer tumors.
2. Will cancer drugs in the future be targeted at the organ where the tumor is found (e.g., breast, lung) or at the molecular driver of the tumor? Why?

Can You Build a Better Brain?

Blueberries and crossword puzzles aren't going to do it. But as neuroscientists discover the mechanisms of intelligence, they are identifying what really works.

SHARON BEGLEY

This would be a whole lot easier—this quest for ways to improve our brain—if scientists understood the mechanisms of intelligence even half as well as they do the mechanisms of, say, muscular strength. If we had the neuronal version of how lifting weights increases strength (chemical and electrical signals increase the number of filament bundles inside muscle cells), we'd be good to go. For starters, we could dismiss claims for the brain versions of eight-second abs—claims that if we use this brain-training website or practice that form of meditation or eat blueberries or chew gum or have lots of friends, we will be smarter and more creative, able to figure out whether to do a Roth conversion, remember who gave us that fruitcake (the better to retaliate next year), and actually understand the NFL's wild-card tiebreaker system.

But what neuroscientists don't know about the mechanisms of cognition—about what is physically different between a dumb brain and a smart one and how to make the first more like the second—could fill volumes. Actually, it does. Whether you go neuro-slumming (Googling "brain training") or keep to the high road (searching PubMed, the database of biomedical journals, for "cognitive enhancement"), you will find no dearth of advice. But it is rife with problems. Many of the suggestions come from observational studies, which take people who do X and ask, are they smarter (by some measure) than people who do not do X? Just because the answer is yes doesn't mean X makes you smart. People who use their gym locker tend to be fitter than those who don't, but it is not using a gym locker that raises your aerobic capacity. Knowing the mechanisms of exercise physiology averts that error. *Not* knowing the mechanism of cognitive enhancement makes us sitting ducks for dubious claims,

since few studies claiming that X makes people smarter invoke any plausible mechanism by which that might happen. "There are lots of quick and dirty studies of cognitive enhancement that make the news, but the number of rigorous, well-designed studies that will stand the test of time is much smaller," says neuroscientist Peter Snyder of Brown University Medical School. "We're sort of in the Wild West."

A 2010 evaluation of purported ways to maintain or improve cognitive function, conducted for the National Institutes of Health, shows how many of the claims for cognitive enhancers are as sketchy as a Wild West poker player with a fifth ace up his sleeve. Vitamins B_6, B_{12}, and E; beta carotene; folic acid; and the trendy antioxidants called flavenoids are all busts, and the evidence for alcohol, omega-3s (the fatty acids in fish), or having a large social network is weak. The Mediterranean diet is associated with a lower risk of cognitive decline, find observational studies, but that hasn't been confirmed in more rigorous, randomized controlled studies, and no one knows whether the benefit comes from what the diet includes (olive oil, fish, vegetables, wine) or what it excludes (red meat, refined sugars, dairy fat). Statins don't help, and neither do estrogen or NSAIDs (aspirin, ibuprofen). Be skeptical of practices that promise to make you smarter by increasing blood flow to the brain—there is no evidence that's the limiting factor in normal people. Yes, you can find individual studies concluding that one or another hype-heavy intervention helps your brain, but the conclusion of any single study is more likely to be wrong than right. (For one thing, scientists and journals prefer positive findings and bury negative studies.) Only by assessing all the evidence from all the studies, as the NIH evaluation did, can you get the true picture.

The quest for effective ways to boost cognitive capacity is not hopeless, however. The explosion in neuroscience is slowly revealing the mechanisms of cognition. "We have accumulated enough knowledge about the mechanisms and molecular underpinnings of cognition at the synaptic and circuit levels to say something about which processes contribute," says James Bibb of the University of Texas Southwestern Medical Center, who organized a symposium on "cognitive enhancement strategies" at the 2010 meeting of the Society for Neuroscience. Greater cognitive capacity comes from having more neurons or synapses, higher levels of neurogenesis (the creation of new neurons, especially in the memory-forming hippocampus), and increased production of compounds such as BDNF (brain-derived neurotrophic factor), which stimulates the production of neurons and synapses, says neuroscientist Yaakov Stern of Columbia University. Both neurogenesis and synapse formation boost learning, memory, reasoning, and creativity. And in people who excel at particular tasks, Stern's neuro-imaging studies show, brain circuits tend to be more efficient (using less energy even as cognitive demand increases), higher capacity, and more flexible.

One of the strongest findings in neuroplasticity, the science of how the brain changes its structure and function in response to input, is that attention is almost magical in its ability to physically alter the brain and enlarge functional circuits. In a classic experiment, scientists found that when monkeys repeatedly practiced fine-tactile perception, the relevant brain region expanded, just as it does when people learn Braille or the violin. Similarly, a region of the auditory cortex expands when we hear a particular tone over and over. (Yes, the spot that processes your ringtone is encroaching on next-door areas.) But when monkeys simultaneously touched something and listened to tones, only the brain region controlling the input they were trained to focus on expanded. In other words, identical input—tactile sensations and sounds—produces a different result, expanding a brain area or not, depending only on whether attention is being paid.

That might explain why skills we're already good at don't make us much smarter: we don't pay much attention to them. In contrast, taking up a new, cognitively demanding activity—ballroom dancing, a foreign language—is more likely to boost processing speed, strengthen synapses, and expand or create functional networks.

By nailing down the underpinnings of cognition, neuroscientists can separate plausible brain boosters from dubious ones. With apologies to the political-correctness police, nicotine enhances attention—that key driver of neuroplasticity—and cognitive performance in both smokers and nonsmokers, scientists at the National Institute on Drug Abuse reported in a 2010 analysis of 41 double-blind, placebo-controlled studies. Nicotine, they found, has "significant positive effects" on fine motor skills, the accuracy of short-term memory, some forms of attention, and working memory, among other basic cognitive skills. The improvements "likely represent true performance enhancement" and "beneficial cognitive effects." The reason is that nicotine binds to the brain receptors for the neurotransmitter acetylcholine that are central players in cortical circuits. (Caveat: smoking also increases your risk of dementia, so while cigarettes may boost your memory and attention now, you could pay for it later. To be determined: whether a nicotine patch delivers the benefits without the risks.

Neuroscience supports the cognitive benefits of stimulants like Adderall and Ritalin, too, at least in some people for some tasks. Both drugs (as well as caffeine) raise the brain levels of dopamine, the juice that produces motivation and the feeling of reward. On balance, finds psychologist Martha Farah of the University of Pennsylvania, studies show that both drugs enhance the recall of memorized words as well as working memory (the brain's scratchpad, which plays a key role in fluid intelligence). They do not improve verbal fluency, reasoning, or abstract thought, however, nor provide much benefit to people with a gene variant that keeps dopamine activity high, Farah found in a recent study.

These limitations suggest two things. First, if you're naturally awash in dopamine and are highly motivated to, say, deduce from its source code how a website was built, then increasing dopamine levels pharmacologically is unlikely to help. Farah found no difference between the performance of volunteers given Adderall and volunteers given a placebo on a battery of cognitive tasks, suggesting that you can get the same dopamine-boosting benefits of the drug by simply believing that you'll do well, which itself releases dopamine. Second, the divide between the mental functions that drugs do and don't improve suggests that psychological factors such as motivation and reward help with memory, but not higher-order processes such as abstract thought. The drugs "will help some people some of the time, but maybe not by a whole lot," she concludes. Fun fact for anyone hoping for IQ in a pill: a recent survey of doctors finds they're more comfortable prescribing sex drugs than smart drugs.

Knowing that Adderall and Ritalin work, when they do, by giving you motivation and a sense of reward from, say, solving a Sudoku puzzle implies that other ways to achieve those feelings will also boost mental performance. That's probably the mechanism by which a whole slew of tricks work. Take, for instance, the "ancestor effect." As a paper to be published in the *European Journal of*

Social Psychology reports, "thinking about our genetic origin"—how Grandpa survived the Depression, how Great-Grandma eluded the Cossacks, et al.— "enhances intellectual performance." The mechanism responsible for that is an increase in confidence and motivation—Adderall without the prescription. Along the same lines, a positive mood—even the kind that comes from watching "Sneezing Panda" on YouTube—can enhance creative problem-solving, finds a new paper in *Psychological Science*. In this case, reducing stress and the resulting cortisol, which attacks the myelin sheath that coats neurons and thus impairs signal transmission, allows underlying abilities to reach their full potential. Finally, being told that you belong to a group that does very well on a test tends to let you do better than if you're told you belong to a group that does poorly; the latter floods you with cortisol, while the former gives you the wherewithal and dopamine surge to keep plugging away.

A year of exercise can give a 70-year-old the brain connectivity of a 30-year-old, improving memory, planning, dealing with ambiguity, and multitasking.

But there's a difference between reaching your natural potential by removing impediments such as stress and actually raising that potential. The latter requires tapping into one of the best-established phenomena in neuroscience—namely, that the more you use a circuit, the stronger it gets. As a result, a skill you focus and train on improves, and even commandeers more neuronal real estate, with corresponding improvements in performance. London cabdrivers who memorize that city's insanely confusing streets (25,000 of them) have a larger posterior hippocampus, the region that files spatial memories, than the average Londoner, neuroscientist Eleanor Maguire of University College London discovered in 2003. Conversely, if we offload our navigational ability onto GPS, we'll lose it.

The rule that "neurons that fire together, wire together" suggests that cognitive training should boost mental prowess. Studies are finding just that, but with a crucial caveat. Training your memory, reasoning, or speed of processing improves that skill, found a large government-sponsored study called Active. Unfortunately, there is no transfer: improving processing speed does not improve memory, and improving memory does not improve reasoning. Similarly, doing crossword puzzles will improve your ability to . . . do crosswords. "The research so far suggests that cognitive training benefits only the task

used in training and does not generalize to other tasks," says Columbia's Stern.

The holy grail of brain training is something that does transfer, and here there are three good candidates. The first is physical exercise. Simple aerobic exercise, such as walking 45 minutes a day three times a week, improves episodic memory and executive-control functions by about 20 percent, finds Art Kramer of the University of Illinois at Urbana-Champaign. His studies have mostly been done in older adults, so it's possible the results apply only to people whose brain physiology has begun to deteriorate—except that that happens starting in our 20s. Exercise gooses the creation of new neurons in the region of the hippocampus that files away experiences and new knowledge. It also stimulates the production of neuron fertilizers such as BDNF, as well as of the neurotransmitters that carry brain signals, and of gray matter in the prefrontal cortex. Exercise stimulates the production of new synapses, the connections that constitute functional circuits and whose capacity and efficiency underlie superior intelligence. Kramer finds that a year of exercise can give a 70-year-old the connectivity of a 30-year-old, improving memory, planning, dealing with ambiguity, and multitasking. "You can think of fitness training as changing the molecular and cellular building blocks that underlie many cognitive skills," he says. "It thus provides more generalizable benefits than specifically training memory or decision making."

The second form of overall mental training is meditation, which can increase the thickness of regions that control attention and process sensory signals from the outside world. In a program that neuroscientist Amishi Jha of the University of Miami calls mindfulness-based mind-fitness training, participants build concentration by focusing on one object, such as a particular body sensation. The training, she says, has shown success in enhancing mental agility and attention "by changing brain structure and function so that brain processes are more efficient," the quality associated with higher intelligence.

Finally, some videogames might improve general mental agility. Stern has trained older adults to play a complex computer-based action game called Space Fortress, which requires players to shoot missiles and destroy the fortress while protecting their spaceship against missiles and mines. "It requires motor control, visual search, working memory, long-term memory, and decision making," he says. It also requires that elixir of neuroplasticity: attention, specifically the ability to control and switch attention among different tasks. "People get better on tests of memory, motor speed, visual-spatial skills, and tasks requiring cognitive flexibility," says Stern. Kramer, too, finds that the strategy-heavy videogame Rise of Nations improves executive-control functions such as task switching, working memory, visual short-term memory, and reasoning in older adults.

Few games or training programs have been tested to this extent, and many of those that have been come up short. Those with increasing levels of difficulty and intense demands on attentional capacity—focus as well as switching—probably do the most good . . . as does taking a brisk walk in between levels.

Critical Thinking

1. What does research say about the role of antioxidants in increasing cognition?
2. Recognize the role of BDNF (brain-derived neurotropic factor) in the brain.
3. Which stimulates synapse formation more: doing a crossword puzzle every day, or learning something new?

With Ian Yarett

Why Do Men Die Earlier?

Genetic and cultural differences combine to cut men's average life expectancies, but new research by psychologists is revealing ways to help men take better care of themselves and extend their lives.

BRIDGET MURRAY-LAW

There's a joke about a man who goes to the doctor complaining that he sees spots. The receptionist asks, "Have you ever seen a doctor?" And he replies, "No. Just the spots."

The joke gets laughs because it reflects a truth: Men are much less likely than women to look after their health and see physicians. They're 25 percent less likely to have visited a health-care provider in the past year, and almost 40 percent more likely to have skipped recommended cholesterol screenings, according to the U.S. Agency for Healthcare Research and Quality. As stereotype would have it, nagging from women is the main reason men ever get their health checked out.

But what's no laughing matter are the statistics on men's poorer health outcomes: U.S. men are 1.5 times more likely than women to die from heart disease, cancer and respiratory diseases, according to U.S. Centers for Disease Control and Prevention data. And they die, on average, five years earlier than women.

Part of this may be genetics. For example, some variants of the Y chromosome may make men more prone to heart disease. But much of it may be masculine socialization, behavioral scientists theorize. "About the difference in life expectancy, we say that one year is biological, and the rest is cultural," says Gilles Tremblay, PhD, a social work professor at Laval University in Quebec City. Research by Tremblay and others has uncovered a cluster of traits frequently seen in men—emotional suppression, aggression and risk-taking in particular—that are associated with fewer visits to health-care providers and higher rates of injury and disease.

"Masculine gender socialization is hazardous for men's health, posing a double whammy of poorer health behaviors and lower use of health care," says Ronald Levant, EdD, a former president of APA and the originator of one of the primary measures of traditional masculinity, the Male Role Norms Inventory (MRNI).

But now research by Levant and other psychologists has revealed something quite different and intriguing: Some aspects of masculinity might actually protect men's health. Men high in traits that are often considered masculine ideals—self-reliance, responsibility, emotional maturity and an even-keeled approach—are more prone to visit their physicians and avoid risky behaviors, findings suggest.

Interestingly, some of these findings on healthy masculinity leading to good health behavior come from research on African-American men, even though they often have less access to health care. Buoyed by the results, the researchers behind them hope that they can be used to teach all men to draw on these positives of masculinity—and perhaps even teach women a thing or two.

Self-reliance—and Cool Heads

One of the researchers pioneering this new work on African-American masculinity and health is Jay Wade, PhD, a psychology professor at Fordham University and president-elect of APA's Div. 51 (Society for the Psychological Study of Men and Masculinity). In a study published in 2009 in the *American Journal of Men's Health* (Vol. 3, No. 2), Wade had 208 low-income African-American men in the New York City area fill out the MRNI and several measures of their health attitudes and behaviors.

After controlling for demographic variables, Wade found that participants who stifled their emotions felt more anxious about and out of control of their health. But those who identified as self-reliant were more likely to think about their health, take steps to take care of it and believe that they could influence their health.

Why might self-reliance exert such power in this group? Wade isn't sure, but he's willing to speculate: "The original self-reliance concept as it was developed is, 'I can do it all on my own. I don't depend on anybody. I don't need anybody.' But it may be that the construct isn't necessarily the same for African-American men. Because of the history of discrimination, it may be more like, 'I can't depend on others in society to take care of me, so I need to rely on myself. And because others—like my family—are depending on me, I *really* need to take care of myself.'"

Jibing with Wade's finding is another from the Men's Health Research Lab at the University of North Carolina at Chapel Hill. In the study, published last year in the *Journal of General Internal Medicine* (Vol. 25, No. 12) and led by lab director Wizdom Powell Hammond, PhD, researchers recruited 610 African-American men from barbershops nationwide and administered the MRNI, among other measures.

Men who scored highest on self-reliance were least likely to delay blood pressure screenings, and those who strongly embraced traditional masculine role norms as a whole were least likely to delay cholesterol screenings. In comparison, those who reported high mistrust of the medical establishment were more likely to delay blood pressure and cholesterol screenings, as well as routine health checkups.

Like Wade, Hammond believes that the particular way African-American men define self-reliance is what makes the difference. "For African-American men, masculinity is tied to their efforts to overcome oppression and a past that involves medical maltreatment—and to increase their access to health-care resources," explains Hammond. "Those who endorse standing on their own two feet want to 'man up' by seeking out preventive services."

This isn't to say that self-reliance is the only positive masculine trait when it comes to health behavior. A new study of 323 college men, led by Levant and published in January in *Psychology of Men and Masculinity* (Vol. 12, No. 1), reveals that some traditionally male traits may actually propel men to seek psychological help from professionals. The stand-out ones, says Levant, are the ability to focus on important matters and not sweat the small stuff, and emotional maturity, which includes avoiding self-destructive behaviors, such as substance abuse and not always expecting to receive what one wants.

"Men who must always get their way, who can't ask for help and who can't ignore the little hassles of life may

have the worst health outcomes," says Levant, who is professor of psychology at the University of Akron.

Amplified Effects

The health hazards of masculinity also loom large for gay men, several studies indicate. Researchers in this area find that gay men who identify with traditional masculinity are more likely to abuse substances and engage in risky sexual behaviors, such as unprotected anal intercourse. Sometimes fueling this risky behavior is "minority stress"—a form of stress that results from oppression of a minority group, in this case, gay men—together with a perception that risky health behaviors are the norm. So finds a study of 315 gay men by counseling psychology graduate student Christopher Hamilton and psychologist James Mahalik, PhD, of Boston College.

The results appeared in 2009 in the *Journal of Counseling Psychology* (Vol. 56, No. 1). And they're backed by results of another study led by psychologist Mark Hatzenbuehler, PhD, of Columbia University's Center for the Study of Social Inequalities and Health, and published in *Health Psychology* (Vol. 27, No. 4) in 2008. In it, Hatzenbuehler assessed levels of minority stress and risky health behaviors among 74 gay men who had recently lost a partner to HIV/AIDS. He found a strong relationship between depression, substance use and unprotected sex and such minority-stress characteristics as internalized homophobia and experiences of discrimination. In comparison, the men's risky health behaviors were largely unrelated to their bereavement—and Hatzenbuehler points out that bereavement is typically associated with mental and behavioral health problems.

"The study shows that minority stress was a unique predictor of adverse health outcomes, even in the context of bereavement," he says.

The results point to a need for large-scale programs to reduce stigma and prejudice, says Hatzenbuehler, as well as individual-level therapy that helps gay men regulate their emotions and tap social support. And that gets back to the core issue of motivating men to look after their health.

Manly Conversations

When men finally do come in for care, health-care professionals, particularly psychologists, have a chance to intervene—and help men improve their health, says Levant. The key, he says, is getting them to see how manliness can work for them instead of against them.

"It almost never works to tell a man to stop being masculine," says Levant. "You need to advise the man to keep up the masculine behaviors that are helpful, but challenge the ones that aren't."

Also important, says psychologist Will Courtenay, PhD, is getting the provider-patient relationship off to a good start. It's all in the health-care provider's approach, he says: Men generally respond better if they think their health-care providers are teammates.

"If the doctor says, 'Where do you want to start?' it immediately enlists the man's involvement and cues him that we're standing shoulder to shoulder and working together on this," says Courtenay, a Berkeley, Calif.-based psychotherapist and masculinity researcher. "And we know that collaborative treatment with active patient involvement is associated with improved outcomes and treatment adherence."

If a patient leans toward the traditionally masculine tendency of active problem-solving, a health-care provider can harness that by skillfully pointing him to tools and strategies, says Courtenay. You could, for example, explain to a smoker how quitting will almost immediately begin healing his cardiovascular system. Such appeals to action and problem-solving may be behind the fact that men are more successful at quitting smoking than women, even though more women say they want to quit—a trend documented in a 2009 analysis in *Nicotine and Tobacco Research* (Vol. 1, Issue Suppl. 2).

Real Men, Real Action

Courtenay attributes men's greater success at quitting smoking to such stereotypically masculine traits as self-reliance, showing what can happen when they put their minds to health improvement. And this is where behavioral researchers hope to intervene with men on a broader, public health level. Men's health researcher Hammond wants, for example, to see the self-reliance findings from African-American men used to craft public health messages focused on action and responsibility.

Past men's health campaigns have been promising, she says, but not focused enough on action. One of them, the National Institute of Mental Health's 2003 "Real Men, Real Depression" campaign, featured men's stories of getting help for depression. In one analysis, published in 2006 in *Psychology of Men and Masculinity* (Vol. 7, No. 1), 209 college men mostly reported finding the materials helpful and educational. But as yet, there is no evidence showing that men sought help as a result of the campaign.

Similarly, the U.S. Agency for Healthcare Research and Quality launched its "Real Men Wear Gowns" campaign in 2008, with an aim to convince men to don hospital gowns and get screened for various cancers and other chronic diseases. Among other recommendations, the campaign offered tips on how to talk to physicians. No evaluation data on the program, however, are available to date. And, says Hammond, the primary message wasn't a "take control of your destiny" call-to-action.

"We have to frame health-care seeking as an act of self-reliance," she says. "The message should be that taking charge of your health is what it means to be a real man. It's about engaging and becoming a partner in your care. You have decision-making power about your health."

One campaign using an action-oriented approach is in Quebec, where suicide is the leading cause of death among 20-to 40-year-old men. Now in its 20th year and held every February, Quebec's Suicide Prevention Week refers young men to a suicide-prevention hotline and 33 suicide-prevention centers. While there are no data to suggest that the drop is directly linked to the campaign, the suicide rate among Quebec's young men has dropped by a third over the past 10 years.

At least one men's health researcher, Gilles Tremblay, thinks the campaign has played a role in that drop. "The campaign sent a message that asking for help is a strong thing for a man to do," says Tremblay. "Now, 15 to 20 years later, providers I work with in mental health are saying more men are more prone to asking for help."

Another benefit of the self-reliance approach is that it appears to work with a variety of ethnic and cultural groups. For instance, nurse and researcher John Lowe, PhD, of the University of Florida, has been using it to train nurses about effectively treating Cherokee men—a group that traditionally values being responsible, disciplined and confident. Lowe describes his approach in a 2002 article in the *Journal of Crosscultural Nursing* (Vol. 13, No. 4). The self-reliance approach has not yet been tested with Latino men, but recent research on this population's resistance to prostate cancer screening, published in January in *Psychology of Men and Masculinity* (Vol. 12, No. 1), suggests the approach might help: In the study of a small sample of 10 middle-aged Latino men—led by Zully A. Rivera-Ramos, an educational psychology graduate student at the University of Illinois at Urbana-Champaign—results indicate that low-income Latino men might respond better to health messages emphasizing that prostate screening does not violate their masculinity. In comparison, high-income Latino men may respond more to messages playing to their role as provider and family protector.

So perhaps—just perhaps—by playing to all men's interests in control and responsibility, health-care professionals and officials have a chance to help them ward off serious diseases and live longer. If the tactic works, the average man will go and see a physician long before he starts seeing spots. And the joke won't be funny anymore.

Critical Thinking

1. Recall the six ways to help men get healthy.

2. Distinguish between men and women as regards visits to health care professionals.

3. What approximate percent of 5 years of life expectancy is genetic and what percent is due to socialization factors?

BRIDGET MURRAY LAW is a writer in Silver Spring, Md.

From *Monitor on Psychology* by Murray-Law, Bridget, June, 2011, pp. 59–62. Copyright © 2011 by American Psychological Association. Reprinted by permission. No further distribution without permission from the American Psychological Association.

More Good Years

Want to live longer—and healthier? These secrets from a sleepy Greek island could show you the way.

DAN BUETTNER

In 1970 Yiannis Karimalis got a death sentence. Doctors in Pennsylvania diagnosed the Greek immigrant with abdominal cancer and told him he'd be dead within a year. He was not yet 40 years old.

Devastated, Karimalis left his job as a bridge painter and returned to his native island of Ikaria. At least there he could be buried among his relatives, he thought—and for a lot less money than in the United States. Thirty-nine years later, Karimalis is still alive and telling his amazing story to anyone who will listen. And when he returned to the States on a recent visit, he discovered he had outlived all the doctors who had predicted his death.

On Ikaria, a mountainous, 99-square-mile island, residents tell this story to illustrate something they've known all their lives: on average, Ikarians outlive just about everyone else in the world.

Ikaria's heart disease rate is about half the American rate, and its diabetes rate is one-ninth of ours.

For three weeks in April, I led a scientific expedition to Ikaria to investigate the reasons for the islanders' remarkable longevity. It was part of my research into the earth's few Blue Zones: places where an extraordinarily high proportion of natives live past 90. Our team of demographic and medical researchers—funded by AARP and *National Geographic*—found that an amazing one in three Ikarians reaches 90. (According to the U.S. Census Bureau, only one in nine baby boomers will.) What's more, Ikarians suffer 20 percent fewer cases of cancer than do Americans and have about half our rate of heart disease and one-ninth our rate of diabetes. Most astonishing of all: among the islanders over 90 whom the team studied—about one-third of Ikaria's population who are 90 and older—there was virtually no Alzheimer's disease or other dementia. In the United States more than 40 percent of people over 90 suffer some form of this devastating ailment.

How do we explain these numbers? History tells part of the story.

In antiquity Ikaria was known as a health destination, largely for its radioactive hot springs, which were believed to relieve pain and to cure joint problems and skin ailments. But for much of the ensuing two millennia, civilization passed over this wind-beaten, harborless island. To elude marauding pirates, Ikarians moved their villages inland, high up on the rocky slopes. Their isolation led to a unique lifestyle.

Over centuries with no outside influences, island natives developed a distinctive outlook on life, including relentless optimism and a propensity for partying, both of which reduce stress. Ikarians go to bed well after midnight, sleep late, and take daily naps. Based on our interviews, we have reason to believe that most Ikarians over 90 are sexually active.

But what about the Ikarians' culture best explains their long lives? To find out, we let visitors to AARP.org/bluezones direct our team's quest. Our online collaborators voted on what we should research next. One day, for example, we interviewed hundred-year-old Ikarians to discover what they'd eaten for most of their lives. The next day we investigated the chemical composition of herbal teas.

In all, we found 13 likely contributors to Ikarian longevity. The formula below may be the closest you'll get to the fountain of youth:

Graze on greens. More than 150 varieties of wild greens grow on Ikaria. Some have more than ten times the level of antioxidants in red wine.

Sip herbal teas. Steeping wild mint, chamomile, or other herbs in hot water is a lifelong, daily ritual. Many teas lower blood pressure, which decreases the risk of heart disease and dementia.

Throw out your watch. Ikarians don't worry about time. Work gets done when it gets done. This attitude lowers stress, which reduces the risk of everything from arthritis to wrinkles.

Nap daily. Ikarian villages are ghost towns during the afternoon siesta, and science shows that a regular 30-minute nap decreases the risk of heart attack.

Walk where you're going. Mountainous terrain and a practice of walking for transport mean that every trip out of the house is a mini workout.

Phone a friend. With the island's rugged terrain, family and village support have been key to survival. Strong social connections are proven to lower depression, mortality, and even weight.

Drink goat's milk. Most Ikarians over 90 have drunk goat's milk their whole lives. It is rich in a blood-pressure-lowering hormone called tryptophan as well as antibacterial compounds.

Maintain a mediterranean diet. Around the world, people who most faithfully stick to this region's diet—a regimen high in whole grains, fruits, vegetables, olive oil, and fish—outlive people who don't by about six years. The Ikarian version features more potatoes than grains (because they grew better in the mountains) and more meat than fish (because the sea was a day's journey away).

Enjoy some Greek honey. The local honey contains antibacterial, anticancer and anti-inflammatory properties. (Unfortunately, the health benefits of Ikarian honey do not extend to American honey, as far as we know.)

Open the olive oil. Ikaria's consumption of olive oil is among the world's highest. Residents drizzle antioxidant-rich extra-virgin oil over food after cooking, which preserves healthful properties in the oil that heat destroys.

Grow your own garden (or find farmers' markets). Fruits and vegetables eaten soon after picking are higher in compounds that decrease the risk of cancer and heart disease.

Get religion. Ikarians observe Greek Orthodox rituals, and regular attendance at religious services (of any kind) has been linked to longer life spans.

Bake bread. The island's sourdough bread is high in complex carbohydrates and may improve glucose metabolism and stave off diabetes.

Do Ikarians possess the true secret to longevity? Well, some combination of their habits is helping them live significantly longer than Americans, who live on average to age 78. We can't guarantee that Ikarian wisdom will help you live to 100. But if Yiannis Karimalis's example is any indicator, it may help you outlive your doctor.

Critical Thinking

1. Explain why people in Ikaria, a very small island, outlive most other people.
2. Name the components of Ikarians' diet that contribute to their longevity.
3. Recall other information you have heard about extending lifespan.

DAN BUETTNER is the author of *The Blue Zones: Lessons for Living Longer From the People Who've Lived the Longest* (National Geographic, 2008).

Reprinted from *AARP the Magazine*, September/October 2009, pp. 22,24, by Dan Buettner. Copyright © 2009 by Dan Buettner. Reprinted by permission of the author via Quest Network, Inc.

This Is Your Brain. Aging.

Science is reshaping what we know about getting older. (The news is better than you think.)

Sharon Begley

Over the years, Timothy Salthouse has tested more than 8,000 people in his lab at the University of Virginia, assessing their memories, problem-solving skills, and other mental functions to see how the brain fares with age. The results have been predictably dismal: after age 25 or so, it's pretty much all downhill. (No news there: Plato wrote that when a man grows old, he "can no more learn much than he can run much.") But something bothered Salthouse about the results, and on a late spring day in his office at the Russell Sage Foundation on New York's Upper East Side, where he has been a visiting scholar this year, he whips out a graph that captures the paradox.

The graph shows two roller-coastering lines. One represents the proportion of people of each age who are in the top 25 percent on a standard lab test of reasoning ability—thinking. The other shows the proportion of CEOs of Fortune 500 companies of each age. Reasoning ability peaks at about age 28 and then plummets, tracing that well-known plunge that makes those older than 30 (OK, fine, 40) cringe: only 6 percent of top scorers are in their 50s, and only 4 percent are in their 60s. But the age distribution of CEOs is an almost perfect mirror image: it peaks just before age 60. About half are older than 55. And the number under 40 is about zero.

One can make a cheap joke out of this (so that's why AIG, GM, Lehman, et al. tanked: the smartest people weren't running them), but Salthouse deduces more counterintuitive, and hopeful, lessons. The first is that in real life, rather than in psych labs, people rely on mental abilities that stand up very well to age and discover work-arounds for the mental skills that do fade. The second is that some mental abilities actually improve with age, and one of them may be the inchoate thing called wisdom, which is not a bad thing to have when running a company. Little of the gloom-and-doom conventional wisdom about what happens to the brain as we age, says Salthouse, "is based on well-established empirical evidence." Instead, he says, much of it seems to be "influenced as much by the authors' preconceptions and attitudes as by systematic evaluation" of solid data.

Insights like that are producing a dramatic, and hopeful, rethinking of what happens to the mind and brain as we age.

Some of the earlier bad-news findings are being questioned as scientists discover that the differences between today's 20-year-old brains and 80-year-old brains reflect something other than simple age, and instead have to do with how people live their lives. And a deeper understanding of normal cognitive aging is producing interventions that, because they target the cell-level brain changes that accompany aging, promise to be more effective than memory exercises and crossword puzzles.

> **A deeper understanding of normal cognitive aging is producing interventions that promise to be more effective than memory exercises and crossword puzzles.**

Take the claim that brain volume shrinks beginning in our 30s. Earlier studies suggested that the prefrontal cortex (just behind the forehead) takes the greatest hit; this is the region responsible for executive function such as forethought, reasoning, and "fluid" intelligence—the ability to figure out, for instance, which letter best continues the sequence G-B-F-C-E. But those data, it turns out, may be skewed by the inclusion of people who have very early dementia—so early that they have no symptoms, explains neuroscientist John Morrison of Mount Sinai School of Medicine in New York, but still have neuronal loss and thus volume loss in their prefrontal cortex. If only truly healthy people were studied, there might be no such volume loss, he says.

Earlier studies also found that myelination, the fatty insulation around neurons, peaks in our late 20s and then declines. Because myelin allows electrical signals to travel through the brain more quickly and efficiently, its loss means it takes longer to connect a face with a name, a book with an author, or any other facts. Its loss also makes the brain "noisier," explains neuroscientist Henry Mahncke of *Posit Science:* "It's like a radio that is no longer precisely tuned to a station. It takes the brain more effort to find that signal, and that takes resources away from memory and thinking." But myelination loss, according to new research, should come with an asterisk. Most of it seems to occur on one specific part of neurons—the part responsible for learning new things. The part responsible for long-term memory shows no such loss.

In fact, a study of rhesus monkeys published this month shows how well the aging brain holds up. The animals' prefrontal cortex indeed loses "dendritic spines," tiny protrusions that, acting as the brain's wide receivers, catch the neurotransmitters that carry signals from other neurons. But there are two kinds of spines in monkeys as well as people. Small, thin ones are responsible for learning and remembering new things (where did I park my car?), and short, stubby ones are responsible for recalling things we've known for years. The brain loses some 45 percent of the first kind—and zero of the second kind, Morrison and colleagues reported in June in the *Journal of Neuroscience*.

That would account for why we have trouble with new memories as we age but not with our core knowledge. "We hypothesize that expertise and knowledge are coded in the synapses and spines that are not lost with age," says Morrison. "This may be how the brain retains what it learned decades ago, and why a professor of cell biology can teach well into his 80s." It may also be why, although most people's ability to reason and solve novel problems declines with age, knowledge holds up just fine, with vocabulary increasing through at least age 60. Emotional intelligence, social skills, and self-control generally improve with age, too.

Although most people's ability to reason and solve novel problems declines with age, knowledge holds up just fine, with vocabulary increasing through at least age 60.

And as always, individuals differ. In general, cognitive processes such as processing speed—how quickly the brain takes in and makes sense of information from the outside world, as well as how quickly signals propagate along a thinking circuit—decline beginning in our 20s, just as our respiratory and immune systems decline. Memory and problem-solving improve into our 20s and then plateau, beginning to decline in our 50s or 60s. But averages hide big individual differences. The scores of some adults in their 60s on memory, problem-solving, and other cognitive tests are above the average of adults in their 20s. As anecdotal evidence, Salthouse gestures down the hall to the office of economist Robert Solow, 86, a Nobel laureate who is as intellectually active as ever and producing research papers that—and I'm going to have to just quote here—"rejected the representative-agent models that more or less impose optimal properties on observed trajectories" in macroeconomics.

We can't all be Solows, even in our 30s—let alone our 80s. But clearly, some brains hold up better than others. Some of the difference may be genetic, but since we can't go back and ask Mom and Dad to bequeath us different genes, the possibilities for intervention on this front are limited. That leaves how we live our lives. Salthouse points out that only about 20 percent of the variation among people in standard measures of memory, problem-solving, and other executive functions is the result of age. The rest—64 to 96 percent on different cognitive test scores, he estimates in his new book, *Major Issues in Cognitive Aging*—reflects factors other than age.

One such factor may be generational. Many of the dismal conclusions about aging come from what are called cross-sectional comparisons: haul 20-somethings and 60- to 80-somethings into the lab, test, compare, repeat. The differences are supposed to indicate what will happen to the first group when they reach the age of the second. But that may not be right. Consider a visitor to Miami. She notices that most of the older people are New York Jews, while many of the younger ones are Latino. She concludes that as people age, they change from Latino to Jewish.

We may be making a similar mistake when we compare young and old brains. The differences may not mean that mental function falls off a cliff as we age. Instead, warns Salthouse, many "age-related differences [in brain function] could reflect generational differences." The fact that more recent generations outperform older ones belies the idea that we are getting dumber, and is so well established, it has its own name—the Flynn effect. As a result, cross-sectional studies finding that today's 80-year-olds don't think and remember as well as today's 30-year-olds may be capturing this generational difference, and thus painting a more pessimistic picture of the aging brain than it warranted. When the same people are measured over and over, says Salthouse, "at least before about age 60" there is "either stability or an increase" in brain function with age.

The recognition that so much of the difference in brain function is due to something other than age has ignited a market in interventions that might postpone, mitigate, or even prevent some of the decline. The largest study of interventions is ACTIVE (Advanced Cognitive Training for Independent and Vital Elderly), which began in 1998. It gave 2,832 adults, ages 65 to 94, either no training (the control group) or training in reasoning, memory, and processing speed in 10 sessions of 60 to 75 minutes each. The reasoning training, for instance, gave people strategies for breaking a problem into easier steps and identifying patterns of relations. The memory training involved strategies to form images or associations: to remember a list of words that includes penguin, scissors, and cupcake, for instance, visualize the bird wielding the tool while pecking the chocolate frosting.

As expected, people got better at what they trained on. In general, the gains were equal to turning back the clock seven to 15 years for reasoning and remembering, and even longer for processing speed. But there was essentially no transfer: getting better at memory did not sharpen reasoning, and faster processing speeds did not improve memory. Somewhat alarming was that after training, most people's performance fell even more precipitously than it did without training. That probably reflects the fact that for brain training to "take," it has to be like aerobics, says Mahncke: "We think that for each core mental ability you want to train, you'll need a booster every nine to 12 months."

Doing crossword puzzles would seem to be ideal brain exercise since avid puzzlers do them daily and say it keeps them mentally sharp, especially with vocabulary and memory. But this may be confusing cause and effect. It is mostly people who are good at figuring out "Dole's running mate" who do crosswords regularly; those who aren't, don't. In a recent study, Salthouse and colleagues found "no evidence" that people who do crosswords have "a slower rate of age-related decline in reasoning." As he put it in a 2006 analysis, there is "little scientific evidence that engagement in mentally stimulating activities alters the rate of mental aging," an idea that is "more of an optimistic hope than an empirical reality." (P.S.: Bob Dole's 1996 VP choice was Jack Kemp.)

What does support mental acuity as we age is the same thing that's good for your heart, lungs, immune system, and muscles: aerobic exercise such as brisk walking. A seminal study by scientists at the University of Illinois found that three vigorous, 40-minute walks a week over six months improves memory and reasoning. It also spurs the birth of new brain neurons, scientists led by the University of Illinois's Art Kramer reported in 2006, and increases the volume of white matter, which connects neurons, in areas responsible for such executive functions as planning.

A seminal study by scientists at the University of Illinois found that three vigorous, 40-minute walks a week over six months improves memory and reasoning.

Walking is free, but Americans spent $13 million on brain-fitness software and games last year, Ambient Insight, a market-research company, reported in April. Nintendo's Brain

Age ($19.99), the Web-based MyBrainTrainer ($29.95 for one year), HappyNeuron's Brain Fitness ($69.95), and the like improve the skills they train, say independent scientists: drilling yourself to hit the right-arrow key when you see a green light improves reaction time, doing exercises in which you decide whether one face matches another will speed up visual processing, and determining whether words in a new list match any of those in an old one boosts short-term memory. But as in the ACTIVE study, it's not clear these improvements translate into a fitter brain overall.

An approach that targets the underlying brain processes might. A computergame-like program from Posit called InSight ($395), for instance, includes an exercise in which you discern which direction a pattern on a screen is moving as a second pattern appears before the brain is finished processing the first. The idea is to turn up the signal and dial down the noise in the brain. "We think it's important to fix the underlying information-processing machine rather than target higher-level functions like memory directly," says Mahncke. "By training the brain to improve its signal-to-noise ratio, information goes through more accurately and faster." A 2009 study found that healthy older adults (65 and over) who used a Posit program based on the same principle, Brain Fitness ($395), an hour per day for eight weeks improved their processing speed to that of 40-year-olds and their memory to that of brains 10 years younger. And a study scheduled for publication finds that such "perceptual training" improves memory in older adults. It's enough to give you hope that, for the brain, aging may become almost optional.

Critical Thinking

1. Describe the characteristics of "wisdom."
2. Infer why new things are forgotten while the past is remembered.
3. Recognize "emotional intelligence" and review why it generally increases with age.

Test-Your-Knowledge Form

We encourage you to photocopy and use this page as a tool to assess how the articles in *Annual Editions* expand on the information in your textbook. By reflecting on the articles you will gain enhanced text information. You can also access this useful form on a product's book support website at www.mhhe.com/cls.

NAME: _____ DATE: _____

TITLE AND NUMBER OF ARTICLE:

_____

BRIEFLY STATE THE MAIN IDEA OF THIS ARTICLE:

_____

_____

LIST THREE IMPORTANT FACTS THAT THE AUTHOR USES TO SUPPORT THE MAIN IDEA:

_____

_____

_____

_____

WHAT INFORMATION OR IDEAS DISCUSSED IN THIS ARTICLE ARE ALSO DISCUSSED IN YOUR TEXTBOOK OR OTHER READINGS THAT YOU HAVE DONE? LIST THE TEXTBOOK CHAPTERS AND PAGE NUMBERS:

_____

_____

_____

_____

LIST ANY EXAMPLES OF BIAS OR FAULTY REASONING THAT YOU FOUND IN THE ARTICLE:

_____

_____

_____

_____

LIST ANY NEW TERMS/CONCEPTS THAT WERE DISCUSSED IN THE ARTICLE, AND WRITE A SHORT DEFINITION:

NOTES

NOTES